Late Admissions

Late Admissions

Confessions of a Black Conservative

GLENN C. LOURY

W. W. NORTON & COMPANY
Independent Publishers Since 1923

Late Admissions is a work of nonfiction. Certain names and potentially identifying characteristics have been changed.

For information about permission to reproduce selections from this book, write to Permissions, W. W. Norton & Company, Inc., 500 Fifth Avenue, New York, NY 10110

For information about special discounts for bulk purchases, please contact W. W. Norton Special Sales at specialsales@wwnorton.com or 800-233-4830

Manufacturing by Lake Book Manufacturing
Book design by Chris Welch
Production manager: Anna Oler

ISBN 978-0-393-88134-9

W. W. Norton & Company, Inc.
500 Fifth Avenue, New York, N.Y. 10110
www.wwnorton.com

W. W. Norton & Company Ltd.
15 Carlisle Street, London W1D 3BS

1 2 3 4 5 6 7 8 9 0

To the memories of

Gloria Cartman Roosley and Leanett Loury Smith,

who were there with me from the beginning.

Preface

We're playing a game, you and I, reader and author.

An aging black academic economist and conservative social critic of some prominence sits down to write his memoir. He is relatively well known, but not a household name. He is occasionally recognized by strangers on the street, but not every day. If the reader does know of him, that reader may know that he has, more than once, publicly reversed his positions on a number of important issues of the day. The reader may know that he has endured more than one public scandal. The reader may know that he is accorded respect in some circles and scorn in others. Perhaps the reader does not know anything about him at all.

Whatever the case, the reader, being skeptical at the outset, will try to discern exactly why this aging black academic economist and conservative social critic is writing a memoir in the first place. That is, the skeptical reader will ask just what story this guy is selling, what image of himself he is trying to get across. What details does the author finesse to make himself look better than he might otherwise look? What embarrassing incidents is he passing over in silence lest they make him look foolish? What impression is he trying to make? The reader will attempt to read between the lines, to locate the fatally flawed, flesh-

and-blood human lying beneath the narrative construct that the author has assembled for the reader's enjoyment and, perhaps, for the author's own self-aggrandizement.

Call this game "the problem of self-regard."

Your role in the game is to search me out. Not the narrative-construct me, the real me.

My role in the game is to get you to call off the search, to convince you that the narrative construct and the man are one and the same. But I can't just ask you to surrender your critical faculties and believe whatever I say. That would be a red flag, a clear indication that I'm trying to pull the wool over your eyes. So I need to find a way to convince you to believe what I tell you about myself, even though you know it's in my interest to portray myself in the best light possible, no matter how improbably rosy that light may be.

My strategy is as follows. I know you are going to be on the lookout for anything that discredits my story about myself: a contradiction, a slip of the pen, an inadvertently revealing detail about my behavior. Since I know that you won't be satisfied until you find this discrediting information, I will dispense it for you freely, openly and undisguised. My bet is that this strategy of self-discrediting disclosure will accomplish two things:

First, it will appease your impulse to find cracks in the edifice of my self-presentation, to search out my contradictions and too-convenient narrative contrivances.

Second, I hope to exploit a paradox that these self-discrediting disclosures will initiate. The more self-discrediting information I deploy, the more credible I will become. I will convince you that I am not lying, because no sane person would invent the discrediting things I'm going to tell you about myself. As you take in more and more such discrediting information, I will accrue a kind of credibility capital that I can spend on incidents that cast me in a more conventionally positive light, because I am reasonably sure that you will then consider me to be a reliable narrator.

A possible objection from you, the skeptical reader: I say that no sane person would invent this discrediting information about himself, and yet I've laid out a rationale for doing just that. If I'm most concerned that you buy into my self-presentation, and if I know that you won't be able to do that unless I disclose discrediting information, then don't I have a strategic incentive to invent discrediting information if I find myself in need of it?

My rebuttal is simple, if distasteful: *I am going to tell you things about myself that no one would want anybody to think was true of them.*

And yet, they are true.

I am going to tell you that I have lied, because I need you to believe me. I am going to tell you that I have deceived those closest to me, because I need you to trust me. I am going to tell you that I have abandoned people who needed me, because I need you to stick with me.

I must tell it all in this memoir, because if I don't tell it all, nothing I say will be heard.

The skeptical reader will have observed that this game has already begun.

Late Admissions

One

I'm standing in my auntie Eloise's living room. It's summer, and Chicago's air is thick with humidity. My shirt is starting to stick to my back. All I want to do is tear off my jacket and tie, kick off the dress shoes torturing my feet, leap into street clothes, and run out to join whoever else in the neighborhood has managed to extract themselves from their homes. But duty calls. Auntie Eloise's living room is beautiful, elegant, just like the rest of her house—like Eloise herself. A baby grand piano sits in the corner. Stained glass–fronted recessed bookcases filled with classics line one wall. With its six bedrooms, its three-car garage, its fish pond and barbecue pit in the backyard, its flowing drapes and French provincial furniture (chaise longues and all), the place is an extension of the woman herself: regal, tasteful, and timeless.

Up the stairs leading from the kitchen is a small, semi-separate apartment where my sister, my mother, and I live. We pay some rent, but less than we were paying before Eloise gathered us up and brought us here. Certainly, in the sort of places we used to live, there were no bookcases, no chaise longues, not much of anything special. And there were a lot of those places. We moved from apartment to apartment, so many that I had attended five different schools by the time I reached the fifth grade. In Auntie Eloise's eyes, this would not do. A "Negro" woman, as she would have insisted on describing herself, of her ambition and vision wouldn't allow it.

Next to me stands my younger sister, Leanett, along with four others. These are my "cousins," a set of siblings whom my aunt took in and adopted as her own. We shared equally in Eloise's beneficence. They had different fathers but the same mother, who was troubled. Raising four children on her own became too much of a burden for her, so she left them to foster care and they were sent to different homes. When Auntie Eloise got wind of this, she decided to gather them up, adopting over the course of a few years first Diane and Jimmy, then Herman, and then little Larry. She was determined to unite them all under one roof. Married to Uncle Moonie but childless, she was doubtless thinking of her own three siblings—my mother and their two brothers, Adlert and Alfred—who were sent to live with different relatives when their mother, my grandmother Nettye, passed away. Eloise just could not abide seeing that family broken up.

I'm ready to bolt, but I don't dare. Eloise herself sits on the sofa before us. At nearly six feet tall, she is imposing even when sitting down. A cigarette rests between her fingers. Smoke swirls ceilingward, and afternoon sunlight pours in through the windows behind her.

She looks at us and smiles.

"So. How was church? What was Pastor Bob's sermon about?"

This is the Sunday ritual, the one we'd been preparing for all afternoon. You better be paying attention. You better not be goofing off in the back row. I'm not expected to recount how I heeded the altar call, went up in front of the congregation, and dropped to my knees, humbled by the power of Jesus. I didn't do that in those years. The Spirit that moved other folks to tears and spontaneous exultation did not quite move me in that way. But that's not what this ritual is about. The point is, you better have something to say when asked a question, because Auntie Eloise expects an answer.

I recount the Bible passage the pastor spoke on, the movements of his speech, where his voice grew excited and where it came low. I recall the shouts of "Hallelujah!" echoing from the pews. I offer up a phrase or two from the sermon verbatim. Or close enough to verbatim. I'm sure Pastor Bob wouldn't consider a little embellishment to be so great a sin.

She stops me midsentence.

"So, what do you think *that* means, Glenn? What's the point of what the pastor said there? How does it relate to you?"

This is not something I've thought about at all. I've got nothing at my fingertips, no rehearsed answer. But silence is not an option, and so I improvise, spinning out an interpretation of the pastor's words that I hope will pass muster. She nods in approval, and I continue on. I think I'm pretty slick. She doesn't even notice I just pulled all that out of my hat.

Only later would I realize that, far from putting one over on Auntie Eloise, I was learning exactly the lesson she wanted me to learn. It had little to do with merely recounting a sermon, little to do even with veracity. Years later, when my own children would stand before me and when I would stand before lecture halls full of students, I would understand what the Sunday ritual was really about. Look beneath the surface of things, and tell us what you see.

But right now I am just trying to get through it, hoping Woody and my other buddies haven't grown impatient and headed off on their bikes to who knows where. I know Woody wouldn't leave me behind if he could help it, but a wave of insecurity washes over me. I tell myself that I would wait for Woody if he were in my increasingly uncomfortable shoes, and in the moment it's true.

Finally, after Leanett (everybody calls her Lee Lee) and the others have performed the ritual to Eloise's satisfaction, we are dismissed. I thud up the stairs, change as quickly as I can, and race out the door.

THIS IS ELOISE'S SOUTH SIDE: 7329 South Michigan Avenue. Park Manor. Black families living in well-kept homes in a neighborhood knit together through a sense of community and kinship. They owned small businesses, performed skilled labor at the steel mills or in the stockyards, and often had a little hustle going to make ends meet. In Uncle Moonie's barbershop, for example, you could get a shave and a haircut in the front room and then slip into the back to buy a little reefer or whatever fell off the back of the truck that week. It wasn't exactly legal, of course, but as far as Moonie saw it, nobody was getting hurt. He was going to take care of his family, and he wasn't relying on the law—even civil rights law—to get that done. "The white man may have let black folks into the schools and restaurants," Moonie would say, "but you can call me when they start integrating the money." Until that day came, he didn't see why he shouldn't earn in the back room what the white man wouldn't let him earn in the front.

And besides, that extra cash helped him keep Eloise living in a style befitting her stature and ambition. That ambition wasn't just for her, it was for all of us. This is the woman who took in four orphans, plus her sister's family. This is the woman who raised funds to ensure two of her nieces, Alfred's daughters, could attend Fisk University, and then made sure they knew the right sorority to pledge when they got there, despite never having attended college herself. This is the president of the Social, Religious, and Literary Guild of our Bethel AME Church, a position that accorded her a certain status in the community.

My auntie Eloise was extremely attuned to all the minute signs distinguishing those of one status from those of another in the black community. She acquired this sensibility from the Great Aunts, a generation of matriarchs that came before her—her mother's five older sisters who, along with five brothers, had migrated up to Chicago from Tennessee and Mississippi in the years after World War I. These people carried themselves with a certain class. They had made a way out of no way, acquiring modest wealth and property through sometimes dubious means.

How you presented yourself in public mattered to them. The thinking was, no matter how someone made their money, they ought to know how to handle themselves, how to communicate that they knew their worth. A man might work in a stockyard, but before he went out for the evening, he knew to bathe, shave, shine his shoes, and dress in a way that reflected his aspirations for himself and for those around him. Viewed in this perspective, the astounding stylishness of the South Side of the 1950s and '60s was in no way superficial, and it was not unexpected. Style reflected ideals and ambitions that might otherwise have gone unexpressed in the often-trying conditions under which we lived.

There was a line, after all. A line between those moving upward and those sliding back into a sordid condition from which one might never break free. A line between nascent bourgeois respectability and hopeless poverty. A line between legitimate (or mostly legitimate) ascendance and backsliding. Eloise stood firmly on one side of that line. So when she saw my mother's marriage to my father fall apart, and then another marriage go the same way, when she saw her sister Gloria (their brother Alfred called her Go-Go because she was always on the move) bouncing around the West Side, moving Leanett and me from apartment to increasingly shabby apartment, Eloise made it her duty to yank us back to the right side of the line before we crossed too far over, to mold us, who were yet without shape, who could go either way.

I SIT ON THE BED in my mother's room in our apartment attached to Eloise's house. It's Saturday night, and these are the last moments I will spend with her before she goes out. Out with her friends, out with a man, to dinner, somewhere.

I can see her face in the mirror as she stands before her dresser, slowly rubbing cream into her arms, the milky white dissolving into her brown skin. She examines her face and sings softly, absentmindedly along with Judy Garland's "The Man That Got Away."

Gloria has a beautiful voice, and as it ascends through the verses with Garland's, it drifts and mingles with the scent of perfumes, oils, and powders. She considers each ingredient carefully before plucking it from the forest of bottles and jars on the dresser. A spray of this, a dab of that. Occasionally she glances back and smiles her sweet smile.

She sits down on the edge of the bed and pulls on silk stockings. I have only a vague sense of where she goes and what she does on these evenings. But I know my mother is a beautiful woman, a desirable woman, and this has something to do with whatever happens when she goes out into the night.

I tell her I need something: a new notebook for school, a new sweater like the other kids are wearing, something.

She stands to approach her dresser and looks back at me through the mirror.

"Ask your father. He should have sent me money last week anyway."

I don't push it further. She knows if he hasn't given it to her, he doesn't have it. Maybe if I'm feeling bold when my sister and I go stay with my father next weekend, I'll ask. But I know what he'll say.

"You need money? Get a paper route."

That's what he did when he needed money, he'll remind me. He went out and got it himself. There was no one he could ask, nor is there now. Not his father, who abandoned him as a baby. Not his mother who died when he was in high school, or his grandparents, who have it hard enough. My father has no Eloise to rescue him if he slips, no gaggle of cousins and aunts and uncles to fall back on. He has nothing but a rigid sense of virtue and self-respect to keep him from whatever disaster waits on the other side of the line. Born Everett Lowry, when a schoolteacher misspelled his name—L-O-U-R-Y—he opted to keep the new spelling. His own father had left him nothing more than that name, and in surrendering it, my dad found a kind of freedom that could be maintained only through the practice of rigorous austerity and personal responsibility. This is my patrimony, what I'll receive from him in place of the money he cannot, in fact, afford to give me.

My mother turns from the dresser and again sits on the edge of the bed. She is lost in thought, singing plaintively.

> *Don't know what happened*
> *It's all a crazy game*

My mother is a kind and generous woman, but her relationship with my father is strained, and that confuses me. There's tension there. Lee Lee and I can feel it, even though we're only kids. They play a game, pretending to be cordial to cover over the tug-of-war raging underneath. So if a stranger with some sad story asks Mama for a hand up, she's inclined to help. But if I want something that costs money, she'll say, "Ask your father." And if I wince, wondering why she would give money to some anonymous drunk but not buy her son that new notebook, that new sweater, she'll admonish me not to judge that drunk. You never know what's behind another person's troubles. "There but for the grace of God go you or me." That's what she'd say. I don't quite understand why this seemingly boundless sympathy does not extend to my father.

My mother is ready. She checks herself in the mirror, making sure every fold of her dress is perfectly in place, making sure her hair frames her face just so.

PARK MANOR. THE SOUTH SIDE. Well-kept lawns, respectable black folks inching their way toward prosperity, values instilled and sustained by church, the family, and common sense. All this is true. It is also a story, the kind you tell yourself in those moments when, indulging in a little nostalgia, you reminisce about the good times. But it is not the whole truth. And if it's a story, it's a cover story, one that obscures the darker undercurrents in the world that shaped my early life, where people walked on both sides of the line.

It is true that Eloise's house was a monument to an ideal for living. It is also true that in that house, our friend Boo-Boo's father, a man suffering from mental illness and alcoholism, shot himself in the head as my horrified, helpless mother looked on.

It is true that on some Saturday afternoons, my mother would pack a lunch, and friends and family would meet at the park, spread out on the grass, and eat her delicious food while cheering on my Little League team—I was a pitcher and third baseman. It is also true that one of my teammates, Paul Shumpert—a nice, quiet kid who lived down the block—would die from a heroin overdose at age eighteen.

It is true that my mother's kindness had no limit. When Cousin Ronnie, strung out and skinny, would knock on our door asking for something to eat, my mother knew he was only there to steal money from her purse. She would invite him in anyway.

Pig, a grade-school nemesis of mine, robbed a currency exchange, shot a cop, and caught a life sentence.

My pal Stevie's friends accidentally shot him in the gut while playing with a gun. They panicked and ran, and Stevie bled out on his mother's basement floor.

Even in the heart of Park Manor's most respectable venue, the church's literary society over which Eloise presided, disreputability snuck in. It was rumored that my uncle Adlert managed to seduce every member of that committee (aside from Eloise, of course). My mother took delight in saying so. Did it happen? It's certainly possible. Tall, well built, intelligent, and handsome, the silver-tongued Adlert, a graduate of Morehouse College and Northwestern University School of Law, had no problem finding women.

Neither did his brother, my uncle Alfred, who eventually fathered twenty-two children by four different mothers. Alfred's appetites may have outstripped the confines of respectability. He was roundly denounced by some of the Great Aunts. But he was quite the patriarch. His sense of duty as a father, stretched thin though it may have been, gave his life meaning. He thought of himself as founding a clan. His models were the biblical prophets. He took "Be fruitful and multiply" literally and seriously. He was, in his way, a quintessential family man who maintained a fierce devotion to each of his progeny. His wives—Betty, Marybell, Rose—all had bills to pay, so Alfred hustled from one job to another in order to take care of all his children. He'd go to the Great Aunts with his hand out, especially Cammie, who'd taken him in after his mother died, and Rosetta, who was the eldest and most prosperous of the bunch. He'd even try to borrow money from my mother when the creditors were on his heels. And he could get it if she had it, even if it cost her son that sweater. That's just how much she loved him.

MY DAD HAS RUN OUT to get something from the grocery store, so Lee Lee and I are snooping. This is a delicate operation. My father is a creature of habit and order. If we leave anything out of place, he'll be sure to notice. That's part of the game; the risk of detection makes it all the more thrilling.

His single-room efficiency apartment—with its tiny kitchenette, a sofa, and a bed that folds down from the wall—is a far cry from Eloise's palace. This isn't my dad's ideal living arrangement, but the spartan conditions suit him. There is no space wasted and no space to waste.

I open his closet. Everything hangs in order. The suits in one section, pants in another, shirts in another, all of them pressed and straight. His ties hang from a rack, all of them evenly spaced. On the floor sits a shoe tree holding probably every dress shoe he's owned since his feet stopped growing, all of them polished, spotless. I move to his dresser and find what is likely the most organized sock drawer that has ever existed, with brown socks to one side, then white, then black, then navy, all of them folded in uniform fashion, nestled like eggs in a carton. Even his under-wear is neatly folded and stacked.

This all strikes me as funny, or at least remarkable, but I do not know why at the time. It will later occur to me that Lee Lee and I may have been the only other people besides his future wife, Constance, ever to see the inside of that apartment. It is not the sort of place set up for enter-taining guests. My father's rigorous arrangement of his most intimate possessions is not done for show or in case someone checks or because his wife insists on it. His sense of order, his discipline, goes all the way down. This is the closest I will ever get to a glimpse of my father as he is when no one is looking, and it is, in essence, no different than the image he presents to the world.

In time, I will understand why he developed this rigorous self-control. Working his way through a degree in accounting and then law school at night, supporting two children, discipline was a necessity and perhaps a comfort, something he could rely on when there was little else to offer him support. Perhaps he acquired it from the high school ROTC, where he excelled. Or perhaps he excelled in the ROTC because he had a tal-ent for discipline. In either case, it was at the root of his self-respect, and he tried to impart it to me constantly through example and instruction.

Which is not to say that my father's entire world can be found within his sock drawer. He takes me to see the White Sox play doubleheaders at Comiskey Park, where we sit in the bleachers. He takes Lee Lee and me out to see the country. We take long road trips out west to Pikes Peak in Colorado and back east to visit family in Buffalo and stand before Niagara Falls. He wants us to see a world not hemmed in by concrete and bisected by impassible highways, checkered with blocks to avoid and hustlers to dodge. We are confirmed city kids, but the city is not all there is. Neither is the endless search for respectability. Out there in the open spaces, Eloise's line between the respectable and the lost evaporates. There seems to be no need for it. Such, anyway, is what I imagine my father is thinking when he takes us on those outings.

Later in life, I will hear a story about the night of my birth. My mother has delivered me, and she is resting in the hospital. Word gets around that I have entered the world, and Uncle Adlert shows up to my father's grandparents' house, which is where he and my mother are living while they save up for a place of their own. Adlert has recently graduated from Morehouse and is on his way to earning a law degree at Northwestern, back when black men simply didn't do such things. My father admires Adlert's prodigious intellect, oratorical genius, and academic achievement, which have become the stuff of family legend, and he envies his prowess with the opposite sex. My father, who would one day aspire to law school himself, feels honored that Adlert has dropped by to congratulate him. Not only that, he's brought along a bottle of whiskey to toast my birth.

Whether due to self-discipline or an indifference to alcohol, my father is not much of a drinker. But Adlert is. He's a drinker and a talker. And as they sit and talk into the night, Adlert proceeds to dazzle my father with storytelling about his varied conquests, even as he drains the entire bottle of whiskey more or less by himself. "In awe and appalled," is how my father will later describe his reaction to this performance. In awe, no doubt, of Adlert's brilliance and his profligate promiscuity. Appalled, no doubt, by Adlert's worrisome display of alcoholic virtuosity. My dad's lesson for me when sharing this tale, I surmised: brilliance without discipline is just not good enough, if one wants to walk on the right side of the line.

Adlert will eventually earn that law degree and become a lawyer of some distinction. Then he'll be disbarred after getting involved in some shady family business cooked up, it is rumored, by one of the Great Aunts, who still loomed over my mother's side of the family. Eventually, and tragically, my uncle Adlert will develop a dependency on alcohol that destroys his life.

FIRST, THERE IS THE COVER STORY. Everett Loury marries Gloria Cartman right out of high school in 1948. In short order, they have two children, Glenn and Leanett. Gloria is a doting mother and a faithful wife. Everett is a hard-working husband and a loving father.

Then there is the real story. My mother returns home from the hospital with my sister Leanett in her arms. Nobody who sees her can ignore the disparities. Where my parents' skin is relatively dark, Leanett's is light. Where my parents' hair is kind of kinky, Leanett's is relatively straight. My mother's features stare up from the swaddling cloth, but my father's face is nowhere to be found in Leanett's. I do not know the extent to which my sister's paternity was the subject of my parents' many arguments. But I do know that my dad refused to acknowledge what was obvious to anybody who looked: he was not Leanett's biological father.

My dad's perceived recalcitrance on the matter escalated whatever tensions were already present in his grandparents' home, where we were all still living. Finally, during a confrontation over this scandalous situation, his grandfather told him, "You can be a fool if you want to, but that is not your child." My father insisted he take it back and, when he refused, a physical fight ensued. I'm not sure whether the fight was about my mother's honor or my father's or something less easily articulable, but soon enough, Everett, Gloria, Lee Lee, and I moved out into our own place. The marriage collapsed not long thereafter.

Regardless of the whispers and snickers, my father never treated Leanett as anything other than his daughter, and she never treated him as anything other than her father. Except for one drunken comment made when Lee Lee and I were older, my mother never spoke of it. Though after divorcing my father, she did marry a man, an old friend we were told, who bore a striking resemblance to my sister.

What led my father to claim Leanett as his own when he would have been within his rights to cast her and my mother out of his life? No one would have blamed him. Was it denial, an inability to accept my mother's betrayal and the humiliation that came with it? Or was it his ironclad sense of duty that led him to do what he thought, maybe beyond reason, was the right thing, whatever the cost? Or perhaps he was simply determined not to see his own paternal abandonment repeated yet again. I do not know. It was not the sort of thing my father, proud and taciturn as he was, would ever have talked about with me.

But if the story my father chose does not convey the absolute truth, I cannot call it a lie, either. Through his stubbornness, through the commitment that maddened his grandfather, through his dedication to raising and loving Leanett as his own, he transformed what would otherwise have been an embarrassing case of denial into a cause for pride: yes, she was his daughter, as surely as I was his son. No other man on Earth could say that and have it mean something.

I'M STANDING IN AN ALLEY around the corner from Eloise's house, waiting. Any minute, Woody should be turning the corner to give me the all-clear signal, letting me know the neighbors have gone out and the house is empty. We've been planning this heist all afternoon, waiting for our opportunity. My heart is beating fast as I look to either side of the alleyway, scanning for passersby who might interfere.

Suddenly, Woody rounds the corner and waves. I jump up, grab the fence with both hands, and hoist my legs over. I have to be fast.

An apple tree stands in the far corner of the yard. I scuttle over to it in a crouch, keeping my head low. I reach up and pick the ripest, reddest fruit I can find with one hand, stretch my T-shirt out with the other, and drop my spoils into it like a basket. I look over and see the top of Woody's head poking above the fence, keeping a lookout. When I've piled as many apples into my shirt as it will take, I hobble back over to the fence and hand the spoils over to Woody, one by one. My shirt empty, I hoist myself back over the fence, take my cut from Woody, and we both run out the end of the alley, laughing. The perfect crime.

Woody is my best friend, and he will remain so for years. Through

high school, through my failed first shot at college, through my first real
job, through the birth of my daughters Lisa and Tamara and that of my
son Alden, Woody will be there beside me.

But at the moment, I'm not thinking about the future. I'm thinking
that we just nabbed a fine haul, and that the neighbor whose backyard
fruit tree we pilfered would be none the wiser. I'm thinking about the
game of stickball I'll play in the alley later that afternoon.

Woody's family is an extension of my own, and I think nothing of
dropping in on them unannounced. Woody's father owns a small con-
tracting and construction business and he has a few years of college
under his belt. Though he never finished his degree, he has the mind of
an engineer. His hobbies alone fascinate me. He sits patiently painting
miniature figurines under a magnifying glass, then arranging them on
a tiny model of a rolling field. As he places a gray figure here and a blue
figure there, he explains the troop movements of the Battle of Vicksburg
and the strategic thinking behind them. In the basement sits a hulking
chunk of metal, a half-assembled automobile engine he is building by
hand for fun. I don't know anyone else in the neighborhood with the
technical know-how even to attempt this, much less someone who would
take pleasure in that kind of arduous work.

He also loves chess. I had been introduced to the game by my dad,
who thought I would enjoy it, given my growing love of mathematics.
As he only knew the rudiments, he decided to turn it into a bonding
experience. We would learn together. He unpacked the board, showed
me how to set up the pieces, and we were off. Naturally, he assumed he
would beat me, regardless of his inexperience. But in our third game, I
took him to checkmate in five moves. With that, he packed up the set,
handed it to me, and wished me well with my new hobby.

Woody's father is much more skilled. When he discovers that I'm
learning the game, he sits me down to school me. I'll not be checkmat-
ing him anytime soon. Woody is annoyed that my attention has been
hijacked by what he regards as a boring game. Why sit inside staring at

a board for hours on end when our bikes are laying right there on the front lawn just waiting for us to hop on and ride? But I'm a goner, an instant chess obsessive, and Woody's dad is showing me the ropes. Soon enough, I'll be poring over books documenting classic matches, challenging whoever shows the slightest interest in the game, and requisitioning a lazy Susan from Eloise's kitchen so I can sit in the bathtub and play both sides of the board without getting up, at least until someone pounds on the door demanding to know just what the hell I've been doing in there for so long.

Woody is really light-skinned. Though he has a Negro grandparent on each side of his family, he nevertheless looks for all the world like your typical white boy. His family has lived in Eloise's neighborhood since before black families started moving in. I would often wonder why Woody's parents never moved away like the other whites had done. Then one day I overheard his mother declare to one of her new neighbors, "We just wouldn't run from our own kind," a comment that confuses me. Sometime later, while rewatching a movie that she loved on television, *Imitation of Life*, my mother will explain to me how someone can "be" black while they "look" white. She'll tell me about people like that in our own family, second cousins living in a fashionable suburb, on whom we would never dare simply drop in, because they are "passing for white."

It would have been absurd for someone with my darker skin tone to attempt to "pass." But Woody's family could have passed. In fact, it soon became clear to me that they *had* been passing in Park Manor in the years they'd lived there prior to Eloise and Moonie moving in. Ultimately, as the neighborhood transitioned from "white" to "black," they chose not to move, and therefore not to continue to "pass," out of a deeply felt loyalty to "their own kind."

How ironic, that they were so ambivalent about their passing! Did this mean my passing cousins felt no such loyalty, or harbored no such doubt? And if not, did their choice make them "less black," or perhaps not black at all? What had seemed an elemental fact of life—that the differences between blacks and whites are visible, inherited, and immutable—now broke apart into something much less certain. And what did this all mean for my relationship with Woody?

At the time of the apple heist, it means nothing at all. I sit on Eloise's front porch and feel the fruit's skin give way between my teeth, taste its sweet flesh and juice. For now, meaning is the thing you pull out of your hat when Eloise asks you about the pastor's words. It winks out of existence just as quickly as it comes. It has nothing to do with Woody and me sitting there, savoring this fruit and this afternoon, just like yesterday afternoon and the one before it and on and on. There will be another bike ride and another game of stickball and another fruit tree and another and another. There is no reason we can see that it won't go on forever, this procession. And despite whatever murmurs emanate from the rooms in the fine houses lining the block, and despite the lengthening shadows, there is no reason for either of us to think that the encroaching darkness coming down just a few hours from now will ever touch us.

Two

arolyn Green. Between classes, I scan the halls for her fair skin and wavy, sandy brown hair. I half hope and half fear that, through the play of bodies and faces, shouts and laughter, her eyes—they're light, almost blue—will meet mine. I lean against a wall and pretend to listen to what a friend is telling me, about which of the freshman girls is looking fine and what teacher is on his case again. I'm pretending to listen, but I can't help looking over his shoulder to try and catch a glimpse of her skirt, or even one of her friends cutting a path through the bodies, a path that might lead me to her.

But even if her eyes did meet mine, even if she beckoned me over to her, I wouldn't know what to do. Whenever I'm around her, I clam up, suddenly unable to think of anything funny or interesting to say. And it's not like I don't know how to talk. Aunt Eloise's ritual has served me well. In my senior year, I'll be voted "Most Talkative," a title I well deserve. I'm smart, and often enough I'm a smart aleck. Bored in class, finishing my work before the others, I have little to keep my mind occupied except for running my mouth, drumming on my desk, and trying to make my classmates and the occasional teacher laugh.

But whatever wit I possess leaves me whenever I'm in the presence of Carolyn Green.

I keep a journal, and the words I wish I could speak to her go there and nowhere else, stopping dead on the page. In English class, we're studying Shakespeare's sonnets, and my inability to speak to Carolyn moves me to compose a poem myself.

Alas, come near and listen to my piece,
About a dream of love with this girl fair,
A love so strong that it will never cease,
To fill my heart and keep a flame lit there.
Yet, dreams are dreams, and ne'er they may come true,
'Less I undo myself and play my part.
I have not valor as the others do,
And words come not to mouth but to my heart.
Yet I do hope that someday I'll see light,
And overcome these feelings I have now.
I'll speak to her and our love will burn bright,
I'll find the courage that I know, somehow.
With hopeful heart and steadfast mind I'll strive,
To win her love and keep my dream alive.

I can barely carry on a normal conversation with Carolyn, so reciting my sonnet to her is out of the question. Instead, I approach my English teacher, Mrs. Tidwell, after class, journal in hand, and read her my poem. I tell her (and myself) that I want her expert opinion on my iambic pentameter, but the truth is that keeping my desire for Carolyn bottled up is unbearable. It has to come out some way, and, maybe a little pathetically, this is the way I've chosen. When I finish, the first words out of my teacher's mouth are, "Does she know?" Mrs. Tidwell has no idea that Carolyn is the object of my unrequited yearning, but there is no disguising that the poem emerged from real romantic torment.

That yearning will replicate and attach itself to other girls at school, but I never felt about them as intensely as I did about Carolyn. And I never did "undo myself and play my part" when it came to her. I just couldn't bring myself to tell her how I felt, and eventually my passions cooled and moved on, though they never died completely. To make things worse, some years later, after graduation, when I told a mutual friend of my feelings toward Carolyn and my inability to express them, she told me that Carolyn once told her that she thought I was the most interesting boy at school.

IN A PHOTOGRAPH OF the John Marshall Harlan High School chess team, I stand in the lower right corner, smiling in a striped collared shirt. I appear to be looking just to the side of the camera. Compared to my six classmates, I look like a mere child who has somehow found his way into the picture. But my presence there is authentic. Due to a combination of intellectual precociousness and a registration error that led me to skip a year and a half of elementary school, I entered high school at age twelve.

Precociousness is a double-edged sword. On the one hand, despite my youth, I excel academically. Classes are a breeze. Even material that makes my brighter classmates wince, like learning Latin declensions, comes easily to me. With that ease, I earn a reputation as a bit of a prodigy, which I revel in. I take any chance I can to display my facility with the material. I can sit in trigonometry class—one of my favorites—and explain the lesson backward and forward almost as well as the teacher can. I can absorb and synthesize whatever equation, text, or concept I'm presented with as naturally as breathing. It is my first taste of the power and the freedom that come with intellectual mastery, and I want all I can get.

On the other hand, looking like a child—being, in fact, a child—among teenagers has its drawbacks. In Little League, I had been a very good pitcher, and I retain my athletic ambitions in high school, thinking that perhaps I'd like to try out for the basketball team. But one look at the Harlan High squad dashes those hopes. Not only are these, to all appearances, full-grown men out on the floor, they're *good*. There is no way my undersized body could handle running smack into one of those brick wall picks or taking a charge to the chest from a two-hundred-pound center.

But worse than that, there is the dating scene. Advanced as I am in the classroom, outside of it I am a social novice, especially when it comes to girls. While my youth makes my academic accomplishments more impressive, it also saddles me with a seemingly insurmountable disadvantage when it comes to dating in my early high school years. The fact is that I cannot translate my gregariousness and wit into credible flirtation, the sort of thing that might lead to a date and from a date to necking and then to who knows where.

The boy in that chess team's photo does not yet have the makings of a Player—someone whose mastery over whatever game is at hand commands the respect and admiration of others. He is not a Gouster, one of the tough, dark-skinned kids who live in the towering apartment buildings to the west of the Dan Ryan Expressway across from Park Manor. You can recognize the Gousters by their loose-fitting pleated pants and knit shirts. Even if he had the wardrobe, the boy in the chess team's photograph would never be mistaken for one of them, with their swagger and fabulous dancing and the switchblades in their pockets. Even as kids, the Gousters ran with legitimate gangsters, and they would sniff that boy out in an instant, as would those fly girls who were always hanging around them.

Neither is he an Ivy Leaguer, one of the light-skinned kids living in the bungalows and low-occupancy apartment buildings on the east side of the expressway, with their starched-collar Brooks Brothers shirts under V-neck sweaters and their tapered pants and loafers. The Ivy Leaguers are nothing but punks as far as the Gousters are concerned, and the Gousters are nothing but thugs as far as the Ivy Leaguers are concerned. What they have in common is that none of them take much notice of the boy in the photograph, as he poses no threat. They regard him, he imagines, with thinly veiled contempt. The boy himself registers these slights and feels a rising urge to make his presence felt, not as a Gouster or Ivy Leaguer, but as a Player of his own making.

TAKE A CONE—a three-dimensional shape with a circle at the base that narrows to a single point. Now imagine taking a flat piece of paper and passing it straight through the cone. You can pass it through at any point along its length and at any angle. Maybe you pass it through so the paper is parallel to the base. Or maybe it's perpendicular. Maybe you pass it through at a 45-degree angle. Consider all the different ways that the paper can intersect the cone.

Now imagine that the part of the cone that intersects with the paper leaves a trace. You'll get a circle if the paper is parallel to the base; a hyperbola if it's perpendicular; or an ellipse if it passes fully through at any other angle. If you pass the paper only part of the way through, you'll get a parabola. These are curves that begin and end at the edge of the paper.

There's nothing particularly magical about any of this. What blows my mind, though, is when my solid geometry teacher, Mr. Reffels, shows me that, if you plot those circles, ellipses, hyperbolas, and parabolas on the x and y axes on a graph, you can take the coordinates and translate them all into the same mathematical formula: the quadratic equation. With parameters appropriately chosen, the coordinates that satisfy some version of the quadratic equation will fall precisely along the trace left by the intersection of the paper's plane with the surface of the cone.

In other words, a cone isn't a cone just because it looks like other cones. There is a deep, underlying order to the cone that is the same everywhere and always. A cone is a cone for a reason that can be expressed in perfectly precise, logical, and elegant mathematical language. Any child can learn to recognize a cone by comparing it to other cones even before they learn to speak. But does being able to point to the cone and identify it mean the child knows what it is? Even if he learns to speak and describes it in words, do those words express what makes the cone a cone?

In an instant, standing before Mr. Reffels's blackboard, I suddenly understand what the child does not. I understand that what I've just been shown applies not only to the cone but to many other things. Three-dimensional shapes, yes, but perhaps more. There is an order beneath the surface of things, and mathematics can help us find it. A previously hidden part of the world has broken open, and I look inside.

SO MUCH FOR MATHEMATICAL GENERALITIES. What about the order in real life? Imagine that I woke up one morning to find myself transformed into a tall, handsome jock, someone who can dunk a basketball but can make neither heads nor tails of solid geometry. Would I be overjoyed, or would I find myself just as frustrated as I am now, but only in another register? Perhaps I'm fortunate that no such metamorphosis ever occurred. But for now, I exist in a state of tension, with a mind a little too advanced and a body a little too stunted, where I am intellectually capable of almost anything and physically capable, it seems, of almost nothing.

I'M MISSING SOMEONE IMPORTANT at Harlan High: Woody. Despite the fact that we're neighbors, we go to different schools. Neither of us attends nearby Parker High, which is in a state of decline. It's no longer the sort of place either my family or Woody's deems suitable. Woody attends the private, all-boys Mendel Catholic Prep, while I have managed to attend Harlan with the help of a little legerdemain. Park Manor falls outside of Harlan's district, but the apartment my father shares with his new wife, Constance, does not. When I register, we put down my father's address instead of Eloise's.

Woody would never have made it at Parker anyway. Looking to all the world like a white kid, he surely would have been brutalized by the

Gousters who inhabit the place. Even if Parker's academics had been up to snuff, it would have been a hazardous environment for someone who stands out the way Woody does. And, proud as he is, he would likely not have had the sense to back down from a fight he was sure to lose. Woody knows how to take a punch, but how many punches can one man take?

Mendel, by contrast, is mostly white. Woody could have pretended to be like one of the other Irish or Polish or Italian kids there. But he takes his family's decision to stick with their own people to heart, and he doesn't even try to pass. If anything, his racially ambiguous appearance prods Woody to double down on his blackness, which he proudly trumpets every chance he gets.

I miss Woody's company at school, but our connection is strong enough to survive our days of separation. On our Little League team, I was a pitcher and he was a catcher. We would spend long afternoons practicing signals and pitches in the alley. While I had the precision and focus to reliably place a pitch wherever I wanted it to go, Woody had the toughness to endure the catcher's physically demanding role. He was a little undersized, but he was sinewy and competed as though possessed. When a runner came hurtling toward the plate, determined to bowl Woody over and knock the ball out of his hands, he would invariably stand his ground, make the tag, and take the hit.

While my athletic aspirations stall out in high school, Woody's are fulfilled. Although I'm bigger and stronger than Woody, I'm still no physical threat to anybody. But he manages to turn himself into an asset on the wrestling squad, working out and cramming in the calories to make weight. He excels through pure grit, ferocity, and an ability to endure pain. By the time he graduates, he'll have a letter sewn onto his Mendel varsity jacket in honor of his achievements on the mat. I will envy him for that.

But no matter our differing experiences, and no matter Woody's athletic accomplishments, we're both odd ducks in our way. Though we have to navigate the halls of our respective schools without each other, we are still always there for one another, lounging in wait on the front lawn with our bikes or trotting out to the street for a game of catch, baseballs in one hand and gloves on the other.

———————————

AS I FOUND OUT LATER, there was a path not taken, one that might actually have led me away from Woody. At some point before I entered high school, my parents had a meeting with an admissions officer at the University of Chicago Laboratory Schools. The Lab Schools were, and remain, a beacon of progressive education. There teachers implemented innovative pedagogical techniques and researchers produced new knowledge about education. One of my public school teachers had apparently passed my name on to someone at the school and informed them that I would make an excellent candidate for admission.

Had I attended the Lab Schools, I undoubtedly would have found myself among other students with my intellectual abilities and proclivities, the kind of kids who, like me, knew their way around a slide rule and a chessboard and thought that spending an afternoon reading the *World Book Encyclopedia* constituted a pretty good time. In an environment like that, I surely would have found myself challenged in ways that were simply beyond the capacity of a public school like Harlan High. I had several excellent teachers at Harlan, but, understandably, more of their energy was expended on those lagging behind than those barreling ahead. While I likely would have been an advanced student even at the Lab Schools, I would have been much closer to the norm there than at Harlan.

That is what I imagine would have been the case, anyway. I never did find out, because I did not end up attending the University of Chicago Laboratory Schools. In a rare instance of consensus, my parents decided against pursuing admission.

I never got a full explanation as to why, but I did get a sense of their reasoning. It was not about the kind of education I would receive. I suspect it had more to do with the kind of social world I would enter at the Laboratory Schools, and the effect my parents imagined it would have on me. Though nested among neighborhoods much rougher than Park Manor, the University of Chicago's Hyde Park campus existed then and exists now as a world apart from the rest of the South Side. In the early 1960s, it would have been an almost entirely white world of students, administrators, and professors. The Lab Schools would have been staffed mostly by white teachers, and my peers would have been mostly the white children of mostly white academics and professionals, with the occasional black, brown, or Asian face dotting the yearbook pages.

Perhaps my parents were worried about racial stigma, about my feeling out of place or alienated because of the color of my skin. It is also possible that, in their meeting, they felt condescended to by an admissions officer who may have arrogantly insinuated that these young, relatively unsophisticated, divorced Negro parents ought to hand over their gifted son to the people who could do for him what they plainly could not. Maybe this person would have suggested that my parents should feel gratitude for the opportunity, as if Everett Loury and Gloria Cartman were less than capable of providing comparable opportunities for their child. I don't know if any of that did happen, but such a scenario is not implausible.

More than the possible condescension of the administrator or the probable realization that their son would be one of very few black students, I imagine my parents would have known that I could not spend four years in Hyde Park's rarified air and emerge unchanged. I would change by virtue of acquiring education, of course, and I'm sure they thought that was all to the good. But what manners and habits of mind would I absorb from the children of these intellectuals and doctors and lawyers? What new tastes would I develop amidst the University of Chicago's imposing gothic spires, hidden away from the precincts of "my people"? Why had Aunt Eloise gathered us up and brought us into her home in the first place, if not for fear that we malleable souls would find ourselves deformed by our environment? While Hyde Park did not threaten to deform me, my parents may have perceived that it had the power to transform me into someone they would no longer recognize and, even more poignantly, someone who would no longer recognize them in himself. Even as a preteen, I was already developing a reputation for being a headstrong smart aleck. Perhaps they worried that one day they would look at my face and see that Lab Schools administrator's arrogant grin slashing across it.

THOUGH I WOULD EVENTUALLY GROW and blend in among my peers, I found myself socially disadvantaged in more subtle ways than my obvious youth. By the early 1960s, the Great Migration was in its final phase. Millions of Southern Negros linked to slavery and its aftermath either by blood or personal experience made their way north to find work in cities such as Chicago and to escape the South's increasingly brutal Jim Crow regime. The Great Aunts were among these migrants. And like many migrants, they set to work assimilating once they got where they were going, shedding their Southern manners and clothes for the sophisticated tastes and dress of midcentury Chicago. By the time I came around in 1948, the only thing that distinguished the Great Aunts from native-born Chicagoans was their accents. The Great Aunts had accrued modest wealth and property and a social network in Chicago. They were established.

And once established, they were in a position to vet, judge, and distinguish between the newcomers, just as they themselves were likely once judged by other black Chicagoans. I often heard the word *country* thrown around to describe someone who didn't dress quite right or who spoke with a too-pronounced Southern twang or who otherwise revealed themselves not to have properly absorbed the habitus of the city. *Country* wasn't a compliment.

It was not lost on me that these "country" people often had darker skin than their city counterparts. This is the early 1960s, well before ideas like "black is beautiful" gained currency. Nappy hair, thick lips, broad noses, and dark skin were not signs of beauty in midcentury black Chicago. The Great Aunts would warn their daughters and granddaughters away from dating men who were "too" dark, lest it become a source of gossip. If a woman were to say, "That nigga is fine," more likely than not she was referring to his light skin tone, his light-colored eyes, or his wavy hair.

Skin color prejudice among black folks could be a self-fulfilling prophecy. The wrong skin tone would not only affect a man's dating life, it could also prevent him, as a pledge, from gaining admittance to a selective black fraternity. This rejection could result in measurable material disadvantage down the road, as the failed pledge would not have access to the informal social and professional networks fraternities are designed to create and perpetuate. Such a situation could then reinforce existing stereotypes about dark skin and "African" features. An observer would eventually notice that, since other well-placed light-skinned friends are willing to give them a job or a loan or a business contact, light-skinned blacks would tend to have more wealth and more resources than dark-skinned blacks. As a result, the former would, in some material way, be more desirable to associate with than the latter. Only later would I come to see the deeper lesson of this self-fulfilling prophecy: observers could be mistaken in thinking of a dark-skinned person as inherently less intelligent, talented, or worthy than a light-skinned person. Nevertheless, these observers would not be mistaken to use skin color when trying to gauge a person's relative prospects of success, given that colorism is sufficiently powerful in the social environment, and absent any other information about a person besides their skin color. That is, skin color prejudice and rational inference need not conflict with one another. Which is not an argument for colorism at all, but merely an explanation of what makes it so insidious.

Indeed, colorism was so insidious that it could worm its way into relations among family members. And at least to some extent, color hierarchies determined the dating pecking order among the black students at Harlan High. While it wasn't quite clear where I fell in that order, it was crystal clear to me that my features excluded me from the highest levels of desirability.

Colorism affected Woody, too. Whereas the prejudice against dark skin was held more or less out in the open, Woody's feelings about his own light skin played out in counterintuitive ways, especially when it came to dating. For all of his toughness, Woody was a romantic, not an aspiring Player like me. When he pursued a girl, he did so with the same single-minded focus that he brought to the wrestling team. And the girl that really drove him wild was Elvie, who was three years younger than Woody, lived in a dicey neighborhood, and had very dark skin.

Woody was intelligent, handsome, amusing, and athletic. I imagine that all those qualities, in addition to his visual appearance being that of a white person, would have made Woody irresistible at the mixers and dances held by Mendel and its sister school. But, unlike me, Woody wasn't interested in wooing multitudes; he forsook all of that for Elvie. While he would check out the girls right beside me, and listen to me go on about whoever I was trying (and failing) to make it with that week, once he found Elvie, he never seriously considered anyone else. He was in love. And being in love, even the many attractive girls who would give him a smile held no real attraction for him.

Elvie was pretty and sweet, and Woody would dutifully take a Chicago Transit Authority bus over to her neighborhood and then walk four blocks past the tenements. This was not the sort of place you wanted to end up stranded after dark, especially if you were, to all appearances, white. Dating Elvie required actual bravery. But I imagine the danger only deepened Woody's sense that he was performing an act of chivalry in tribute to his beloved.

I found the whole thing baffling.

Since I was a child, I had watched Adlert and Alfred seduce their way through the South Side. Adlert was very clear about it. Despite his professional accomplishments, he told me, point blank, that life's goal was to "get as much pussy as you can." Whether he was joking or not, he certainly walked the talk. And I took his advice quite seriously. But at the time, the most pussy I could get was exactly none. There was no denying it: I was failing. Meanwhile, my best friend was set up for what could have been a wildly successful sexual career, and he refused to capitalize on it, preferring instead to pursue Elvie, a girl who (through no fault of her own) put him in physical danger, occupied his every waking thought, and blinded him to the many dalliances and pleasures that awaited him.

I had no doubt that Woody's feelings for Elvie were sincere. They had to be, or his behavior would have struck me as deranged rather than merely puzzling. Woody loved Elvie dearly, so much so that he eventually married her. It was real. But I suspect that her skin color played a part in Woody's attraction to her. Whether due to Elvie's modest upbringing, her dark skin, or some other factor, Woody's parents did not approve of the relationship. They would have much preferred that he dated someone else. Woody fought them on it and prevailed. If his parents had been passing, then chose to stop passing when more black families started moving into the neighborhood, was Woody not simply following their lead? Wasn't this his way of sticking with "his own kind"? Didn't his racially ambiguous appearance and his sense of pride compel him to ensure that no one would mistake him for anything other than a black man?

I would not have had the language to articulate such questions at the time even if they had occurred to me. And whatever the answers, they would not negate the reality of Woody's feelings. The relationships of the adults in my life were always complicated, their tensions often palpable, their reasons for being together sometimes obscure. Against that backdrop, Woody's attraction to Elvie was pretty conventional, especially in the sense that, the reality of his feelings aside, it signified something larger about his own sense of social belonging. Anyone doubting Woody's affiliation with other black people only had to look at the girl standing beside him.

Three

I'm doing this for love. Or if not love, then sex. Or if not sex, then whatever I can get. I'll take anything at this point—a kiss, a touch. I'm standing on the lot of a filling station and auto body shop on the South Side, just a garage and a few pumps with a handful of cars parked outside. I ride my bike past it often. Woody and I used to play stickball in the alley alongside it. There's a '61 Chevy with South Carolina plates that's been sitting in the lot for a while now, and some neighborhood kids tell me the guys in the shop have been messing with the ignition. You don't even need a key to start it, they say. Anyone can just hop in and drive it off the lot.

I badly want a car for all the reasons any seventeen-year-old wants a car. I want to cruise, to impress my buddies, to pick up girls, to go where I want when I want. But I've got something more specific in mind right now. My former high school's prom is coming up, and Sandra has asked me to go with her. I had taken her to my senior prom the year before, when she was a junior. Now that I'm a graduate, a college man (though just barely), I imagine I'll be that much more desirable to be with and to be seen with. Man, it would be great to pick her up in my own ride. I'm practically an adult. I tell myself it's only fitting that I show up in style. Not to mention, that Chevy, with its big back seat, would create the space for some interesting possibilities after the dance.

Skinny, bookish, and plain-looking, Sandra is not physically remarkable. But I like her, and anyway she is my best option. In high school, I was the brainy, funny kid, a math tutor and the captain of the chess team. It was a recipe for academic success but a toxic brew where girls were concerned. I frittered away four years on unrequited crushes and failed romantic entreaties, and I managed to graduate both a valedictorian and a virgin. Now that I'm a college freshman and I *still* haven't gotten any, the situation has gone from depressing to unbearable. Things aren't looking any better at my current school. The Illinois Institute of Technology, with its focus on science, engineering, and design, is not exactly a hotbed of coed sexual liberation. Drastic measures are in order.

I've already asked Alvin, my mother's third and current husband, if I could borrow his car for the prom, and he turned me down flat, as I don't even have my license yet. My only legitimate option is off the table. That Chevy has been sitting in the filling station lot for weeks now. It's late in the afternoon, and the station is closed. My plan is to get in, drive off, and stash the car somewhere it won't be noticed. Then, on the evening of the prom, I'll pick up Sandra, dazzling her, I'm sure. We'll dance, hold each other close, and when we drive off, I won't even have to propose that we pull over somewhere secluded to spend some time together. It'll be understood. She'll be thinking the same thing. Then, early the next morning, before the station opens, I'll return the car. Just as mysteriously as it disappeared, it will reappear. No harm done.

This is a solid plan. I approach the filling station, glancing around to make sure no employees are lurking. But, by the time I hear the engine roar and feel the steering wheel vibrate beneath my palms, the plan has changed. It occurs to me that, as long as I've got the car, I might as well take advantage of it. Neither Mom nor Dad is going to have the money to buy me one of my own anytime soon, and neither will I.

The next week is a bit of a blur. I keep the car parked well clear of Mama and Alvin's house, where I'm living while I work at Burger King and sometimes manage to attend classes. I don't want to have to answer any awkward questions. But in every spare moment, I'm behind the wheel and cruising, usually with Woody riding shotgun. Now that I've upped my game, there are plenty of people I want to see. Girls who had turned me down in the past, or who I never had the guts to ask for a date in the first place. The guys from school, who can't believe that I'd somehow gotten my hands on a ride, and who stand around admiring it and asking if they can drive (hell, no). In my own mind, I have ascended to the next echelon of status, that of a Player. No matter that it's all temporary.

When prom night finally rolls around, I'm full of confidence. And, as I know from observing the smoothness with which Adlert and Alfred operate, confidence is the best aphrodisiac there is. I check myself in the mirror. I have my suit together; my hair is looking good. My mother stands admiring me, telling me how handsome I look, how I'll sweep Sandra off her feet. I leave the house excited, imagining how her skin will feel on my skin, worrying a little that I'll fumble while trying to unclasp her bra.

I'm still thinking about that bra clasp when I hear the siren and see the flashing lights in my rearview. I pull over, and the police officer gets out of his car and walks over to mine. He asks to see my license. I tell him I don't have it on me.

"This your car, sir?" he asks.

"Yes, officer."

"Where are you from?"

"South Carolina," I say, remembering the out-of-state plates.

"Where in South Carolina?"

"Columbia," I tell him. It's the only city in South Carolina I know of.

"Mm-hmm."

He tells me to step out of the vehicle.

As I sit in the back of the squad car, now officially under arrest, it occurs to me that I have done something incredibly stupid. This wasn't a foolproof plan; it was a harebrained scheme. What had I been thinking? More ominously, what will my father say?

At the station, I call him and explain as best I can where I am and why. Later, Adlert will help me out. He has already been disbarred, so he can't officially represent me, but he still has connections within the court system. This is Chicago, after all. If you know somebody who knows somebody, you're good. He'll plead my case: "A good kid, valedictorian, attending the Illinois Institute of Technology. He knows he messed up. You don't really want to send this promising young man to the county lockup, do you?" Though Adlert is in a state of professional disgrace, his lawyering must be as sharp as ever, as I do not spend a single night in jail, and the offense will eventually be expunged from my record.

But at the police station on prom night, I'm knotted with worries. Sandra will be understandably hurt and upset. Not knowing that I had been arrested, she'll think I simply stood her up on prom night. Her older brothers will threaten to kick my ass, and I'll never really be able to apologize. Whatever hopes I still have for making it with her evaporate.

As we leave the police station, my father is quiet. There is no yelling. Instead, he tells me that I am starting to remind him of Gerald. Gerald is his half-brother, a drunk and a fuckup, unable to hold a job or provide for his family. They have the same mother, Leotha, but different fathers. My dad is forever buying groceries and running them over to Gerald's apartment to make sure his children don't go hungry. The humiliation of being arrested, the frustration of inadvertently sabotaging my own plans for Sandra, the possibility of jail, none of it is quite as bad as hearing my father compare me to Gerald, who is disappointment made flesh. I know I'm not as bad as Gerald. But the mere thought that my father might think I am fills me with shame.

THE NEW BAUHAUS SCHOOL of architecture looms large over the Illinois Institute of Technology. In the 1930s, it merged with the Institute of Design, which was founded and run by László Moholy-Nagy, a force within the Bauhaus movement who came to Chicago by way of London after fleeing the Nazis. The campus was designed by Ludwig Mies van der Rohe, and his S. R. Crown Hall that houses the architecture department is a masterpiece in glass, concrete, and steel. Every bench and building seem to communicate that this is a serious place where serious people come to study their craft.

Besides the intimidating minimalism of IIT's structures and grounds, there are the students. They walk briskly from class to class, sporting crew cuts, slide rules hanging from their belts, and pocket protectors nestled into their button-down shirts. Almost all of them are what we would call "white ethnics": Polish, Italian, Jewish, Greek, and Slavic. Many of those who are Chicago natives came up through Lane or Tilden, renowned and specialized technical high schools that had prepared generations of working-class Chicago kids for the rigors of engineering, mathematics, and physics.

At this time, IIT is not about the shaping of young people into free-thinking citizens or the cultivation of aesthetic sensibilities or the Socratic method. This is a science boot camp. In the first year, everyone takes calculus, physics, chemistry, and biology. Sit, pay attention, learn your equations, and God help you if you fall behind in your coursework. I've got a natural aptitude for these subjects, but natural aptitude is not enough in this environment. Success here requires long hours of disciplined study, hunched over notes and textbooks. It requires unwavering focus.

Before my first semester at IIT, my father presented me with a gift of $1,000, a considerable sum of money in 1965, and especially considerable because he was probably only making around $10,000 a year. Scraping together that much cash could not have been easy, and despite his obvious eagerness to see me out on my own and off his expense book, he wanted to make sure that I had a little something extra to transition into adult life.

That transition is not going well. I do okay for the first part of my first semester, but things quickly go to pieces. I start spending most of my time hanging out with Woody, who had enrolled at IIT along with me, and with my new friend John, a transplant from New York with a taste for vodka and reefer. John is one of the few other black people on campus. He's light-skinned, from a well-to-do family, and he carries himself with a certain swagger and braggadocio. He tells me he plays chess, but after I decimate him in game after game, it's clear he's barely a novice. As an amateur boxer, he's much more formidable. For some reason, I think he'll be as easy to take in the ring as he is on the chessboard, but I abandon that notion, along with boxing itself, after John pops me in the face a few times with his wicked left jabs and I see stars.

I rarely make it to class now, and when I do, I sit and stare at the calculus lessons on the board, utterly lost in a math class, the place where I often felt most comfortable in high school. I'm three assignments behind in chemistry, and I've stopped bothering to tell myself that I'll catch up eventually. The more I fall behind, the more attending class becomes a psychologically fraught experience. I had been the brightest kid in any grade at every school I'd attended up to now. I know I have the ability to understand this material. Why am I flailing while my cohorts seem ready to meet the challenge? As the missed classes, missed assignments, and flunked exams pile up, so does the guilt. Sitting through lectures that I barely understand only amplifies the awful feeling that I am embarrassing both myself and my family, so I often skip them rather than endure the suffering.

I know this is a losing strategy, that I can't continue in this way and expect to graduate. Things will change next week, I tell myself. I'll buckle down and put all this angst behind me.

I'M THINKING VAGUELY ABOUT the chemistry exam I should be studying for as I pick up the carton resting between my feet and take a sip.
Orange juice and vodka, a screwdriver to go. I'm feeling the effects of
the drink, plus the joint John and I shared before we hopped in his car.
We're headed toward the Robert Taylor Homes, a massive complex of
housing projects about ten blocks from campus. They sit a few miles
north of Park Manor and just to the east of the Dan Ryan Expressway,
which Mayor Richard J. Daley built in order, among other reasons,
to cordon off that black neighborhood from the white ethnic enclave
whence Daley originally hailed. That enclave provides Daley the voter
base that allows him to run the city essentially as he wishes, a state of
affairs that will last for twenty years. The Robert Taylor Homes stand
there, cheek-by-jowl with that expressway, as a monument both to the
efforts of midcentury reformers who took up the staggering challenges
of black integration and poverty, and to the resistance and resentment of
the city's white working class.

One cannot fault the ambition and ideals embodied by the Robert Taylor Homes, but rolling up to them now, you can't mistake the
place for anything other than a ghetto. The neighborhood and the towers themselves are run by gangs like the Disciples and the Blackstone
Rangers, and on the street you can see these gangsters keeping watch
over prostitutes and street dealers and whatever other services make
up the area's black markets. Anything you desire can be got for a price
right there on the avenue, as long as you keep your eyes open and your
wits about you. I know a little something about life in Chicago's public
housing projects because my uncle Alfred, his wife, Marybell, and their
brood of seven kids had lived for years in the Ida B. Wells Homes, just
a couple of miles northeast of Robert Taylor Homes. Mama, Lee Lee,
and I would often visit them there.

John and I have come to take it all in, the sordidness and the vitality
alike. But specifically, we're looking for girls to pick up for a joy ride, and
this is a target-rich environment. It's a beautiful mid-autumn evening,

the sweet spot where the damp summer air has dried up but the bitter winter chill has yet to set in. There should be plenty of fine women out and about, as there usually are in this part of the hood. I'm still living with my mother and Alvin, but when I'm out cruising with John, looking for girls and sharing a laugh, I feel like I'm far away from home. And that's not the only pastime we share.

Besides the girls, there is always the game of pool. Along with vodka and marijuana, my friendship with John is built on competition, and he doesn't mind putting a few dollars down on a game. He's eager for me to show him around the South Side's pool scene. We often find ourselves in one of the many black-owned storefront pool halls. Occasionally women come into these places, either on someone's arm or looking to be on someone's arm, but I don't go to the pool hall for the women. I go for the men. Because the men play for money, and as I play, observe, and sharpen my game, I find I can take that money home with me with some reliability.

And I need it. Burger King is not known for its generous compensation packages. But I also do some work at IIT as part of my financial aid package. This involves brushing and maintaining the dean's private pool table, which is behind a locked door. It's a beautiful table, flawless, perfectly level, sporting a new felt covering without a single divot and cushions that are perfectly intact, which is perhaps to be expected at an engineering and design school. The balls are made of ivory and provide perfect elasticity of collision. If you strike the cue ball straight, it will stop dead in its tracks when it collides with another ball.

But here on the South Side, I'm far away from the oak and ivory of the dean's private table. I enter a South Side pool hall, and I'm hit by the smell of cigarettes and the sound of chatter. The Players gather around one table, bragging and dogging each other. In the corner a group of older men sit chattering about the Watts Riots of the past August. Light from low-hanging lamps above the table filters through the stratified smoke suspended in the air. Racks of house cues line one wall. I pull one from the brackets, hold it in place, and test it, rolling it on a table to check for the telltale wobble that indicates warped wood. I run my left hand over a cone of white chalk. The cue must move smoothly through my fingers as they form the perfect bridge. A pool player's bridge is like a horn player's embouchure. It's the foundation on which his entire game ultimately rests.

Before each shot, I press my left palm flat on the table. My thumb and index finger gently wrap around the cue, which extends over the knuckle of my left middle digit. I draw the cue back and forth slowly with my right arm, the lower part of which swings like a pendulum while the upper part remains perfectly still (or at least that's the goal). I try to keep my shoulder stationary, allowing the lower and upper arm on my right side to form a perfect right angle. I focus on striking the cue ball with a smooth, continuous, unhurried motion—with finesse—to allow the tip of the cue stick to bounce back off the cue ball, imparting whatever English (high or low, left or right) I have decided to apply.

In the time since I began hanging out at pool halls, I've picked up a range of different games and the specific skills required to win them. There is eight-ball, where a player takes either solids or stripes and attempts to sink all of their set and then the eight ball itself. There is nine-ball, where players shoot the balls off in sequence from number one to nine. Whoever sinks the nine ball wins. Making a ball on the break and running the remaining balls off without my opponent ever getting a shot is one of the best feelings I've ever experienced. Doing it from rack to rack while my opponent sits helpless and fuming as all his money makes its way into my pocket leaves me feeling like a god! There is bank pool and one-pocket and straight pool and many others, some of them played on ordinary pool tables and some, like snooker and three-cushion billiards, that require special, rarer tables. I learn as many of these games as I can, fascinated by the drastic shifts in tactics and technique required by even subtle differences in the rules.

I love the implicit geometry and math of the game, its logic and clarity, and the rush I get from a perfectly executed run. The extra cash doesn't hurt, either. But the social world of the pool hall soon becomes an attraction in itself. A black pool hall in America is a little like a black barbershop. Men come in to hang out, talk culture, talk politics, and talk shit. They gossip and mull over their triumphs and defeats. Old guys sit, talk, read the paper, and, often enough, demolish young guys like me on the felt.

Working men come in to blow off steam after a long shift, and they mingle with the Players who live their lives on the other side of the line. The Player is a hustler, a gambler, and a would-be pimp. You can spot him in every pool hall. He's tall, slim, and slick, with a gold tooth, Jheri curled or conked hair, and a cigarette dangling from the corner of his mouth. He sports a feathered fedora and well-shined wing tips, pleated pants, a knit woolen shirt, and a tweed jacket. More Gouster than Ivy Leaguer, the Player's got swagger. He walks with a lilting step and talks in a smooth patter. He could be a high-yellow nigga or he could be blue-black; they come in all colors. He takes a swig of cognac (no cheap wine here) from a bottle in the brown paper bag discreetly tucked away in his jacket pocket.

If a guy who, say, drives a pretzel truck for a living should wander in at eight o'clock on a Friday looking a little tipsy, you can watch the Players converge on him like vultures. A Player who knows what he's doing will get the truck driver into a game, put two dollars down, and lose. Then he'll lose again and again, and then maybe win one, and then lose again, all while upping the bet to five and then maybe ten dollars. The truck driver is feeling pretty good. He's winning more than he's losing, so why not put a twenty down on a game? He's feeling confident, maybe even a little cocky. Then the Player starts to play for real, and pretty soon the strutting truck driver is just another sucker who has lost everything he "won" off the Player and then some. Watching these hustlers operate is one of the things John and I most enjoy about cruising the pool hall scene.

Of course, not all Players carry themselves like wannabe Iceberg Slims. Some months after we first started hanging out together, John and I get wind of a bowling alley up in Milwaukee equipped with quality pool tables and a steady supply of mediocre amateurs just begging to have their money taken. We figure we'll at least be able to make enough to pay for gas, probably more, and we'll get a story out of it. And we do get a story. Here it is: some toothless hillbilly from Kentucky we had pegged as a rube took every penny I had. Now that guy could *really* shoot. This time I was the sucker. I suppose that's what I get for judging by appearances.

I'm not yet a Player at the pool table, but neither am I a mark (at least not usually). I can hang. Nobody's chasing me off or treating me like a kid. Maybe I can't get anything going with the girls. Maybe I'm floundering at college. But at the pool hall, I can compete. Whatever masculine validation is denied me elsewhere, I can reclaim a little of it on the felt.

IT'S A SATURDAY AFTERNOON, two or three o'clock, and I'm hanging out at a pool hall across from the Roberts Motel. The motel will soon acquire a reputation for offering first-rate music, food, and entertainment to black clientele on the South Side. But it also offers the same kind of service any other motel offers. Most of the couples who check in there don't have any luggage with them.

This pool hall has a three-cushion billiard table, a rarity, and the proprietor is an older guy who's very serious about this challenging, elegant game. So I sometimes come in just to watch him play and learn some technique. I'll never be as good as him, but the precision required for three-cushion billiards is so extreme that getting even a little better at it will work wonders for the rest of my game.

I look up from my table and through the pool hall's big glass windows I see my mother across the street. She is in full flower, beautiful, busty, and hippy, with a form-fitting dress and a stole of some kind draped around her neck. She is on a man's arm, and that man is not her husband. In fact, I don't know who this guy is. I watch as they cross the street and head toward the pool hall. When they enter, it feels as though the world I have built for myself here is being trespassed upon by visitors from another planet. The pool hall serves as a workshop for my still-burgeoning masculinity, and the presence of my mother and what I suppose is her "date" reminds me that, in age, I am little more than a child.

Mama sees me, approaches, and awkwardly introduces the man. He shakes my hand, looks me dead in the eye, and grins. His face betrays not a hint of shame. He seems a little too amused by this coincidence, a little too happy to see me. He's running his hands along my mother's shoulders, along her hips. With every touch and caress, he seems to be daring me to say something. And he challenges me to a game of eight-ball.

I want to tell this smug motherfucker exactly where he can shove that eight ball. I want to grab him by the neck and toss him out in the street, where he belongs. I want to tell him that if I see him again, he won't be walking away under his own power.

But those words won't come out. Instead, I smile weakly and say, "Sure. Let's play."

I rack. The surge of anger and adrenaline sharpens me up. Soon enough, I knock a ball into a pocket, then another, then another. That smile of his is still on his face, but I think I see it fading a little. He should know, you don't walk into my house like that and put your hands on my mama. Since I can't hit him, I'm going to do the next best thing: I'm going to humiliate him in front of the woman he came here to impress. I'm going to wipe that smile right off his face.

I sink the final ball of my set. To win the game, I just have to take care of the eight, and I've calibrated my previous shot to leave me in an ideal position. The only thing sweeter than making a really tough pool shot is putting yourself in a position where you don't have to attempt one, which I've done to perfection.

But as I get my cue into position, I start thinking. And then I can't stop thinking. I want to win so badly. I want it too much. And for some reason I can no longer quite understand how to do it. What looked like a simple side-pocket shot a second ago, what in fact *is* a simple shot, suddenly becomes confusing. Am I supposed to strike the cue just right of center to send it to the left, or is it the other way around? Do I have to hit the cue ball low, so it stops in its tracks after striking the eight, or does that risk accidentally sinking the cue, which would result in a loss? I can feel all the confidence draining out of me. In other words, I'm choking.

The worst thing about choking, about allowing pressure to short-circuit your judgment, is that you're aware it's happening, and you can do nothing to stop it. Whatever talent, skill, and confidence has gotten you to where you are vanishes out from under you. You find yourself suddenly and absurdly unprepared, as though stricken with spontaneous amnesia, unsure of how you got where you are and clueless about how to get back. Think of the prototypical anxiety dream. You are sitting to take a final exam in a class you have somehow forgotten to attend all semester. Any answers you write down are hopeless guesses, and with each impotent response you progress inexorably toward your own doom.

I draw my cue back to strike, and before it even makes contact with the ball, I know it's a bad shot. The eight caroms off a side cushion instead of dropping into the pocket. That smug smile seeps back into the man's expression and, with the Player's swagger, he finishes me off.

My mother and the man leave soon after—I cannot now recall how they made their exit. Perhaps they're heading back to the motel across the street, or perhaps they're going their separate ways. I stand in the middle of that pool hall feeling violated, my rage toward the man, my mother, and myself surging inside me and crashing against waves of shame. I want to scream and smash the big glass windows. That man made a sucker out of me, just as he was making a chump out of Alvin by spending the afternoon in a motel room with his wife, my mother. Mama had also made a sucker out of my father, I think. Who knows how many times she stepped out on him before Lee Lee's birth forced him to reckon with the truth. I feel a wave of contempt for my father rise in me. Just as his grandfather had insisted, Daddy allowed himself to be played—to be made into a mark. Well, at this very moment, standing at that pool table amidst my humiliation, I silently swear that I won't ever again let that happen to me. There are Players and there are suckers. I know which one I want to be.

I stifle any impulse to act out, and when my anger ebbs a dull sense of desolation is left in its wake. As the sound of blood rushing through my ears subsides, I hear only the occasional clack of ball on ball, the squeak of chalk on cue tip, the low murmur of chatter among the Players.

If someone watching the game out of the corner of their eye, perhaps one of the old timers practicing his billiards, had asked what had happened, I would have shrugged my shoulders and said, "I choked." And he would have known just what I meant. I lost to that man, sure enough. But I also lost to myself. In some sense, my mother and the man only activated a confrontation with an internal enemy who had lately emerged—in the pool hall, at school, seemingly everywhere—and with whom I was ill-equipped to compete.

MORE AND MORE, I find myself thinking of Charlene Teague. Even as I'm scheming to "borrow" the Chevy and seduce Sandra, as I'm sitting through lectures at IIT in a half-stupor, and as I'm working on my pool and chess games, Charlene drifts into my thoughts.

We met several years ago in choir rehearsal at the Bethel AME Church, where her mother, Mrs. Mary Teague, is a stalwart of the usher board, one of those women in starched white uniforms and gloves who, with meticulous dedication and propriety, show parishioners to their seats and keep the service running smoothly. The role suits Mrs. Teague, as she is rigid and a little severe in her ways. She is not a bad woman. She takes the Gospel seriously and loves everyone accordingly. But she is an old-fashioned, tough-minded Southerner and not someone I want to cross.

Charlene herself is anything but rigid. She is sweet, pretty, and shy, with a figure I find absolutely irresistible. Though I don't go to church as often anymore, I find ways to see her. After getting off the second shift at Burger King at eleven o'clock at night, I wander over to her house, still in uniform and probably smelling of grease and french fries. I knock softly on her window, and after a moment it slides open and she leans out, dressed for bed, her breasts enticingly close to my face. She listens as I spill out my problems, my inability to get a handle on IIT, my menial job, my ever-growing sense that things are not quite going my way. I can talk to her about these things, and she knows just what to say to soothe me.

One night, I move in for a kiss, and she reciprocates. Not many nights after, I ask if I can come in, and she says yes. She shares a room but not her bed with her younger sister, Monica. Her parents are asleep, so I crawl in through her window as quietly as I can. In another minute, I'm in bed with her and my uniform is on the floor. Though I've been mentally preparing for this moment for as long as I can remember, neither of us are quite sure what to do with each other. For information about the mechanics of the act itself, I've had to rely on the bragging (and, I'm now realizing, wild exaggerations) of friends and cousins. But eventually, after much groping and fumbling, we manage to figure it out. Afterward, we lay in bed, happy and nervous. Monica doesn't stir, though I suspect she's aware of my presence. I don't know what Char is thinking, but I'm thinking this has been a long time coming.

This becomes our routine. I get off work, knock on Charlene's window, climb in, and we make love. Not every night, but often enough. After so much trying and so much failing, the idea that sex with someone I find so desirable is now a regular part of my life seems unreal.

I have no real plans or ambitions for my relationship with Charlene, we're just enjoying each other's company. And I am enjoying her company very much. We go out to the movies sometimes, or to Friday night dances at the union hall just down the street from where she lives, but I'm always careful to have her back home before her curfew, lest I run afoul of Mrs. Teague. Her father, Lincoln, is less of a worry. A quiet man from Tennessee, every day he wakes up early, takes two buses for ninety minutes to reach a facility where he works as a janitor, then takes the ninety-minute bus ride back home, where he eats dinner and then sits in his chair in the living room, smoking a pipe and reading the newspaper until retiring to bed at nine o'clock. You could set your watch by Mr. Teague's routine, and Charlene and I more or less do. We can be sure that, by the time my Burger King shift ends, both parents will have been asleep for hours.

It's an evening in June, the night air still thick, and I approach Charlene's house. Despite the humidity, the breeze is a welcome respite from the Burger King kitchen's punishing heat, and I'm relishing the mixture of quitting time's relief and the anticipation of another night with Charlene. I knock on the window, and it slides open. Charlene knows exactly how long it takes me to walk from work to her bedroom, and she's ready for me. As usual, Monica is fast asleep. I hoist myself into her room, and Charlene sits smiling on her bed.

I make a move toward her, but before either of us can say anything, her bedroom door swings open, revealing the silhouette of her father, a rifle cradled in his arm. Charlene and I both yelp, and before either of us can do anything more, her quiet, gentle father is shaking me by the shoulder with his free hand, both relieved that I'm not a burglar (or worse) and a little perplexed by my presence in his daughter's bedroom.

"Son, don't you know I could have shot you?"

A few minutes later, part of me wishes he would have. Nothing fatal, just enough to send me to the hospital and spare me the scene playing out in the Teagues' kitchen. Charlene's mother is awake now, and she is *irate*. The ordinarily controlled and polite Mrs. Teague has transformed into a fury in a nightgown, railing at her daughter, cursing Charlene's irresponsibility, asking aloud how she could have raised "that kind of girl," and bemoaning her daughter's foolishness. Mr. Teague and I are mere silent spectators to this scene of holy matriarchal terror, and Charlene can do little but weep, offering weak protestations and apologies, until finally, apparently unable to bear any more, she blurts out, "But Mama! We're getting married!"

This is news to me. Charlene and I have never even discussed the subject. Why would we? I almost say as much, except that Charlene's "revelation" has managed to silence Mrs. Teague.

"Right, Glenn?" Charlene asks.

All three Teagues look me in the face, and I realize I have no options. I don't want Charlene's mother turning on me, and while I've never heard her father so much as raise his voice, I wonder if his thoughts would turn to that rifle if it transpired, falsely or not, that I'd taken his daughter's virginity and then lied about my intention to marry her. Not to mention that I'd be selling out my darling Charlene, whom I really do love.

"That's right, Mrs. Teague," I say. "We're getting married."

No one seems particularly elated by our improvised engagement announcement, but at least no one is yelling anymore, and Charlene's tears have subsided. There will be time to straighten all of this out, I think to myself. Once tempers have cooled, we can sit down and have a calm discussion about what happened. Charlene and I can plan out how we'll tell her parents that, while we are very much an item, we have no real plans to marry. We can tell them that there will be plenty of time for thinking about marriage in the future. After all, she is only fifteen and I am only seventeen. We are both so young.

Years later, I'll wonder if Charlene knew even then that we did not have as much time as I thought. Was she just trying to quell her mother's rage? Or was that a cover story of its own, a convenient domestic eruption that allowed her an opening to raise with me what would soon become a pressing concern? Did she know even then what I wouldn't find out for months? Did she know she was pregnant?

Four

The R. R. Donnelley & Sons printing plant occupies a dozen or so buildings along Chicago's lakefront. Thousands of employees working across three shifts set the type, print, trim, bind, pack, and ship everything from black and white legal documents to full-color magazines like *Sports Illustrated, Time,* and *National Geographic.* Mail order catalogs and telephone directories are printed there. Men ferry hand trucks loaded down with plates from station to station on a deafening shop floor echoing with the clacking sound of metal on metal, the grinding of machinery, and the shouts of workers. Concern for fire hazards limits smoking, which virtually everyone does, to restricted, enclosed areas. Empty trains pull into the tracks that run alongside the plant's campus, awaiting loads of bound documents to be shipped out across the country.

In the office, where I work as a clerk, laborers drop off their time sheets, which I record in a ledger before handing them off to a runner, who takes them down to a pool where they're coded into punch cards by rows upon rows of women sitting at their desks. While my job is fairly menial—all it requires is the ability to type, add, and not fall asleep at my desk—I find R. R. Donnelley endlessly fascinating. The operational logistics that keep the place running smoothly are mind-blowing in themselves, requiring tight coordination among everyone from the floor managers to the typesetters and engravers to the clerks to the technicians, all of whom work in concert with dozens of specialized machines, each of which has one task, and each of which must function perfectly in order to get a single job done.

In my idle moments, I sometimes sit and watch the printing plant's choreography play out, as men glide across the floor to the machines' groaning, lurching rhythms. Forklifts haul pallets full of bound documents to and fro. In the cafeteria and break rooms, office workers like me mingle with the skilled workers who possess deep knowledge of every aspect of the printing process. These men are Polish and Italian and Irish and Jewish and black, all of them with hard, glovelike hands shaped by a lifetime of physically arduous labor. In a city that's 35 or 40 percent black, almost all the union-protected craftsmen who make the big bucks are white. But Ed Faulkner is an exception. I stop to chat with Ed if he's on a break, sipping a cup of coffee, with a pack of cigarettes rolled up in the sleeve of a T-shirt straining to contain his enormous biceps, and a dog-eared copy of Frantz Fanon's *The Wretched of the Earth* sticking out of his back pocket. Ed Faulkner, I learn, has just been promoted from ink man to apprentice roll tender. He's a deeply thoughtful, disciplined, and ambitious brother.

Ed had spent some years in prison, where he got an education in the anticolonial movements that are presently remaking the world. I like him. He's a self-taught black intellectual of the sort that's quite common on the South Side. They read books, though often not the books you'd find on a college syllabus. You'd find them on the shelves of the black bookshops like the one my mother's cousin, Danny Boy, owns. His bookshop is stocked up on radical and Afrocentric literature, often revisionist in nature, some of it a little crazy in its historical and political claims, maybe a little conspiratorial in its mindset. This is the Chicago of Elijah Muhammad's Nation of Islam, and the writings of Muhammad and his followers get ample shelf space. The ideas in these books color a lot of the casual talk I hear at family gatherings, in pool halls, and from the mouths of the bow-tied black nationalists handing out tracts on the corner.

These ideas have a way of seeping into every sort of conversation, such as those heard at Aunt Eloise's house, which is like Grand Central Station. Holiday or no holiday, people gather there on weekends to cook over the big barbecue pit or hang out in the living room and kitchen. Often, the men take their drinks to a room upstairs and smoke a little something. The talk quickly turns to politics and religion. They mull over black nationalists' demands for a Republic of New Africa, which would encompass five Southern states and funnel reparations payments to its all-black citizenry. They parse Bible verses and debate whether African Americans are the "true" descendants of the Old Testament's Israelites. There will be much skepticism as to whether NASA had actually landed men on the moon. "You really believe that shit?" Alfred will ask. I'll keep my amusement to myself. Yeah, I really do believe that shit.

These ideas color a little of Ed's talk, too. He's read Fanon and Ellison and Baldwin and Malcolm. We'll sometimes hang back after a shift, play a game of chess, and talk. I would never say this to Ed, but when we sit across from each other, the two of us hunched over the board, quietly contemplating our strategies, I sometimes feel as though we both came to R. R. Donnelley for the same second chance. Now out of prison, he's turned his life around. The printing plant pays its most skilled laborers, including Ed, quite handsomely, and Ed's got a wife now and owns his own home. I don't do too badly, either. Now that I have Charlene and a newborn to take care of, the money doesn't go all that far, but it goes far enough.

More than a salary, though, R. R. Donnelly offers me a shot at redemption, one less drastic than Ed's but no less necessary. I had dragged myself through to the end of the semester at IIT. Citing my dismal grades and attendance, the school's administration asked me to leave, but that was a mere formality. If I had stayed, I would have been throwing my money away. And with a child on the way, and Charlene so young, I would need all the money I could get to support my new family.

I feel the shock of these two events deeply. Charlene's pregnancy isn't a "failure," exactly, but neither is it a welcome surprise. And dropping out of IIT is, after all the angst, something of a relief. I no longer have to white-knuckle my way through lectures I can't understand or live with the stress of unwritten papers and unread textbooks hanging over my head. With that relief comes a corresponding shame, the mirror image of which materialized on my father's face when I had to tell him, in two successive conversations, about Charlene and about IIT. When I told him about IIT, he shook his head and informed me that, having blown the thousand dollars he had painstakingly squirreled away for me, I would never get another cent from him. The pregnancy he could at least understand, even if he didn't approve. After all, he and my mother got married while she was pregnant with me. Still, he admonished me, "Do the right thing. Be a father to your child. But do not marry that girl."

There was something peculiar about my morally fastidious father counseling me against marrying the young woman who was to be the mother of my child. I would have expected "the right thing" to include a hasty wedding. But I don't believe my father approved of Charlene. Her parents were fresh out of the South and uneducated. A pregnant girl would have created an intolerable scandal at DuSable High, where she was enrolled. So Charlene would soon drop out and end up getting her GED. My father had no real sense of who Char actually was. He must have thought back to his own marriage to my mother and how that turned out. He had seen my poor judgment set me back far enough already. I was his son, but I was also a college dropout and an unmarried soon-to-be father who had, not so long ago, stolen a car and gotten arrested. If remaining unmarried was not exactly the most "honorable" choice, I can see how it made pragmatic sense from his perspective. If I'm being generous (to myself), I imagine he also thought there was still potential there to be wrested from the grip of the enemy inside me that seemed intent on wrecking my life.

These conditions do not make for a happy engagement, though Charlene and I still enjoy being with each other. Illegitimacy's gray cloud hangs over Charlene's pregnancy, and her mother's disappointment is palpable. My mother does not judge me, but she is less than thrilled at the way her first grandchild is coming into the world. She and Mrs. Teague act as emissaries who collaborate on the preparations for my child's birth. If some agreement has to be made concerning financial support or any other practical matter, it is brokered by them. You could not imagine two people more different in their habits and sensibilities than my brash, vivacious, wonderfully profane mother and the austere, dutiful, deeply religious Mrs. Teague. There is plenty of drama— arguments about who said what and how they said it, disputes over who was responsible for this or that—but they are now family of a sort, and they find a way to work with each other, if only for the sake of their children and grandchild.

Charlene had kept her pregnancy from me and her family for as long as she could. But even after that, it had to remain a secret from the rest of the community. An usher's unmarried teenage daughter could not show up to church with a bulge under her Sunday dress. The only person outside my family I could tell about my situation was Woody, who was managing the workload at IIT better than I had. Our exchange went like this:

"She's pregnant?"

"Yeah."

"She's pregnant."

"Yeah."

"You're fucked."

That about summed up my feelings.

When Charlene gives birth to our daughter, Lisa, I am not at the hospital. I have no concept of the responsibilities waiting for me, no concept of what will be required of me beyond what I observed in my own father. He has set an excellent example, but I am in no way prepared to apply whatever parenting lessons I have subconsciously absorbed from him. My initial response to the position in which I put myself was denial. I knew the baby was coming. I wasn't delusional. But at some level, I could not accept the reality of the situation. This was not supposed to happen to me, and so a part of me could not accept that it *was* happening to me. I was still too ashamed to look Mrs. Teague in the face and apologize for what I had done. How, I wondered, at just eighteen years old, could I raise another human being?

Clearly, this was not going to be a traditional arrangement, at least not at first. Charlene and I would continue to live separately, she and little Lisa with her parents and me with my mother. I would contribute a monthly sum of money, but Charlene and her parents would actually care for the child most of the time. Which is not to say that I was absent. I spent time with my daughter and my girlfriend over at the Teagues, and I did come to delight in holding Lisa, in making her giggle, and all the small joys of fatherhood. But whatever anxieties I shed when the pressure of school fell away came roaring back tenfold when I looked at my young family.

Once IIT was finished with me, I had to find something to do with myself. Burger King wasn't going to cut it once the bills started rolling in. And besides the money concerns, the idea of living with my mother and working part-time at a fast-food joint while my girlfriend sat with our infant daughter at *her* mother's house was too shameful to contemplate. Such things simply weren't done in Aunt Eloise's orbit. A part-time job was fine if you were working hard in school. But if you didn't have classes to attend and studying to do, daughter or no, you had better find real work. Idleness would not be tolerated.

It's not like finding work was difficult. At the time, Chicago benefited from an overheated national economy and a thriving midcentury industrial boom. I had a high school diploma, a little bit of college under my belt, and I was smart. Looking through the classifieds in the *Chicago Tribune* one day, I saw that R. R. Donnelley & Sons was looking for a timekeeper. I knew that they employed many South Side residents. Mrs. Teague was already working there as a laborer in the pressroom.

So I circled the ad, went in for an interview, and within days I had a full-time job at a good wage with the promise of overtime.

The job itself is simple. The timekeeper sits in a room in the monotype department. When a typesetter is done with his shift, he drops off his timecard, and the timekeeper records the hours he's worked and what wages he's due. If a typesetter has worked overtime or exceeded any benchmarks, the timekeeper estimates his bonus. The extra pay depends upon the nature of the job. Setting one kind of type is more demanding than setting another, and changing the typeface requires more work. A reference book in the office lists how much typesetters are paid per hour for various tasks. The timekeeper looks up the rates, adds up the time, and writes the data on a card, which will then be picked up and coded onto an IBM punch card that someone else feeds into a machine somewhere else on the campus.

And that's the job. I am indirectly responsible for the typesetters getting paid, but I have no discretion in the matter, so no one complains to me about the size of their paycheck. I am just a human calculator performing no task more complex than simple multiplication. For that I am paid around $6,000 a year (about $55,000 in 2024 dollars), a respectable wage. I am living with my mother and her husband Alvin and Lee Lee, so I am not paying much rent. Even after covering costs for Lisa, I still have a little bit of money left over.

A 1965 WHITE CONVERTIBLE Plymouth Sport Fury. I go to the used car lot with my mother, she cosigns the papers, and it's all mine.

I have a car.

But the paint job won't do. So I immediately take my brand new (used) car down to the same auto body shop where I had stolen the car that got me arrested. They don't know I was behind it, and I don't volunteer the information. They do good work and they do it cheaply. I get it painted bronze with silver pinstripes down the sides. I get the Playboy Bunny heads inlaid on the headrests—it's 1967, after all. I install an eight-track player with a reverberator that puts a booming echo on my music. I want everyone to hear me coming, because this car and the guy driving it need to have all eyes on them. Especially the girls' eyes.

When I'm out cruising in my Sport Fury with Woody, both of us a little high, the sound system bumping, pulling over to talk to a group of girls hanging out on the sidewalk, I feel free. I'm free from the Glenn who pays bills and struggles to be a partner to Charlene and a father to Lisa, the Glenn weighed down by the heaviness of the situation he's gotten himself into. That other Glenn recedes when I'm leaning out the window of my Sport Fury trying to charm four different women all at once, and often enough succeeding. That other Glenn only shows up when it's time to go home or when he avoids eye contact with Mrs. Teague while handing over grocery money. That other Glenn is frustrated and unfulfilled. He doesn't sit around gossiping and cracking jokes and running the chessboard at the R. R. Donnelley cafeteria table with his buddies Ed and Chuck, another black guy, about my age, who works alongside me. I'm learning to live with the disjunction between the two Glenns. I'm even learning to like it.

I also find that I like feeling the bulge of a thick wad of cash in my pocket. I pick up every extra shift I can get at R. R. Donnelley, and it's good work, but making real money there takes years of training, of working your way up, of waiting for the right spot to open up. And I need money now, not five years from now. Every day, Lisa is getting bigger, and Charlene and I can't live apart forever. Mama and Alvin's house has only two bedrooms, one for them and one for Lee Lee. I sleep on the back porch. It's enclosed and heated and perfectly comfortable, but it's not exactly what I envision for myself. Luckily, I come across what seems like a great way to make money fast: Holiday Magic.

I see Holiday Magic advertising around the neighborhood, and it makes me curious. They sell cosmetics, but they're also looking for salespeople, and the ads promise fast money and a lot of it. So I lay out $150 for a two-day seminar at one of Chicago's most luxurious hotels downtown. On the first day, the front of the hotel is choked with luxury vehicles of the kind I'd dreamed of owning since I was a little kid. And out of them step men in tailored suits and Italian loafers, with big rings on their fingers and gold watches on their wrists. Inside the hotel's enormous conference hall, which is packed with hundreds of other would-be entrepreneurs, these impressive men ascend the dais, and they testify. They testify to the riches they have reaped in the few short years since they started with Holiday Magic. They testify to the way their lives have changed, how they have risen from a hell of overdue notices and bare cupboards to a heaven of fat wallets and vacations at resort hotels in far-flung locales. They had nothing, but thanks to Holiday Magic, they now have everything.

If this had been the Bethel AME Church, you would have heard murmurs and shouts of "Amen!" echoing back from the crowd, and I would have been among those shouting loudest. Using the techniques we would learn over the next two days, we would transform ourselves into sales machines that turned Holiday Magic's powders and creams and lipsticks into hard cash. What better evidence could there be of the Holiday Magic sales system's efficacy than our own enthusiasm? Just listen to us clap and holler at the tales of wealth and luxury emanating from the stage. An hour ago we had no idea these minor moguls existed, and now we counted their successes as our own.

We attend workshops and lessons and lectures, all of them designed to sell us on the virtues of Holiday Magic and the infallibility of their sales strategy. The exercise that makes a believer out of me occurs during lunch on the second day: Go out into the streets of downtown Chicago and get ten dollars from a stranger. You can't take it from them, they have to give it to you willingly. We're to open with the following lines, "Sir, I lost my wallet. I don't have any way of getting home. I ask you to trust me, and I know that's the hardest thing to ask." We're taught that telling someone you have a problem makes you a sympathetic figure. Everyone at the seminar is well dressed, so no one looks like a homeless person or a drunk. You look trustworthy, which makes you even more sympathetic. You look directly into this stranger's eyes and you tell him, "I need your help." That gives him the opportunity to help you, which gives him something in return for his money. All of a sudden, he's demonstrated to you and, more important, to himself that he's the kind of person who goes out of his way to help somebody in need.

I go out into the street and within a half hour some nice man is taking a ten-dollar bill out of his wallet, handing it to me, and wishing me a safe trip home. It is the most empowering feeling I've ever experienced. All I do is talk to him and tell him that I have a problem and he can help me solve it. Like that, I'm a richer man than I had been that morning. There is no reason to be poor. I can make money fall from the sky if I'm smooth enough, and there is more of it than I could spend in a lifetime floating around out there waiting for me to grab. As soon as I slide that guy's bill into my pocket, I'm sold on Holiday Magic.

Now, we learn that, while of course you can make good money selling cosmetics and accessories, the real money comes when you start building a team. You can become a common distributor by purchasing a set of Holiday Magic products at a discount, selling them to customers at full price, and keeping the profits. But for $2,500, you earn the right to become a master distributor. That enables you to start recruiting other master distributors yourself, and when they pay the $2,500 fee, $500 of it goes straight to you. The more people you recruit, the more money you make. All you have to do is sell them the same vision of prosperity that you just bought yourself.

I walk out of the hotel at the end of the conference's second day with a load of makeup under my arm and some marketing materials, including a bumper sticker that encapsulates Holiday Magic's message of uplift and self-motivation: "Rise Above It!" As I drive south, I start tallying up all the women I know. They all have potential. Potential as sources of income for me, yes, but also potential to change their own lives, to get theirs. I can start selling the makeup in my trunk immediately, but I have my sights set on becoming a master distributor.

In order to do that, I need $2,500. That's nearly half my annual salary, and I don't have it just lying around. There's only one person I can think to ask: my father. True, not so long ago, he told me never to ask him for money again. I can understand why. I had let him down terribly. Now I want to show him that I'm worth a damn. I wouldn't be asking for him to just *give* me the money. This is a business loan. I would pay him back. Still, I know it will take some convincing, so I prepare a sales pitch. When I'm not at the printing plant, I'm crafting my appeal and working on my visual aids. I have a plan, and I'm going to give him a formal presentation to show that I don't take his willingness to hear me out for granted. I'm working up what I call a "neighborhood self-help plan," in which I show how, under my guidance, Holiday Magic can help keep black money in the black community and revitalize our neighborhoods. We'll rise above it, just like the bumper sticker says.

He agrees to meet with me, and I'm fully aware of the stakes, not just for my financial future but for my relationship with my dad. I'm ready to prove myself. When I begin to explain how Holiday Magic works, Everett Loury breaks out into laughter. He laughs and laughs, and I never get anywhere near my formal pitch. The poster board on which I have diagrammed and bullet-pointed how I'm going to single-handedly elevate the South Side sits unused. I don't know if he ever utters the words "pyramid scheme," but he makes clear that, no, he will not be investing any of his money in either my "neighborhood self-help plan" or Holiday Magic, which is obviously a scam.

Amused by my naivete, my father pats me on the shoulder and sends me on my way, empty handed. Seeing Holiday Magic now through his eyes, the spell lifts. I was not so different from the nice man who gave me the ten dollars. But I held on to that bumper sticker. I had paid my money, and I got some hope in return. But if I was truly going to rise above it, I'd have to find another way.

DESPITE LIVING UNDER DIFFERENT ROOFS, and despite the near-constant presence of parents in both houses, Charlene and I still manage to find ways to be alone together. By the end of 1967, she is pregnant again. After the shock and ensuing drama of the first pregnancy, the second doesn't feel as explosive. But soon there will be another mouth to feed, more visits to the doctor, more bills, more everything. Even with my wages from the printing plant and the help of my mother and Mrs. Teague, we are still teenage parents who are barely keeping things together. When Charlene tells me the news, I'm filled not with elation but with anxiety and dread.

Charlene and I have a discussion. Afterward, I take $200 out of the small sum of money I've been able to save and give it to her. I've asked around discreetly and found a name. He's said to do good work, though there are no guarantees. You meet at an anonymous motel room somewhere far from your neighborhood, where no one will recognize either of you. Or if you're lucky, you're snuck into an office long after the last official patient leaves and the staff has gone home. With anonymity and illegality comes risk. Risk of a botched procedure, risk of discovery and prosecution, risk of all the things that can happen when a vulnerable young woman puts herself at the mercy of a powerful man. There is nothing calculated about these risks. Everything is left to chance.

One night, Charlene leaves home with the $200 in her purse. When she returns, the money is unspent. At the time, I do not know how to feel about Charlene's decision, though I understand why she made it. In

June 1968, when I see my youngest child Tamara's beautiful face for the first time, I quietly thank God.

Though the money is unspent, there is still a price to be paid. When, after three months of pregnancy, Charlene begins to show, she essentially goes into hiding again. Another pregnancy brings with it more shame, and the upright Mrs. Teague does not want the gossip mill to spin back up again. This is the cover story: When Tamara is born, Mrs. Teague tells church friends and family the child belongs to a distant relative in Mississippi, a girl who got into trouble and sent the baby up to be raised by the Teagues. Such things were not uncommon. Still, it's not very convincing. People can put two and two together. While neighbors and the church usher board go along with it so as not to give offense, everybody knows that child belongs to Charlene and me. After a while, Mrs. Teague allows the cover story to die a natural death.

While my reputation does not suffer in the way that Charlene's does, I no longer feel like the golden child who breezed his way through school, picking up praise and accolades like loose change from the street. I am nineteen years old now with two baby daughters and a high school diploma. When the girls start growing and the Teagues' modest home can no longer accommodate all the people living there, what will happen? Aunt Eloise's line between the respectable and the sordid looms into view. There will be no cover story that can account for what waits on the other side of it. The dark side of the line seems to have a gravity all its own. As Everett Loury knew, escaping its pull requires more than smarts, just as even Adlert's considerable smarts were not enough to keep him from being dragged down. It has become clear that, if I'm to step up in the way my father would have me do, then playtime must end.

Five

In late August, Chicago feels like a swamp. The hot, humid air hangs low on the street, trapped by the concrete and high-rises, and on a windless day the atmosphere is so thick you almost feel you could grab a piece of it with your hand. Still, it's my nightshift "lunch" break, and I need to get out of the printing plant for a while. My small office offers little respite from the thunderous noise of the machines on the shop floor, and tonight it's starting to get to me. I drive two miles uptown and pull over close to Grant Park, a grassy expanse bordered by Lake Michigan to the east and the luxury stores lining Michigan Avenue to the west and the Art Institute to the north and the Field Museum to the south. I've heard there's a scene going on there, and I want to see it for myself.

For days, anti-Vietnam protesters have been gathering around Chicago, dancing, smoking reefer, chanting protest chants, singing protest songs, and planning for the massive march on the Democratic National Convention that soon will lead to a brutal response from the Chicago Police Department. News cameras will capture Mayor Daley's police indiscriminately beating unarmed teenagers in the street as they try to make their way across town from Grant Park to the International Amphitheater, where the pro-war Hubert Humphrey will clinch the nomination over the anti-war Eugene McCarthy to run against Nixon.

If tensions are running high for these protesters, I'm only vaguely aware of it. Most of them are about my age. If I had wandered into the park and joined them, nobody would have blinked. Like almost everyone I know, I'm against the war. But my skepticism has little to do with a thoughtful critique of US involvement in global affairs. The guys in the shop factory are blue-collar working men. They have no time for the hippies and yippies out there getting high while they're working long, hard hours on a dirty, sweaty shop floor. And, despite our racial and ethnic differences, I can identify with those guys. Maybe they have their doubts about the war, as I do. But they're not about to go out into the street and burn their draft cards. And neither am I. Like most of the people in my family and social circle, I'm fiercely animated by a sense of outrage at the race situation, Nixon, the Republicans, and Vietnam. Even my moderate father, who served in the ROTC and who was drafted into the Army for a two-year stint in the early 1950s, has no love for that war. My sister is determined to marry Levi James Mann III—everyone calls him Trey. He's an Army volunteer serving in the 101st Airborne Division, a straight-arrow spit-and-polish man gung ho on the war in Indochina. My father regards him with utter disdain. Anyone who would voluntarily wade into the bloodbath in Vietnam is a fool in his eyes, someone who must hold his own life cheaply, and certainly not someone fit to marry his daughter. He feels so strongly about it that he will refuse to attend their wedding. And while he may be a little hard-hearted in his refusal, he's eventually proven right. My sister's husband will come back from the war a damaged man, and their marriage will quickly fall apart.

I sympathize with the protestors, but in an hour (give or take), I'll have to be back at my desk at the printing plant. That fact alone represents an uncrossable divide between me and them. If I ditch work and devote my time to their cause, the consequences will be swift and severe, both for me and for my family. I have worries that feel more immediate than Vietnam. The war is raging, but the semester is starting, and I'm enrolled in a few classes at the community college. This means I'll have to figure out how to balance school, work, fatherhood, and, at some point, sleep. Within a month, life will become a blur of classrooms, the printing plant, study sessions in the library carrels, the occasional nap, and meals eaten on the fly, often enough from a can.

Southeast Junior College, the community college I attend, doesn't have a campus of its own. It's housed in a spare wing of the Chicago Vocational High School, a massive building teeming with students. A bell rings and students file to their next class as though they themselves were still in high school. The rec room and cafeteria at CVHS are raucous and crammed full of people hanging out and playing noisy games of bid whist. Between classes, students sprawl out on the lawn in front of the building, smoking cigarettes as music plays from the cars idling on the street. I don't look out of place among them, but I rarely have time to join them. I'm all too aware of what may happen if I lose focus. It's already happened once when I was at IIT, and I have neither the time nor the money to afford another slipup.

My shift at R. R. Donnelley usually begins at four in the afternoon, so I head straight from class to the printing plant. I get off around midnight, head home to my mother's house, grab some sleep, wake up, drive over to the Teagues to see Charlene and the kids, then walk the quarter mile to the CVHS campus and hit the library. That schedule is almost manageable. But whenever there's overtime available, I take it because I need the money. Some mornings I have only three or four hours to get home and rest before the cycle starts over again.

Despite the balancing act my life has become, I'm buckling down and acing my classes with relative ease. The coursework at Southeast Junior College can't compare to the rigors of IIT, and so no spirals of doubt and shame suck me down and away from my studies. Anyway, I have little time for the kind of introspection that opens the door to self-doubt. There is always another exam to study for, always another overtime shift to pick up, always another bill to pay, always another and another and another.

BY THE TIME 1969 ROLLS AROUND, it no longer makes sense for Charlene and me to live separately. But money is still tight, and it will take a little more saving before we can afford to rent a place of our own and pay for day care so Charlene can get a job. That means I'll have to move in with the Teagues, and for that to happen, we need to get married. There is no way Mrs. Teague is letting Charlene and me live under the same roof without a ring, no matter how many kids we have together.

So one Saturday afternoon, Charlene and I put on the best clothes we have, walk into Pastor Bob's office at the Bethel AME Church, and exchange vows away from the eyes of the congregation, our extended families, and most everyone else. A walk down the aisle and a white dress and a big reception are out of the question. There are no flower girls, bridesmaids, or groomsmen, and no relatives come in from out of town. The Teagues and my mother are present. My father does not come, not because he is any longer opposed to the wedding, but because he has something else to do, and this is not the sort of event for which one cancels plans.

Moving in with the Teagues brings its own stresses. There are now seven of us, including Char's sister, living in a three-bedroom house. I chip in for rent and groceries, and after providing for Lisa and Tamara, paying for tuition and books, and saving a little bit, there is no money left over. Charlene and I begin to argue regularly, and there is nowhere to go to cool off, no private space to repair to in order to get my head together. I turn one corner, and I see Mr. Teague sauntering toward the living room, his pipe in hand and the evening paper tucked under his arm. I turn another corner, and there's Mrs. Teague. Whatever she's doing, she does not look overjoyed at my presence.

Luckily, these arrangements don't last long. Within six months, Charlene and I move into our own place. It's a modest apartment in a newly built, moderate-income housing complex near Jackson Park. It's nothing to brag about, but at least we don't have her parents breathing down our necks. Even if we haven't achieved marital bliss and our finances are still stretched to the limit, at least we have the place to ourselves. It's our first home together. We have fun shopping for cheap furniture, buying groceries together on Saturday mornings, and taking the girls for strolls in the park. The lakefront is nearby, and picnics on the beach are a favorite summertime activity. Char, although she has only a GED, secured employment at the post office. Mama and Mrs. Teague take turns babysitting for us from time to time. Life is hectic, but, on the whole, things are looking up.

WORKING THE THIRD SHIFT at R. R. Donnelley had its benefits. For one, I got to hang with my man Chuck. As soon as we met, we took to one another. We'd sit during "lunch" breaks (which happened around four in the morning) and shoot the breeze, talk about movies, about music, whatever. If we were both working on payday, we'd leave work together, cash our checks as soon as the bank opened, and get breakfast at a nearby diner. Often enough, we'd head back to Chuck's apartment, take a few hits off a joint, and listen to some records: Smokey Robinson, Curtis Mayfield, the Temptations, Crosby, Stills, Nash & Young, the Beatles, and James Brown were some of our favorites. Occasionally, Woody, who had landed a job at the plant on my recommendation, would join us. When I got home after these sessions, Charlene would be irate. "Where the hell were you? You got off work hours ago." I understood. She's home with the kids, and I'm out getting stoned to "Papa's Got a Brand New Bag." It doesn't seem fair. But all I could tell her was that Chuck and I had a hard week, and we needed to take some time to chill. I was seeking respite, somewhere that was neither school nor work nor home, and Chuck's apartment offered it.

Chuck was an attractive man—tall, physically powerful, and handsome. He was also extremely intelligent. He loved reading the classic

Russian novelists, which impressed me. A masterful talker, Chuck would take over and command the conversation with a sure hand if there was ever a lull at the cafeteria table where we'd hang out with some of our other black coworkers. He was also gay. We never talked about his sexuality, but we didn't have to; it was obvious. I don't know if he was ever fully open about it with anyone at the printing plant, though I doubt he was. Homosexuality was not something that could be discussed freely, and especially not around the sort of hypermasculine men who worked at the printing plant. I did wonder, though, how he went about his business. He couldn't go about it the way I did, cruising up to whatever girl was on the street, trying to coax and cajole her in broad daylight. He must have had his hangouts and a circle of people with whom he could talk about sex, maybe even with the same brazenness and raunchiness that all the straight men I knew talked about their conquests.

I never did find out, though, because somebody murdered Chuck. They bludgeoned him to death in his apartment, possibly in the very same room where he and I would sit listening to James Brown. One night, I came into work and found one of our regular cafeteria companions crying. She told me that Chuck was dead, and then I was crying, uncontrollably. There may have been an investigation, I don't know. I took his death hard and harbored many unanswerable questions: Did Chuck know the man who murdered him? Was it a break-in? A hookup gone wrong? Did Chuck invite the man who killed him back to his apartment to smoke a joint and listen to some records, as he had invited me? Despite his imposing physique, there was no hint of violence about Chuck. He was gentle by nature, and I could not believe that he would have done anything to provoke whoever killed him. But I never got any answers. All I was left with was the bare fact that my friend was gone.

It wasn't unheard of for gay men to be assaulted during what they believed would be an ordinary sexual encounter. I imagine it was even more common than we—straight people—knew at the time. I don't know if that's what happened to Chuck. But if it was, then the secrecy

around his sexuality played a part in his death. I could not have understood what Chuck's life outside the printing plant was really like, but I
knew something about sex and secrecy. Adultery was commonplace on
the South Side. Which is not to say that everyone cheated, but for the
most part it wasn't surprising when you found out someone had. Who
was concealing that little something on the side from whom was a constant source of gossip. For all the pain infidelity could cause, it seemed
to be an endemic part of the social world I was born into. It had been,
after all, directly responsible for my sister's birth.

Seeing my mother with that man in the pool hall may have changed
me, but it didn't exactly change my opinion of her, since I knew that
other men had always been around. No doubt she went out of her way
to make sure Alvin never knew, but as far as I know, she never lied to
me about her own appetites. In fact, she even gave me advice on the
matter, tongue in cheek: "If caught, deny everything. No matter what
they say they saw and what they think they know, deny it. If they catch
you naked in bed with her, deny it."

I'm sure Mama was just trying to look out for me, but the assumption
was clear: at some point, I would need that advice. Maybe she knew
something about me, and thought she was offering counsel from one
Player to another. Or maybe she simply thought that most people were
just like her. Whatever she may have thought, she was Adlert and Alfred's
sister. If her brothers' attitude toward sex—quantity over quality—was
wrapped up in their ideas about what made a man a man, sex had to be
equally central to Gloria's ideas about what made a woman a woman.
She delighted in tormenting my father by wearing something provoc-
ative when he came by to pick up Lee Lee and me as kids. And when
Daddy married prim, slim, and severe Constance, Mama raged that this
new wife wasn't half the woman she was, didn't have her figure, couldn't
satisfy my father the way she could.

Why tease Daddy with what he couldn't have and then get jealous
when he went somewhere else to get it? Why was my mother constantly

seeking male attention? I didn't understand. One day, Lee Lee and I got to talking about it. She reminded me of our mom's upbringing, bouncing around to different relatives before finding stability, being separated from her sister and brothers, whom she loved intensely, growing up essentially without a father while knowing that her father had gone off and started another family, and then being treated essentially as a stranger by that family. "Of course she's got issues," Lee Lee said. "Who wouldn't?" It never occurred to me to ask these same questions about Adlert and Alfred, who had the same childhood as Mama. Didn't they have "issues," too? And wasn't Adlert's "pussy" advice to me tainted by those "issues"? Interestingly, what frustrated me in my mother's behavior was the same thing that made me look up to her brothers.

AT THE END OF EVERY SHIFT, I drop off the timesheets with the typing pool workers, who will code all the data onto punch cards. Getting to that office requires an elevator ride upstairs into a different world, far away from the noisy, hectic factory floor and the men with dirt under their fingernails. Naturally, I get to know the women in the typing pool a bit. They're just starting their shifts and I'm just ending mine, so we stand around and chat for a little while before I head out and they sit down to work in earnest. Out of all of them, I most look forward to seeing Janice Brazan. She's shapely with glasses and dark brown skin. It's easy to see that she's a good girl, but she has this mischievous glint in her eye and enjoys playing coy. I sometimes invite her to get a coffee or breakfast in the cafeteria, and we get to know each other. Pretty soon, I start planning what I'll say when I approach her and checking myself in the bathroom mirror when the end of my shift approaches.

Even before things turn physical, we both have a sense that we're more than just friends. She doesn't know that I'm with Charlene, and I'm not about to tell her. In my mind, my flirtation with Janice has nothing to do with Charlene, and vice versa. As a Player, such things shouldn't matter to me. Even when I start visiting Janice at her mother's modest home, I don't let on about Charlene. And once things get physical between us, I know I can't let on about Charlene. As far as Janice knows, we're just work colleagues who have struck up an office romance, maybe one that will lead to something more. Though Janice is a couple years older than me, I'm more experienced. I have little intention of allowing things to blossom into a full-blown relationship. I have little intention about anything having to do with Janice, but I do know that I want to keep things going. When I leave Janice's mother's home after one of our trysts, I can't help thinking about when I'll get a chance to tell my uncles about it.

STUDYING ACCOUNTING SEEMS LIKE the right course for me. My father had earned a degree in accounting and now he's working for a regional office of the IRS and sweating his way through law school at night. The world's always going to need accountants, I figure, and the math involved is a cinch for me. I even start to enjoy learning about the ins and outs of the tax code, depreciation formulas, and why one asset is taxed in one way and another is taxed differently. These are the mechanisms that generate the vast majority of the federal government's income, and studying them is like reading the schematics of the state's engine. After earning some more credits at the community college, my plan is to transfer to the University of Illinois's Chicago Circle campus so as to finish my bachelor's and start a career following in my father's footsteps.

Since I'm studying so hard and doing so well at the community college, I decide that I'm ready for more advanced mathematics and sign up for a two-semester sequence in calculus. After a semester of straight A's, I'm feeling confident in my abilities. I no longer have any fear that I'll end up shirking class and succumbing to self-doubt.

The instructor is Professor Andres, a retired engineer and graduate of Northwestern who's teaching here seemingly purely for the love of it. Not only does he love it, he's really good at it. He has a gift for making the abstract propositions of calculus comprehensible, in much the same way that Mr. Reffels unveiled the relationship between cone segments and the quadratic equation. But the possibilities inherent in calculus go far beyond the cone. I'm mesmerized by the lectures, by the subtle connections among algebra, geometry, and trigonometry that the mastery of calculus lays bare. When I sit down to study for the class, I'm driven by something deeper than the desire for a good grade. I want to *know* this material, truly know it, understand it inside and out. Whatever it is that's driving me has little to do with the applicability of what I'm learning, how it will help me in life, how I will be able to use calculus in some practical endeavor. I only know that I need to master it.

My desire to understand Professor Andres's calculus lessons regularly drives me to his office. I sit with my notes and the textbook and ask him a question. Before he's half through answering it, I understand where his response is going and finish his thought for him. After several weeks of regular appearances at office hours, we start chatting more informally. He asks me about myself, where I'm from, what makes me so interested in calculus. I tell him the basics: South Side, married with two young kids, working full-time, and trying to make something of myself after a false start. Naturally, he's intrigued. Many students here regard community college as a fifth or sixth year of high school. They're content to coast through. One of the few guys engaging with the material seriously is, well, me. I'm smart, but on paper I'm prime drop-out material. And yet.

Something about my persistence and abilities must impress Professor Andres. He knows about my plans to apply to the University of Illinois, but he lets me know there are other options. He hands me a phone number and tells me to call it. Northwestern has a program for people like me: talented inner-city kids who haven't taken the most traditional path to college. Professor Andres tells me he's recommended me, and that they're expecting my phone call. That is, if I'm interested.

The idea of attending a place like Northwestern has never even occurred to me. Situated on the shore of Lake Michigan in Evanston, a

suburb to the north of the city, Northwestern is one of the top universities in the country. I have no idea what goes on in a place like that, but in
my mind, it's a temple of knowledge where distinguished professors toil
away on complex and obscure problems while the well-heeled children
of the elite sit in rapt attention in oak-lined lecture halls and stay up at
night in their dorm rooms debating the big questions. Uncle Adlert had
attended Northwestern's law school, and it had only added to the stories
and legends that surrounded him. Consequently, the place has an aura to
it, and I believe being associated with the school could impart the same
aura to me. So yes, I tell Professor Andres, I am interested.

MY LIFE WITH CHARLENE IS TUMULTUOUS. There is always an argument brewing, and the pressures of school and work don't leave me with
much patience when I return home. I try to enjoy my time as a father,
but there is always some distraction, some task, and the ceaseless drag of
exhaustion. Things with Janice are so much simpler. We flirt at work,
and we fool around at her mother's place when I have the chance to steal
away from home. There is no past and no future there, at least not for
me. My time with Janice exists suspended in a no-time zone, floating
above the rhythms that dictate the rest of my life. She asks nothing of
me but my presence. Together we are light and effortless.

So I cannot quite understand it when Janice tells me that she's pregnant and how far along she is. I cannot understand it, or I don't want to
understand it. Janice and I don't get together all that often, and we don't
have sex every time we do get together, and as I think back through what
we did and when, it just doesn't seem to me that I could be responsible for
that pregnancy. But Janice is not a liar, that much I know. When she tells
me there are no other men, I have to believe her. Just as the pregnancy is
unthinkable, it is equally unthinkable that Janice would try to trick me
into claiming a child that wasn't mine. She's not that kind of girl. Even
so, I deny it, and that brings an end to the relationship.

The denial is all-encompassing. I never tell Charlene, never tell any-body. The baby isn't mine, I think to myself, so what is there to tell? Janice was just a fling, something that began and ended and now exists only in our memories, which is as close to not existing as something can get. I keep my head down, go to work, go to school, keep my interac-tions with Janice brief when we see each other at the printing plant. But that baby is coming. And when it does, I know I'm going to hear about it one way or another.

Finally, I do hear about it, via a court summons. And finally, I have to tell someone, so I tell someone who will understand: Mama.

My mother comes with me to the courthouse, where a court-appointed counselor informs me of my options. I have the right to deny paternity, and that will involve standing before a judge and stating that I am not the father of the child. In essence, I would have to accuse Janice of sleeping around, lying about it, and then trying to trap me into footing the bill. I would not want to insinuate that, because I do not believe it to be true. I don't believe the child is mine, but at the same time, I don't believe that Janice is lying. The tension between these two ideas has reached its sticking point. Though in my heart I am unsure, I tell the counselor that I'll forgo that option, forgo the paternity test, and claim the child—a boy, Alden—as my own.

Though I am responsible for Alden in the eyes of the state, I deny any sense of responsibility to myself. The impossible tension remains lodged inside of me and refuses to resolve itself. I agree to make child support payments, and my mother agrees to act as a go-between when necessary. We both agree that Charlene need not be told, at least not yet. I do not ask my father's advice on the matter. I know what he would say, and I know what he would do in my position, because he has already done it. He's a better man than I would prove to be.

My child support is due to Janice at the beginning of each month, and at the beginning of each month I put it off. I cannot face it. Money is so tight that if I pay, Charlene is sure to notice. The spiral of denial and shame that confronted me at IIT has returned as the specter of my illegitimate child's face, which I can imagine, but which I have not yet seen for myself. I tell myself I will take care of it somehow, tomorrow, next week. But signing my name to the check will register Alden Loury and Janice Brazan as a reality, and that I cannot yet bear. So, irrationally, I consign the unavoidable reckoning to some hypothetical future.

That hypothetical future smashes into the present when someone appears at my front door notifying me that I am delinquent in my child support payments, and that legal action will follow, including seizing part of my wages, if I don't make good. Charlene is home, and she overhears the conversation. When she asks what all that was about, I'm too shaken to think up a plausible denial. I break down and tell her.

The following months are a kind of domestic hell. But I tell myself that we'll get through it, that eventually she will forgive my transgression and learn to live with it. She'll have to.

IN DECEMBER 1969, Fred Hampton, a leader in the Illinois chapter of the Black Panther Party, was shot dead in his bed during a predawn raid on his apartment conducted by a Cook County tactical team. The Chicago Police Department and the FBI had been on the scene, as well. Hampton had been an extremely effective activist and a political prodigy. Even if I didn't subscribe to the Panthers' brand of radical politics, it was hard for me to believe that his killing could be justified.

Where I was skeptical of the official story, many other black folks in Chicago were enraged, and none more so than the Panthers themselves. Meetings were being held around the South Side to try to decide what to do in the wake of Hampton's death. Woody got wind of one, and he somehow convinced me to go along with him. I was disturbed by Hampton's murder, even angry. But attending a political rally was not the way I wanted to use what little free time I had at my disposal.

Being political neophytes, neither of us knew many of the participants at this rally. We were all very agitated, determined to fight the good fight, even to the point of being arrested if it came to that. Judging by his demeanor, Woody was among the most zealous of those present. Despite his zeal, it took courage for Woody to attend the meeting, given how white he looked.

I had no doubt that Woody's feelings were authentic, but I found myself doubting that he fully grasped the pain, frustration, anger, and self-doubt many of us felt in moments such as these, when the seeming intractability of American racism made itself felt by such vicious means. Every person in that room probably felt that their life could have been taken just as easily as Hampton's, and for offenses far less grave than threatening Chicago's political hierarchies, or for no offense at all. Woody may have felt a similar precarity but, I allowed myself to wonder, was the threat as real to him as it was to us?

A critical moment came when the leaders interrupted their speech-making to solicit ideas from the crowd. Woody had an idea and enthu-siastically raised his voice above the murmur. But before he could finish his first sentence, he was cut short by one of the dashiki-clad brothers in charge, who demanded to know how a "white boy" got the authority to have an opinion about what we black people should be doing. That was one of our problems, the man said. We were always letting white people "peep our hole card," but we were never privy to their deliber-ations in return.

A silence fell over the room. The indignant brother asked if anyone could "vouch for this white boy." More excruciating silence ensued. Now it was my moment of truth. Woody turned plaintively toward me, but I would not meet his eyes. I refused to speak up for him. He was asked to leave the meeting and did so without uttering a word in his own defense.

I stayed, but I didn't hear anything anyone else said after that. All the rage, the calls to arms, the strategizing passed right through me. I had betrayed my friend. And for what? If I suspected that Woody had been, in some sense, passing for black, then I was forced to confront the fact that

I, too, was passing—hoping to be mistaken for something I was not: a black radical. To proclaim before the other black radicals in the audience that this "white boy" at my side was in fact our brother would, I feared, have compromised my own chance of being received among them as a genuine peer. Who, after all, was there to vouch for me?

In truth, I didn't care about the men and women at this rally. I had no idea who most of them were. What had seemed important was that I was there, in solidarity, within the embrace of my people. Vouching for Woody would have led, I feared, to the withdrawal of that embrace, and so when the moment came to stand by a friend who had so often stood by me, I chose "my people" instead. As soon as Woody walked out the door, I knew I had chosen poorly. It would not be the last time.

Somehow, Woody and I remained friends. We never spoke about the incident. He never let on how he felt about it, and I never told him how badly I regretted abandoning him. Perhaps he understood the dilemma, understood that racial solidarity forces a choice and requires a sacrifice. I had made a sacrifice of Woody, but a sacrifice to whom, and for what?

IN THE SPRING OF 1970, the US military begins its incursion into Cambodia. The illegal expansion of the Vietnam War into a neighboring country provokes a renewed wave of protests and strikes on campuses around the United States. Focused as I am on getting myself through the semester, I'm only vaguely aware of what's going on. I know only that I have to study for my calculus test at the end of the week, and by 4:00 p.m., I'll have to go back home and try to get some sleep so I can be at work by 11:00 p.m., after which I'll head back to campus at 7:00 a.m. to get some more studying in before class starts later that morning. Between the protest and the ordinary noise of the junior college campus, studying out in the open is impossible, so I head to the library, only to find that the librarian, fearful of the protesting, rampaging throng, has decided to barricade herself inside. Furious and exhausted, I bang on the door, assuring her that I just want a quiet place to study, and demanding to be let in. Eventually, she relents.

In the spring of 1970, after submitting an application and transcripts and sitting for an interview, I learn that I will be admitted to Northwestern University in the fall on a full scholarship.

In the spring of 1970, I see a photograph of Alden for the first time. The face staring back at me, without a doubt, is mine. The next time I see him it will be in the flesh, and he will be a grown man.

Six

My capacity for infidelity is now the subject of common knowledge within my marriage. Charlene knows that I have fathered a child by another woman. And I know that Charlene knows that I know that she knows. All the time I'm spending out of the house now—at work, in class, and losing myself in Northwestern's beautiful, brand-new library—allows Charlene to imagine the worst, even though she knows that, with forty-plus hours a week at the printing plant and a demanding course load of four classes per semester at Northwestern, I wouldn't have time to cheat even if I wanted to. For a long time, when I stagger in the front door, practically dead on my feet, I'm greeted with squeals of delight from Lisa and Tamara and silent glares from Charlene. These looks remind me of the humiliation I've visited on her, even as she tries to search out signs of the next one.

But, slowly, we find ways to reconnect and have fun together. In the hour or so I have between dinner and sleep, we talk while watching television. We go out to the movies and see whatever's playing. Once in a while, if my schedule allows it, we leave the kids with Mama or Mrs. Teague and go out to eat or hang out at Woody and Elvie's place, where we listen to music (Motown, Crosby, Stills, Nash & Young, the Rolling

Stones, and Chicago), smoke a little weed, burn some incense, and drink Boone's Farm apple wine.

Char and I also love to go out to blues clubs. The South Side has dozens of tiny clubs with bare-bones stages and, often, sawdust on the floor. Five dollars gets you admission to the club and a "setup" consisting of a bucket of ice, glasses, and a Coca-Cola. The rum we put in that Coke costs extra. Char is underage, but either nobody notices or nobody cares. These clubs host crooners and bands that might have a little local reputation, but no one on the level of, say, the great B. B. King or Muddy Waters, the Mississippi-born Chicago blues legend. It doesn't matter to us, though. Even the third-tier acts we see are pretty damn good.

And the show is only half of it. The audience is filled with every type of person you can find on the South Side, from men dressed in elegant suits to Gousters who probably have a blade on them to working stiffs like me and Char, dressed to the nines for a night out. There are sometimes prostitutes leaning against the bar. These places have a funky, guttural quality. People are smoking, talking, and laughing or sitting quietly absorbed in the music. If the number has the right tempo, people leap to their feet and dance right at their tables or in front of the stage. Sometimes when the band is cooking, the whole place feels like it's swaying, swiveling, and rocking on its hips. People come to these joints to release some pressure after a long week, which is exactly what Char and I do, too.

It is not a storybook relationship, and it never will be. The only thing we can hope to do is move forward and forget, to the extent possible, that each of us knows what we know, and try to build something new.

MY LIFE AT THAT TIME was as divided as the City of Chicago itself. On the South Side, below the Loop, Chicago's central business, shopping, and cultural district, I lived a life not very different from the rest of the area's black working class. I worked long hours at a factory and lived with my wife and children in close proximity to any number of relatives and friends, whose lives more or less resembled mine. My South Side existence was concerned with keeping food on the table, raising my kids, trying to keep the peace with my wife, visiting with my parents, aunts, uncles, and cousins, and playing a little bit of chess or pool when I could find the time.

My life on the North Side could not have been more different. Sometimes I'd drive along Chicago's lakefront up to Northwestern in the early mornings, through the quiet, leafy Rogers Park neighborhood of the Far North Side and into Evanston. Often enough, my beloved Sport Fury was in the shop or broken down or with Char if she needed to use it to get to work or run errands. In that case, I'd take an hour-long ride on the elevated train, where I'd sit with a book in my lap and a pencil in my hand and get some studying done. I'd slough off the lingering residue of family drama and workplace agitation and mentally prepare myself for the challenging ideas and equations that awaited me on the university's campus. If my schedule allowed it, I would arrive well before my first class of the day and enter the library.

I'd look forward to these hours, where I'd get some peace and quiet away from the cacophony of the shop floor and the turmoil and sweet noise and ceaseless errands of life at my apartment. I came to feel at home in the library, where I would sit and be still. I would either study or just wander through the stacks, pulling down whatever books and journals seemed interesting and absorbing whatever was in them before hustling off to a lecture or seminar. If I was looking for something specific, maybe an article in a mathematics journal, I'd go to the card catalog, look up the journal, track it down in the stacks, then photocopy it for later study. If I had an hour or two between classes, I'd often head back and do it all over again. The same kid who spent many an afternoon leafing through the encyclopedia now had a world-class research library at his disposal. Pulling down volume after canvas-bound volume, I was in heaven.

Whatever plans I had to continue my path to accounting vanished soon after I started at Northwestern. The place was an intellectual smorgasbord. Every week, I encountered an idea I had never known existed, a piece of history or political theory that made me reconsider who I was and the circumstances into which I was born, an equation that unscrewed the top of my head. Soon I settled on math as my major with an economics minor. I was a happy surprise to my teachers in those subjects, who found an ardent and skilled pupil in this slightly unusual, slightly older transfer student. In fact, I was a surprise to myself. I had always known I had a head for numbers, but here I was at one of the best schools in the country, and I was absolutely acing it. Whatever anxieties I had about being able to compete with the polished kids with their prep-school educations vanished as my teachers would ask a question about some principle of economics or set theory, and I found my hand flying up to answer while the rest of the students puzzled over it.

Besides all the math, for the first time I was learning something about European intellectual and literary history. I found myself especially taken with the stories and novels of Franz Kafka and Thomas Mann. The existential philosophy of Sartre and Camus fascinated me. They argued that existence consists of the struggle to hew meaning from a world that is essentially without meaning, to make yourself into whatever you will become and to attempt to do so without succumbing to bad faith and the temptation "to merge with the anonymous crowd and to flow comfortably along with it down the river of pseudo-life," as Václav Havel would later write. That was my story, wasn't it? The pull of the other side of the line wasn't merely about respectability. It was about the constant effort needed to live in good faith: to exercise control over my being, to take responsibility for my life, and to make myself into whatever I would be. I had already gotten a taste of what could happen when I let the currents of life determine my course. At Northwestern, I was learning to use my oars, and I paddled like my life depended on it, because it did.

I was also introduced to political theory for the first time. In a course called Capitalism, Socialism, and Democracy, we read Adam Smith, Friedrich von Hayek, Milton Friedman, and Karl Marx, among others. Most of our readings of Marx concentrated on the *Economic and Philosophic Manuscripts of 1844*, which had appeared in English only about fifteen years earlier. Here Marx first sets out his ideas about alienated labor and the mechanisms through which capitalism converts the laborer's time and effort into surplus value borne to the market in the form of commodities. Commodities are nothing but fragments of the laborer's life that have been alienated from him and invested in objects from which the capitalist profits.

I was deeply affected by the ambition of Marx's critique, how seriously he took the worker's part in the creation of value, and how rigorously he pursued that relation between labor and value. Marx calls the relationship between the laborer who sells his labor and the capitalist who uses it to turn a profit "exploitation." The laborer is paid just enough so that he can replenish his energy and come back to the factory the next day where he sells his labor to the capitalist who uses it to enrich himself even further.

Marx was not being taught in the economics department. He was no longer taken seriously as an economic thinker. But the moral dimension of capitalism, which interested me, was not something I often heard discussed in my economics lectures and seminars. For that I had to go elsewhere. After all, wasn't I a laborer, in Marx's sense? I spent at least eight hours every day at R. R. Donnelley. While I worked behind a desk instead of out on the floor, I was still contributing to the company's bottom line in some way. I began to think more about questions of economic justice. Which is not to say that I was radicalized by Marx— hardly. But reading him and the others convinced me there was more to know than just the equations.

All this effort and excellence in the classroom soon attracted the attention of my professors. Marcus Alexis, an extremely distinguished black economist recently arrived at Northwestern, dubbed me El Bad One, and that's how I felt standing in front of the class scribbling out an equation on the blackboard, leaving most of my classmates in the dust: like a bad motherfucker. Rob Masson had come to Northwestern as an assistant professor, fresh from UC Berkeley, and it showed. He was a flower child, lecturing in jeans, cowboy boots, and an open-collar shirt instead of a jacket and tie. But no matter what he was wearing, his talent couldn't be denied. He may have seen a little bit of himself in me, another gifted outsider. Donald Saari, one of my math professors, was a mentor. I aced his course on real analysis. He was interested in using math to solve analytic problems in economics. We'd sit and shoot the breeze, with him learning about the unusual student in front of him, and with me soaking up whatever wisdom about mathematical economics and academia he had to offer. I dropped by his office whenever I could. There were some things you couldn't learn in the classroom, little nuances and tricks of the trade, important papers I should check out, and tidbits about the current state of the field (and, okay, some gossip). Don was happy to share it all with me.

While I was fascinated by the quantitative techniques of midcentury economics, my Principles of Economics teacher Jonathan Hughes, an economist and historian, was at pains to remind me that economics is a *social* science. While formal models can generate incredibly powerful economic analyses, he taught me not to forget that there are human beings on the other side of those numbers and formulae, human beings who bind themselves to each other through families, communities, institutions, and nations. His book, *The Vital Few*, and especially the book by his mentor, the great British economist Sir John Richard Hicks, *A Theory of Economic History*, are brilliant demonstrations of the idea that, while history and economics are deeply interwoven, one is not necessarily reducible to the other. Becoming an economist means (or should mean) more than doing math, though Hicks did plenty of that. It should mean thinking deeply about the complex texture of the social fabric that makes the transactions we study meaningful. Jonathan Hughes never tired of saying so.

Up there in Evanston, far from R. R. Donnelley, where not so long ago I had contemplated starting on a management track to enter the white-collar side of the business, my sense of what I was and what I could be was changing. The more challenges my teachers placed before me, the higher I rose to meet them, and the more pleased and encouraging they became. The hazy future I had envisioned for myself—something about an office, something about a job, closing a briefcase at 5:00 p.m. and not opening it again until 9:00 a.m. the next day—was dissolving in the ether. The feelings of power and mastery I experienced while dominating an opponent on the pool table or relieving that stranger of his ten dollars on the street were nothing compared to what came over me at the blackboard or when breaking down a challenging philosophical concept. It was an intoxicating sensation, and I never wanted it to end.

It had to end, of course. Every day, I would have to get back in my car and drive to the South Side, to work or to my apartment, where Charlene and the kids were waiting for me. But when I made the trip back to the South Side, part of me remained uptown. My books and papers began to colonize the kitchen table. At the printing plant, my supervisor Emil, a big Polish guy, was so impressed that I was trying to better myself while working at the factory that he allowed me extra breaks during my shift so I would have more time to study. With Emil's consent, the shop floor foreman would let me use the typewriter in his relatively quiet office to put finishing touches on the papers I had to write for my literature and philosophy classes. All those white ethnic guys at the printing plant seemed to be rooting for this black kid from the South Side who was determined to "Rise Above It!" I still enjoyed working at R. R. Donnelley, enjoyed the camaraderie of my colleagues and watching the entire sprawling, balletic operation. Even so, the satisfactions of life there could no longer compare to what I found uptown. Leaving the factory feeling like I had done a good day's work now had to compete with sitting in a theoretical economics classroom and hearing myself praised by a future Nobel laureate, knowing that even when I wasn't present, I was the subject of conversation among the young faculty members doing the most advanced research in their fields.

How could a printing plant measure up to that? How could anything?

MY ECONOMICS PROFESSORS aren't the only ones who see promise in me. I'm attracting plenty of attention from my math teachers as well, so much so that I'm starting to think about a career in mathematics. They've got such high hopes for me that Don Saari enlists me to compete in the annual Putnam Competition put on by the Mathematical Association of America. It's one of the most prestigious tournaments of its kind in the world. In the Putnam Competition, undergraduate entrants have six hours to complete twelve extremely challenging math problems, and entries are scored on a scale of one to ten per question, with partial credit given for some partial answers. Every entrant competes individually, but they and any other student chosen represent their home department. It's almost a team sport, and I am tremendously honored that my teachers would select me to represent them in this high-profile (at least among mathematicians) challenge.

I take it very, very seriously, and so do my teachers. I come in for extra training sessions in which Don and others walk me through the kind of problems I might encounter, drill me on strategy, and give me the confidence that good coaches impart to their players. When the day of the competition rolls around, I feel ready. I have my mentors' backing, and I truly believe that I'm one of the most talented math students at Northwestern, and, who knows, maybe the country.

By the time someone calls "pencils down" at the end of the sixth hour, I have solved precisely zero problems. None. I had absolutely no idea how to begin to formulate responses to most of the twelve queries, and I was unable to satisfactorily complete any of them. The entire six-hour ordeal is one of the most humiliating and devastating of my life up to that point. Afterward, totally demoralized, I sit and ask myself how this could have happened. How could I have so sorely misjudged my own abilities, and why did my teachers buy in? How could I have choked so badly? I've let myself down, and though everyone is magnanimous and kind in their consolations, I feel I've let my teachers down. Later, I will learn two facts that will take some of the sting out of the loss. First, the winner of that year's competition was able to solve only five and a half of the problems. Second, the median number of correct answers among test-takers nationwide that year was precisely zero!

Before the Putnam Competition, I had been interested in economics, but I still saw myself as a future mathematician. After the Putnam Competition, I have my doubts. This stuff is pretty difficult and the people who are good at it are *really* damn good. If I'm sweating this hard over an undergraduate math tournament, am I going to be able to take the next step?

THE MORE TIME I SPENT AT NORTHWESTERN, the more fascinated I became with the most abstract, theoretical aspects of economics. It's there where I could really put my math to use. I learned how certain economic problems that had bedeviled scholars for centuries were now being formalized using sophisticated mathematical techniques. We were living in an incredibly exciting time for the discipline. I learned about Kenneth Arrow and Gérard Debreu and their work in general equilibrium theory, and about John von Neumann's pathbreaking work on the theory of games. Professors would share dog-eared copies of working papers with me, which is where I learned about a place called the RAND Corporation and its research division. My professors brought to my attention the work of David Blackwell, a true genius who developed techniques such as statistical decision theory, stochastic control theory, and discounted dynamic programming. I fell in love with these techniques, with the elegant mathematical proofs that undergirded them, and with the audacious, often counterintuitive results they generated when applied to practical problems by first-rate minds.

In other words, I was beginning to learn what economics was, what it *really* was. I came to see that apparent truisms of the field—like "There's no such thing as a free lunch"—express deep, profound truths about society and the way people interact with each other, truths with consequences that are in no way obvious once you tease out their implications. Advanced though I was for an undergraduate, I had caught only a glimmer of the monumental intellectual task that economics had set for itself. One way to appreciate the richness and complexity of human behavior and interaction is to immerse yourself in it, to experience the world and pay attention to your place in it. But another perspective is to understand that relying only on our idiosyncratic, first-person experiences of the world sometimes conceals more than it reveals about how and why people do what they do. Beneath the seeming chaos and irrationality of transactions and interactions among individuals are layers and pockets of order. Economics tries to understand that order, to formalize it, and to learn from it. In the same way that knowing what a cone looks like will tell you only so much about why a cone is a cone, economics was beginning to show me that relying on my own haphazard thoughts and intuitive feelings could take me only so far in understanding the world's immense complexity. If I wanted to do that, if I wanted to truly understand, I had to go deeper.

Of course, whatever understanding I would manage to attain through the study of economics would itself occur on the apparently chaotic and irrational surface of a world that I was so keen to see in its full complexity. And surface disorder often posed its own challenges that had nothing to do with the efficiency of markets or the logic of incentives. For example, it so happened that the brilliant David Blackwell was African American. I was thrilled to learn this. He began his professional career in the 1940s at Howard University, a laudable institution, but one that was viewed as marginal by white mainstream academics. He was black at a historically black university, where heavy teaching loads detracted from the time he was able to spend doing research and publishing. Somehow, though, he did manage to publish groundbreaking work. But his brilliance was ignored until his publications in the field's top journals made it impossible to ignore him any longer. Eventually he was offered a position in the statistics department at Berkeley in the 1950s. He became the first black American to hold a tenured position at that university. It occurred to me that, had his skills and research been assessed on their own merits, and had Harvard and Princeton and Yale not been blinkered by their own prejudices, Blackwell would surely have ascended to the kind of position he deserved much earlier. He lost time that he would never get back, and so the discipline lost out on what he could have done with that time. In one sense, this is a lesson about opportunity costs. But what was the "opportunity" there? And how did all this relate to me?

When I began reading Blackwell's lectures and papers at Northwestern, and when I learned about his story, I had the idea that some of the techniques he pioneered might be useful in studying inequality. Specifically, I thought his research on dynamic stochastic systems might be employed to model how the distribution of income within a society evolves over time. So I wrote him a letter in which I sketched out some rough ideas, and I sent it. To my surprise and delight, he actually wrote back. He was noncommittal but generally encouraging, telling me to keep at it. To him, my ideas probably looked a little undercooked—they almost certainly *were* undercooked! But my person-to-person contact with him did affirm, in some small way, that I might eventually have something to contribute.

I'M NOT THE ONLY BLACK STUDENT at Northwestern. There's a cadre of others, and I've tried to make friends. Really, I have. We're cordial enough, saying hello, maybe stopping to chat for a bit, nodding as we pass. But the more I get to know my fellow black Northwesterners, the more I'm convinced that skin color is about all we have in common. And sometimes, given how light-skinned many of them are, there's not even that.

These are not the kind of black people I grew up with on the South Side. They're both more and less sophisticated than us. They've seen more of the world, but less of the streets. They carry themselves with a nonchalance that communicates how comfortable they feel in Northwestern's rarefied air. And they should feel comfortable, since most of them are the children of doctors, lawyers, and professors, members of the black bourgeoisie whose lives growing up were not as different from those of their white peers as they would have me believe. Black radicalism rolls off their tongues, but as far as I'm concerned, it dies in the air. For all their talk about revolution, I happen to know that these children of privilege spend plenty of time partying and playing bid whist in the student lounge, instead of sharpening their intellects in a way that could actually help move forward the political visions to which they claimed to be committed. How radical can you be, I'd ask myself, if you show up to campus in a Benz, as I saw more than one of them do?

Everything I appreciate about Northwestern, the tremendous opportunity it represents, the rush of ideas I immerse myself in every time I make my way uptown, the sheer joy of learning, none of it seems to mean anything to them. They have nothing but contempt for all that I find electrifying about the place, and they let me know it. One day, I approach one of these "brothers," dizzy with excitement after having read Friedrich Nietzsche for the first time, needing to vent some of my thoughts about the German philosopher. When you read Nietzsche for the first time, you want to talk about it. But I'm met with a snort of derision and something about how reflecting on mankind's "will to power" is something "for white people." Don't I know, he seems to say, that reading European philosophy *isn't what black people do?*

Walking away stunned, I soon grow angry. This blasé little rich kid means to tell me what black people do and what they don't? Funny, I've never seen him or his ilk in any of the black pool halls or black barber shops or black bars or black churches or black neighborhoods on the South Side where I've spent my entire life. I can't detect in his speech any of the familiar intonations and idioms that I've heard spoken by black men and women my entire life. And I sure as hell can't imagine him clocking into the third shift and then heading off to the library and then to class, as I've been doing for years, putting in the kind of work I learned how to do from watching my father and Uncle Moonie make a life out of nothing. I try to imagine what would happen if he walked into the upstairs room during a barbecue at Aunt Eloise's house and tried to sell Alfred and Adlert and the cousins on his ideas about blackness. Getting laughed out of the place would be the best possible outcome for him.

Which is not to say that I think I'm more authentic than him because those spaces, conversations, and ways of being make up my own experience of blackness. I don't think that. I'm not more authentic because I show up to campus wearing the same jeans, boots, and flannels I wear to R. R. Donnelly instead of the latest fashions that he and his Ivy Leaguer cohort wear. But I know that my desire to read books written by some dead white geniuses doesn't make me any *less* black than he is. To him and his cadre, I imagine, a degree from Northwestern is just another rubber stamp on their path to respectability, a good job, and a nice house in the suburbs. Nothing wrong with it. But the thought that someday they'll all sit around in their well-appointed living rooms and reminisce about their time in "the struggle" makes me ill. This brother wouldn't know struggle if it pinned him down and sat on his head. I know something about struggle. Uncle Moonie and Aunt Eloise and my mother and father know about it, and so do Charlene and the Teagues. Nietzsche knew about it, too. Which is what I wanted to talk about with the brother. But maybe he wouldn't have understood what I meant.

I'm feeling a little alienated on campus, but I do find my people. They're in a billiard room in the basement of the administration building. I begin spending my lunch hour there, getting into straight pool tournaments with the other students. I've earned my spurs in black pool rooms on the South Side, where the competition is fierce and I often played above my level. Some good players are here, too, but nothing like what I'm used to. Soon enough, I acquire a reputation as a sharpshooter and a bit of a character, dramatically cursing the heavens when I miss an easy shot and celebrating when I hit a difficult one. I show some swagger, and the other students find it amusing, not least because I can back it up on the table.

This isn't a black pool hall, but it's not a white pool hall, either. The only thing that we all have in common is our status as Northwestern students and our love of the game. Not racial belonging but shared interest and camaraderie lead me to these new friends, and the billiard room becomes one of the only places besides the library, the classroom, and my professors' offices where I feel comfortable on campus. One day, I'm lining up what should be a winning shot. We're playing for a little money, so I *really* want to win. I pull back, strike, and miss badly. I'm taking a German class at the time, and without thinking, I slap my forehead and exclaim, *"Wie kann das sein?"* How can it be? The entire room cracks up at this black guy from the South Side remonstrating himself in German.

BY THE TIME I REACH MY FINAL YEAR at Northwestern, I'm enrolled in graduate-level lecture courses in both economics and mathematics. I'm one of only two undergraduates in either of these classes—everyone else is a PhD student. And still, I find that I'm able to keep up with the best of them. It's clear to the professors who have taken me under their wings that I have a future as an economist, and that's becoming clear to me, as well. More and more, grad school comes up in our conversations. When the time comes to consider where I'll be applying, they have some concerns. Marcus Alexis, Rob Masson, Jonathan Hughes, and pretty much all my other economics teachers are liberal Democrats. They're Keynesians, which means, among other things, they believe that allocating resources via the central government can be an efficient means of solving large-scale economic problems. At this time, the University of Chicago is one of the top economics programs in the country, but it is also, somewhat unusually, dominated by an approach to the discipline that is quite skeptical of government regulation and quite bullish on the ability of relatively unencumbered free markets to efficiently distribute resources. I soon come to understand that this difference of outlook is one of the key fault lines in the economics profession. Figures like George Stigler, Milton Friedman, and Gary Becker loom large at the University of Chicago, and their economic ideas have given them entrée into a world of political and policy influence unmatched by any economist since John Maynard Keynes himself, whose ideas informed FDR's New Deal programs.

Simply put, the University of Chicago is a place that produces economists who are often brilliant and also politically conservative. Marcus and the others are quite explicit: It wouldn't be a tragedy if I ended up studying at the University of Chicago, but neither would it be the best possible outcome. They don't want to see me become a free-market ideologue bent on dismantling government regulation. Moreover, they think I need to get out of Chicago and see a little bit more of the world. It may be time to broaden my horizons, they think, and with my family and my South Side life just a few blocks away from Hyde Park, perhaps they're a little worried that I'll have too many distractions pulling me away from my studies.

They also, somewhat unbelievably, warn me away from Harvard. I mean, who wouldn't want to go to Harvard? *It's Harvard!* Their concerns aren't ideological, they're pedagogical. Graduate students at Harvard, they tell me, hardly get any time at all with their advisors, who are too busy churning out papers and traveling to conferences and meetings to concern themselves with guiding and shaping the young people ostensibly in their charge. Harvard can be an intimidating place even for tenured faculty, and because I'm coming from where I'm coming from, my teachers worry I'll get lost in the shuffle or make mistakes that could easily be avoided with a little sage counsel. They're high on the economics department at MIT which, I'm told, has a very different culture from Harvard's, one that is much more hospitable to graduate students.

I take them at their word about Harvard. I don't see what's so bad about Friedman and the rest, but then I'm not particularly motivated by politics. I've seen the names of the schools beneath the bylines on all those incredible articles that I've been reading: Harvard, Yale, Berkeley, MIT, and the rest. The idea that, within a few months, I could be affiliated with such places, could have their names below mine in *Econometrica* or the *American Economic Review* makes me impatient. I still don't quite know what it means to be an economist, to devote my life to research, but I badly want to find out. Imagine a life where I don't have to squeeze economics in during breaks at the printing plant, and I don't have to push through exhaustion in order to work on a problem set. Whatever the rigors of grad school, there's no way they could be more physically and emotionally taxing than these last three or four years.

I work closely with my mentors to craft my grad school applications, send them off, and then spend months trying not to think about them or when I'll hear back. I'm made aware that, talented though I am, I am also in competition with some of the most promising students in the world for a few precious spots.

Eventually, in the spring of 1972, the envelopes begin arriving. Seemingly every time I open my mailbox, there's another one of those names: Harvard, University of Chicago, Berkeley, and MIT. They're all acceptances. Each time a new one shows up, I feel a fresh wave of validation. Whatever confidence in my abilities I had lost during the Putnam Competition debacle returns many times over. My joy is matched by that of my mentors, who take great pleasure in watching my hard work pay off. Their genuine pride in me is a lesson I take to heart. Advanced seminars aside, my real graduate education begins there, seeing the look on Marcus Alexis's face when I tell him about yet another yes. That look, that smile, that twinkle in his eye, is an expression of his own commitment as a teacher, one who has mastered his subject and has taken on the responsibility of passing on the knowledge to others.

With all the options laid out before me, I settle on MIT in Cambridge, Massachusetts. I'm told that MIT's economics department is one of the best, if not *the* best, in the world. Over the past twenty-five years, its faculty and the students they've produced have revolutionized economics through the development of methods that have formalized and made comprehensible formerly indigestible problems in the field. It is a serious place led by a serious man, Paul Samuelson, an undeniably brilliant Jewish economist whose career had been hamstrung by antisemitism while he was at Harvard. He responded by publishing pathbreaking article after pathbreaking article, taking a job at MIT, and putting together a faculty stacked with the most innovative economists he could find, many of whom would go on to win Nobel Prizes, many of whom were also Jewish, and many of whom had faced some of the same obstacles as Samuelson.

Hearing how Samuelson dealt with prejudicial treatment—by outworking, outmaneuvering, and outthinking everyone else—attracts me to MIT almost as much as its status. Marcus, who has faced plenty of prejudice as a black economist, believes I'll be treated fairly there, but he warns me that fair treatment means no one will take it easy on me just because I'm black and I've had some struggles in my life. Which is not to say the economics faculty at MIT don't find the idea of a black prodigy enticing—they go out of their way to recruit talented African Americans. But the quality of the work is all that matters there, Marcus tells me, and that makes me want it even more. For all the rigor, MIT is uniquely committed to graduate education. There, Marcus says, the faculty keep their office doors open. Samuelson and his colleagues have made the guidance and shaping of professional economists a high priority in the department. If I've got a question or a problem, someone will be there who can help. I'm encouraged by this. Though I've made good—dean's list in all six of my trimesters at Northwestern, a bachelor's degree approaching, a new career path opening before me—the failures leading up to my turnaround still weigh heavy on me. I still have something to prove.

Mama, Lee Lee, Adlert, Alfred, Aunt Eloise, and Uncle Moonie, they're all so proud of me. Not only another college graduate in the family, but a graduate of Northwestern. Not only a graduate of Northwestern, but a PhD student at MIT, and then a professor, and then who knows. Such things are a rarity on the South Side, and the people who made me what I am have now acquired weapons-grade bragging rights. The person I'm most looking forward to telling about all this is my father. After putting him through the disappointments of my arrest, dropping out of IIT, and the unplanned pregnancies, I need to show him that I'm still worth the faith he once had in me, that I'm not another iteration of his wastrel brother, Gerald. He's told me he's proud of the progress I've been making at Northwestern, but when I tell him about my admission to MIT, he beams. It is clear to me that he's proud—truly proud—of what I've done.

After I inform the family, after the graduation party, after all the talk of the future, I still have one last person I want to tell: Woody's father. As a would-be engineer, the kind of guy who builds car engines from scratch as a hobby, he'll especially appreciate what admission to MIT means. I drive down to Park Manor, knock on his door, and tell him the news. He's overjoyed—he knows he has a hand in this success, as well.

LEAVING CHICAGO IS A BIG STEP. This is the only home Char and I have ever had. Almost everyone we've ever known lives here or nearby. We're still young and inexperienced, without a sense of what really goes on in other parts of the country, never mind the rest of the world. Charlene is nervous. She'll be leaving behind her family and friends to come with me, and once we settle in Cambridge, me and the kids will be the only people she'll know. She'll have to establish herself, get a job, find a way of making a life while I spend long hours in the library and the classroom. But she knows what this opportunity means for me, for all of us, and she goes along with it.

Not that I really present our move to Massachusetts as a choice. When she expresses her worries about the distance from her family, I brush them aside. I don't really think things through when it comes to listening to Char's anxieties. I'll be arriving in Cambridge on a mission, but there is nothing driving her except her desire to stay with me and keep our family together. I have to hope that that will be enough to sustain us.

I could live my entire life on the South Side. Plenty of people do it. And no doubt I would find a way to carve out a rich and satisfying existence for myself. Up until a couple years ago, I don't know that I had contemplated anything different. But now that a new future has opened up for me, I grab it with both hands. I'll leave behind what I have to and keep what suits me. As for those hardscrabble stories (and cover stories) of life on the South Side, I'll dine out on them in the elevated environs of the elite academy. As for all of those unsavory things I've seen and done, I'll pass over them in silence.

Seven

When I pull into Cambridge, Massachusetts, at the end of the summer of 1972, I am coming in hot. Marcus Alexis had encouraged me to apply for a Ford Foundation doctoral fellowship for minority graduate students. Because Marcus was on the selection committee, he figured I'd probably have a good shot at getting one. I flew from Chicago to New York City to interview for it, and they gave it to me. At twenty-three years old, this was my first time on an airplane and my inaugural encounter with the streets of Manhattan. I was in awe of those steel and glass towers that seemed to be reaching for the sky wherever I looked. The fellowship paid my tuition and provided a small stipend—just enough money to cover living expenses for Char, the kids, and me so that, with her salary also in hand, I won't have to hold down a job during my first year of taking classes at MIT.

I'm about to begin a steep professional and intellectual ascent. I know this, and I'm excited by the thought. But I'm also apprehensive. A sense of foreboding comes with my excitement because of something else I know: that I have something to prove, to the world and to myself. I wear this mix of excitement and anxiety ostentatiously. I want anyone who sees me coming to know where I'm coming from. I take two imprints of the bumper sticker I so admired during my stint at Holiday Magic, and

I slap one on either side of an olive-green attaché case filled with books and papers that I lug around everywhere. It's my motto, announced in bright orange letters on a black background: "Rise Above It!" It's my message to the world and to myself. The stakes are precisely that high for me. Either I'll rise above it, or I'll get pulled to the other side of the line.

The "It" that I am determined to rise above is the lingering doubt I have about my abilities. The "It" is my racial and social class background, something which I would never disown but which I feel, nevertheless, that I must somehow transcend. The "It" I'm determined to surmount is whatever distractions that would divert me from this challenging and important work. Even as a neophyte, I can sense that I'm at the cutting edge of something truly great, and, while I don't know exactly where this all leads, I know I must steel myself for the tasks ahead. This is what I remind myself of daily. And this is what I tell anyone who's bold enough to ask me about those stickers on my briefcase.

But there is another It that I don't talk about, not to anyone. I hardly even acknowledge it to myself. That It is my weakness for temptation, the inclination I know so well to indulge my appetites, which has almost derailed me. That It is the problem of my growing self-regard, which can become an all-consuming egotism that distorts my moral judgment and is sometimes difficult to disguise. That It is the enemy within. I have no inkling now of what I would only fitfully come to understand: that It cannot be risen above through sheer intelligence, hard work and study, or via the admiration of one's peers. For now, I'm not even trying to rise above that It. I'm merely pushing it down.

No one here knows anything about that side of me—the dark side. All they know is what I allow them to see: a curious, brainy, sublimely confident black guy proudly from the South Side of Chicago, with a wife and two kids in tow, who tears it up in the seminar room. Here Northwestern repeats itself, but at a much higher level. Same as always, I'm quick during lectures with the good questions to show the professors that I understand whatever problem is at hand, I'm quick to the blackboard in study sessions with classmates to demonstrate my chops, and I'm an eager participant in the after-class and lunchtime exchanges where students kibbitz about the theories and techniques we're being taught. Although I'm far from the only African American in the economics program—two are in my cohort and others have preceded us—I'm outperforming all of them, and most everybody else to boot.

I'm learning from some of the finest economists of the day. There's Paul Samuelson, of course, riding high from having been honored with a Nobel Prize in 1970. There's also Franco Modigliani, Bob Solow, Peter Diamond, and Robert Merton, all of whom will someday receive Nobel honors for work they're doing now. I often see a young Stanley Fischer, an Israeli monetary economist, hustling around campus with his shirt-sleeves rolled up—he'll eventually serve as the vice-chair of the Federal Reserve and the governor of the Bank of Israel. Solow ends up advising my dissertation, with Diamond and Fischer as second and third readers. Then there's the development economist, Richard "Dick" Eckaus, who is not quite as distinguished as some of the others, but I often find myself seeking him out for his wisdom and counsel in matters that aren't, strictly speaking, economic in nature. Martin Weitzman, Bob Hall, and Peter Temin are among the younger tenured faculty whom I encounter during my first year in the program, whose offices I would visit to talk about economics research.

The stories Marcus told me about this place turn out to be true. It's a hothouse environment or, if you're not quite up to snuff, a pressure cooker. There's a lot of math, and they throw the most difficult material they can at us: matrix algebra, multivariate calculus, differential equations, separating hyperplane theorems, probability theory and advanced statistics, convex analysis, and the optimal control of dynamical systems. They do so not because they're trying to pummel us with equations, but because these are the cutting-edge technical methods that they expect us future MIT-trained economists to master. They're not going to take it easy on anyone, and I thrive on the challenge.

And as Marcus suggested, it's impossible not to notice the Jewishness of the place. Samuelson, Modigliani, Solow, Diamond, Fischer, Eckaus, Temin, Weitzman, and many others: all Jewish. The culture is not religious, nobody is praying in the hallways, and few wear yarmulkes or even discuss religion. But it's in the air. Many of the faculty members are self-consciously aware of what it means to be a Jew in the upper echelons of a discipline and an institution that, not so long ago, would have done its best to keep them out. And concomitantly, they are quite aware of what it means for me to be an African American when there are so few black people operating at their level and even fewer with my working-class background. These Jews who are my teachers and fellow students are almost all liberals. They believe in the power of public institutions to enact social good, to balance the scales, and to bring the promise of the civil rights revolution to fruition. Most of my professors are keenly aware of the urban crises affecting African Americans, and because they occupy positions of relative power within their institutions, they're trying to do what they think is best to advance the racial equality agenda. Accordingly, while starting each year with an incoming class of twenty-five or so, the department elected to create three additional spots specifically for black students. One of these slots is occupied by me when I arrive in 1972, though I suspect that my strong performance at Northwestern would have stood me in good stead in the admissions tournament, regardless.

As my time at MIT progresses, the faculty let me know that they are quite happy with that decision, at least in my case. Some feel I'm proof that their outreach program is working. Others see my performance as evidence that special programs may be unnecessary. These are the early days of affirmative action, when it is controversial even among liberals. As I excel, and as word gets around, Dick Eckaus occasionally takes me aside to warn me that being a talented black economist would bring with it some expectations. Advanced mathematical analysis may live in my heart, he declares, but I must remember that there will always be some who assume that I should address issues of racism and discrimination. I will not have the luxury to concern myself only with epsilons, deltas, and the limit as t goes to infinity. An elite black economist (which is what he's sure I will become) will also be expected to address himself to poverty, to have something to say about race, inequality, and social justice. The message I draw from this advice is that, like it or not, in the classroom and on the conference lecture circuit, I'll unavoidably be seen as an emissary from my race.

It is a little strange to hear this slightly older Jewish economist tell me what will be expected of me as an African American. But many of the Jews here came to the profession as outsiders facing their own sets of expectations. Who would know better what it's like to have to grapple with the perhaps ill-informed assumptions of your peers about what you can do and what you should be doing? Even so, no one expects them to work on "Jewish issues," nor should they. I eventually come to understand that Dick isn't telling me all this because he thinks I should be working on "black problems." He's merely trying to prepare me, outsider to outsider, for what is to come.

Along these lines, I have an interesting exchange early in 1973 with two Jewish graduate students, Steven Shavell and Meir Kohn. Even though I'm still only in my first year, I've come to their attention. They ask me if I know of David Blackwell. I tell them it so happens that I do. They stress to me that pretty much every mathematically oriented economist on the planet knows of Blackwell's fundamental contributions to technical areas such as the theories of dynamic programming and optimal statistical decisions. In making those contributions, they stress to me, Blackwell had shown that a black social scientist could operate at the highest level. He did not need to present himself as a "black statistician." He had established himself as an excellent statistician, full stop. Be like David Blackwell, they tell me. Master the techniques, prove yourself as a social scientist, and resist the seduction of working mainly on problems of particular concern to African Americans. That is how I can best use my talents as an economist to advance the interests of my race, they say.

I have mixed feelings about this advice, both from Steve and Meir and from Dick. I appreciate that everyone is trying to look out for me, and I have no doubt they all have the best of intentions. These are the world's expectations, they're telling me, and I can assent to them or I can buck them. But the deeper message for me in all of this, whether intended or not, is clear: Either I would be a black economist working on black issues or a black economist pointedly *not* working on black issues. That is, I'd either make my race into a career or I'd be preoccupied throughout my career by avoiding my race. I don't much care for either option, but trying to think my way out of this double bind gets me nowhere. So I put these idle thoughts aside, pick up my notebook, and dig into another problem set.

BY DAY, I WAS INDISTINGUISHABLE from any other grad student at MIT. You could find me hunkered down over a photocopied journal article, scribbling on a yellow notepad in the library, sitting in a seminar room, or popping into a professor's office. By evening, I was a father and husband. Charlene's job had her working as a secretary at the nearby Draper Labs, so it was sometimes my duty to pick up Lisa and Tamara from day care. There were a few other married students in the program, but I was virtually the only one with kids. While the rest of my cohort convened at the bar after a day of study and lived in the traditional, semiferal manner of American graduate students, I was picking up groceries, helping Char prepare meals, and tucking the kids into bed. Occasionally, I'd join some of my colleagues for a quick beer, but I always felt a little guilty doing so. After all, there were people who depended on me being home at our small garden apartment in Watertown, so I usually was.

MIT attracted people from around the world, many of whom were naive when it came to race relations in America. Some of the international students took an interest in me, especially the Europeans. The other black graduate students in economics were not so different from the cliques of black students I encountered at Northwestern. They had middle-class backgrounds, and it showed in the way they carried themselves, their reference points, the way they dressed, and the way they talked. It was probably just as obvious, even to the Europeans, that there was nothing middle class about me. And yet I was proving to be one of the top two or three students in my class. That made me an interesting, anomalous, and somewhat enigmatic character.

Curiosity got the better of one of these Europeans, Pentti Kouri, a tall, gregarious Finn who sported a shock of red hair, a well-groomed beard, and a winning smile. He was also a very brilliant young economist-in-the-making. We got to talking after class and during lunch, and pretty soon Pentti, consciously or not, decided to make a project of me. He invited Char and me to a cocktail party at one of those old mansions on Brattle Street near Harvard Square that he and his wealthy European friends rented out. The conversation bounced from Hayekian economics to opera to Husserlian phenomenology to Shakespeare to the French Revolution and any number of other topics in which they were all fluent. It was a display that was at once self-consciously erudite and natural— that's just where the conversation drifted when they opened the wine and got loose. To say that Char and I had unsophisticated tastes is an understatement. Where we came from, people drank Boone's Farm and listened to pop music and the blues. We didn't know anything about French wines, classical music, fine art, or any of the other refined pleasures that came as second nature to Pentti and his friends, all of whom had been raised in an environment where going to the symphony or the museum and arguing about Beethoven's late quartets or the paintings of Renoir was simply what one did. These young men and women were products of the European haute bourgeoisie. Char and I were products of Chicago's black, working-class South Side. I could talk economics and I could fake my way through phenomenology based on my coursework at Northwestern. But I was keenly aware that my knowledge in these other areas was lacking, as was Charlene's. I'd chime in occasionally, but the two of us mostly sat silently observing the others.

Our silences were not the same, Char's and mine. I studied Pentti's crew, absorbing all the talk and all the references, picking up on their mannerisms, turns of phrase, and attitudes. I not only wanted to be able to participate, I genuinely wanted to know what these Continental sophisticates were talking about. I not only wanted to know, I needed to. I'd track down a book or borrow a recording of a Mahler symphony from Pentti to make sure I'd be able to contribute next time. It was like learning a second language. After some immersion, I wasn't fluent, but I could understand what was being said and even join in the conversation. At times I felt like the talented Mr. Tom Ripley, Patricia Highsmith's chameleonic autodidact (minus the murder and fraud). As I moved between worlds, slipping in and out of the persona of a Bordeaux-sipping cosmopolitan who enjoyed musing about the links between Goethe and Thomas Mann, I experienced a thrill.

Char's silence, on the other hand, was induced by anxiety and awkwardness. I was the reason we got invited to these soirees. Char was there because it would have been rude for the others to exclude her. But she felt excluded all the same. Having earned only a GED, she was in over her head once the conversation moved from pleasantries to economics and pretty much any other subject. Initially, the others made some effort to involve her, but no matter how hard they tried to conceal it, she and I both suspected they looked down on her. One evening, she sat in a chair in the corner of the living room for three hours as the rest of us talked and drank and debated and circulated. I don't think she said a single word between "hello" and "goodbye." I could have turned the conversation to a topic she would have been able to discuss, but I didn't. In fact, I was mildly embarrassed by her timidity. I was too eager to soak up everything Pentti and his friends were laying out. I could feel myself growing and deepening, and I did not want to be held back. So I let Charlene sit there, ignoring her obvious discomfort.

Besides Char, I was the only other black person at some of these gatherings. My race was an interesting fact about me, but if I hadn't been steamrolling my way through the seminars, I doubt the Europeans would have taken much notice. I took pride in their interest, though I could never say such a thing aloud, and I could never *ever* say it to another black student. I wasn't proud because I needed the validation of white Europeans. I was proud because my talent made me stand out, allowed me to rise above it, made me a person worth seeking out and knowing. Evidently, I was becoming a Player in the big-league economics game, and I was proud of that.

Aunt Eloise had imparted to me her finely tuned sense for subtle class distinctions among black folks. I could tell that many of those at MIT grew up wealthy, at least relative to me. Uncle Moonie had his businesses and Aunt Eloise had her palace, but I grew up in an apartment that was entered from up the back stairs of that palace, sharing a bed with my sister until I got too old. After that, I slept on a couch. Many of my fellow black students knew which fork to use with which course and what wine went with what dish, and I undoubtedly had a chip on my shoulder about all of it. Maybe I envied their sophistication, or at least I wished to avoid the occasional embarrassment that arose from not having it. But I found that whatever I lacked in social graces was more than made up for by my uniqueness. I was rough around the edges, and that fascinated the Europeans who had never met someone who came up the way I did.

I was naive in my own way about race and class. While I could tell most of the black students were middle-class, I simply assumed most of the white ones were rich. When the end of spring semesters approached, plenty of them mentioned that they were heading off to their families' summer homes. As it happens, Rosetta, one of the Great Aunts, actually had a summer home herself on Lake Michigan, but no doubt the other students would have been shocked if they knew she financed it, in part, by fencing stolen goods. So when Roger Gordon, a white fellow student, invited me to visit his family's home in Marblehead, Massachusetts, I envisioned some seaside colonial manse with a Rolls Royce in the driveway. Instead, I was surprised to find a lovely but very modest house. His father wasn't a surgeon or a CEO, as I had expected. He was a shopkeeper and part-time lobsterman. Roger, his beloved son, had made the family proud by winning scholarships so he could afford to attend Harvard and MIT. That made Roger an outsider in my book, and I was happy to welcome him to the club.

IMAGINE A PIECE OF PAPER HELD FLAT, parallel to the ground. Imagine a curved surface that is swooping down from above the paper, touching it at a single point, and then swooping back up. Now imagine a second curve swooping up from below the paper, touching it at the same point, and then swooping back down. Both curves kiss the paper at the same point, but on different sides. Now, notice that, if these two curves are kissing the same plane at the same point but on different sides then, when you take away the paper, the curves must be kissing each other.

This graphical image illustrates one of the most profound insights of economic theory. For we can think of the first curve as representing alternative consumption possibilities in an economy. The point at which the first curve touches the plane is where the consumption of goods and services results in as much satisfaction for all households as can be achieved, within the limits of their budgets, at prevailing market prices. And we can imagine that the second curve represents the production possibilities of an economy. This second curve touches the plane at a point where the economy is producing the most profitable combination of goods and services that is technically feasible at prevailing market prices. When supply equals demand in all the markets, what's produced equals what's consumed, so the two curves touch at the same point.

Economic efficiency is achieved whenever consumer satisfactions cannot be uniformly improved, given an economy's production possibilities—that is, whenever it is not possible in that economy to reach a point that lies on or above the first curve (more satisfactions) while also remaining on or below the second one (technical feasibility). A fundamental theorem in microeconomics, dating back to the eighteenth-century writings of Adam Smith, states that under ideal conditions, a competitive market equilibrium will be efficient in this sense. These ideal conditions can be satisfied only if the plane (piece of paper) where those two curves fall into equilibrium and kiss one another can be identified with market prices for all relevant goods and services. Because, after all, two curves that kiss the same plane at the same point must be kissing one another! It follows that no point can simultaneously lie above the upper curve (generating greater household satisfaction) while lying below the lower curve (being technically feasible to produce). This is because the two curves in question do not intersect except at the point where they both kiss the intervening piece of paper that otherwise separates them.

When Paul Samuelson stands in front of the class and explains this principle—in words and equations—my head cracks open. Like Mr. Reffels's lesson about the cone, what I had been able to understand only dimly suddenly becomes illuminated from within. Samuelson's formulation shows, with elegance and beauty, how producers and consumers can effectively communicate with each other, not through their words but through their actions in the market. It is the price system that does the talking. As Samuelson explains, the slope of a plane depicted by that piece of paper contains all the relevant information needed for consumers and producers to efficiently coordinate their activities. Consumers can adjust their buying of goods to take into account the costs of production, and producers can alter their offerings of goods in response to what consumers are willing to pay. When each side takes the position of that piece of paper as fixed and beyond their control and responds accordingly, they will act "as if led by an invisible hand," as Adam Smith had put it, in such a manner as to produce a socially efficient result.

———————

I COME HOME ONE EVENING in the fall of 1973, my second year of grad school. Charlene and I start chatting, talking about our days. She mentions that she had seen me earlier walking down the street with a woman and asks me who it was. "A friend from MIT," I tell her. "We were talking about a lecture."

This is a lie. The woman is a friend, but she is not from MIT. She's from Chicago, and before Char and I got together, this woman and I dated a bit. In the years since, we fell out of touch. Now she was visiting Boston, supposedly on business, and she wanted to catch up. So we spent the afternoon walking around Cambridge reminiscing about our friendship and playing with the idea of renewing it.

Char had recognized her immediately. She knew exactly who that woman was, and she probably guessed what we were talking about. Now that I've compounded my guilt by lying, Charlene springs her trap. She is livid. A terrible fight ensues. She curses me out, calls me names, and tells me I'm no kind of man. I curse her out in return. We go round after round, screaming at one another while the kids cower in their room. Finally, I throw up my hands and tell her that I've had enough and I'm going to stay at the YMCA. I have studying to do, I tell her, as I stuff some clothes in a bag and storm out.

If the lie about my old girlfriend had been the only issue at play, the fight might have fizzled out. While I'm sure we still would have fought (we now fight constantly about everything and nothing), I might not be stomping down the street on a chilly night, swearing under my breath, and thinking about how I'll soon be sharing a bathroom with a hall full of other men. The move to Cambridge has exacerbated the tensions that had always been present in our relationship, and now everything is coming apart. I knew within a semester that MIT was exactly where

I was supposed to be. I've excelled, made new friends, and discovered capabilities I never knew I had. But the only reason Charlene is here is to be with me. I spend my days learning about problems of a technical complexity a nonspecialist couldn't begin to understand, which means that there is only so much of my life that I can share with her. The more I grow, the better I get as an economist, the further I drift from Charlene, the more frustrated she becomes, the more we fight.

After a couple of days at the YMCA, I return home and knock on the door. Char answers and tells me I can't come in. "What do you mean I can't come in?" I ask her. "I'm paying rent here. I want to see my kids." After more arguing, she finally lets me in, and sitting in the living room I see Bernadette. "Bernie" is a friend of Char's who also works at Draper. They've become close over the last year, but something about the friendship seems off to me. She's always acted a little coldly toward me, though I can't think what I would have done to offend her. I get the sense from the way she carries herself that Bernie is a lesbian, and deep down, I've come to suspect that she has designs on Charlene. Maybe her coldness is jealousy, or maybe Char has told her about our rocky past, about Janice and Alden. Either way, she does not look happy to see me.

Whatever the reason, seeing her there sets me off. I imagine Char sitting and listening as Bernie pours poison into her ear, telling her she should leave me, telling Char that she and the kids can come stay with her for a while until things settle down. I have no proof of this. But what I do know is that I have lost control of the situation, and control is what I want. Our life in Cambridge is supposed to be about me, after all, about my career, about my brilliance. In my mind, Char has a role, which is to take care of the kids, take care of the home, and be a good sexual partner. In trying to keep me out and inviting this interloper into our living room, I think, she is shirking what I take to be her duty.

My egotism has become insufferable. My narcissism reigns. The world begins and ends with me. That is what I think. I have no room in my head to consider the kind of challenges Charlene is facing, the loneliness and isolation she must feel, not only at Pentti's dinner parties but here, in the home she is supposed to be sharing with her partner. It does not occur to me that, even if Char has no intention of carrying on an affair with Bernie, she may well be looking for intimacy I'm no longer interested in providing.

The argument continues. Eventually I trudge back to the YMCA.

FOR A WHILE I DIDN'T TELL ANYBODY at MIT that I had moved out and was living at the YMCA. But eventually it became too much for me to carry alone. Phyllis Wallace, a black woman from Baltimore, was an economist who taught at the MIT Sloan School of Management. Phyllis served as an academic advisor to me and many of the other black students in the economics program. She hired me as a research assistant my first summer in Cambridge, and we got to know each other pretty well. I felt I could talk to her about what was going on in my life. One day, I went to her office, closed the door behind me, and told her everything—well, almost everything.

"Oh no, no, no," she said. "This is a catastrophe of unimaginable significance for the future of your family, of your children. There are troubles in every marriage, but you two need to find a way to work it out and get past this."

I knew Phyllis was right. If Char and I let things continue in this way, there would be serious repercussions down the line. Someone needed to step up, be the adult, and figure out a way to mend the relationship.

But neither Char nor I were up to it. I continued to live at the YMCA through February, and in that time, we only drifted further apart. By March, I had rented an apartment in Beacon Hill. And not the nice part of Beacon Hill. The people who lived at the bottom of Ivy Street didn't exactly take pride in their neighborhood. The sidewalks were covered in dog shit. Just getting from the street to my front door was like running an obstacle course. And once the weather warmed up, the smell of it wafted in through the windows.

Char and I worked out a way of splitting expenses for the kids and a schedule that would allow me to spend time with them. Meanwhile, I poured myself into my classes and research. My marriage wasn't the only relationship in my life going sour. I was also having increasing trouble relating to many of the other black students at MIT. Some of them complained privately that they encountered racism within the department and among other graduate students. It wasn't hard to imagine that they may have endured some insensitivity at the hands of older faculty or international students who didn't understand the subtleties of race in America. But I had never witnessed anything at MIT that rose to the level of racial antipathy. When I heard these complaints from my fellow students, I didn't dismiss them, but neither did I hear anything that was all that alarming.

And I doubted very much that racial insensitivity could have accounted for the uncomfortable fact that many of my black peers were not performing that well. They were holding on by their fingernails. In seminars, they often sat silently taking notes rather than raising their hands and engaging with the coursework put to us by our professors or asking questions that showed they had a grasp on the material. That behavior suggested—rightly or wrongly—that they were not as swift as those who participated more actively. If you wanted a reputation within the department, if you wanted respect, you had to step up to the challenge in the moment it was offered.

I was always raising my hand, always asking good questions, always eager to sink my teeth into a problem, and I was rewarded for it. Those rewards materialized in ways both quantifiable, like research assistantships, and unquantifiable, like slaps on the back and burgeoning friendships with faculty. Whether they admitted it or not, every student at MIT wanted the affirmation of the faculty, wanted to be viewed by them as a peer rather than a pupil. As I began to receive that sought-after currency, I began to sense resentment from some of my black peers. Not all of them, but some. Casual conversations could grow tense seemingly for no reason, and I began occasionally to feel unwelcome in some ostensibly "black spaces."

Things came to a head at a meeting of the Black Graduate Economics Association, of which I was president. It was a mostly ceremonial title, and I had been elected by my peers on the strength of my academic performance and because, at least at first, I was well liked. The BGEA had decided to send letters to black congresspeople offering up our services as black economists. Some of us had ambitions to work in government, and it was a pretty standard thing to do. Charlene had been asked to type up the letters and mail them off, and it turned out she had committed a mild faux pas by addressing the women as "Congresswoman" instead of the standard "Congressman" in the letters' salutation.

Julianne Malveaux, who went on to become a well-known commentator and university president, was another black graduate student in MIT's economics department. She decided to make an issue of it, calling out Charlene by name and saying the error should be laid at my feet. When I objected, Julianne proposed that I be removed from my position as president. I was irate. Who was Julianne Malveaux to stand up there and say my wife's name? Char and I may have had our problems, but we were still married, and I wouldn't have her disrespected. Nor would I have myself disrespected! I earned my position, I thought, and this was a shady way to remove me.

I let my emotions get the better of me, and I cursed at Julianne in public. She complained vociferously, accusing me of "sexism." Needless to say, I lost the position. I probably should have told myself to rise above it, but I wasn't thinking.

The entire affair devastated me, not because I was no longer president but because I felt abandoned and ostracized by my fellow black students, who were forced to take sides, and as a majority sided against me. Exploding at Julianne made me difficult to defend, but no one had tried to intervene on my behalf (and Char's) before then. I went to see Dick Eckaus, who was the faculty advisor for the outreach program that brought black students to MIT. I hadn't once come to his office in such distress since the day I arrived. I was doing just fine academically. If I had a question about course material, I'd usually ask Bob Solow, with whom I had become close. But I needed to vent, and I knew Dick would hear me out.

After I told him about all of it, he told me a story about Paul Samuelson. I already knew that Samuelson had left Harvard because of the antisemitism there.

"And I have no doubt that's true," Dick said. "He was a twenty-eight-year-old genius who was the victim of antisemitism. But he also made a lot of enemies on his own merit. He could be an asshole. He didn't suffer fools gladly. If he thought someone was an idiot, he'd let them know. And some of those 'idiots' were fifty-year-old full professors of economics at Harvard. So yes, there was antisemitism, but Paul made himself easy to dislike."

That part of the story I hadn't known.

"You're like a black Paul Samuelson," Dick said. "You're a standout talent, and that's going to rub some people the wrong way. It's not fair, but it's true. You carry the burden of having to attend to their inability to deal with your talent. Don't gratuitously offend them."

I took what Dick said to heart. Despite what happened, I still wanted to be part of black life at MIT. I wanted to gather together with my black friends and peers. But there were still little moments of friction. One Friday night, I was invited to a party full of black grad students and medical students and law students from the Boston area. I arrived fresh from a lecture, and I was buzzing with excitement about it. The music was banging, people were dancing and bumping and drinking, all of them trying to blow off steam and forget about the pressure of grad school for a night.

I spotted my great friend Ron Ferguson, who had graduated from Cornell and entered MIT at the same time I did. I ran up to him. "Man, you wouldn't believe this lecture," I told him. "This guy was talking about the asymptotic behavior of stochastic dynamical systems, Markov chains and so forth. He stood up there and proved this and he proved that." I described all of this in an animated fashion to an amused Ron. I must have been talking loud enough to be heard over the music, because after a couple minutes, one of the partygoers strode over, a bigger guy with a few inches on me. He looked me in the eye and said, "Nigga, the reason we're having this party is 'cause we don't want to hear that shit."

I wrinkled my brow. If I wanted to talk about Markov processes, I was going to talk about Markov processes. That didn't make me any less "black." Who was this guy to tell me what to do? As I was opening my mouth to say exactly that, I felt Ron's hand on my shoulder. "Let it go, bro," he said. "Let it go." I rose above it that time, but I needed the help of a friend.

Eight

I t's the end of spring semester, 1974, and I need a break.

The previous six years had been a marathon. Finishing my under-graduate degree while working more than full time, taking on the pressures of graduate school, and then splitting with Charlene have worn me out mentally, physically, and emotionally. Luckily, Marcus Alexis comes to the rescue. He's running a summer program at UC Berkeley for minority students in economics, and he's secured a well-funded grant and hired me as a teaching assistant. So during the six weeks from late June to early August, I inhabit a swank apartment just off Telegraph Avenue, a stone's throw from campus. I've temporarily escaped the cloistered life I'd lived since before Lisa was born—the life of working, studying, hus-banding, and fathering full-time—and have entered a sunshine-fueled, ultrahip bacchanal that I had not known existed. It is a liberating expe-rience that changes me. Though the spirit of the '60s is dead throughout most of the country, it is alive and well in Berkeley, where rock and roll, free love, and weed still occupy the forefront of the culture. The weather is perfect. The fruits seem sweeter, the flowers more colorful, the sounds and smells more vivid and exotic than I'm used to. My sun-kissed sum-mer of love feels almost like a rebirth. A zest for life seizes me. By day I tutor students, attend lectures on economics at Berkeley, and make an occasional drive down to Stanford for their math–econ workshops. By night, having concluded my professional responsibilities, I hit the town. There's action everywhere, and I'm ecumenical in my activities. At one club I mingle with the flower children while listening to hard rock; at another I hit the dance floor and boogie-down to some funky tracks with the other black folks. I pursue the single life with gusto, and I love it. By summer's end, whatever my marriage license says, I know Char and I are done for good. But I have no idea how the demise of our marriage will affect Lisa and Tamara. And my son, Alden, is barely an afterthought.

Aside from Marcus and another economist who is also teaching in the program, nobody in Berkeley knows me. I can be whoever I want to be, say whatever I want to say while out here. Char and I are still sharing the financial burden of maintaining a roof over our kids' heads and food on their table. But I've left her with the burden of taking care of the kids and finding new housing for herself. In my heart, I want to be a good father to Lisa and Tamara, but this new taste of life as a single, unencumbered man pulls my thoughts away from them and toward the seminar rooms and nightclubs. I feel responsible only to myself, free from any constraint. I know that condition can't last forever. (And even if it could, would I want it to?) The end of my marriage is, at some level, a relief. There simply isn't enough common ground there to hold Char and me together, our mutual love for the kids notwithstanding. But it soon becomes clear to both of us that our breakup is also a tragic failure that points toward an uncertain and challenging future. Char won't stick around Cambridge for long, I know. There is very little there for her. And when she leaves, she'll be taking Lisa and Tamara with her back to Chicago. After graduating from MIT, I'll be on the academic job market, ending up who knows where. I know I'll feel their absence, as I do when I'm in Berkeley. But it is hard to deny that life will be better for them in Chicago, with all their kith and kin at hand to offer support. I want my kids to have a relationship with my mother and father, Aunt Eloise, and the rest of the family, and that's not going to happen while they're living so far from Chicago. I don't want to damage my own connection with them in the process, and yet that is exactly what I'm doing. How much of their lives am I missing out on? The situation is distressing to think about. Berkeley gives me a respite from reckoning with the consequences of this sad turn of events between Char and me.

I do have to return to real life eventually. At the beginning of the fall, I'm back at MIT and no longer able to escape myself. I still enjoy being single, but Cambridge is no Berkeley. Acting with the same impunity in Cambridge as I do in Berkeley, sleeping with whoever is ready and eager, is neither advisable nor possible. At times, I get pretty desperate, which is the kiss of death where dating is concerned. Without the comfort of anonymity and the transgressive ethos of the counterculture, my game slips. Early that fall I do manage to meet a woman in Cambridge who shows some interest, and one night a group of us black grad students decide to go bowling. Before leaving the house, I disguise the stench of my own desperation with a healthy spritz or two or three of English Leather cologne. I then show up to the bowling alley, unaware that I positively reek of the stuff. Early that evening, a friend crinkles his nose and asks, "What's wrong with Glenn? It's like he bathed in cologne." Another guy replies, within earshot of my date, "Cut the brotha some slack, man. He just tryin' to get himself some pussy!"

After my triumphant summer in Berkeley, all I can do is try to find the humor in my humiliation. I'm only glad that Adlert and Alfred aren't here to witness my shudder-inducing lack of swagger.

LINDA DATCHER LOVED GAMES. Any kind of game. Card games, board games, party games, anything that would put her skills, smarts, toughness, and wit up against a worthy opponent. It could be chess, or it could be charades, it didn't matter. Linda was an athlete. While a student at an elite Quaker high school in Baltimore, she excelled at basketball and lacrosse. If facing Linda on the court and field was anything like sitting across from her at a Risk or Scrabble board, then I feel sorry for the young women she competed against. She was ferocious, a born competitor. She refused to give up on anything or anyone.

Later, at Swarthmore, Linda continued with lacrosse and turned that same intensity toward math, economics, and black studies. As I would have predicted had I known her then, she succeeded wildly. Her impressive academic record at Swarthmore gained her admission to MIT's doctoral program in economics where I ended up, with the department's encouragement and support, tutoring her in microeconomic theory during her first semester, the fall of 1974.

I was skeptical about Linda at first. I expected, when I sat down to walk her through some of the material she was learning, that she'd eventually show herself to be like the other middle-class African Americans at Northwestern and MIT. But it turned out that her upbringing was much more like mine than theirs. In some ways, she was even less advantaged than I was. Her father, Griffin Datcher, was a sporadically employed house painter. Linda had grown up in a dilapidated home that the bank was forever threatening to take from her parents because they always had trouble making the mortgage payments. Even as a graduate student, Linda would dutifully take money from her meager Ford Foundation fellowship stipend and send it home to help them out financially.

Despite being steeped in the black studies canon of those days, radicalism wasn't Linda Datcher's thing. This said more about her temperament than her politics, because she certainly leaned to the left. But first and foremost, Linda wanted to see through the rhetoric to the root of things. She wasn't satisfied with spouting slogans. She was too even-keeled and levelheaded for rabble-rousing. She lacked the requisite rage, which didn't preclude her from sympathizing with, for example, the anti-apartheid struggle in South Africa. After all, one hardly needed to be a radical in 1974 to see the egregious racism and brutality of the South African state for what it was.

We began talking about all these things and more during our tutoring sessions. Her life and mine, where we came from and where we stood. We'd linger after study sessions to talk about this or that. She was learning economic theory and statistics from me. But I learned a lot from her, too. She had a fantastic record collection and an encyclopedic knowledge of modern jazz. She would put on records and school me—she especially favored the great pianist McCoy Tyner, whose cascading left-hand technique and dramatic solos provided key elements in John Coltrane's classic quartet. Keith Jarrett, Chick Corea and Return to Forever, Wayne Shorter, Herbie Hancock—these were among her favorites. Linda even enjoyed playing some piano herself. She wasn't an innate musical talent, but she loved the instrument just the same. She would book time in one of MIT's piano rooms to keep up her rigorous practice regimen.

Soon enough, Linda and I were friends, and then we were lovers. Her intensity in all her endeavors translated to the bedroom, where she was very enthusiastic. She happened to live in Beacon Hill, too, though her modest apartment was located in a nicer part of the neighborhood. On hot summer nights, the sound of music and laughter from the bistros lining Charles Street drifted into her windows, not the smell of excrement. We wasted little time moving in together. I found it easy to respect Linda—she was thoughtful, witty, funny, and sharp. Without question, she could hold her own at any dinner party, whatever the company. And she'd relish it.

Things were going so well with Linda that I took her back to Chicago to meet the family. We all had dinner at Aunt Eloise's house, and I could tell that opinions on Linda were divided. My mother and Eloise were noticeably skeptical. They were both a little old-fashioned in their ways. They had ideas about a woman's role in a relationship, and Linda didn't quite fit in with them. She was not the most stylish dresser, and she was not a conventional beauty in their eyes, although I found her very attractive.

When dinner was over, rather than staying to clear the table, wash the dishes, and clean up with the other women, Linda went with me to the living room where the men were watching a football game. This seemed to annoy Eloise and Gloria, though they didn't say anything to either of us. The men found it weird, too, but they loved it. So did I! As a former athlete and recovering tomboy, Linda was every bit as invested in the game as they were, cheering and cursing, arguing about what the quarterback should have done and praising a coach's adept adjustment. And when talk turned to politics, she was animated and well informed.

Mama's fourth husband, Mack, was there taking it all in. Mack was from Birmingham, Alabama. He had a dark complexion and spoke with a twang. He was "country." He could seem pretty unsophisticated at times, but he was sharp in his own way. He had the delightful habit of nicknaming everyone. He would invariably refer to my mother as "Little Lady," for instance. He dubbed Eloise "The Queen," which pretty much captured the state of things. As Mack watched Linda arguing good-naturedly with Uncle Alfred about a play, he turned to me and said, "Man, you have hit the jackpot. You got a woman who loves the game, and it doesn't get any better than that."

That pretty much captured the state of things, too.

At some point, Eloise took me aside. She was concerned. Not about Linda, but about Lisa and Tamara. She was worried about what would happen to them without their father around. Her tone was sober.

"You have to act like a boyfriend to those girls until they're old enough to get real boyfriends themselves," she told me. "Send them flowers on their birthdays. Surprise them with little love notes. They don't have to be long, but they do have to be sweet. If you don't do this, if you don't show them how much you love them, they're going to spend their entire lives going from man to man looking for the father they didn't have."

I assured her that I would. You don't say no to Aunt Eloise. But I only half understood what she was talking about. The idea that Lisa and Tamara would one day go on dates with boys was beyond my reckoning. They were still toddlers, and I was still caught up in the business of becoming a high-flying economist. I didn't really grasp what Eloise meant by me playing the role of boyfriend. Shouldn't I simply be their father?

What I would not understand for some time, not until it was too late, was this: Eloise was trying to tell me that Lisa and Tamara needed to be shown how men ought to treat them. If they were treated with sweetness and kindness by me, their father, they would accept nothing less than sweetness and kindness from other men who might enter their lives. Not wanting to "cast their pearls before swine," as Eloise would say, they would rightly reject those men who did not meet the standards they had been taught from a young age to expect.

I still had a lot to learn about life. Eloise was not making a parenting suggestion with her intervention but explaining a basic principle, one that had been taught to my mother and her by their own harsh experience with a father who had abandoned them and allowed his new family to treat them poorly. Eloise, through sheer force of will, had managed to turn the tables and shape her world to suit her. When she met Uncle Moonie, he was not quite the industrious man I knew growing up. He was a heroin addict in his youth. But Eloise saw potential in him, and she made clear that he could keep her or he could keep shooting up, but not both. So Moonie kicked cold turkey and, as far as I know, never again touched anything stronger than marijuana. Aunt Eloise wanted Uncle Moonie, but she was going to have him the way she wanted him or not at all.

My mother, for all her strengths, did not have that same ability to impose herself on the world. When Eloise warned that my daughters would bounce from man to man looking for their father, she may well have been thinking of Mama. It seemed that whenever Mama got together with a new guy and then discovered something wanting, she simply went elsewhere to find it. She left behind her a trail of divorces and abandoned relationships. She was always looking for the next thing. Almost as soon as she found it, she found it lacking.

If only I had been able to see my daughters not as the small, inno-cent children they were but as the women they would become, perhaps Eloise's wise counsel would have penetrated more deeply, as it should have. But at the time, I was stymied by my problem of self-regard, and I couldn't see much beyond the end of my own nose.

BACK AT MIT, by the spring of 1976 my dissertation is nearing com-pletion. It's a collection of essays that apply the mathematical analysis of random dynamic systems to problems of inequality. I first got an inkling of the idea that one might fruitfully use stochastic process techniques to study inequality when I was an undergraduate. These thoughts had led me to write to David Blackwell with my half-formed ideas. Now the years of thinking are paying off. My dissertation committee agrees that it's a great success, and I'll work on crafting these essays into articles suitable for publication over the course of the coming years.

My dissertation, "Essays in the Theory of the Distribution of Income," consists of two separate studies. At the end of the first (which I called "A Dynamic Theory of Racial Income Differences"), when summarizing the implications of my ideas, I coin the phrase "social capital." It describes one of the effects I'm trying to capture. My goal is to elaborate a simple model of income dynamics that takes account of social externalities in the acquisition of human capital. These spillovers occur because individ-uals are connected to one another via bonds of social and psychological affiliation. One result of this is that it is easier for people to acquire pro-ductive traits when they are socially linked with others who have been successful. I theorized that such communal networks of connectivity would, in a society like ours, reflect racial identity dynamics.

When economists talk about human capital, they are referring to the productivity-enhancing traits individuals acquire through education, training, work experience, or some other route. These skills boost one's earnings potential, and the analyst can use them to explain differences in earnings among individuals: one simply measures the human capital, correlates that to individuals' earnings, and in this way accounts for any disparity. My social capital notion extends this idea by imagining that the skill levels of those to whom a person is connected partly determines the level of skill that person ends up acquiring, himself. My idea is that human development is not just *transactional*. It's not just people buying stuff out in the marketplace. It's also *relational*. It's people interacting with one another inside social networks.

The role played by the family in the process of human development is the clearest illustration of this point. The maturation of the infant, from before birth, is nested within this web of relations. You can't come in and out of that web based on changing budgets and prices. It's woven out of intimate connections among people and reflects their own self-understandings, affiliations, and identifications.

Such considerations are particularly relevant, I think, to the study of persisting racial inequality because race is entangled with notions of identity and social meaning. It carries significations and connotations. It conveys implicit understandings. Those meanings are reflected in how people connect, how they associate with one another, how they bond, how they marry. The social construct of race does not even come about unless people behave in a way that reproduces race. Through bearing children, that is, people are deciding to produce and reproduce the underlying physical differentiation that is the basis for race.

I am proposing a theory where skills—how well you do on a test, how much knowledge and experience you have—determine wages. I go on to theorize that patterns of racial inequality will emerge that have this social capital aspect to them whenever the processes through which skills are acquired are influenced by social relationships and not fully accounted for by economic transactions, especially when those relationships are rooted in racial identity.

My hope is that this model could help us understand how inequality between racial communities takes root and persists across generations. If we learn enough about that, we might also be able to figure out how to alleviate inequality's most devastating effects. Concerning public policy, I argue that attending only to market-mediated transactions (via racial antidiscrimination laws, for example) and not to informal social relations (via racial integration strategies, for instance) would mean failing to achieve racial equality, even in the very long run. This is an important insight in 1976. But the sheer challenge of formulating the models themselves is equally attractive to me. My analysis is highly technical and that's important to me, too. I develop an elaborate structure of definitions, theorems, and mathematical proofs. I take pride in that because, while I want to make a valuable contribution to society and to black Americans who suffer under unequal conditions, I also want to contribute to my field. I want to make a name for myself as an economic theorist, one that will be cited by generations of scholars working on these tenacious problems. And I want to be known as a "black economist," someone who works to liberate his people. Above all, I want to be like David Blackwell, someone whose brilliance inspires awe. By the time I finish my dissertation, I come to believe that I've found a way to do all these things.

LINDA AND I WERE ENJOYING OUR TIME together immensely. One spring break, we treated ourselves to a trip to Bermuda. I snuck a few joints into my suitcase. When we passed through customs, my heart nearly stopped when security searched through my things. Luckily, they didn't find the weed. But I got another scare when we arrived at the resort, turned on the TV, and saw a news report showing a man being led to a police car in handcuffs because he had been caught with a quarter ounce of marijuana, a paltry amount. I went straight to my suitcase, grabbed the joints, and flushed them down the toilet.

Linda knew how to have fun. We rode around town on scooters, soaked up the music and the vibrant pastel colors, and relaxed on the beach. It was romantic. We even enjoyed all the British snootiness of the place. But I was dumbfounded and mildly annoyed when the restaurant at the resort informed me that I would have to wear a jacket in order to be seated for dinner!

Soon enough, though, I had to make a decision. With my dissertation nearing completion and my degree all but assured, it was time to start applying for academic positions. Linda was two years behind me. We both understood that I would most likely be leaving Cambridge. If our situations were reversed, she would have done the same. Academia often imposes distance between loved ones who must take positions in different cities. It's one of the downsides of the profession. But we knew what we had was strong enough to last. We'd figure something out.

The invitations to interview came rolling in, and job offers arrived not long after that. The University of Michigan, UC Berkeley, Northwestern, Harvard, the RAND Corporation, and Bell Laboratories all came back with offers. I quickly decided to turn down the RAND and Bell Labs offers, because I wanted a teaching position. Harvard was tempting, but in my mind it couldn't compete with Northwestern. They offered me plenty of funding, plus I would once again be close to my family. There was also something appealing about returning to my city and my alma mater in triumph, the hometown boy made good. It was all the sweeter that I was being hired by my former mentors, the teachers who had first shown me my true potential and set me on a path to realize it.

Six years earlier, I had been a community college student working at a printing plant. Now I was a professional economist with a PhD from the best economics program in the world and a reputation as a rising star in the field. Within a few years, Northwestern's economic theory group would be at the bleeding edge of the profession, and I would be a part of it. Roger Myerson and Bengt Holmström—both future Nobel recipients—were brought in around the same time I was. Paul Milgrom was hired a little later than me. He heard I had been doing very well, and he dropped by my office. "What's your secret?" he asked. I mumbled something, not really knowing what to say to this guy who was even greener than I was. He would eventually go on to get a Nobel of his own—turns out he didn't need my advice!

The senior member of the Theory Group in those years was Stanley Reiter, an abstract mathematical economist who headed up MEDS, a research center on Managerial Economics and Decision Sciences. Stanley would have every young professor in the department come to his office and present their research at his blackboard. It was a rite of passage, and it was legendarily intimidating. Whatever you were working on, he'd want to see it, inside and out. He'd stop you at the blackboard, make you go back, get into the nitty gritty, and demonstrate exactly how every part of your argument worked. If there were any flaws in your reasoning, any weak spots at all, he would find them. And he could be withering in his criticism. If he thought your work was trash, he would say so to your face. "That was underwhelming" was a formulation he was fond of.

So when he summoned me to show him what I was working on, I was terrified. This wasn't grad school anymore. I was surrounded by heavy hitters, and Stanley had handed some of them their asses. I didn't know what was going to happen. At the time, I was working on a paper about how the degree of competition between firms affects the rate of technical progress in an industry. It was a problem various economists had worked on, and I had found a clever way to approach it. I had constructed an elegant framework that captured the economic issues at play, but I was worried that it wouldn't wow Stanley because the math wasn't all that deep. What made it impressive (I hoped!) was that it took what had seemed like an impossibly difficult problem and, by means of some artful modeling choices, reduced it to an exercise in arithmetic.

I stood at the blackboard, and Stanley sat and listened as I explained the argument and began sketching out my graphs and derivations. I kept waiting for him to interrupt me, but he just sat on the edge of his chair, concentrating on what I was saying. After I finished, he said, "That was gorgeous. Congratulations." Relief washed over me. I'd passed.

What I showed Stanley on the blackboard in his office ended up becoming my second big article, "Market Structure and Innovation." It made quite a splash when it appeared in the *Quarterly Journal of Economics* in 1979, and has since garnered almost two thousand citations. My name was now to be found at the top of papers that some awestruck kid sitting in a library somewhere would photocopy and study and puzzle over, just as I had so often done.

I was immersed in theoretical economics, obsessed with it. I thought about it constantly, doodling equations on scrap paper just to entertain myself. Back when I had been an undergraduate, the economic historian Jonathan Hughes had warned me against getting so caught up in the abstractions of economic theory that I lost sight of humans and history. Shortly after I returned to Northwestern as Jon's colleague, he once again took me under his wing.

"This is a university, not a factory. All kinds of things are happening here that you have no idea about," he told me. "Don't just live here, in the economics department. Don't eat lunch with your economics colleagues. Go to the faculty club and sit at a table with physicists and historians and anthropologists. There are really smart, really interesting people here. Talk to them about your research and listen when they talk about theirs. Live large, and open up your mind."

Jon connected me with a graduate student in the history department who wanted to read Marx with an economist. He was studying the impact of colonialism on African economic development. His particular interest was in how the introduction of money-mediated exchange affected people's decisions about production and consumption. I took Jon's advice to heart and agreed to form a two-person study group with this student. The would-be historian and I read big chunks of Marx's three-volume, unfinished magnum opus, *Capital*. Though I'd read a little Marx as an undergrad, I was afraid that I'd be forced to endure hundreds of pages of ideological propaganda. What I found instead was a herculean effort to systematically analyze the advent of modernity and the transformations in social and economic relations that attended the rise of capitalism. I couldn't help but be impressed with Marx's breathtaking intellectual ambition and range. He was dealing with big, essential problems in the history of economic development and applying his interpretations directly to the world he lived in. Even if reading *Capital* didn't turn me into a Marxist, it gave me an appreciation for what so many others saw in his work. And seeing how a smart young history student thought about Marx gave me an appreciation of the rigor and intellectual seriousness of other disciplines.

Jonathan Hughes helped me to widen my intellectual vision. He wanted me to see the kind of thinker I could become, one grounded in our discipline but not confined by it. I might always be an economist at my core, but I didn't have to limit myself to graphs and equations. In fact, if I wanted to achieve the best of which I was capable, I couldn't afford to limit myself. I'd have to read the big books and grapple with them. I needed to open myself as much as I possibly could to the best that had been written about culture and society throughout the ages. This was Jon's wise counsel that, to my everlasting benefit, I have taken to heart.

NORTHWESTERN IS LOCATED JUST NORTH of Chicago proper, but I'm living in the city. When I move back, I rent a stylish one-bedroom loft in the fashionable Lincoln Park neighborhood. It's got track lighting, a fireplace, exposed brick, and a balcony with outdoor seating. A spiral staircase with a wrought-iron railing leads up to the bedroom and bath. A window opens up a bar area connecting the tiny kitchen to the living room. I want to turn this place into something special, but my design sense is lacking, so I ask a friend to help: Lynnise. Lynnise is the woman I had been casually dating when Charlene became pregnant. She was the woman who had come to visit me in Cambridge and who Char had spotted me with on the street, and she was the woman who inadvertently precipitated the end of my marriage.

Now that things are over with Charlene and I'm back in Chicago, I don't see any reason I shouldn't call up Lynnise and reconnect. Linda is still at MIT. Even though we write and talk on the phone and she comes out to visit occasionally, there are a thousand miles between us. But Lynnise is right here, and I feel like there is something left to explore with her. Mama and Aunt Eloise, still lukewarm about Linda, are constantly talking Lynnise up. She's an artist with a real visual sense, so I ask her to help me decorate.

With her guidance, I buy a giant lamp with a marble base and chrome arc that ends in a glowing orb, a maple-wood table setting for four, bar stools to go under the living room side of the kitchen counter, a bearskin rug to lay out in front of the fireplace, and a four-poster brass bed. I buy a stereo with a nice turntable and some big speakers, and I start putting together a record collection, which includes a lot of jazz that Linda has turned me on to and plenty of R & B. When the dimmers are low, the fire is roaring, and Marvin Gaye is crooning "I Want You" through the sound system, my apartment becomes the ultimate bachelor pad. The brand-new Buick Skyhawk I've bought for myself completes the picture.

After I get everything together, I invite Uncle Moonie over to check out the place. We enjoy a smoke and some idle chitchat. Then, amidst much ceremony, I put on John Coltrane's masterpiece, *A Love Supreme*. We sit in silence as the record plays. His eyes close, and he's swept up in the music. He's never heard it before in its entirety. Anyone can tell you about the first time they heard *A Love Supreme*, and Uncle Moonie's initiation is happening right now, in my crib, at my behest. Eventually, he says, "You're gassing me, man. You're blowing me away." I had come up in Uncle Moonie's barbershop, a boy shining shoes and running errands. That was where I first heard bebop, Charlie Parker, Thelonious Monk, and Charles Mingus, which was what all the coolest cats were listening to at the time. Now I've returned to Chicago as a man, with a new career and a chic apartment. Now I'm the sophisticate, introducing my beloved uncle to a sound he's never heard before. I feel proud and grateful that I can return the favor, at least in some small way.

Uncle Moonie is here to check out my pad. He's also here to drop off some weed, which I had requested. It's nice to have a connection in the family. But I've undertaken a little botany experiment and planted some seeds in a pot on the back patio. A fully grown cannabis plant would really put the finishing touch on the place.

I CONTINUED TO FLOURISH AT NORTHWESTERN, working on a flurry of papers that I would complete and publish over the next few years. One of them developed out of my dissertation, but others I worked up for the sheer intellectual challenge. For example, I published a paper showing that something called "the minimum-border-length hypothesis" does not explain the shape of black ghettos. In another paper I proposed a solution to the so-called "cake eating problem" when a decision maker is uncertain of how much "cake" there is to "eat." This is not quite what it sounds like. It's not about dietary practices. Suppose you have a resource that is in limited supply (i.e., a "cake"). You can use up (i.e., "eat") more of it today, but then less will be left for tomorrow. So when deciding how much cake to eat today, you want to account for your desire to have some left for the days to come.

If you know how much cake you have altogether, then it's relatively easy to figure out how much to eat and how much to save. The answer depends on how much value you place on additional consumption, and on how heavily you discount future enjoyments. But suppose the supply of a limited resource is unknown when a decision must be made about how much of it to consume today. Because you don't know how much cake you have, you don't know exactly when your supply will be exhausted. And yet, you want to make it last as long as you can while satisfying your desire to eat some every day, for as many days as possible. So how should you proceed?

I used an elegant modification of some standard techniques in the calculus of variations to provide an answer. Figuring out how to optimally exploit a limited resource of unknown quantity turns out to be a rather subtle problem. And, of course, it's not primarily of interest to aficionados of baked goods but rather to fossil fuel companies and those managing their strategic petroleum reserves. They care a great deal about this puzzle. My theoretical approach to the problem attracted interest in some prestigious quarters. One summer the much-lauded economic theorist Joseph Stiglitz invited me to spend time with him as a visiting scholar at Oxford, where he was teaching. When I showed him a draft of the cake eating paper, he shook his head and said, "I've been working on this with my students for five years without making much progress. And now you've pretty much solved it. Mazel tov!"

"The Optimal Exploitation of an Unknown Reserve" appeared in the *Review of Economic Studies* in 1978 to wide acclaim. It was my first publication in a top economics journal. That was the sort of problem I was interested in: knotty, seemingly intractable theoretical dilemmas that I could clarify with maximum elegance. That was also, perhaps not coincidentally, the kind of problem that the most prestigious economics journals and departments were interested in. Work on the hard problems—better yet, *solve* the hard problems—and you get rewarded. I began to receive offers to travel and give lectures and invitations to review my peers' work. My profile was rising.

My first summer at Northwestern, Marcus Alexis again invited me to be involved in his program for minority economics students, this time as a faculty member. The site of the program had moved from Berkeley to Evanston. Linda was getting close to finishing up at MIT, and she came out to join us as a teaching assistant. It was fun to show Linda around Chicago, taking her to old haunts and introducing her to many of my life-long friends and acquaintances. We spent time with Lisa and Tamara, too, and they grew more and more comfortable sharing their father with his new friend.

At the end of the session that same summer, I threw a little party at my Lincoln Park pad to celebrate the conclusion of the program and to give the students a chance to mingle with faculty in a less formal setting. I knew these teens and twentysomethings would get a kick out of their professor's hip accommodations.

Everything went great. Students and faculty alike had a good time drinking a few beers, listening to music, and talking about life and economics. It was only later that I gathered Marcus was miffed. He had noticed my little botany experiment out on the patio. It wasn't a full-grown pot plant, but the telltale five-point leaves were large enough that anybody who knew anything could see what it was. Any college student in the 1970s would *definitely* know what it was. Marcus thought it outrageous that I was openly engaging in an illegal activity—no matter how harmless—in full view of the students.

Maybe Marcus was right. I could see his point. Still, I was annoyed. These Pollyannaish objections to my hobby played into a larger pattern in his attitudes that got deeper and deeper under my skin as my time at Northwestern went on. He had snobbish tendencies, and they were grating on me. His family was from the Caribbean and he grew up in Brooklyn, but for all his race-consciousness and his work recruiting and mentoring black students (including me!), he had a problem with the ghetto. He would sometimes speak contemptuously of "chicken bone-picking, jack-kneed preachers," and about black "thugs" who would beat and rob you as soon as look at you. I came to think he just didn't like a certain kind of poor black person.

This condescending attitude was complicated, at least in my mind, by the fact that he had a white wife. And in the 1970s, I had a white wife problem. I didn't like the idea of black men marrying white women. I was skeptical of the claims white women were making about their own political oppression. When I was helping Phyllis Wallace put together her book, *Women, Minorities, and Employment Discrimination*, back at MIT, there was a little tension between us over the matter. I would ask her,

"Why 'women' before 'minorities'?" I thought white women who married white men (as most of them did and do) were keeping all their social capital "in the family," so to speak. Yet they wanted to trot themselves out as victims alongside blacks. But, I would tell Phyllis, white women were actually winning their fight for equity, while blacks were still struggling. Rightly or wrongly, I thought at the time that white women who married black men were using their husbands' racial status to playact as oppressed people. And I didn't like it when black men let them do it.

I may have been wrong about that, and who Marcus chose to marry may well have been none of my business, but he was trying to meddle in my romantic life, as well. His wife had a black best friend, Elaine, whom she met in law school. Marcus and his wife were very keen to see the two of us together, and we eventually did start dating. But Elaine and I were never going to click. She was too much like the black students I had encountered at Northwestern and MIT. She was preppy and dainty and snooty. She had some of the same distasteful prejudices against poor black people that Marcus had. When we would drive to my apartment, she'd insist that I not cut through any of the poorer neighborhoods bordering the Dan Ryan Expressway but instead take the scenic Lakeshore Drive. That way, rather than having to hear the music and sounds of the streets and to see the kind of people that I grew up around, she could look at all the nice shops and restaurants that bordered Lake Michigan. I was disgusted by the suspicion that she wanted, in effect, to pretend poor black people didn't even exist. Neither did I much care for her unnerving habit of reading the poetry of E. E. Cummings aloud to me in bed.

When I told Elaine it wasn't going to work, she was heartbroken. Marcus was also unhappy, and that only put more distance between us. What could I tell him? Elaine and I weren't a good fit. That's just the way it was. By this time, he was chair of the economics department, and I was starting to feel as though I was under his thumb. He never retaliated against me in any way, never tried to hinder my career or undercut my position in the department. But he was always there, and I couldn't help but feel that he always viewed me as that kid who landed at Northwestern fresh from community college. I was no longer a kid, but I still had a lot of growing to do as an economist. I started to think that Northwestern, as great as it was, might not be the place for me to do it.

By the time I started looking for an exit from Northwestern, Linda had finished her PhD and taken a job as an assistant research scientist at the University of Michigan's Institute for Social Research. The economics department at Michigan extended an invitation to me to come out as a visiting professor in the fall semester of 1978, and I took the opportunity to put a little distance between me and Marcus and get closer to Linda. Michigan had offered me a job out of grad school, and they made clear during my visit that they were not done trying to bring me aboard. In some ways, Michigan would be a step down from Northwestern. It was and is one of the best public universities in the country, but it would still require that I teach bigger classes. The bureaucracy of the place was unwieldy, to say the least. And there was nothing at Michigan that could compare to Northwestern's Theory Group. But there was Linda pulling me toward Ann Arbor and there was Marcus pushing me away from Chicago. Marcus had mentored me as an undergrad and guided me toward grad school. For that I would always be grateful. Despite my dalliances in Chicago, I knew that Linda was my future. Marcus was my past. Northwestern tried to keep me in Evanston by granting me early tenure in 1979, but I was convinced that it was time to move on.

Nine

By the early 1980s, Detroit has become a basket case. The city has been on the decline for at least a decade, since the midcentury manufacturing boom began to slow and well-compensated union jobs with pensions and good benefits began evaporating. Now the Motor City is enduring widespread poverty and seemingly uncontrollable crime. There are areas where it's simply not safe to go, no matter the time of day. In late 1981, police begin deploying helicopters early in the morning to patrol a neighborhood where somebody has been raping young girls on their way to school. I live thirty-five miles down the road in Ann Arbor, but Linda and I spend a lot of time in Detroit. Most of the crime there happens within African American communities; its perpetrators and its victims are black.

It seems to me that the first and second order of business for any politician in or around Detroit should be getting violent crime under control and ameliorating the increasingly abject living conditions in the city. But when I open the paper one morning, I see that John Conyers, the Democratic congressman whose district includes a good chunk of the city, is holding House Judiciary Subcommittee hearings about police brutality. I don't doubt that there are instances of police brutality in Detroit—I grew up seeing it in Chicago. It's a problem. But poverty and violent crime are tearing Detroit apart, not police brutality. Conyers had been a labor lawyer who fashioned himself into a leader of the black community. Now, with his city imploding, he's trying to build a national profile for himself as a civil rights leader. Well, I think, what about the people whose rights are being violated by muggers, thieves, and murderers? What about those little girls dodging rapists on their morning walks to school? Where is their House subcommittee?

Reading about Conyers's cynical assumption of the civil rights mantle only confirms some thoughts I've been having lately. The Civil Rights Movement, such as it is, has lost its way and is verging on irrelevance. It has maintained a single-minded focus on searching out and exposing racism, but in the meantime black inner-city neighborhoods are deteriorating at an alarming rate. Terrible public schools leave even those teens who manage to graduate unprepared for college. Many black kids live in unstable one-parent homes. Cycles of unemployment leave people dependent on welfare or crime, none of which does anything to improve the sometimes-treacherous conditions in which many African American people live. It seems to me that white racism can take us only so far in explaining these maladies. At some point black leaders are going to have to stop hunting for racists and start looking within the communities they are supposed to be leading for the causes of and solutions to these troubles.

I am haunted and disturbed by these thoughts. When I begin saying things like this in casual lunchtime conversations with my Michigan colleagues, they don't quite know what to make of it. They're almost all liberals, and I suppose I'm a liberal, too. At least that's how I've always thought of myself. The economics department is also all white. They know who I am and where I come from, so if they have any strong objections to what I'm saying, they may be keeping it to themselves, not wanting to give offense or to presume to instruct their black colleague on black issues.

But my errant thoughts about the state of poor black communities and the inadequacy of civil rights leadership aren't going away. They nag at me. As an undergraduate, I discovered publications like the *New York Review of Books*, the *New Republic*, and the *Atlantic*, and in grad school I began to consume the essays and reviews in these places voraciously. I pored over the incisive reflections and commentaries of erudite thinkers, many of them academics who were turning their intellects to the problems of the day. Jonathan Hughes had counseled me not to limit my thinking to theoretical economics, and these magazines presented a model for how experts working in relatively obscure areas of academic specialization could nevertheless engage with real-world issues in a public forum. Their example inspired me.

Now that I've got an idea that I think needs to be heard, I set it down on paper and send out a couple little essays to some small publications, and they actually print them. One of these essays, "Responsibility and Race," based on a Black History Month lecture I gave at Hillsdale College, is set to appear in the magazine *Vital Speeches of the Day*. In it, I argue that African Americans need to stop blaming the troubles in their communities on racism and start taking responsibility for their own lives rather than relying to such an extent on the largesse of welfare programs. Voters' willingness to foot the bill for these programs will someday come to an end, I say. Ultimately, if black people want to thrive, we can only depend on ourselves to make that happen.

Before the essay comes out, I show it to my economics department colleague, Frank Stafford. Frank, a centrist Democrat, has a cautious and conservative disposition. After reading my essay, he invites me to his office and closes the door. Being a labor economist, his room is piled high with computer printouts generated from the various statistical studies he's in the midst of. He has a worried look on his face. "You're raising some interesting points here, Glenn, but you need to be very, very careful about saying this kind of thing in public." Frank reminds me, as if I need reminding, that I'm black and I'm a rising star in the profession, one who works on labor market inequality but also on economic theory.

He's afraid the essay could make it seem like I'm on "the wrong side" of the inequality debate. He anticipates that the negative blowback will distract me from my theoretical work. In other words, I'm beginning to sound to him like a type: the "conservative black economist," that dreaded figure whom Marcus and all my other teachers at Northwestern warned me not to become.

I nod and thank him for his concern, but in truth I have no idea what he's talking about. Black economist—sure. But conservative? I'm just stating the obvious. I'm not concerned about what a conservative or liberal would say. I'm thinking about Black Muslims standing on Chicago street corners, about Malcolm X's speeches, and about my uncle Moonie. I'm asking myself: What would they say? They probably thought that, given the country's history, it was a very bad idea for black people to depend on white people to bail us out of our problems. They would have insisted that nobody is coming to save us. Although Moonie would never have described himself as conservative, he had very little sympathy for people with multiple children out of wedlock who spend their days roaming the streets instead of looking for work, who sit on their butts waiting for a handout from "the white man." My uncle would tell those people what he told his own kids when he caught us still in bed at ten o'clock on a Saturday morning: Get up and get busy. That really is no different, I think to myself as Frank drones on, than what I'm arguing in my essay. Whether you label it "conservative" or not, how could it possibly be wrong for a black economist to say this?

Frank has some objections to the actual argument, but they don't trouble me. What I find disturbing is his counsel to me not to speak my mind. Why bother to think deeply about the hard problems if I'm not allowed to share the fruits of my reflections? In any case, these are just little essays, I tell myself—a hobby. My real job—my passion—is economic theory. Nothing is going to change that, I think. Besides, I don't consider myself to be all that conservative. Sure, I think the free market solves problems that a centralized economy never could. But I am keenly aware of the free market's limitations. In fact, the bulk of my doctoral thesis is spent identifying market imperfections and advocating for equality-enhancing policies.

As my second year at Michigan comes to a close, two things happen: I receive and turn down an offer from Princeton. My work has attracted the admiring attention of the theorists and the more applied types in their economics department. It's an attractive offer, but there is no job for Linda in Princeton. More important, though, my paper "Intergenerational Transfers and the Distribution of Earnings" is published in the profession's leading journal, *Econometrica*. This is a breakthrough event for me. That paper, adapted from the second essay in my dissertation, employs state-of-the-art mathematical techniques to formulate an original theory of inequality. It focuses on the long-run implications of a simple fact: The development of a child's human potential is constrained by the economic resources available to that child's family. I speculate that, under those conditions, the redistribution of income from rich to poor families can make a society, at one and the same time, both more equal *and* more productive. I conclude that the reformer's goal of equality and the economist's ideal of efficiency needn't be in conflict once such intergenerational influences are taken into account. Frank's concerns notwithstanding, I assure myself that this self-consciously egalitarian theoretical argument could hardly be the work of a "conservative," black or otherwise.

Conventional economic theory teaches that there is a trade-off between equity and efficiency. Markets, left to their own devices, may produce more inequality than is desirable. But when a government intervenes to reduce that inequality, it necessarily decreases efficiency. The economist Arthur Okun called this the "leaky bucket" problem. Imagine that you have two wells, one full and one dry. Suppose that, to transfer some water from the full well to the dry one, you must carry it in a bucket and, in the course of this transfer, some of the water inevitably spills. As a result, you can only reduce the inequality of water between the two wells by also reducing the amount of water that is available overall.

My paper points out that this trade-off does not necessarily hold once one takes account of the intergenerational connections between parental wealth and a child's development. Children born into poor families may inherit little or no material wealth from their parents, true enough. But neither will those parents be able to invest much in their children's human development. The children of rich parents, on the other hand, inherit more than financial wealth. Crucially, their parents can afford to make greater investments in their acquisition of personal skills. The rich parents pay for extra tutoring, an expensive prep school, music lessons, outings to the theater and to museums, and so on. When the child matures and makes use of those skills and that knowledge to generate value, these investments in their child's human capital pay off in the form of increased economic success. The potential return on such investment is so great that it can even outweigh the value of inherited wealth.

It's clear, then, that unless there exist perfect markets for loans to underwrite the cost of human capital investments for poor children, the intergenerational impact of parental success on the child's development will greatly advantage the rich and thus increase social inequality. My argument is that society's overall productivity is also reduced if the gain from investing a bit more in a typical child's development is greater in poor than in rich families. Moreover, I show that one can always devise a redistributive policy that moves wealth from rich to poor families, which, at the same time, raises overall productivity. This outcome is because appropriately using taxes to reduce the inequality of family incomes leads, over time, to poor children developing their capacities to create value that is more on par with their rich peers, with gains to the poor more than outweighing losses to the rich. Over the course of generations, inequality can be decreased in this way while enhancing overall efficiency. With the publication of this conceptual argument in such a high-profile venue, I believe I have taken a big step toward plugging Arthur Okun's leaky bucket.

This is essentially an argument for the centralized, limited, targeted redistribution of wealth. It's the sort of idea a certain kind of conservative economist might dismiss out of hand, but one can't simply brush aside the theory I devised. "Intergenerational Transfers and the Distribution of Earnings" will turn out to be the most influential contribution I make to academic economics. An article that gets cited a couple dozen times is considered a success. This article will eventually rack up *over* 1,500 citations. Almost six years in the making, when this paper finally comes out, I feel like I've come into my own. I even flatter myself by imagining that David Blackwell, the brilliant black statistician whose discounted dynamic programming techniques I employ in the more technical parts of this paper, would be proud of me.

WHEN I ARRIVED AT THE UNIVERSITY OF MICHIGAN, I knew things were going to be different than they were at Northwestern. This was my first up-close experience with a big state school, and Michigan was the mother of them all. The university was a sports mecca. This I knew, of course. But I was not prepared to feel the floor vibrate beneath my feet, like in the first stage of an earthquake, as I stood in my office on a fall Saturday afternoon. The football fans' celebration after a touchdown sent literal shockwaves through the ground that could be felt miles away from the stadium. Neither was I expecting to find an economics department as close-knit as this one. I had no choice at Michigan but to violate Jon Hughes's commandment not to eat lunch with other economists. Whoever from the department was on campus usually ate together, seated at a big round table in Alumni Memorial Hall, where we gossiped away about the profession. Since no one wanted to go straight back to work after eating, we often gathered behind the venerable old economics building and played stickball with a plastic bat and wiffle ball for a half-hour or so before returning to our business.

Michigan may not have been quite as elite a place as Northwestern, but I enjoyed the camaraderie immensely. The department had pursued me and hired me with tenure, so I felt fairly relaxed entering this new environment. One day at lunch, my colleague George Johnson, a red-haired, red-cheeked jokester who enjoyed a good drink and a good pun, looked at me and said, "You know, you're a fine economist, man. You're truly outstanding. I suspect we would've hired you even if you'd been Jewish." Everyone laughed. The joke was not that Jewish economists couldn't get hired at Michigan, but that there were so many of them in the department already. I took it as the great compliment that, I believe, it was intended to be. It was George's way of telling me that, at Michigan, I would be valued and respected for my abilities, not just for my race.

I've always craved belonging. I longed for my father's approval. I would sit at my uncles' feet and dream about the day I could match their feats of sexual conquest. And I would haunt those South Side pool halls practicing my bank shots hour after hour to prepare myself for opponents, in order to win, yes, but also to gain their respect and that of whoever was watching. I would sit in the math classes at Northwestern and take every chance that presented itself to raise my hand and speak out, to show my professor and classmates—and myself—that I had an iron grip on the material. Now I have become a tenured professor at a first-rate economics department with a growing list of impressive publications and a seemingly unlimited future. The undersized child, who had to poke fun at himself and make jokes in high school to cover over his own self-perceived inadequacies, had grown into a man accepted and admired by his peers. When I searched myself, looking for that enemy within who had shadowed me through my failures and missteps, he was nowhere to be found.

LINDA WAS WELL ESTABLISHED by the time I got to Michigan, but she wasn't working in the economics department. Instead, she was at the Survey Research Center, a unit housed within the university's Institute for Social Research and funded by large grants from foundations and federal agencies. Data was life for the dozens of researchers at the SRC. They spent their days writing up questionnaires, administering surveys to huge groups of people, then collecting, organizing, and analyzing the data. Linda's beat was to work on the Panel Study of Income Dynamics. This was a massive longitudinal study that surveyed the same five thousand families year after year. The data it produced gave Linda and other researchers an opportunity to track income and expenditure changes over time, which was a costly and labor-intensive endeavor that yielded a trove of measurements that were otherwise impossible to come by.

Talking to Linda about her work and hanging out at the SRC gave me a new perspective on some of the theoretical ideas I had about inequality and social capital. As a theorist, I mainly dealt with abstract equations and models. To actually see the data, along with all the work that went into collecting it, helped keep my feet on the ground. It is one thing to propose theories about inequality. But testing one's theory against reality is another thing altogether. These surveys were completed by people out there in the world living their lives. Seeing the results was a stark reminder of what Jon Hughes always stressed to me: economics is a *social* science, one dealing with the behavior of actual human beings. How do people really spend their time? What bequests do they leave to their children? How did they find their current jobs? How many hours did they work last year and at what wages? Linda had ready access to all of this data before it became generally available to others, and she put it to good use, publishing papers about the intergenerational effects of education and economic success, about who benefits from minimum wage legislation, and about the tenure-duration of employees who find their jobs through personal referrals.

On campus and at home, Linda and I would bounce ideas off one another and test our various hypotheses. We became informal collaborators on our respective research projects, true intellectual partners. She wasn't a mere sounding board who would sit and listen politely as I rambled on. She'd challenge my assumptions, suggest routes of inquiry I hadn't considered, and help me think through the implications of my theoretical ideas. I would do the same for her. I may have had more mathematical ability, but she had a way of bringing my lofty theorizing back down to earth, of keeping me in touch with the lived realities that undergirded the equations.

Ann Arbor was nice, but it was a little sleepy for our tastes, and to be honest, a little white. While there were parts of Detroit that we'd dare not enter, the city held a lot of attraction for both of us. We'd drive in to get a good soul food meal on Livernois Avenue, or to hang out at the Northwest Community Center. The NCC was great. It had a gym, a swimming pool, racquetball courts, chessboards, and all manner of other diversions. We both took music lessons there, Linda on the piano and me on saxophone (though I never could get a decent tone out of the thing). I may have been bigger and stronger than Linda, but I wasn't any quicker. Her athleticism made her an even match for me on the racquetball court—and I hated losing! We'd head into the city for a concert at the Detroit Institute of Arts or to check out one of the jazz and blues clubs along Eight Mile Road or if we just wanted a break from the charming college town life of Ann Arbor.

Sometimes I'd head into Detroit alone. I'd go to play chess or to hang out at a bar and have a drink. Sometimes I'd cruise the avenues of Detroit's east side, finding myself in parts of town that felt like the neighborhoods in Chicago I used to explore with Woody and my IIT buddy John. The bars and clubs there were a little rough around the edges, the people much like those I grew up with in Chicago. When I went on sojourns deep into Detroit, I wouldn't dress in the khakis and button-downs I wore to my Ann Arbor office. I'd dress to operate. Not quite like a Player, but close enough. My manner would change. No longer a professor inhabiting the role of the genial colleague or kindly mentor, slang would seep into my speech. Part of this change was self-protective. I didn't want to come off like a tourist or, worse, a mark. But it was also a natural reversion to a mode of speech I had grown up using, and I liked the way that made me feel. My "ghetto vernacular" would come out when I was around other black folks who talked that way. It was as natural as breathing, and I'd hardly notice when I did it.

As I grew more comfortable in Ann Arbor, my trips to Detroit would involve women. I'd flirt sometimes with attractive visitors to the Northwest Community Center, maybe engaging in some repartee over a game of chess. (Yes, black women play chess!) But things could go further, and Adlert's dictum—to get as much you-know-what as you can—would often reassert itself. With Linda back in Ann Arbor, I could find myself on a mission in pursuit of the meaning of life as my uncles saw and practiced it, a mission that I had by then adopted as my own.

MY WORK ON THE CAKE EATING PROBLEM, along with other papers I've published, makes me something of an expert on the economics of exhaustible resources. So my dissertation advisor, Bob Solow, commends me to staffers at the National Research Council who then ask me to serve on a committee studying oil and gas price regulations. As a result, I get to know Ed Erickson, an economist at North Carolina State University who does a lot of consulting with the Natural Gas Supply Association, an industry lobbying group. Ed and I really hit it off. So the NGSA proceeds to hire me as a research advocate to develop arguments against federal caps on the wellhead prices of natural gas. Deregulation is all the rage by the end of the 1970s. Railroad freight and trucking rates were freed up during Jimmy Carter's presidency. (The Interstate Commerce Commission, where Marcus Alexis serves as a commissioner for the last two years of Carter's presidency, saw its brief completely revised.) Statutes are being enacted by Congress, and talk about deregulating energy prices is in the air. Since there are still provisions in place that the industry wants to see rescinded, they have set out to produce research, to develop a legislative strategy, and to organize meetings with the various interest groups that could help them. They want to hire me to be a Player on their side of this public relations tug-of-war.

I begin attending meetings in Washington, DC, and Houston, where representatives from Exxon, Chevron, Gulf, Texaco, and a host of other energy companies gather to discuss research and strategy. I produce a study assessing the benefits and costs of regulations. The study circulates among members of Congress who are looking at the numbers behind the industry's proposals. It concludes, of course, that the costs of regulation outweigh the benefits. The white guys I'm working with on this project are lawyers and analysts from the regulatory policy offices at the big oil and gas companies. This industry, centered in Texas and Louisiana, is politically conservative by nature. Over the course of many months of meetings, lunches, and evening drinks, a few of them begin to ask me where I see myself going in the future. I'm this rare bird, a black MIT-trained economist who translates complex technical analysis into plain English that even a congressional staffer can understand. When, during happy hour after a ten-hour day around the conference table, I share my ideas on the state of urban black communities and the foundering of the Civil Rights Movement, it soon becomes obvious to me that they've never heard a black person say such things. They're excited to hear my perspective and that pleases me. Unwinding in their company, I find, somewhat to my own surprise, that I am quite comfortable doing business with the fossil fuel industry.

After Reagan defeats Carter soundly in 1980, the zeal in some quarters for deregulation evolves into the Reagan Revolution, pushing economic policy further to the right. By now I've begun reading the *American Spec-*

tator, which, under the auspices of editor Emmett Tyrrell, had become a proponent of supply-side economics. Supply siders think that, beyond a certain point, high taxes are inefficient. They are dubious about calls to redistribute wealth. It is better to let businesses and individuals keep their money and spend it as they see fit than for politicians to decide how those resources are allocated. The theory is that free markets distribute resources in a more rational way than any central authority (including the government) ever could. I'm not a free-market zealot, but I can appreciate the logic behind these ideas. It's all a question of balance. As I argued in my thesis, some government intervention can be a good thing. But, as I know from my study of the oil and gas industry, overregulation can hinder growth. I can see that the government is insulated from market forces that weed out ineffective practices. This often leads to bad public policies that hurt the people they're supposed to help. Such thinking doesn't seem like mere ideology to me. Rather, it's a natural implication of the basic economic principles that emphasize the role of prices, incentives, and enterprise. A business founded on mistaken principles and that cannot cover its bottom line goes bankrupt rather quickly. But a government, whether it actually delivers what it has promised or not, can always dip into the public coffers to underwrite the cost of whatever it undertakes. As a result, bad policies with enough political support (like energy price regulations) can remain in place long after they've effectively failed.

I'm also aware that deregulation can lead to price increases, which can hurt consumers, especially poor consumers who struggle to keep food on their table and a roof over their heads. Those people can't afford to pay higher energy bills. The NGSA knows this, too. What is more, they know that if millions of poor and working-class people are suddenly unable to afford to heat their homes in the winter, the industry will find itself on the wrong end of an embarrassing public hearing. So their deregulation proposal protects low-income energy consumers: if prices go up, households below a certain income threshold are to get tax credits making up the difference. I am asked to go to New York to present this plan to the governing board of the NAACP and to solicit its endorsement. My argument is straightforward: Reagan is busy making good on his promises to reduce the influence of the federal government. Further deregulation is coming, one way or another. The gas companies are just trying to speed it along. There are "gains from trade" to be had here for black people. The endorsement of a decidedly left-leaning organization like the NAACP would give the gas companies something that carries weight with Democratic legislators. In return, lending their support to the industry's proposal would allow the NAACP to protect its vulnerable, low-income constituents. I see it as a win-win, so I agree to pitch the idea.

I may have underestimated the political subtleties of the situation. When I get to New York, the governing board gives me thirty minutes to make my case. They listen politely, but in the end they vote our proposal down. The partisan battle lines are getting more and more stark with Reagan in the White House. I get the sense that the NAACP doesn't want to be seen colluding with rich, conservative organizations like those I'm there representing. They have other political irons in the fire with Democrats who they would rather not irritate by doing anything that could be viewed as pro-Reagan.

They may also have other matters on their minds. The former NAACP executive director Roy Wilkins, a legendary civil rights leader, has just died. As it happens, his funeral is to be held that day, right across the street from our meeting place, at the Community Church of New York. While the governing board may not like who I'm representing, they like me enough to invite me to join them at the funeral. Standing under the cathedral's vaulted ceilings, I see a procession of black notables including Jesse Jackson and Harry Belafonte. President Jimmy Carter delivers a eulogy, calling Wilkins "a great and noble leader." I'm just another face in the crowd compared to them. Still, I'm exhilarated to be there. It's not lost on me that, without the ferocious efforts and moral clarity of people like Wilkins, I likely would never have received the education I got and therefore wouldn't have been in a position to attend the kind of meetings that led me to rooms full of accomplished African Americans such as this one. It's a powerful moment, and one that drives home the fact that my people stand at a crossroads. There will be more funerals like this one as the years go on, each of them marking the passing of the first generation of civil rights pioneers. Who will step in to complete their work?

AS MY INVOLVEMENT WITH the natural gas industry continues, travel becomes a more frequent part of my professional routine. I don't mind it. In fact, I start to view it as one of the perks of the job. I'm getting out to see new people in new places, and I'm doing it on the company's dime. Besides handsome remuneration for the work itself, there are first-class airplane tickets, sumptuous meals, open bars, and nice hotels in cities that often have plenty to offer after the day's business has concluded. There's a sense that the tumult of the '70s that rocked the petroleum industry is over and boom times are ahead. The oil and gas companies see big profits coming, and they don't mind spending money on anything they think will help their bottom line, including research consultants like me.

I imagine Aspen, Colorado, doesn't exactly have a thriving club scene, but what it lacks in nightlife I'm sure it more than makes up for in sheer natural beauty. So when I get an invitation to go there for a gas industry meeting, I gladly accept, and I decide to bring a companion. It won't be Linda, who has a scheduling conflict and can't join me. Instead, I decide to bring a woman Woody had introduced me to during my most recent stint in Chicago, a beautiful, light brown–skinned free spirit who is into new age spirituality. I want to depart from Chicago, so Linda and I make the drive out to visit my family before I make the trip.

I had called a travel agency to book the tickets, so I ask Linda to drive me by the place while I pick them up. The streets are crowded with cars, and I tell her not to bother looking for a parking spot. I'll just run in and run out while she drives around the block. After a few minutes the travel agent has my information and I've paid, and just as she's printing out the tickets, Linda walks in. She happened to find a parking spot right after I got out of the car. "Two tickets, departing from O'Hare," the agent says, well within Linda's hearing.

The agent hands over the tickets, and I prepare to go into denial mode. Admit to nothing. Linda had definitely heard the agent, and she definitely saw that there was more than one ticket. For a moment the tension is unbearable, and I brace myself for whatever is to come. But she doesn't say anything about it. We get in the car, I slip the envelope with the tickets into my backpack, and we continue on as though nothing has happened.

When I was at Northwestern and Linda was finishing at MIT and starting at Michigan, she knew there were other women in my life. We never talked about it, but I could tell that she knew. Nuances of phrasing and well-placed silences let me know that she knew. In the same way, I knew that there were no other men in her life. But Linda also knew that she was a priority for me, that while she may have had to share me while we were living apart, she had no real rivals. I was, in my way, committed to Linda. Distance guaranteed that she would never come into contact with my flirtations, flings, and lovers.

Now that Linda and I live together again, what she knows about my involvement with other women and what she doesn't has become, paradoxically, less clear to me. Until now, I assumed that she knew nothing about what I get up to when I occasionally go to Detroit alone. No strange women ever call the house asking for me. I never carry on with anyone in Ann Arbor. But her nonreaction to the second ticket throws me. If she feels shock or anger, she completely suppresses it. She now knows for sure that there is someone in my life I'm not telling her about. I know that she knows. She knows that I know that she knows. But, amidst this intersubjective game of tacit consent and thinly veiled deceit, neither of us ever lets on that we know what we know, even though my infidelity has now become common knowledge between us. If she had exploded at me upon seeing the second ticket or said anything at all about its existence, I would have figured out a way to handle it. But her poker face gives me neither admonishment nor permission. Whatever game we're playing, I realize that Linda understands more about its rules than I do.

Perhaps, having met my family and observed the way I go about in the world, Linda has accepted that I am my mother's son, my uncles' nephew. Perhaps she has come to some self-negotiated understanding concerning my faults and appetites. She knows—she must know—that I'm not going to leave her for whatever name is on that other ticket. Perhaps she thinks there is nothing to be gained by forcing the issue. I imagine she may think that, whatever my intentions, I'm disrespecting her with my behavior. Perhaps she is, even now, wrestling with whether or not she is disrespecting herself by staying with me. Linda's an economist, so maybe she has crunched the numbers and gamed things out. She could leave me and go out in search of another partner, someone without my habits. But who knows if she would find someone with whom she could share what she and I share: sympathy, compatibility, ease, intellect, and love. Or she could stay and make the best of things, either accepting my faults or trying to figure out a way to address them and change them. I am, in effect, trading on my confidence that she will make the latter choice.

None of these thoughts I'm having rise above the level of speculation. I'm not about to broach the issue in the car. If I had thought about it more deeply, I might have reflected that, when the Player plays, someone gets played; someone assumes the role of the sucker, someone gets hurt. I might have realized that, in my pursuit of the Player's path, I have turned Linda into that sucker, a hapless victim, a mark. Unselfconsciously, I have interpreted her silence about the second ticket as acquiescence, as a willingness to assume the role I have heedlessly assigned her. She surely deserves better, but, at this time, I am simply incapable of such an honest self-assessment. I meet the new age girl at the airport, and we have a nice time in Aspen. When I return, I tell Linda about the meetings and the research and some of the characters from the gas company who I meet, about the fresh air and mountains and the elevation. I don't mention anything about the new age girl, and she doesn't ask.

Ten

Every American academic of distinction (and plenty of those without it) thinks about "the call." Some, craving the affirmation that it brings and becoming obsessed, think about it constantly and spend long hours strategizing how to get it. Most of these aspirants never do. Others view it with indifference. They can afford to; they're just that good. A chosen few of them end up getting it without even seeming to try. In any case, however distinguished or confident the scholar may be, they all know that to get the call means one has finally arrived. So everybody thinks about the call.

My Michigan colleague George Johnson would play on this universal awareness, poking fun at people in seminars and faculty meetings when he sensed that they were getting too full of themselves. If someone was droning on and on in an especially self-promoting way, overselling his modest theoretical insight or exaggerating the importance of some empirical finding, George would pick up an imaginary phone, affect a stentorian basso profundo, and intone, "Hello, this is Dick Caves calling. We'd like to welcome you aboard."

Richard Caves was the chair of Harvard's economics department in those years. There is no institution in America that carries the same prestige as Harvard. Some places are just as good, in terms of the objective quality of the research they produce and the achievements of the scholars they train, but no other place carries quite the mystique that Harvard does. One could come up with all kinds of explanations for this prestige, but none would quite capture why the Harvard brand occupies the place it does in America's cultural imagination, and why students and researchers everywhere aspire to be associated with it. Whatever the source of the mystique, the simple fact remains: when the call from Harvard comes, you take heed.

When my phone rings in Ann Arbor one day early in 1982, it's not the voice of Dick Caves that I hear on the line but that of Thomas C. Schelling. Tom is a legendary economist, a game theorist whose work on the competitive dynamics of arms races has influenced the US military's Cold War nuclear strategy. He's a true original, with research interests that range from bargaining to war to addiction to housing segregation. There is no course of study you could take to become a thinker like Tom Schelling—he's part economist, part military strategist, part psychologist, and part wizard. Wherever he directs his attention, he invariably shows himself to be a master of the strategic analysis of complex human interactions, which he expresses in beautifully precise prose. I've known about and admired his work for over a decade. When I eventually meet him, I'll think that he looks like he belongs behind a computer bank at NASA, with his crew cut, horn-rimmed glasses, and white button-down shirts. He's witty and ironic, with eyebrows that dance on his forehead when he's making an arch observation. I'll discover, much to my delight, that he's also playful. You know Tom's come up with an especially counterintuitive insight when he gets a little glint in his eye and a mischievous grin spreads across his face. But right now, as I begin the second semester of my third year at Michigan, he's just a voice on the other end of the phone, asking how I'd feel about moving back to Cambridge and joining the faculty at Harvard.

By early 1982, word has apparently gotten around that, after a detour at the University of Michigan, I might be eager to take the next step in my career. I had already said no to Princeton a year earlier. In fact, I had already said no to Harvard twice before, once for grad school and once right after MIT. But now Harvard is looking to retool its ailing Afro-American Studies department, and Tom serves on the committee whose job it is to recruit new faculty worthy of the institution. The chair of that committee is the distinguished black historian Nathan Huggins, who has recently taken the helm in Afro Studies at Harvard. Apparently my *Econometrica* paper on intergenerational transfers had gotten their attention, and my writing on the dynamics of racial income differences has piqued their interest. I'm just six years past my PhD and they're offering a joint appointment as full professor of economics and of Afro-American Studies. The appointment would make me the first black tenured professor in the history of Harvard's economics department. I like the sound of that. In the past, the timing hadn't quite felt right for Harvard. But now it does feel right, and I have the sense that if I say no a third time, they won't be calling again.

Of course, I have to talk it over with Linda first. After some back and forth with Tom and Nathan, they assure us that they'll create a two-year postdoctoral fellowship for her at the Kennedy School while she looks for permanent employment. Linda likes the idea of going back to Cambridge, but there is a nagging issue. "I'm not going to be the dutiful girlfriend who just follows you around the country," Linda says. I know what she means. Once again, I'm asking a woman to pack up her life so I can pursue my own ambitions. And though she doesn't say anything about it, that second airplane ticket hovers in the background of the conversation. Linda is a respected economist in her own right, with a promising future, and she wants some assurances before making a decision that will affect her career, too.

By now, whenever I envision the future, Linda is there sharing it with me. So while it is a call from Harvard that leads me, finally, to ask for her hand in marriage, I am also doing so because I want it. We both do. She says yes.

By the end of spring 1982, I begin making plans to return to Cambridge in triumph.

BY SPRING 1983, my "triumphant return" was beginning to feel more like a dismal failure. When I accepted Harvard's offer the year before, I saw myself ascending to the pinnacle of my profession. I had a prestigious appointment at the country's most prestigious institution as the first black person to be tenured in that economics department's history. Now, at a mere thirty-four years of age and having already published groundbreaking work in technical economics, I was poised to contribute to the intellectual history of my people. It seemed when I arrived in Cambridge that I had faced the crossroads dividing the economist from the *black* economist, and that I had found a way to walk both paths. I was soon to be disabused of this overconfident assessment.

I was newly recruited as senior faculty in Afro-American Studies alongside Nat Huggins and the literary scholar Werner Sollors, both of whose work would become central to the field in the coming years. The department was housed in a modest repurposed bungalow located on Dunster Street, just south of Harvard Square. My office was in a room that would have been the front parlor, just to the left off the entryway. The Civil Rights Movement titan Bob Moses had an office next to mine. The race studies community at Harvard was collegial, and I got to know my way around. Over in the sociology department, Orlando Patterson had just published his magisterial study *Slavery and Social Death*, a book that would have a profound influence on me and pretty much every other scholar who thought about slavery and its legacy. These were deep thinkers armed with a staggering breadth of knowledge, all of them tackling big questions about race, about culture, about history, about the nation. My conversations with them opened a new world of ideas for me. When I came to Harvard, I hadn't really understood what one could learn from writers like Emerson, Thoreau, and Melville. I hadn't really given much thought to the enormously complex ways that immigration and assimilation, nativism and pluralism had shaped the American project. Talking with Harvard colleagues in the Afro-American Studies department and beyond, reading their work and attending their lectures, I started to understand that political, philosophical, and literary imagination could play just as powerful a role as raw economic forces in shaping our experience of the nation, and even that "raw economic forces" aren't immune to the influences of that imagination. I was invigorated by this humanistic perspective. I started to add philosophy and sociology and literature and history to my regular reading diet of economics journals. I could just imagine Jonathan Hughes slapping his forehead: "Finally, he gets it!"

While Afro-American Studies was opening up new intellectual terrain for me, the economics department began to feel suffocating and intimidating. The atmosphere was cold. As my mentors at Northwestern had warned me, the doors to my economics colleagues' offices were almost always closed. Their rooms lined a hallway that was itself hidden behind huge oak doors. They were guarded by secretaries who refused entry to any unexpected or unauthorized visitors. I faced a daunting task when I first arrived at Harvard. Often it felt like I was facing it all alone. My appointment carried with it a set of expectations not just about what I was to do there but about what my presence represented. I was to perform at the highest level as a technical economist, but I was also expected to help safeguard the institution's investment in the serious study of African American life, society, and history. It was an enormous burden to carry and there was virtually no precedent for doing this. My Afro Studies colleagues, though supportive, had no clue about the workings of serious economics, and my economist colleagues, though not unwelcoming, seemed distant and aloof.

The pressure had been turned all the way up, and I was starting to sweat. Maybe I was even starting to choke. Suddenly, I found that I was at a loss for my next big idea in economic theory, the breakthrough that would prove that I deserved the enormous spotlight that had been turned on me. Sure, I had scattered thoughts here and there, and I wrote a few new papers on nonrenewable resources and imperfect competition, but there was no Big Idea. Nothing I was working on just then was going to change the world, and I knew it. Moreover, my intellectual life was becoming increasingly disjointed, bifurcated, and riven by the divide between the pristine incisiveness of my economic models and the subtle ambiguities of narrative and imagination that characterize the humanistic exploration of the black experience. Now, at the pinnacle of the American academy, I began to have doubts about what I was doing there. I had published some noteworthy work already, no doubt. But what was next? I sat there in my departmental office in Littauer Hall, waiting for insight to come, and I didn't see any sign of it on the horizon. After making my way past the department's front desk, through its oak doors, and hearing my footsteps echo down that long, empty hallway, I would sit forlornly in my room, working on ideas that I was no longer sure mattered, feeling for all the world like one of Kafka's doomed protagonists. I knew that I was drowning, but I did not know exactly how, or whom, to ask for help.

To make things worse, I was watching former Northwestern colleagues Paul Milgrom, Roger Myerson, and Bengt Holmström churn out blockbuster paper after blockbuster paper in top-tier venues like *Econometrica* and the *American Economic Review*. They, guided by the formidable Stanley Reiter and his collaborator at the University of Minnesota, Leonid Hurwicz, had transformed Northwestern's Math Center into ground zero for some of the most exciting new techniques in the field. The theories of mechanism design and incentive compatibility were being invented, and the study of bargaining and of auctions was being revolutionized there. It was obvious to me, even then, that these explorations of the interplay between information and incentives in the design of economic institutions would determine, to some extent, the future of economic theory. I began to wonder: Had leaving Northwestern's Theory Group been a mistake? It seemed that every time I cracked open a new issue of a big journal, I saw the name of someone I knew, whereas mine was nowhere to be found. For the first time since I was an undergraduate, I began to doubt that I had what it takes to be a Player in the big league economics game.

Michael Spence, by then the chair of the economics department at Harvard, had asked me to co-teach a graduate course in industrial organization with him. Spence had made his reputation by essentially creating a subfield in economics called signaling theory while he was still in grad school. He would eventually receive Nobel honors for this contribution. Each of us selected material for the seminar participants to read, and we would trade off leading classes. I was confident in my ability to lead the students through the articles I had selected, but Mike had put a bunch of big books on the syllabus, like Alfred Chandler's *The Visible Hand*. These texts were full of detailed, seemingly endless case studies on how large corporations conduct their businesses, and such was my insecurity that I felt I had to know this material inside and out if I was going to hold my own in a room with the likes of Mike Spence. So I spent hours and hours poring over the readings, often working late into the night and forgoing much-needed sleep. By the time I walked into the classroom the next morning, I was a wreck. Sleep deprived and lacking confidence, I got the job done, but only that. Whereas I would normally reel off a lesson with zeal, the sentences unspooling from my tongue with ease and mastery, now I found my speech halting, my words falling flat. The grad students would fire off questions, eager to demonstrate, as I had always been eager to demonstrate, that they understood the material. As I groped around for responses to their open-ended queries and comments, I suddenly felt like something less than a full professor.

I began to spend more and more time in my Afro-American Studies office and less and less time in the economics department. I began to skip their faculty meetings. Standing before my blackboard or poring over my yellow pads and scrawling out equations, I was overcome by a sense of panic. None of it seemed good enough to live up to what was expected of me or to what I expected of myself or to what I saw my peers doing. My research questions just weren't big enough, I felt; my insights were insufficiently deep and original. Along with this terrifying suspicion that I could not measure up came an old, familiar feeling: I really was choking. Whereas, before, I had rushed headlong to meet the challenge of being a "great economist," now I was watching helplessly as I lapsed into a spiral of avoidance and diffidence. Suddenly, I did not feel great anymore. Once again, I was back in that IIT lecture hall where I floundered, back in that pool hall facing off against my mother's lover and coming up short. Deep down, I still knew that I knew how to do what I was there to do, but somehow I had lost the thread. I had forgotten how to make it real, how to ask the right questions, how to balance both sides of the equation, how to sink the shot. To make matters worse, I was all alone in my misery. I couldn't tell anybody about the terror I was feeling, not even Linda.

I began to avoid going into Littauer Hall. I feared that if I spent too much time hanging around the economics department, my colleagues— all of whom I imagined to be meeting and exceeding the expectations that Harvard's imprimatur carried—would sniff me out for the fraud I was now beginning to suspect I might be. I tried not to think about what was going on behind the closed doors of those faculty offices, about the groundbreaking work my colleagues were surely perfecting as I hid away from them, hoping my absence would not raise too many questions, distracting myself from the task at hand by exploring the various Afro-American Studies literatures. I had entered Harvard believing I had resolved the contradiction of the black economist, but now I was as confused as I had ever been about what path I should walk. The enemy within had returned with a vengeance.

BY THAT SUMMER, word must have gotten around again. My former dissertation advisor at MIT, Bob Solow, and his wife Bobby (really!)

invited Linda and me to their place on Martha's Vineyard to go out on what we thought of as their yacht and hobnob with whatever bigwigs were around. The "yacht" was really a modest sailboat with sleeping quarters below deck, but Bob and Bobby were immensely proud of it. Neither Linda nor I had ever before been on a sailboat. We spent a lovely morning on the water learning to sail, with a cool breeze blowing and the sun glinting off the waves.

Later, Bob and Bobby took us to a cocktail party at the sprawling home of the great sociologist Daniel Bell. The place was stuffed with intellectuals and luminaries whose names I had read in all the magazines of opinion I had been consuming. The fabled social critic Irving Kristol was there, along with noted urban sociologist Nathan Glazer and a half-dozen other people whose names I knew but whom it never occurred to me that I would actually meet. This was the Vineyard social scene, and I was drinking it all in.

Once we made the rounds, Bob pulled me into a corner. "I've heard you're not all that happy at Harvard," he said. I began to equivocate, but he stopped me. "They put you in an impossible position," he said. "You're a once-in-a-decade talent, and they set you up for failure by giving you a frontline role before you were ready, before your work had a chance to mature." Hearing this hurt a little. I respected Bob immensely, looked up to him as a mentor and a model for what a great economist should be, and he was telling me I wasn't ready for the big leagues. At some level, though, I knew he was right. I had five or six good papers to my name, one of them a potential classic. But Harvard had hired me with tenure. I knew the work I was currently doing wouldn't pass muster at that level, and the pressures of my joint position weren't helping.

Back then, MIT's economics department had an unofficial policy. They would never hire their own students right out of grad school. But if one of the department's top students went out and made a real name for himself, after a decent interval, he could be offered a job at MIT and welcomed back into the fold to help ensure the department's preeminence.

Bob suggested that the door would be open to me if I did want to come back. I could return to a place where I had flourished, where hardcore technical economics permeated the atmosphere, and where I wouldn't have to worry about the impossible expectations that went along with the Harvard post. I could do my research and write my papers and teach graduate students at a place where that was the coin of the realm. And I could grow at MIT, become the economist I wanted to become, the "black Paul Samuelson," as Dick Eckaus had put it (though I seriously doubt that Bob, Samuelson's close collaborator and lifelong colleague, would ever have put it quite that way).

Standing at that party and looking around at all the luminaries, thinking back on the morning out on Bob's sailboat, I saw his point. I didn't need to go through all the angst, trying to be all things to all people. I could just do what I did best. Maybe I could become an epochal figure in economics. That was what I wanted. One day, just after arriving at Harvard, I had told Tom Schelling, who was starting to become a close friend and confidant, that I aspired to win the John Bates Clark Medal, a very prestigious prize in the field, awarded every year to an economist under the age of forty. I was in my midthirties. Tom was bullish about that prospect. I still had time to make it. But I wasn't going to win any Clark Medals with the kind of derivative work I was then doing. Bob said that if I was willing to commit solely to social science—no more little essays, no more Afro-American Studies—I could "come home" to MIT. They were prepared to offer me a tenured position. "Think about it," Bob said. Then we rejoined the party.

Later, back in Cambridge, I got another call about MIT. This one was from the theorist Peter Diamond, another mentor and a member of my dissertation committee. It was about the offer. "We think you're on a promising trajectory," he said. "If you put your nose to the grindstone and concentrate on your technical work, everything will be fine. However, I need to be honest with you. You wouldn't be getting this offer if you weren't black."

The conversation ended shortly after that. At first, I didn't know what to make of it. I didn't take offense. Peter was a friend, and I believed he wanted to let me in on conversations that were happening behind closed doors. I didn't think he was racist for telling me this. But the implications were clear. First, he thought I should know that I was not yet at a level where MIT would have offered me a position based purely on my accomplishments. They were making an exception for me. Partially, I'm sure, out of respect and affection and a belief that I could fulfill my promise. But partially because they wanted to diversify their faculty. They had standards, and in hiring me with tenure at this time, they would be mildly compromising those standards. The second implication I drew from Peter's comment (which may not have been in his mind at all) was that, if I went to MIT and failed to measure up those standards, it would be seen not only as a personal failure but as a failure of "my people." I would be failing my race.

Linda and I spent a long time talking about it, but it was really no choice at all. I couldn't go. Say I didn't measure up, and I never produced anything of note again. Then I'd be viewed as a charity case at MIT. Everyone would know I was there only because I'm black. That would be absolute misery for me. I would be the black guy who didn't work out, proof that their attempt to open the doors to this most demanding discipline at the highest level was a failure. I would spend my days puttering around, attending to my business, and watching younger colleagues pass me by.

I couldn't stand that idea. I couldn't bear the thought of being condescended to or merely tolerated. I'm not that guy. I wanted to sink or swim, paddle or drift along the current of life, on my own terms. So I called Bob Solow and thanked him for the offer but told him I would figure out a way to make Harvard work for me. Tom Schelling's bullish perception of my Clark Medal prospects helped me to persuade myself that this was the right move. At the time, I had no idea how fateful for my career, and for my life, that decision would prove to be.

NOT EVERYTHING WAS GLOOM AND DOOM in Cambridge. I was white-knuckling my way through another year in the economics department, but by the end of 1983, I was meeting people. Tom Schelling would invite me to events at the Kennedy School where he'd introduce me around. Some of these people, it happened, were conservatives. The political scientist James Q. Wilson was often there—his ideas about crime and policing would influence a generation of criminal justice policy in American cities. The psychologist Richard Herrnstein was occasionally around, as were the brilliant biologist E. O. Wilson and even, rarely, Senator Daniel Patrick Moynihan, whose 1965 report, *The Negro Family: The Case for National Action*, sounded an early alarm about black domestic instability that was still ringing in the 1980s. Tom introduced me to the couple Stephan and Abigail Thernstrom, an historian and a political scientist, respectively, who quickly became close friends to Linda and me. They would check in with us to see how we were doing, have us over for dinner, and treat us almost as family. In their scholarship and writing, they could be scathing to the liberal targets of their critiques. But as human beings, they were warm and inviting, often going out of their way to help if either of us needed anything at all.

The atmosphere at Harvard's Kennedy School was completely different from that of the economics department. As a professional school, its ultimate focus was on mastering the art and improving the practice of government. Public management and public leadership mattered at the Kennedy School. Politics, social ethics, and history mattered there, too. Analytic virtuosity was prized, but not for its own sake. The Kennedy School conservatives were hardly the foaming-at-the-mouth right-wing ogres their liberal opponents made them out to be. I found them thoughtful and open-minded. There was more collegiality at the Kennedy School than there was in the economics department, more of a sense that everyone was there to share and debate ideas. Perhaps that was due to the nature of the school, whose purpose was to fund research but also to train current and future leaders and policymakers. Faculty there could get just as much respect from their colleagues for writing a big article in the *Atlantic* as they would for a publication in a top-tier scholarly journal. They proceeded from the notion that new ideas could and should be presented in such a manner as to influence the public discourse and the making of public policy.

Back in the economics department, I was still stuck. Tom had noticed that I wasn't handling my dual role very well. He saw that I was struggling. One day, I finally poured out all my anxieties to him. I told him about the excruciating self-doubt I was experiencing, about my fear that I had peaked, that my best work was behind me. I had no idea what was next, and I was worried that my career as a serious Player in economics might be over.

It all came out. I couldn't stop myself. And when I had finally wound down my tormented monologue, Tom *laughed*. I was stunned. I was standing before him baring my soul, and he was *laughing* at me? Where was the humor in my tortured confession?

After a moment, Tom recovered, looked me in the eye with that impish smile, and said, "Do you think you're the only one? This place is full of neurotics hiding behind their secretaries and their ten-foot doors, fearful of that dreaded question: What have you done for me lately? There are no prizes big enough to quell the panic these guys feel when someone tells them, 'Okay, I saw your paper in *Econometrica* three years ago, but what are you working on *today*?' We're all neurotics here, terrified that someone is going to ask us to justify our existence. Relax. Just relax and do your work."

Tom's pep talk did calm me down. I had my troubles, but at least I now knew I wasn't the only one. Somehow, I doubted that Tom was as neurotic as he made himself out to be. But he could be hard to read. He suggested that he felt the same pressures that I did, yet he seemed so steady and confident. His little smiles and ironic comments, his ability

to see every situation and problem in its entirety, his apparent impervi-
ousness to petty rivalries or nagging insecurities—all of this conveyed a
sense that he hovered slightly above the fray. He always seemed to be in
absolute control of his emotions. With his strategic brilliance and utterly
illegible demeanor, he could have made an outstanding poker player.

Or a spy. And Tom was clearly fascinated by spies. He kept a shelf outside his office where anyone could take or leave a book, and it was loaded
with the spy novels that Tom devoured by the handful. His favorite was
John le Carré's *A Perfect Spy*, a brilliant, dark psychological portrait that
describes all the manipulation and secrets and alternate identities that go
into the making of a figure who survives only by means of subterfuge
and evasion. It would be tempting to see Tom's taste in literature as a
"tell," an inadvertent revelation of what made him tick. I found him to
be a comforting presence, almost a father figure. But I had to wonder
what was going on beneath the surface.

IN OUR SECOND YEAR AT CAMBRIDGE, Linda landed a tenure-track
position at Tufts, just a couple of miles from the Harvard campus. We
were both glad that she had permanent employment at an excellent
school, but my troubles at Harvard persisted. While Tom's pep talk had
helped center me, I still wasn't producing work at the level I should
have been.

Tom recognized that I was still in distress, and he confessed that my
distress was now distressing him. "I brought you here," he said, "I would
hate to think that I'm responsible for putting you in this situation." He
seemed genuinely troubled by my pain. It wasn't Tom's fault, of course,
but he wanted to fix the situation anyway. He knew I was interested
in questions that outstripped economics, questions of culture, politics,
policy, and social theory. "Why don't you come to the Kennedy School?
We can figure out a way to get you here, and believe me, we would be
thrilled to have you."

I jumped at the chance. Some kinks would need to be worked out. I'd have to officially resign from the economics and Afro-American Studies departments and then be rehired by the Kennedy School, such were the tangled dynamics of Harvard's intrainstitutional system. I would not be able to teach graduate-level economics courses anymore, except as part of a team, nor would I be allowed to chair dissertation committees in economics without the department giving its permission on an ad hoc basis. That made me a little sad. My mentors meant so much to me, and now I could not play the same role in quite the same way for other young would-be economists. But the benefits outweighed the costs. I'd have the freedom to pursue broader intellectual interests, and I'd have an institutional home where the faculty were collaborative and supportive. I had choked in the economics department, there's no denying it. But there was no reason to keep choking. I could start fresh at the Kennedy School. And Tom's confidence in me helped me to believe that I would succeed there, despite having failed elsewhere.

Abigail, who then served as an adjunct instructor in the government department, was very happy I was joining the Kennedy School's faculty. When I gave her a copy of "Responsibility and Race," the little essay I'd published in *Vital Speeches of the Day*, she took it seriously, and she loved it. She didn't see that kind of writing as an interesting sideline to my "real" work as an economist. She encouraged me to keep at it. Whatever her feelings about me personally, she was also a former leftist who was becoming a conservative. She was in the midst of writing what would become her book *Whose Votes Count?*, a very critical assessment of key civil rights initiatives like the Voting Rights Act and affirmative action. It's likely that she saw in me not only a new friend but a fellow traveler in the making, someone who was willing to call out the failures of the Civil Rights Movement while the liberal establishment averted its eyes.

Abigail thought my ideas needed a bigger audience, that *I* needed a bigger audience. Marty Peretz, the brash, boisterous, and incredibly self-confident owner of the *New Republic*, was a fixture around Harvard. His magazine didn't have huge circulation numbers, but the people who did read it were influential. Marty taught classes on government and foreign policy, and he had purchased the *New Republic* using funds provided by his wife, an heir to the Singer sewing machine fortune. In fact, he purchased a lot with that money, including a gorgeous house on Brattle Street that was lined with priceless works of art that looked as though they should be hanging in a museum somewhere. Abigail had pressed my essay on Marty and cajoled him into meeting me for lunch one day. I was a highly regarded black economist who was criticizing the present-day Civil Rights Movement from a relatively conservative position. And I could *write*. Surely that would appeal to Marty's taste for controversy.

It turns out she was right. I met Marty for lunch. He grilled me about my past and my work, asked me where I stood on this and that issue, and tried to figure out exactly how this black working-class guy ended up with a PhD from MIT and tenure at Harvard. We talked about "Race and Responsibility." He liked it, but he thought there was a lot more to the idea than was coming through in that essay. He suggested substantial revisions. If I expanded it a bit more, gave it more teeth, it could make a good piece for the magazine.

I was excited by the prospect of writing for the *New Republic*. By now I had more of a sense of what Frank Stafford meant when he said I would be seen as a conservative. But I decided I couldn't worry about that. If my ideas about race, poverty, and the black family and my criticisms of black leaders were conservative, then so be it. I happened to think my ideas were correct, and I happened to think that if policymakers actually were to listen to my analysis of the situation, and if they were being honest with themselves, they would find it hard to disagree with me. And besides, now that I was meeting and talking to some unabashed conservatives, I found that they made a lot of sense. I didn't agree with them about everything, but they were smart, and they didn't have the knee-jerk skepticism toward the free market that many of my colleagues in Afro-American Studies, brilliant as they were, nevertheless clung to.

After my talks with Bob Solow and Peter Diamond, I knew that publishing an explicitly political piece in a high-profile venue like the *New Republic* would signal to the world that I was devoting more time to my "little essays" and less time to technical economics. This wasn't social science, but it was deadly serious. The issues I was pointing to in black communities, I thought, needed to be addressed immediately. Black lives were needlessly languishing, and black bodies were piling up in the streets. Black leaders needed to step up, and they weren't doing it. Clearly, this was a huge opportunity. I began to see that there was more than one way for me to make my mark. My self-consciousness and insecurity had gotten the better of me in the economics department. I didn't know if I was failing there because I really wasn't good enough or because I merely feared that I might not be good enough. The outcome was the same regardless: I wasn't producing. And I couldn't just sit there not producing. That wasn't me. I had to do something. I had to find a way to make Harvard work for me, and this was it. I was pushing all my chips in.

IN THE SUMMER OF 1984, I'm on my way to attend a meeting of black leaders in Washington, DC. This consortium of officials from major organizations would periodically come together to consider matters of mutual interest. I'm here because Phyllis Wallace, my mentor from MIT, has invited me. She knows about the drift of my recent political thought—I'd shown her an early draft of my *New Republic* essay. I'm calling it "A New American Dilemma," after the Swedish economist Gunnar Myrdal's 1944 study *An American Dilemma: The Negro Problem and Modern Democracy*. Phyllis was alarmed by this draft and basically said to me it would be great if I could sit down with some of "our leaders," share my concerns with them, and listen to theirs in return. So she had me added to the agenda for this meeting of the civil rights coalition.

It's a hot day, but that doesn't really faze me. The fact is, I'm sweating from more than just the heat, because I'm fearful of how people might react to what I'm about to say. We meet at the Urban Institute, which is housed in an indistinct gray stone office building in Northwest Washington. The meeting is taking place in a seminar-type room without a podium, just a long table with chairs all around it. Maybe a dozen people sit at the table with a dozen more scattered at the periphery.

When it's my turn to speak, I don't move to the front of the room, I stand up in my place. I speak without notes. My draft article had circulated beforehand, so I just emphasize my main points. Everyone is attentive. No one betrays the impatience they must be feeling with the presumptuous upstart now lecturing them. The fact that I plan to publish this piece in the *New Republic*—not a popular venue for most left-liberal African Americans—surely rubs them the wrong way. I imagine that they view my notable achievements to date as the fruit of the civil rights struggle. There may be a sense of despair, I think, for these leaders who are now confronted by someone like me, a product of their efforts who seems to have gone off the rails.

I'm nervous but also excited, maybe a little arrogant in my assertiveness. I speak with an edge in my voice, with the words coming too quickly, with my emotion—my anger—showing through. I know what I'm saying flies in the face of what they believe. Still, I want to emphasize that I think *they* are the ones who have lost their way, and I'm not at all hesitant to say so. I'm not hiding from the truth as I see it, nor am I apologizing for it.

Looking around that room I see some familiar faces: Benjamin Hooks, head of the NAACP; John Jacob, who leads the National Urban League; Eddie Williams, president of the Joint Center for Political and Economic Studies; historian Roger Wilkins; politician Julian Bond; and Coretta Scott King of the Southern Christian Leadership Conference but, more important, representing the legacy of Martin Luther King Jr. Looking out at their faces, these leaders whom I'd seen on the evening news, some of them since I was a child, I feel proud to be there, despite knowing that these luminaries are not very happy with me just now. Clearly this is a key moment in my career and in my life. Important people want to hear from me.

I feel a certain pride and a certain trepidation. And something more: I am energized by the prospect of their anger. I'm declaring that the emperor has no clothes. But unlike the naive child of the folktale who has no idea he's calling power to account, I know exactly what I'm doing, and it excites me. I'm certain that I see something important that the others also know to be true but will not or cannot admit.

We stand there in the summer of 1984. Ronald Reagan is completing his first term, and we can all see he's going to win reelection in a landslide. Two decades have passed since the heyday of the civil rights achievements of the 1960s. It is time to take stock. Where have we blacks gotten ourselves to? High up in my speech, I throw down the gauntlet: "The Civil Rights Movement is over!" I assert that problems of the lower classes of African American society, plagued by poverty and joblessness, are, at the end of the day, not remediable by the means which had been so effective in the 1960s: protests and petitioning for fair treatment. What we now face, I suggest, is a new American dilemma.

I allow that racism continues to hinder black people, but I think it has been constrained by civil rights legislation and evolving norms. By contrast, citing a long list of statistics, I describe the problems of black communities, and I argue that these problems—single-parent families, early and unwed pregnancy, criminalized youth, low academic achievement, absence from the labor force—now limit our ability to seize upon opportunities newly available to us. I openly call this a social pathology in the so-called black underclass. I conclude that this social pathology needs to be addressed and, crucially, that the methods of yesteryear's civil rights protests are not an effective means of doing so.

When I finish my talk, the sweat beading on my brow, some among the assembled have questions:

"Well, Professor Loury, don't you think some of these so-called pathologies are themselves the consequence of our people having been denied equal rights and victimized by discrimination?"

"Professor Loury, can you not see that the things you're saying here are precisely what the conservative Republicans can be heard to say in their derogatory, stereotypic renderings of African American life?"

"Professor Loury, don't you realize it's more complicated than that?"

I have responses to these questions, but I've noticed something disturbing. Coretta Scott King has tears in her eyes. They well up and roll down her cheeks. Those tears are her only commentary.

Here is the widow of the Reverend Dr. Martin Luther King Jr., a woman who, more than any other single person, embodies the black freedom struggle in America. No, she is not an intellectual leader, nor a political actor in any meaningful sense, nor a strategist. But her words and her very presence nonetheless carry a unique gravity. I don't take her response to mean that my argument must be mistaken on the merits. I don't see her as a serious social critic. Still, this is Dr. King's widow, an icon who represents something almost sacred. Her husband had been murdered simply for trying to serve his country, his people, and his God, and at the young age of thirty-nine, only a few years older than I am now. I feel honored by her presence. In fact, she sits directly beside me. I have only to look down into her face to see those tears.

Still, I am perplexed. Why is she weeping? What had I said that could have brought about this kind of response? It does not occur to me to reflect and to try to understand the role that my speaking in this way plays within the larger social drama, to contemplate the difference between merely being right about the movement and being helpful to it. At this moment, I have not even begun to consider which of these alternatives might be more important to me.

Nor does it occur to me to look within myself for my motivations in writing and speaking as I do. I am angry, enraged by what I see as the dishonesty of these leaders and the media and the liberal commentariat. I am ashamed of the way these failures within black communities—whatever their cause—reflect back on me and those of us living (publicly, anyway) on the right side of Aunt Eloise's line. I am afraid that in those failures I see a distorted version of my own image. And yet, I also believe there is a conspiracy of silence about all of this. I know that conspiracy does not extend to the pews of the black churches where many pastors sermonize, lamenting the nature of life on the streets of their cities. Such sermons decrying the ill effects of "loose living" are being preached weekly to African Americans. But on the talk show circuit, in the lecture halls, at the political podiums, and in the demands and representations of black leaders, it seems to me that no honest assessment of these conditions is being made, except when it might serve to indict white society for what had gone so horribly wrong.

Where will the future take us? What will happen to these communities, like the one I was raised in on the South Side? What will become of the people living in the housing projects that I explored back in Chicago, where so many of my people live and, often, languish? And what will become of the kids dependent on schools where most of them aren't learning how to read or to do algebra? I fear that if we don't get it right, we will find ourselves dealing with these very same issues two or three generations down the line.

There is no word that could describe my emotions as I watch Coretta Scott King cry. I want to offer her comfort, but it is not my place to do so. That is for the others. As I have more or less announced, I have a different role to play, other enemies to seek.

THE DAY THE ISSUE OF the *New Republic* containing "A New American Dilemma" comes out, in December 1984, I bundle up against the cold and walk over to Out of Town News, a fabled newsstand in Harvard Square that carries magazines and newspapers from every corner of the world. If you're looking for the news from China, Nigeria, or Sri Lanka, this place has it, along with seemingly every glossy magazine printed in the English-speaking world. I pull a fresh copy of the *New Republic* off the rack, flip to my piece, and smile as I read my name across the page. There is no turning back now.

Eleven

On June 11, 1983, Linda and I got married. The year before, while we were still in Ann Arbor, I took care of a small legal matter that would have impeded our union: getting a divorce from Charlene. There were times, after our separation in 1974, when I considered trying to reconcile with Char for the sake of the kids. But that was never a realistic option. As the years went by, the distance between us only widened. Our relationship was long over. If it wasn't for Lisa and Tamara, we probably wouldn't have had any contact at all. But, while we were separated, we had never actually gone to the trouble of getting divorced. Divorce is expensive, time-consuming, and painful, so we just didn't do it. Linda knew the situation, and for a while it didn't seem to bother her, but clearly Charlene and I had to bite the bullet and sign the papers in order for both of us to move on with our lives.

By the time of the wedding, all of that was in the past. The ceremony was organized by Linda's sister, Rhonda, and took place at an Episcopal church in Baltimore. Rhonda was Linda's maid of honor and Alvin Headen, a friend from my MIT days, was my best man. My mother and father, Aunt Eloise, my sister Lee Lee, and my daughters Lisa and Tamara flew in, as did my maternal grandfather, along with his wife, Pearl. They made the trek from Chicago, much to my surprise. Despite having caused so much pain to my mother and her siblings, my grandfather, Adlert Miles Cartman Sr., had tried over the years to develop some sort of relationship with me, though there was and always would be some distance between us. I knew that he was proud to claim me as his own because he kept a copy of my dissertation displayed in a place of honor in his living room. I had set that copy aside for my mother, but he took it away from her, saying that he'd be the better custodian. Given how disorganized her life was, he imagined that she'd not be able to lay her hands on it six months hence. He may have been right about that. But, the damn thing was so technical, I doubt he could have made heads or tails of it, either. Nevertheless, he wanted me to know that his grandson's educational accomplishment meant the world to him, and that pleased me. Still, he and I were never really close. I just couldn't get past what I knew about the trauma he inflicted on Eloise, Adlert Jr., Alfred, and Gloria. Auntie Eloise had forgiven him, by all appearances. She took delight in his occasional visits to her glorious manse and was given to grand pronouncements like: "That's your grandfather. We must honor him." But Mama wore her wounds less graciously. She would sometimes seethe with anger at the mere mention of his name. And she complained incessantly about his wife, the woman whom he had left her mother for; the imperious woman whom Mama would sardonically refer to as *Aunt Pearl*, with her upper lip curling ever so slightly and her voice quaking.

After the ceremony and reception, Linda and I hopped into a limo for the hour-long drive down to Washington, DC. We spent a romantic night in a boutique Georgetown hotel and departed the next morning for our three-week honeymoon in Jamaica—twenty-one glorious days of rum drinking and ganja smoking, feasting on roasted suckling pig, laying in the sun on pink sands, snorkeling, reading, playing ping-pong and backgammon, and making love. Linda was developing an interest in African and Afro-Caribbean art. She took the opportunity to buy a few pieces to start a collection. It was exactly the right way to commence our married life, full of things we had discovered together and shared.

My first marriage had everything working against it. If Charlene and I hadn't produced the kids, Lisa and Tamara, the relationship probably would not have lasted all that long. We weren't right for each other. But Linda and I were right for each other. Everyone could see it—even my mother and Eloise eventually warmed to her. My father was Linda's biggest fan. He respected her steady temperament, her intelligence, and her work ethic. He could see that her pragmatism and coolheadedness balanced me out, and he'd been very pleased when I told him we were getting married. Linda loved him right back. She called him Big Ev, partially as an affectionate joke about his slight physical stature, but also because she respected his toughness, self-reliance, and no-nonsense attitude. She saw a determination in him that she found lacking in her own father, who never seemed to be able or willing to do what was necessary to provide stability for his family. Both Everett and Linda had come from nothing and made something of themselves, and they recognized that struggle in each other.

ON TUESDAY NIGHT, NOVEMBER 6, 1984, after my scathing speech before the civil rights leaders at the Urban Institute and before the publication of "A New American Dilemma," Linda and I are sitting on a sofa in Bill Kristol's crowded living room. We're all here to watch the election returns. As the anchorman calls state after state for Reagan, the jitters that had been palpable earlier in the evening dissipate and a sense of elation takes hold. Reagan is not just defeating his Democratic opponent, Walter Mondale; he is *crushing* him. Whenever another state goes red, cheers erupt. Bill Kristol, the son of Irving Kristol, is now an assistant professor at the Kennedy School, but he'll soon depart to join the second Reagan administration, which is at this moment being resoundingly voted into office.

Another state turns red, another cheer erupts, and I'm cheering right along with them. The other guests at Bill's election party, most of them anyway, are neoconservatives, right-leaning intellectuals, politicians, and policy experts who retain the old conservative commitment to capitalism and the free market but with a deep interest in social theory and philosophy. They didn't have the knee-jerk anti-intellectualism of the old conservatism. How could they? The key figures in the movement all had PhDs and, at one time or another, taught at elite universities. They were forward-looking, interested in the ways that free markets were responding to social developments and vice versa. Many of the movement's originators, like Irving Kristol himself, were former socialists who had become disillusioned by the failures of the left and its seeming blindness to the indispensable role of market innovations. As has become clearer and clearer to me in recent years, in my attitudes toward social policy and economics, I'm a neocon, too.

In the '60s and '70s, I believed the Vietnam War was a mistake, and in the '80s I still do. But Vietnam is over—American troops left Saigon almost a decade ago. Not only do I think that communism is doomed to fail from an economic perspective, I have come to see, in the left's equivocations about the repressive, murderous nature of the Communist regimes now in power, a form of infantile wishful thinking. The left seems lacking in the conviction necessary to defend our civilization. They seem to harbor contempt for the very political order that protects their right to critique capitalism, American militarism, and the other political developments in the West that they tirelessly inveigh against. I thought a similar fecklessness was true of black leaders, as well. The black leaders whom I had chided at that meeting this past summer were trying to keep the embers of the Civil Rights Movement aglow, and meanwhile black communities were collapsing all around them. By the mid-'80s I'd begun to think that these formerly great crusaders could offer nothing more than their same old bromides about oppression. Such grievance-mongering had worked well enough for them, after all. They were in positions of power and prominence. Never mind that almost anybody who looked around could clearly see that their prescriptions no longer aligned with the situation on the ground. Irving Kristol famously described a neoconservative as "a liberal who's been mugged by reality." That line fits me perfectly.

While I may be a neocon, Linda is most assuredly not. As Reagan buttons up another state, I pump my fist in celebration, and Linda just sits there, silently and impatiently seething.

AT MY MEETING WITH Coretta Scott King and the others, I had already gotten a glimpse of how my new political awakening would be taken by black leadership: not well. I was now in a position of some prominence, and as such it was supposed to be my duty to represent my people and to toe the line on race. I was refusing to do that. Instead, I was aligning myself with the neocons, the Reaganites, and the other political factions who would shake their heads and ask why it was that poor black people couldn't seem to get their act together. Viewed from the perspective of the black leadership, this was a defection that went beyond promoting one policy over another or voting for a Republican over a Democrat. It had to do with who I was, and with my obligation to the noble legacy that I was inheriting. That is to say, they took my conservative turn as a betrayal.

I bristled at the idea that I could be betraying anyone by simply out-lining what black communities had to do in order to get themselves on track. But, in truth, a lot more was at stake for me in my public stand than just policy. I saw the emerging generation of black intellectuals and leaders as constituting a coherent political class, one that was anointed and groomed to determine the fate of black America. These elites were crafting and promoting the company line on race. They were the new Negro Cognoscenti, who presumed to tell the rest of us what "real" black people were supposed to think, and what was best for us. I was expected, but disinclined, to follow the lead of these well-heeled spokespeople for the race. I saw in them another iteration of the "brothers" at Northwestern who grew up comfortable and coddled and then assumed the mantle of black radicalism in order to assert the authority their race supposedly granted them. No longer campus radicals—they had never been true radicals—they were now political opportunists who showed up to the urban crisis in order to make an impassioned speech and talk to the news cameras. When the reporters had their quotes, these "leaders" turned back around and went home. They were once again dictating what and who was truly black, how a black person talked, what they cared about, and what they said. Only now they were getting paid for it.

Back in college and grad school, I had no choice but to swallow whatever contempt I felt toward these people and to keep my own counsel. But things had changed. Now I had a platform. I believed in the ideas that I was putting forward but, more than that, I took delight in throwing the hypocrisies of the Negro Cognoscenti back in their faces. They had convinced the country—or at least liberals and the left—that their concerns ought to drive the national agenda on race. As far as I could see, they had driven that agenda into a ditch. The polite thing to do was to pretend this disaster hadn't happened, that either everything was basically fine or, if it wasn't, white racism was to blame. But I was no longer interested in being polite, at least as far as my writing and speaking went. Look where politeness had gotten us.

The *New Republic* piece was a hit at the Kennedy School. My new colleagues congratulated me when they passed me in the halls and on campus. They had brought me in because they thought I could be a Player, and I immediately showed them I was exactly that. I was fitting in there in a way I never did in the economics department. Edith Stokey, the Kennedy School's executive secretary, took to me immediately and ensured that I got whatever support I needed. She was actually much more than a "secretary." She had studied for an economics PhD at Harvard, taught introductory economics classes to the public policy master's students, and cowritten a popular textbook with a renowned analytical economist at the Kennedy School, Richard Zeckhauser. Her administrative role required her to deal with big personalities and big egos, and she managed all of them with a flinty severity cut with warmth and a playful sense of humor.

Almost immediately after "A New American Dilemma" came out, Irving Kristol asked me to write something for the *Public Interest*. Kristol was a cofounder of the journal. He'd made his career partially through the force of his own ideas and partially through his preternatural skill as a promoter of others who shared them, as a scout who could identify and cultivate talent, and as a connector who knew the value of introducing like-minded people to each other. He and his wife, historian Gertrude Himmelfarb, wielded the soft power of social and political influence like masters, throwing dinner parties where up-and-comers could meet the old guard, where writers could meet editors, and where politicians and policymakers could let their hair down. Arguably, the movement (if it was indeed a movement) called neoconservatism had originated in the pages of the *Public Interest*. Not everyone who published there was a neo-con. Kristol published pieces he thought were interesting and important. But given what I was to write for the magazine, if there were any doubts as to where I stood, they would soon be put to rest.

The essay I sent to Kristol was called "The Moral Quandary of the Black Community." It made the consequences of the dilemma I had described in my prior essay explicit: If black communities were going to overcome poverty, soaring out-of-wedlock birth rates, and high incarceration rates for black men and youths, the change would have to come from within those communities themselves. There were two places the community could look for the source of those problems, inside or outside. Outside were the forces of white racism. Without denying that racial prejudice was still a real problem, I argued that it could not account for the continuing dysfunction in black communities. Black people needed to take responsibility for their lives instead of relying on the next government program to bail them out. Real solutions would have to come from inside, via the long, hard work of changing community standards and morals. I suggested that the efforts of black leaders to extract concessions from the government have done little to aid black communities and, I implied, everything to aid the leaders themselves. In that sense, and ironically, these black communities were indeed being exploited—by their supposed advocates. Black leaders who pointed their fingers at, as I called it, "the enemy without" were looking in the wrong place, and many of them knew it. They needed to refocus their attention on "the enemy within," I argued—on the behaviors, habits, and patterns of thought that were ultimately responsible for the black community's problems.

In saying this, I knew whereof I spoke. I knew about the enemy within the black community—its agents dwelled on the other side of Aunt Eloise's line. You could find the enemy lurking in the gangs that controlled the projects not so far from Park Manor, in the drunk laying on the sidewalk who begged my mother for change, in the relatives and friends who had succumbed to addiction or cycles of welfare dependency. These people were not themselves the enemy. We had been taught to think of them as victims, and in some ways, they were victims. No one can doubt that a black child is going to have a hard time getting ahead if she is born to a single mother living in a housing project where most of the other residents are unemployed, underemployed, on their way to or from prison, or otherwise living on the margins. Those disadvantages are not the fault of the child. But if she is not taught to take responsibility for her own life, to claim her life as her own, to work to live a better, more productive life than those she grew up observing, then she risks falling into that same rudderless existence. That failure to take personal responsibility for one's fate, I theorized, is the enemy within.

The enemy is an observable, large-scale social phenomenon, but it lives within the individual. It can be allowed to fester, or it can be defeated, but it feeds on decisions made or not made by ordinary people. I had not fallen prey to the enemy in the guise my *Public Interest* essay described. I had been taught to work hard and do for myself from a young age. I was surrounded by family and friends who, flawed though they may have been, nevertheless nurtured me, supported my development, and taught me how to become self-reliant. But neither was I free of the enemy. In my successes and failures, the enemy's influence waxed and waned. It appeared in my faltering confidence and my ballooning ego; when I choked and when I grew enamored of my own brilliance.

There is the cover story and there is the real story. Both are true.

The cover story is that I, Glenn Cartman Loury, iconoclastic black intellectual, had launched a necessary critique of the modern-day Civil Rights Movement, one that sought to reorganize the priorities that guided black America.

The real story is that doing so allowed me to salvage my sense of self-worth, which had been badly damaged by my failures as an economic theorist.

The cover story is that my now public conservatism was an unavoidable consequence of my carefully thought-out political and economic analysis.

The real story is that I reveled in playing the bad boy, in drawing the ire of those for whom I had contempt. I loved the fight. I loved the feeling of righteous anger the fight inspired and the perorations that anger fueled.

The cover story is that I was professionally successful, living a stable life, and happily married to Linda Datcher Loury. In that respect I was an exemplar of the very virtues I described.

The real story is that I was not who I appeared to be. Not at all.

THE COVER STORY IS THAT I am in Washington, DC, to attend a series of meetings in my capacity as a research consultant for the natural gas industry. I spend the weekend ducking in and out of hotel conference rooms, presenting my economic research about nonrenewable resource use, and helping industry representatives craft policy proposals for legislators.

The real story is that, at the big dinner that wraps up the weekend's events, I catch the glance of a pretty young woman. I've seen her around talking with one group of executives or another, immersed in the business at hand. Now that business has concluded and everyone is loosening up, I find my attention drifting from the conversation at my table. I spot the woman across the way just as she looks up. Our eyes meet, and neither of us looks away immediately. We both smile.

A few minutes later, I see her get up and head to the bar, and I follow. I'm working out what I'm going to say when I approach her, but by now I know that what I say is less important than how I say it. Confidence is key, of course, but I'm also well trained. Those sales techniques I learned in the Holiday Magic seminars I attended way back when have paid off in ways that have nothing to do with money. Speak in a calm, even voice. Smile. Hold eye contact. Most important, make her feel as though she has the opportunity to help you with something. Make her feel needed.

Later that night, up in my hotel room, our clothes strewn everywhere, the two of us laying side by side, staring at the ceiling, and catching our breath, I reflect that, while getting a stranger on the street to hand me ten dollars had felt good, this felt better by orders of magnitude. And it isn't just the physical gratification that feels good. It's the excitement that comes from the adventure of entering an unknown situation with an unknown person and betting that I can charm my way past whatever reservations she may have. I don't get any particular thrill from gambling, but the rush I feel when putting my pride on the line and coming up with a "yes" must be something like what a gambler feels when he goes all-in on a single hand and wins. The act of seduction is what tempts me. Sex with an attractive stranger is, in some ways, just a nice bonus.

Which is not to say that I'm above paying for sex. I am not. It's the '80s, and with all the money flowing into the natural gas industry, debauchery is a semiregular, quasi-official part of the consulting gig. The guys from Texas know how to have a good time, and when I'm in their neck of the woods, they'll take me around to Houston's finest strip clubs. Occasionally, someone will dial up an escort service, and the party will come to us.

I also have no moral qualms about paying for sex. With my economist's way of thinking, it's easy to persuade myself that prostitution is nothing more than a transaction between consenting adults. Back in Chicago, my friends would have made fun of anybody paying for sex, as though they weren't Player enough to get it for free. But, I would have told them, everybody pays for it one way or another. It's just a question of what form the payment takes. You pay a prostitute in cash, but if you want to seduce a woman, you pay in other ways. You pay the bar or the restaurant, you pay the cab driver if you take a cab or the gas station if you drive yourself. If you get a hotel room, you pay for that. Not to mention the opportunity costs—you could be doing something else instead of spending all that time and money on seduction. Even if you're married, each partner is paying in one way or another, each of them expending their resources on the costs associated with having a life together: a mortgage, bills, car payments, vacations, nights out. I don't look at the resources I devote to my life with Linda as an investment in sex, but sex is part of our married life, and so I am, in an indirect fashion, paying for sex with her just as she is indirectly paying for sex with me. What's morality got to do with it? Apparently, all it takes for me to brush aside the ethical issue of prostitution is a PhD from MIT and the willingness to ignore the moral implication of my thinking: in this I'm no different from a prostitute myself.

I sometimes find myself sitting alone in a hotel room. The conference is over for the day, but it's not yet late. I'm feeling listless, unable to concentrate on a book and bored by the prospect of an evening spent watching TV in bed. So I go down to the lobby entrance, get into one of the taxis waiting out front, and tell the driver to take me to wherever a guy can find a companion for the evening. In some cities, I know exactly where these companions can be found. When I spot the line of women in high heels and short skirts pacing the sidewalk, their sequins shimmering under the headlights of oncoming traffic, the driver slows. I roll down my window, and a woman leans in asking if I'm looking for a date. As

I open the door, she suggests that her friend could join us, making it a party of three. The more the merrier, I tell her.

Back when I joined the faculty at Northwestern and assembled my Lincoln Park bachelor pad, I had invited my uncle Adlert over to check out the spot. He immediately saw its seductive potential, and he was almost as excited about it as I was. He slapped me on the back and told me the place would be irresistible to any woman who set foot in it. Some weeks later, he paid me another visit, and he brought a gift: a beautiful paisley smoking jacket with a matching ascot that he had owned for years. It radiated suave sophistication and Hefneresque cool, and now he was handing it on to me, as I would make better use of it than he now could. As perverse as it seems, I was moved by the gift, which I took as an acknowledgment on the part of this man I so admired, this master of his craft, that I had ascended to his stratospheric level of seductive prowess. He was passing me the baton. The smoking jacket remained a treasured possession for years, a reminder, for good or ill, of who I was and where I came from.

I get my two companions back to my hotel room and we spend a wild few hours together. After they leave and I'm left alone once more, I smile and think that I cannot wait to tell Adlert about this one.

ONCE I CAME OUT AS A CONSERVATIVE, I emerged from my professional doldrums. Now I was an authority on race matters, a fixture in the Rolodexes of reporters who wanted to know the conservative line on public housing policy or the crack epidemic sweeping through black communities or any other issue that could conceivably have a race angle. I was happy to oblige. I must have been irresistible to journalists who knew I could be relied upon for a snappy quote and who may have looked at my blackness as a rare credential. Invitations came in to give speeches on race and politics rather than economics, and I found that practically any organization with a conservative bent wanted to have my name associated with it. Leon Wieseltier, the literary editor of the *New Republic*, would regularly send me books to review, and the *Public Interest* and another conservative magazine, *Commentary*, continued to publish my essays.

There were costs to this ascent, though. My apparent overnight transformation from technical economics whiz to right-wing public intellectual was puzzling to some of my liberal friends and colleagues. Wasn't I the guy who almost got kicked out of a party for talking too ardently about Markov processes while everyone else was trying to relax and forget about school? How had I become what I had become? Most of my friends took it more or less in stride and maintained their ties with me, even if they gave me hell for this or that essay or public statement.

But not everyone was able to swallow it. The political scientist Martin Kilson received his BA from Lincoln University and PhD from Harvard in the '50s, joined the faculty at Harvard in the '60s, and went on to become the first black full professor in the university's history. By the time I came around, he had more or less ceased to produce significant scholarship, but his very presence was a historical achievement. He was a terminally rumpled, grizzled old leftie and a voracious consumer of all things having to do with African American culture. If a black person had written it, painted it, produced it, performed in it, or laid hands on it in any capacity, he seemed to be aware of it.

Not long after I came to Harvard, he invited Linda and me up to his summer home in Dublin, New Hampshire. The dining room table was piled with newspapers and books of all kinds—the entire place felt like the study of a great scholar. We all spent the weekend talking about black history, about the interconnections between Pan-Africanism and black Americans' liberation. We talked about Marcus Garvey, the Masons and other fraternal organizations, the AME church, the black middle class, and the works of W. E. B. Du Bois and E. Franklin Frazier.

He laughed at my jokes and treated Linda and me with such warmth. We hit it off and developed a really interesting relationship. As the man who had broken through one of the American academy's major color lines, he prized the fact that I was the first black tenured professor of economics, part of the next phase in our people's progress. We were penetrating into the elite institutions, and he saw me and our relationship in those historical terms.

Marty had great hopes for me, and when I came out as a neocon and a Reaganite, I dashed those hopes. He made it known that, in his view, I had completely sold out. He cut me off. This was a source of great pain to me. I mourned our friendship. I found out that he had called me a "pathetic black mascot of the right." Apparently, I was a credit to the race only if I was playing for the right political team. Not long ago, I had been an exemplar of the progress of black people in America. Now that was no longer the case because I had written a few essays he disagreed with? In his view, I thought, my politics had nullified my achievements and maybe my blackness, as well. I resented that he had grown so bitter toward me when I was just trying to further the progress that he seemed so much to value.

I knew Martin Kilson wasn't the only person who felt that way about me: a sellout, a mascot, a cover story for racist right-wingers. But neither was I the only black conservative in America. Not long after I took the Harvard job, an offer came in from Clarence Thomas. I had first met Thomas at a conference at the University of Pennsylvania's Wharton School. He was a protege of Senator John Danforth of Missouri, and he had recently become the head of the Equal Employment Opportunity Commission. Thomas asked Linda and me to submit a proposal to become consultants to the commission in order to advise him on civil rights oversight in employment and economic development. The role didn't pay very much, but that was beside the point. It was really an invitation for us to develop a relationship with him, and I was intrigued.

Thomas had been a black radical in his college days, but he started to drift rightward after attending Yale Law School. He was hardly the most conservative person in the Reagan administration, and he occasionally butted heads with some other Reagan appointees because, as he told me, he may have been a black conservative, but he was still black, and he thought some of his colleagues' advocacy for "colorblind" policies was either naive or disingenuous. At the time he had not yet fully developed his views on race-conscious public policy. He thought that some of the Reaganites' attempts to eradicate it entirely went too far. Some within the administration had objected to the 1982 extension of the Voting Rights Act, which President Reagan signed into law. Thomas thought vetoing the extension would have been madness, not only because it would be politically unpopular but because it was also the wrong thing to do. The law wasn't even twenty years old. In his view, and in mine, it was entirely appropriate that it remain on the books, at least for a while longer.

Thomas told me that if I ever found myself in Washington, I should give him a call. So the next time I was in town, I did just that. We met a few times. Once we went out to dinner and then back to his apartment for a drink. He had recently split with his first wife, and he told me that he was having some trouble getting dates. His job in the Reagan White House did not sit well with the single, almost entirely liberal women of Chocolate City. I sympathized with him, but I was not about to tell this powerful new friend about my own nocturnal activities in Washington.

MY NIGHTTIME SOJOURNS ARE not limited to the road. Some nights, back home in Boston, I shed the jacket and tie and change into street-wear: jeans and sneakers, a loose-fitting T-shirt, and cap with the brim turned to the side. In the neighborhoods where I hang out, places like Mattapan, Jamaica Plain, and Roxbury, looking like a Harvard professor is a liability. Dressing and even speaking the way I do around my colleagues and friends in and around academia will not fly there. These are the years of the crack epidemic, and anyone who looks like an easy mark and smells of money risks getting robbed or worse. I need people to know they're in the presence of a serious Player.

188 GLENN C. LOURY

But my change of outfits isn't only a gesture of self-protection. There is something I'm not getting from my life in academia or my life with Linda. As much affirmation as I receive from my new role as a public intellectual, from my teaching at the Kennedy School, and from my marriage, there is something they cannot provide that I've found in the black working-class neighborhoods and housing projects of Boston. I go there to buy marijuana. I'm not a heavy smoker, and I'm sure I could find a more convenient way to get it, but I don't want my Harvard colleagues finding out about my use of it. I use weed in the same way anyone else uses a glass of wine or a scotch at the end of the day. It helps me to unwind and relax. But it's illegal and there's a stigma attached to it. I get the sense that even my liberal colleagues who support legalization in principle would look askance at me if they found out I like to get high every once in a while.

What I could not explain to these colleagues is that my taste for marijuana is not just about the feeling I get from it. It's a part of the culture I come from. I think not only of Uncle Moonie, who used to tell us kids that the funny-smelling cigarettes he smoked were his "asthma medicine," but of the many, many men and women I grew up around in Chicago, about the upstairs bedroom at Aunt Eloise's house where the uncles and cousins would pass around a joint while talking politics, about the camaraderie and laughter shared over a spliff among friends like Woody and John and Chuck. Smoking weed was just part of life on the black South Side, which is not to say that everyone did it—my old friend Ed Faulkner had foresworn its use because he didn't want to violate his parole rules, and my fastidious father would never touch the stuff. But no one was surprised when someone broke out a stash.

So while I change my clothes and travel to these slightly sketchy neighborhoods in order to score a little marijuana, I'm also going for everything that comes along with it: the company of black people who remind me of home, and to tap into part of myself that my colleagues and friends in that other part of my life can never touch. There are available women there, and sometimes that is part of the appeal. But I make friends there, as well. There is Eddie, a slightly older guy with conked hair and jet-black skin who stands about five foot six and possesses a gorgeous singing voice. Eddie sells trinkets, costume jewelry, and perfume off a table he sets up in front of a greasy spoon diner run by a Korean family on Washington Street near Dudley Station. He doesn't have a vendor's license, but he's a charming, affable guy, and the cops leave him alone. The owner of the restaurant loves Eddie and almost considers him a part of the family. He's good for business, too, as his wares and funny sales patter draw passersby over to the restaurant.

Eddie's also a chess hustler. He'll play five-minute chess for a buck a game with anybody who will sit across the board from him, which is how I first get to know him. We hang out frequently, playing chess and talking about life and music. Eddie is a devotee of the amazing a cappella group Take 6, as are Linda and I. So when they come to town to perform at Tufts, I convince Linda that we should buy Eddie a ticket and take him with us. Eddie has never spent any time outside of the ghetto, but on the night of the concert, he manages to locate the auditorium on Tufts's leafy green campus in suburban Medford. With his slicked-back hair and inner-city bearing, he stands out among the middle-class folks in the crowd. But he is so happy to be there and so grateful to Linda for accommodating him that he couldn't care less. After the show, we wander down to the front of the stage to meet the group, and they listen with amusement as Eddie effuses about the performance and their music. Eddie will talk about that show until his dying day, which comes, sadly, not long after. He was a diabetic without access to good health care. What began as a minor infection of his left foot went untreated and raged out of control. The foot had to be amputated. Ultimately, that infection took his life. The Korean proprietor of that diner wept as he told me the story of Eddie's demise.

My friendships with people like Eddie carry a deep meaning for me. One night, a guy named Ralph challenges me to a game of chess. Ralph is slick, a neighborhood Player. He drives a nice car, flashes his money around, and brags endlessly. Whatever he does for a living, I'm pretty sure it's not legal. Still, I like the guy. I appreciate the swagger. We put down a hundred dollars on the game and start playing while Eddie holds the stakes. The whole time, Ralph's barking away, trying to throw me off. "Who do you think you are, Harvard professor? This is how we play chess in the hood." He slams his pieces down: "Check, motherfucker!" But I beat him, and he demands a rematch. So we play, and he continues talking away. He does manage to put me on defense, but he can't close out. He overextends himself, wildly pushing forward the pawns protecting his king. When the smoke clears after my withering counterattack, he's a pawn down and has no idea how to negotiate the endgame. I take the second game out from under him. Furious, he demands a third, and it's more of the same. "You don't know when to break in the center," I tell him. "Your pawns are weak. You're toast, nigga."

After the third win, I clean Ralph out. The money doesn't mean much to me, and I doubt it means much to him. I want to win because I want to win. I want to show him I'm not a chump; nobody can chase me off the board. Eddie has been watching all three games, and he loves it. He loves that I'm a black Harvard professor who can hang on the corner, that I won't be intimidated. In truth, I love it, too. I love that I have the respect not only of the elite intellectuals at the Kennedy School but the drug dealers, hustlers, and working men in the projects. Nobody else but me, I think, could do what I'm doing.

IT NEVER CROSSED MY MIND that someday I might be called to account. If anybody looked into what I was doing with my life, what would they find? Linda knew what she knew. She knew about that second airline ticket. She handled our household finances, so she would have seen some questionable credit card charges. She never asked why I took Adlert's paisley smoking jacket with me on business trips, as I sometimes did.

She didn't press me about where I went in the evenings and what I did when I got there.

If I had bothered to think about it, I might have noticed that I was living a double life. There was my official existence, with its job and wife and friends. And then there was a parallel life, an unofficial world in which the normal constraints of my existence no longer held sway. There were no real rules in this unofficial world. There was no pressure to disguise my appetites and demands for gratification—the satisfaction of my desires, my ego—for anything other than what they were. What would, say, a vetting committee—the avatar of all things official—think if they stumbled onto the world I had concealed?

This division between official and unofficial was not as clean as I would have liked. Perhaps if I had ever thought consciously about the pains I took to keep these worlds separate from one another, that fact, so obvious in retrospect, would have made itself known to me. But I was a victim of self-delusion, or self-aggrandizement. I had integrated the schism between my official and unofficial biographies so thoroughly into the way I moved through my own life that I could not see the tenuous nature of the divide, or how readily I could cross to the other side of the line.

Twelve

I n fall 1985, Linda and I were living in Princeton, New Jersey, where I was spending two semesters on leave from Harvard as a visiting faculty member at the Institute for Advanced Study. The IAS is a legendary institution. Its faculty have lifetime appointments and no teaching responsibilities. Their only job is to conduct research in an environment designed to foster total intellectual freedom. It had been home to the likes of Albert Einstein, Kurt Gödel, and John von Neumann. I suspect I received an invitation to spend time there because of my correspondence with Albert Hirschman, who was on the faculty. Hirschman was a great economist and political theorist, but he was more than that. He had fought the fascists in Spain and helped artists and intellectuals escape from Nazi-occupied France. He was a genuinely heroic figure who, at seventy years old, looked as fit and tan as ever.

I had begun writing to Hirschman after I read his classic book *Exit, Voice, and Loyalty.* He had been on the faculty at Harvard before going to IAS. Tom Schelling, a great admirer and former colleague of his, encouraged me to reach out to him. I thought Hirschman's exploration of the ways that individuals can influence the organizations of which they are a part might have some bearing on African Americans who find themselves dissatisfied with the direction of black politics. Such a person could not literally "exit" (he would always be black), but should he exhibit "blind loyalty" (stick with the group in the name of solidarity no matter what) or exercise "voice" (speak out regardless of consequence and try to change things from within)? Hirschman argued that markets influence organizations mainly via the force of "exit" (because firms lose customers when their products are uncompetitive), while politics operates mainly via "voice" (as contending parties endeavor to build winning electoral coalitions via acts of persuasion). In this context, he emphasized the virtue of genuine (as distinct from blind) "loyalty," defined as the inclination to eschew "exit" in the face of an organization's failures and to exercise a critical "voice" on behalf of needed reforms, notwithstanding the predictable negative reactions from one's colleagues (or one's coalition). This, as I saw it, was the course of action that I had embraced with my criticisms of black leadership.

The IAS put me in touch with many fascinating people. The political philosopher Michael Walzer and I became friendly. I'd read his book *Spheres of Justice* before arriving in Princeton. I had the opportunity to talk with him about the two books he was writing that year, a collection of biographical essays on public intellectuals called *The Company of Critics*, and an elegant piece of communitarian political theory entitled *Interpretation and Social Criticism*. I also met Bernard Lewis, the eminent, controversial historian of the Middle East, who was friendly with many of the neocons with whom I was forging connections. One of the appeals of the IAS was precisely that it enabled me to meet and talk to people like this. It allowed me time to listen, to think, and to write without worrying about teaching or administrative duties. I had been awarded a fellowship by the Guggenheim Foundation in support of my year's leave from the Kennedy School. Having no encumbrances at all, living in a different city, and being ensconced within a community of brilliant, diverse scholars felt like a kind of vacation, albeit one where I constantly confronted new, unfamiliar, and challenging ideas. But that was half the fun!

Still, I was living in Princeton, New Jersey. For all its charms, the city didn't offer much in the way of diversions. The IAS was an intellectually dynamic place, but it was also rather stuffy. There were afternoon teas, and on Friday evenings a semiformal dinner would be served in the cafeteria. But how many afternoon teas can one person attend? I needed something to break the monotony. So on some afternoons and evenings, I'd skip out on tea or dinner, get in my car, and head to nearby Trenton. If I was feeling adventurous, I'd make the drive to Newark or, God help me, Camden. These were cities with rough edges and black neighborhoods where I could cruise and find some action: women, weed, whatever was around.

I was also at that time involved with Janine, a fellow economist. We had met at an event where I was presenting a paper, and we hit it off. She lived in DC, but she would sometimes take the Amtrak up to New Jersey, and I would play hooky at the IAS or make up some excuse to Linda and steal away for a few hours to meet her. We would maybe get a meal and talk or go to the movies and fool around in the back row. Sometimes we would get a motel room for the afternoon. We didn't always have sex. I thought she was beautiful and interesting, and I enjoyed her company. Our favorite activity was hanging out at a bowling alley and pool hall on Route 1, halfway between Princeton and Trenton. She would invariably wear a pair of skin-tight jeans that showed off her irresistible figure to perfection. We'd hang out while I shot around on a table. Occasionally, if someone wandered in, I'd play a friendly game against a challenger. But mostly, Janine and I just went there to blow off steam.

I had several such affairs with women, whom I would see on and off. Many of them were quite accomplished. One was a Chicago lawyer who worked for the state, whom I'd met at a conference at Rutgers and with whom I'd find ways to get together. Another was a program officer working for a big philanthropic organization. There were others, too. Some of these women actually knew each other, but Linda didn't know about any of them. Which is not to say that she didn't know something was going on. How could she not? I was clever enough about covering my tracks and inventing uncheckable alibis, but she was too smart not to have put the pieces together. I knew she knew, but neither of us said anything about it to each other.

My life with Linda, my "official" social life, my (infrequent) contact with my daughters, my academic responsibilities, my teaching, my writing, my speaking engagements, all of that was more than enough to keep me busy. Yet I wouldn't hesitate to get involved with another woman if I found her alluring in one way or another. The truth was that I was becoming bored with my official life. The secrecy and illicit nature of these affairs was part of the attraction just as much as the sex and companionship I found there. That was something that, by definition, I could not get from my marriage and my job.

IN JANUARY 1986, I was summoned to Washington, DC. I had forged a relationship with the great Robert Woodson. Bob had been active in the Civil Rights Movement in its heyday, and upon meeting him, I could see what made him such an asset. He was (and still is) staggeringly energetic. He could talk a mile a minute, but he was actually tackling the big problems while others sat around chatting about them. He thought that social entrepreneurship within black communities—grassroots initiatives, undertaken at the local level, focused on meeting residents' most pressing needs—was key to solving some of the vexing urban problems in the areas of housing, education, and violent crime. And he was a big believer in faith as an antidote to the hopelessness and moral turpitude of the ghetto. As an entrepreneur and a man of faith himself, he practiced what he preached. He believed in consulting experts, but he had no time for academics who sat around debating metaphysics and theory while there was work to be done. I liked that Bob was a man of action with an instinctive disdain for self-regarding black elites, and I appreciated the funny, occasionally profane rants he reserved for those "race hustlers" he perceived to be getting in the way of progress, trying to sweep the problem under the rug, or making speeches when the moment called for deeds.

For all that, he was adamant that African Americans were every bit as capable of excelling as anyone else. We had done it before, he reasoned, during Reconstruction and throughout the early twentieth century when, of necessity, black people built thriving businesses and communities in the midst of violent oppression. Believing that we couldn't do these things for ourselves, that we needed the help of the government and white benefactors in order to survive, was tantamount to racism in Bob's view. Like my uncle Moonie, Bob was not a big fan of racial integration as a solution for the problems of black communities. He thought that, given the chance, black people were fully capable of taking care of themselves.

Bob's prescription for black revitalization—faith, entrepreneurship, education, and self-reliance—found natural allies in Reagan's White House. He had become good friends with Representative Jack Kemp, a Republican from the state of New York, and the two of them came up with the idea to assemble a group of older black Republican businessmen and young guys like me and call it the Council for a Black Economic Agenda. Woodson and Kemp got us all together and used their considerable skills as political operators to engineer a meeting where we would present an enterprise-driven, free-market plan for black empowerment to the Reagan administration.

That is how I found myself, on an afternoon in mid-January, sitting in the White House's Cabinet Room with my fellow black notables and Woodson, Kemp, Attorney General Edwin Meese, Vice President George H. W. Bush, and Ronald Reagan himself, who sat right beside me. Bush sipped a cup of coffee, the end of his necktie tucked into his breast pocket, and lamented that Benjamin Hooks, then the executive director of the NAACP and a Republican, had accused the administration of being the enemies of black people. Bush professed not to understand why Hooks was so adamant in his opposition when they had all been able to work well together in the past. Where was his sense of party loyalty? It was almost as though Bush was flummoxed by the idea that Ben Hooks had his own political constituency to attend to.

We presented our ideas endorsing the administration's proposal for tax-free enterprise zones in inner-city neighborhoods and put forward some ideas about fostering self-reliance. I know I spoke up several times, but in truth, I had a hard time focusing on the meeting. Sitting that close to the leader of the free world had a slightly intoxicating effect.

I'm not sure if anybody in the White House ever acted on our proposals, but I recognized we were now all involved in matters that were both quotidian and historical. Republicans were trying to improve their standing among black voters, and they could now say they were literally listening to the concerns of African Americans—we were the (self-appointed) Council for a Black Economic Agenda, after all. I was sincere in my belief in our plans, but it was also clear to me that the meeting, besides being an opportunity for making policy proposals, was also part of a national messaging strategy. Still, a few days after the meeting, Reagan would deliver a speech marking the first national holiday honoring Martin Luther King Jr. That was a meaningful event to my mind, one that transcended the politics of the moment.

I had worried that I was no longer a Player in economics, no longer one of the figures at the center of the discipline. But I was now a small Player in a much bigger game, with proximity to real power. *Esquire* magazine put out a list that year of influential Americans under the age of forty, and they included my name. People making big decisions about the course of the nation were asking me what I thought about things. I had never had political ambitions per se. I saw myself as an economist and a social critic. Now that I found myself so close to the levers of power, the thought that I might one day pull them was impossible to ignore. No cogent plan about my political future ever formed in my mind—I wasn't daydreaming about running for office—but as I got to know people such as Jack Kemp and Clarence Thomas, and as they continued to show interest in me, it became clear that yet another path was opening up.

WHATEVER I SAID at that White House meeting, it must have left a good impression. When Linda and I got back to Boston after our year in Princeton, we received an invitation to return to the White House for a state dinner honoring the prime minister of Pakistan. It's doubtful that either Reagan or Bush wrote the guest list, but their aides must have thought well enough of me to approve of my attendance. I suspected that Bill Kristol had something to do with the invite. He was by then the chief of staff to William Bennett, Reagan's secretary of education, and it's possible that he made sure my name came up when ideas for invitees were being bounced around.

Linda was no fan of the Reaganites, but she put her criticisms aside for the evening. It was a state dinner, and we two working-class black kids had an invite. We both thought it was cool. We went down to Washington, checked in at The Hay-Adams, a luxury hotel, got dressed, and took a cab to the White House, where we discovered that only limousines were allowed to enter the gates and pull up to the dining hall. Anyone seeing us trudge our way up the drive on foot would have marked us as newcomers to Washington in a second.

When we entered, we discovered that I was seated at Reagan's table and Linda was seated at Bush's. Only one person was sitting between me and Reagan: the prime minister. I knew then that the administration must have had their eye on me—you couldn't have found a more visible spot in the room. The place was full of politicians and dignitaries and more than a handful of actors and celebrities. Eugene Fodor, a pop-classical violinist and former child prodigy who was enjoying mainstream success, served as the evening's entertainment. After the meal, the performance, and some short speeches, people began filling up the dance floor. As Linda and I made our way over to each other, George and Barbara Bush, who looked like they were having a great time, tried to persuade us to dance. We demurred. The foxtrot they were doing was not the kind of dancing we were used to.

When the evening ended, Linda and I faced a dilemma. We got a cab to take us to the White House, but there was no way to get one back without making the long walk down to the street. It didn't seem like a great way to end an otherwise auspicious evening. Without a limo, we were stranded. Standing there trying to get some help from the white-gloved doorman ushering people into their rides, we must have looked about as stuck as we felt, because Howell Heflin, the senator from Alabama, who in 1991 would join forty-five other Democrats and two Republicans to vote against Clarence Thomas's confirmation for the US Supreme Court, realized our predicament and very kindly gave us a lift to The Hay-Adams in his limo before he and his wife went on their way.

The Monday following the dinner, I went into my office at the Kennedy School. It seemed like the entire building knew about my attendance at the dinner. There had been a small item in the *New York Times* listing the guests and the menu, and my (misspelled!) name was right there in black and white. Tom Schelling, whose office was right next door to mine on the third floor of school's main building, found me in the halls and let me know that people were talking.

"Some people are a little concerned about your right-wing affiliations," he said.

You're being groomed for politics. You're an outstanding black economist, and you're not yet forty years old. I just hope you keep things in perspective. I understand your criticisms of affirmative action but remember that this debate isn't just about race. It applies to women. It applies to veterans. You need to remain level-headed. Don't let your gut drive you. People are going to be looking to you for leadership, and what you say will have resonance and influence. Be mindful that when you speak, your words could have consequences beyond what you intend. Play the long game and don't get emotion confused with analysis.

Tom had never before criticized my politics. In fact, we agreed about a lot of things. Conservatives were in and around the Kennedy School, some of them, like James Q. Wilson, more controversial than me. Tom's stature was such that if he had wanted any of them gone, they would have been gone, but he had good relations with all of them. I understood that he was counseling caution and small-C conservatism in my recommendations, should I continue to find favor at the White House.

I believe Tom was also, in a characteristically indirect way, speaking from personal experience. In the 1950s and '60s he had produced pathbreaking work in game theory that had helped to influence the direction of the Cold War and the conflict in Vietnam. Military advisors knew who Tom was. While working on his nuclear war satire *Dr. Strangelove*, director Stanley Kubrick had even consulted Tom about the so-called doomsday machine, a commitment device intended to deter a missile attack from the Soviet Union by automatically launching a counterstrike, thus eliminating any possibility of human indecision. Tom believed that his work could help stave off disaster and aid national defense, so he continued to write his papers about conflict strategy, and he continued to influence people all the way to the top, including his former colleague at Harvard's Center for International Affairs, Henry Kissinger.

In a way, Tom respected Kissinger. He saw in Kissinger a brilliant tactician and student of great powers conflicts. But he was wary of Kissinger's ambition and attraction to power. Tom didn't think him trustworthy. When Nixon and Kissinger engineered the military incursion into Cambodia in 1970, Tom became incensed. Besides being illegal, he thought it was a disastrous decision that would prolong the war and kill innumerable people for no good reason. Tom even led a group of Harvard faculty to meet with Kissinger, by then Nixon's national security adviser, to declare their opposition to the invasion. After that, Tom shifted away from work that had military applications and instead turned his scholarly attention to domestic problems like housing segregation. I believe he wanted me to think carefully, perhaps more carefully than he had, before I began advising people whose decisions affect millions of lives. I couldn't control what they would ultimately do with my advice, but my name would be associated with whatever outcome ensued.

Tom was also addressing my tendency to adopt a tone of righteous indignation. I could come off as angry when I spoke about what I saw as deficiencies in black leadership and problems in the black community because, well, I *was* angry. But such was my tone that I sometimes found myself faced with the accusation that my prescriptions for black America were heartless or that I believed black people were lazy or inferior. Nothing could be further from the truth. I knew African Americans were anything but lazy—I was raised by some of the most industrious people I had ever met. If I believed that black people were lazy or incompetent, it would have made no sense for me to expend so much energy championing the development of their skills and abilities. I always believed—and still believe and will believe until the day I die—that black people are every bit as capable, intelligent, and hardworking as anybody else. The only difference, I thought, was in the degree to which the latent capacities of struggling communities were being nurtured and developed.

If any of my critics had wanted to see what a truly remorseless attitude toward those falling behind looked like, I would have introduced them to my father. He loved the film *Patton*, starring George C. Scott. He especially loved the opening scene. In it, Patton is preparing his troops to go to war. He paces before them, an enormous American flag serving as his backdrop. At one point, trying to get the men's blood up, reveling in the brutality and carnage of war, he growls out the line, "We're not just going to shoot the bastards. We're going to cut out their living guts and use them to grease the treads of our tanks." Despite his skepticism toward the Vietnam War, despite his contempt for my sister Leanett's broken military man of a first husband, my dad *loved* this idea. He didn't love violence as such, but he subscribed to the notion that life itself is warfare and that the man who learns to love the war would be the man who triumphs in the end. Though Lee Lee and I were grown by the time *Patton* came out, he made us watch it more than once, wanting, I think, to show us what he thought it took to survive, and perhaps to tell us something about himself that he could not say in his own words.

As director of its Kansas City Service Center, my dad had clawed his way up the ladder to a top administrative position within the Internal Revenue Service. On one occasion, when my sister and I went out to Kansas to visit him for his birthday, we somehow began talking about the urban crisis, about the black people languishing in broken communities like those we were familiar with from the South Side. He inveighed against "these do-nothing, lazy-ass, stupid niggers who will sit and, with their hand out, collect a welfare check, who will just as soon rob you blind as say good morning to you, who are constantly complaining about what somebody hasn't done for them or hasn't given them. I have no time for them whatsoever." His wife Constance wholeheartedly agreed. It would have made even the most hardened right-winger clutch her pearls. But this wasn't a partisan political sentiment on my dad's part. He was a life-long bureaucrat who unequivocally rejected the anti-tax, small government mantras of the Reaganites. This attitude of his transcended electoral politics. It was the bitter product of a hard life. It was what sustained him while so many of his contemporaries had fallen by the wayside.

My sister replied, "If you saw a woman starving in the gutter with a baby in her arms, would it really matter if she was a good person? Wouldn't you feel something for her? Wouldn't you help?" Leanett was her mother's daughter, through and through.

"I don't have time for that," he said. "The time it takes me to reach in my pocket and pull something out and give it to them is time I could have spent doing something productive. If you ever see me laying in the gutter and you have some place to go, I want you to step right over me and keep on walking."

I knew who my father was and how he went about things. And it was strange to me that he was saying this to my sister, knowing in the back of my mind how he had claimed her as his own, loved her, devoted himself to her, taken pride in her accomplishments, and never wavered in his commitment to her. I knew my father had the capacity for mercy, but I was shaken in that moment by his utter lack of sympathy. The notion that Everett Loury would ever need the help of his children or anybody else was unthinkable, but could he not see that not everyone possessed his iron will and discipline? And I wondered: Did he have my mother in the back of his mind when he talked this way?

And yet, in that moment, I also admired him. I respected the purity of his anger. Earlier in his life, he would have had every reason to be bitter about the hand he had been dealt. Abandoned by his father, left to fend for himself, married to an unfaithful woman, and carrying the burden of two children when he was barely in his twenties, he could have lashed out. But he never openly blamed Mama for his troubles, and he never blamed me or Leanett. Yes, he would become frustrated with us, and often with good reason. He was a hard man, but he did not turn his rage on us. Whatever anger roiled inside of him he used to fuel his relentless pursuit of his goals. His anger was a resource, as was his pride, and like every other resource my father possessed, he would not fritter it away or misuse it. It was too precious.

I recognized my father's anger in myself. Though I did not possess his extreme discipline and capacity for self-denial, I had found a way to channel my anger into something productive. I could deliver a speech on race matters in the United States as fiery as a Baptist preacher's sermon, though I would not go as far as my father in my condemnations. I wanted my audience to understand and to feel what I believed was at stake. These were real people we were talking about in America's ghettos, not statistics. Human beings were suffering, and the fact that many of the so-called leaders of black America were profiting from that suffering enraged me. They needed to see that they did not have a monopoly on righteous anger. Likewise, I occasionally felt that my conservative compatriots needed to be reminded that poor black people were not some abstract social problem or useful props for ideological point-scoring, but flesh-and-blood human beings.

My anger had its uses, then, but I also liked how it made me feel. When I felt embattled or attacked by an opponent on a panel or at a debate, I could summon up an overwhelming verbal barrage that was equal parts head and heart. This side of me would come out especially when I felt as though someone was questioning the validity of my blackness, as Martin Kilson had, and as many others would go on to do. I was not going to pretend to be some disinterested observer pontificating on the race question from atop the ivory tower. These were my people.

It was ironic, though perhaps appropriate, that I located the source of my verbal acuity in the African American oral tradition as it was practiced in my family. I was raised by gifted talkers who signified and played the dozens. There was Adlert's universally acknowledged oratorical genius, but my adopted cousin Jimmy was also a phenomenal signifier. He was constantly cracking on people, inventing clever, improvised rhymes that would have been infuriating if they hadn't been so funny. His nickname for me was Black Walrus because I was a little overweight. I didn't love that, but I also couldn't deny that it was funny, just like practically everything else that came out of his mouth. When he or any other member of the family decided to start goofing on you, you had to be ready to give back as good as you got. It was all in fun, but it also sharpened my tongue at an early age, and I made sure to keep it sharp.

MY STAY AT THE HAY-ADAMS on the night of the White House state dinner was actually my second visit to that hotel in as many months. The first happened in June, when I was in Washington for a meeting of the publication committee of the *Public Interest*. By then I had published a handful of pieces with them, and I was asked to join the committee in order to help select submissions to be published by the magazine. I was in august company on that committee. Irving Kristol, Daniel Bell, Nathan Glazer, Daniel Patrick Moynihan, James Q. Wilson, and the Berkeley political scientist Aaron Wildavsky were all there. We spent a day in a conference room at The Hay-Adams weighing the merits of the submissions and putting forth our recommendations. I was the youngest person by well over a decade, and the only black face in the room. I was flattered that these intellectual heavyweights regarded me as one of their own.

After the publication committee meeting wrapped up and we all had dinner, I went on to my next appointment. I had been for some time corresponding with a young woman named Pamela Foster. While she was still an undergraduate at Smith College, she had written me to get my opinion about some idea or another that she was working on for a class, and we kept in touch. We would go back and forth about politics, and she had some sharp, intelligent things to say. There was nothing unusual about the correspondence. I had many such exchanges. After graduation, Pamela had moved to New York, but she was working in a middling position at a job she didn't much like, and she had asked me for advice. Instead of responding at length, I told her we should talk about it in person and invited her to meet me in Washington at The Hay-Adams bar.

I had never met her in person, but when I walked into the bar, I spotted a woman sitting at a table that had to be her. She was stunning, and she was dressed exquisitely. A white collar peeked out of a tight velvet top. She wore a plaid skirt, white bobby socks, and patent leather shoes, all of it perfectly complimenting her hourglass figure. She stood to greet me, and when I watched her sit back down and cross her legs, I trembled inside. I was instantly attracted to her. I suppose Kristol or Bell or any other member of the publication committee could have seen me sitting there with her, but that could be explained. She was a young black woman interested in politics and seeking career advice from a thoughtful mentor—perfectly innocent.

OVER DRINKS, WE DO DISCUSS POLITICS and her career. And as we talk, I'm also working out a game theory puzzle in my mind. I desperately want to get this woman up to my hotel room. I hypothesize that she also wants to come up to my hotel room, but she does not want to appear cheap or overeager. If I proposition her too early, too directly, she'll believe I think she is cheap and overeager, and she'll say no on general principles. Game over.

My solution to the problem is not to state my intent outright but to reveal it progressively in such a way that I can plausibly disavow my true intent at any point without receiving an explicit rejection. The rule is this: so long as there is no rejection, the revelation of intent can progress. Once I cross a certain threshold in this progressive revelation of intent without receiving a no, I can make the proposition explicit with a sufficient degree of confidence that I'll receive a yes.

So a dance begins in which I advance and retreat. We talk about politics. I answer her questions and ask some in response. I ask about her professors at Smith, about her classes, slowly getting a little more personal. I make a joke that is maybe a little bit serious. I ask about her romantic partners, and I watch her eyes. Is she avoiding eye contact? I hope not. That's the last stop before no. But she is holding eye contact. She is smiling and laughing. I deploy a double entendre, and she laughs again, and I ask her what's so funny. "Nothing," she says, and smiles. I note that I am advancing more than I am retreating. I let her catch me looking at her legs, and she does not try to cover herself up.

At some point, I believe the threshold has been crossed. I don't really know if it has, but I decide that even if I get a no, it's okay, because I find that I really do like Pamela. The worst-case scenario is that I've made a new friend. So I suggest that we continue the conversation up in my room. And she says yes.

When we enter the room, she excuses herself to the bathroom and takes her purse with her. I sit and wait and wonder what's taking her so long. Finally, she emerges wearing nothing but a bra and a slip with no panties. In working through the many permutations of the seduction problem, I had not considered the scenario in which the intent to seduce was mutual.

That night, I devoured Pamela Foster. I was voracious. We both were. I was enraptured by her. This is the zenith, I thought. This conquest and consummation would be my crowning achievement. If I hadn't before, I had certainly now earned Adlert's paisley smoking jacket. It could not possibly get any better than this.

Thirteen

I t was the 1980s!

Shortly after my affair with Pamela Foster began, Tom Wolfe published his hilarious novel *The Bonfire of the Vanities*, which satirizes the social world of Wall Street bond traders of that day. The novel's central character, Sherman McCoy, is near the pinnacle of the financial services industry. He is around the same age as I was at the time. He brims with a confidence and a sense of entitlement that, had I been thinking about it, I would have recognized. True, I wasn't executing multimillion-dollar trades. Nor could I have afforded McCoy's lavish Upper East Side co-op apartment. But laying claim to Pamela made me feel like I was at the apex of personal fulfillment, a Master of the Universe, just like Sherman McCoy. There was nothing I couldn't do, nowhere I couldn't go, no reward above my station. That socially awkward, brainy but undersexed kid I once was had now become a Player. As far as I was concerned, I was Glenn Fucking Loury, and the world was mine.

When Pamela and I parted ways the next morning at The Hay-Adams, we promised to remain in touch. I knew then that this was no one-night stand. I wanted more, and I would make sure that I got it. Over the ensuing months, she would hop on an Eastern Air Lines shuttle flight from New York up to Boston and I would pay. I'd put her up in a nearby hotel for a night or two at a time. We would go out for dinner somewhere and then make love, after which I'd drag myself home late. If I happened to be in New York for a meeting or a conference, we would try to get together at night. I was exalted by the sheer ecstasy of it all. Pamela was exquisite. She was young and eager. She was an inquisitive and creative lover. I just couldn't get enough of her, and she seemed really to be into me. She wanted so fervently to please me and wanted me to know that was what she wanted, which made me want to please her all the more.

All through the fall of 1986, I was wrapped up in Pamela. I barely tried to keep it quiet. I was constantly making excuses to Linda. Surely, she'd noticed that airline and hotel charges on my credit card bills didn't always match my official travel schedule. She had to know something was going on. But I didn't give a damn. I wanted what I wanted. If she chose to leave me, so be it. Pamela's vivaciousness and glamor was what I wanted, what I thought would fulfill me, what I felt entitled to. Linda still had everything that first attracted me to her, but, I thought, didn't I deserve more?

Some years earlier, Harvard had initiated the W. E. B. Du Bois Lectures. These were an annual sequence of talks featuring scholars and civic leaders who had made significant contributions to African American life, culture, and history. This prestigious, high-profile lecture series was organized by my former Afro-American Studies colleague Nat Huggins and funded initially by a grant from the Ford Foundation. Its audiences included prominent scholars from around Boston and elsewhere. That year's lecturer was the civil rights activist Marian Wright Edelman, founder of the Children's Defense Fund and one of the organizers of Dr. King's Poor People's Campaign. I showed up to these lectures with Pamela on my arm. This was brazen, even for me. Friends and colleagues were in attendance there, some of whom knew Linda well. Linda was not just my wife. She was a fellow academic economist who was teaching right up the road at Tufts. Just a decade earlier, we'd both been graduate students at nearby MIT. And there I was, walking in with

Pamela as though there was nothing unusual about it. At the receptions following each lecture, we drank wine and chatted, and I introduced her around. Why not? This beautiful twenty-three-year-old woman was just a friend, after all.

Nothing was said openly at the time, but later Bob Solow confided that bringing Pamela with me had left a bad taste in some people's mouths. He was not alone. The neoconservative writer, Midge Decter, would convey to me a similar concern about a different public appearance with Pamela. What I was doing with my marriage was my business, of course. But bringing this young woman out to an official event like that was, they both said, unseemly. Anyone could see that Pamela was more than a friend or a mentee. Whatever the delusions that had seized me at the time, the cover story I was telling my colleagues wasn't covering up anything at all. Like Linda, they had to have known what I was doing, but I was so focused on this new conquest that I never bothered to think about who knew what.

But what, exactly, *was* I doing? I was humiliating my wife in public for one, and she didn't deserve that. She had done nothing wrong to me. She had never betrayed or mistreated me in any way. She was betting all her chips on me. News of my appearance with Pamela was sure to get back to her, and she'd surely have to confront me about it. What would I say then? I was acting like a criminal who wants to get caught, but I was not a very sympathetic criminal. In truth, I didn't want to get caught so that I would have to stop. Rather, I wanted to get caught so that I could keep doing what I was doing. I imagined that getting caught would end the marriage. Getting caught would make my job easy. I lacked the courage to broach the issue with Linda squarely. I wasn't ready or able to leave her of my own volition, even though I'd already suggested to Pamela that I might. Still, if push came to shove, and Linda gave an ultimatum demanding that I stop the affair or leave, I knew the choice I would make. The marriage would end.

AROUND THIS TIME, Bill Kristol invited me out to dinner. He wanted me to meet Alan Keyes, a black diplomat working for the Reagan administration. Keyes had studied political philosophy at Cornell under the tutelage of Allan Bloom, who was himself a protégé of the brilliant émigré philosopher Leo Strauss. Strauss and Bloom were both charismatic teachers at the University of Chicago's Committee on Social Thought. They had a following of devoted, mostly conservative students, some of whom ended up in influential positions in the government and policy world. At the time, Strauss and Bloom were mostly unknown to the general public, but that would change with the publication of Bloom's blockbuster, *The Closing of the American Mind*, which served as a searing and erudite cannon blast in the culture war of the 1980s.

Keyes was plenty searing himself. Kristol thought that Keyes and I, as up-and-coming black conservatives, ought to know each other. Keyes was a firebrand who spoke in excoriating terms about the liberal policies he abhorred. He struck me as a little tightly wound, especially for a diplomat, but I understood why Kristol wanted us to meet. He was giving me another connection within the Reagan administration. The dinner was interesting, but I was more intrigued by the signal it sent than by anything that was said. I had passed two tests, the Cabinet Room meeting and the state dinner, and Kristol wanted to keep the door open.

Not long after that evening, Bill let me know there was a rhyme and reason to all these invitations and meetings and dinners. A job was opening up. Secretary of Education William Bennett's second-in-command, Under Secretary Gary Bauer, was planning on leaving, and it was Kristol's job as Bennett's chief of staff to find a replacement. He told me that if I wanted the job, it was mine. Bennett would have to interview me, and there would be confirmation hearings. I had met Bennett previously, and he and I got along well. He had a sharp mind and a sharper tongue.

I liked him. Although he made his name as a crusader for family values and public morality, behind the scenes he was a bit of a hedonist. The first time I saw him in a private setting, I was astonished by his appetite for alcohol. Who was I to judge? I had my own appetites.

I was being tapped for a fairly senior position in the executive branch. If some task took Bennett away from Washington, as under secretary I would attend cabinet meetings in his stead. Whereas I had previously done analytic studies of policy or offered theoretically informed propositions about policy, I would now be in a position to actually make policy. Kristol was not just offering me a new job, he was offering me a chance to put some of the ideas I had written about in my articles and papers into practice. The only African American among the administration's cabinet-level appointees who would outrank me would be Secretary of Housing and Urban Development Samuel Pierce. I told Kristol that I was indeed very interested.

When I told Tom Schelling about the potential White House job, he was happy for me. He told me that if it was something I wanted, I should do it. The Kennedy School was generally encouraging when one of its own moved on to a government position, because that increased the prestige of the school and ensured they would have the ear of another person in power. This wouldn't be like leaving for a different academic appointment, Tom assured me. If I found that working for the government didn't suit me, I could always come back. All the angst I felt about choking in the economics department was fading from memory now. It seemed that, after a brief hiccup, my professional ascent was back on track.

THE NEW YEAR WAS APPROACHING, and Pamela had to make a decision. The lease on her New York apartment was ending, and she had to renew it or find a new place to live. She still wasn't happy with her job. So I suggested that she give up the apartment and move to Boston.

I would rent a place for her, provide her with an allowance, and help her meet people who could get her started on a career in broadcasting, which was what she wanted. I liked the idea of having Pamela nearby and accessible. I would have my home with Linda and a retreat where I could repair whenever I wanted to indulge myself in Pamela's arms.

She came up soon after New Year's Eve. I rented a fifth-floor penthouse apartment on Union Park Street in the South End neighborhood of Boston, with a rooftop terrace and a gazebo. It was a home away from home where the two of us could spend time together without constraint. It wasn't too far from the Harvard campus, but it was distant enough from my house and Tufts that I didn't have to worry about Linda driving by while I was walking around with Pamela. We would go out or just hang out at our pad, smoke weed, make love, or enjoy the view from the terrace. It was a kind of parallel domestic existence I had designed to meet my needs.

I set about trying to establish Pamela in some kind of job. I had a friend, Pastor Earl Jackson, who ran a Christian radio station on Cambridge Street where I did a short weekly segment—*The Loury Report*—in which I put forth my conservative perspective on whatever topic I felt like talking about. Pastor Earl, a fellow black contrarian, happened to mention that he needed a DJ to fill the nine-to-midnight slot at the station. All they would have to do is announce the songs and keep the gospel music going. That sounded like a fine entry-level position for someone interested in broadcasting, so I recommended Pamela, and she got the job. I did not, of course, tell Pastor Earl about the nature of our relationship.

One night, I was visiting her at the studio during her shift. We were just hanging out and talking in the booth. Usually, the studio was empty at that time of night, but Pastor Earl had forgotten something in his office, and he came back around 11:00 p.m. to retrieve it. It was late on a weeknight, and there I was hanging out with my "friend." Not long after, Pastor Earl let Pamela go from the station. He called me to tell me the news, then he said that he would be praying for me, and he hoped I would get my life in order.

I knew what Pastor Earl meant, but as far as I could see, my life *was* in order. Even if he had confronted me about it directly and told me that I was disrespecting my marriage vows and living in sin in the eyes of God, I doubt I would have listened. I was a Master of the Universe. Having a beautiful young woman at my beck and call was what I deserved. Anyone could get married, but who could pull off what I was pulling off? Again, as much as I enjoyed sex with Pamela, it was not exactly the sex that attracted me to this arrangement. The thrill of having a liaison that no one—not Linda, not Tom Schelling, not Bill Kristol—knew about was enough to justify the expense and trouble required to keep Pamela around.

And it could be plenty of trouble. After Pamela lost her job at the radio station, she had little to occupy her time. She would sit around at our apartment smoking weed, polishing her résumé, and dreaming up new career paths for herself. It seemed like every time I walked in the door she had decided on a different plan. She was barely out of college and still trying to find herself, and she wasn't having much luck with the search. After a while, sitting there and listening to her talk about the virtues of some new career trajectory, all the while knowing that by the next week she would have abandoned that idea in favor of another, wore on me. If she had been taking steps to make progress on any of these paths, I doubt it would have bothered me. But from where I sat, it looked like she wasn't doing much more than getting high and daydreaming.

Things outside the bedroom may have been getting a little tedious, but that wasn't enough for me to consider breaking things off with Pamela. I was a worldly professor; she was a twenty-three-year-old girl. What did I expect we would have to talk about after we discussed her senior thesis for the fifth time? But the entire arrangement was still worth it to me. And besides, it's not like Pamela and Linda were the only women on Earth. If I wasn't getting all that I wanted out of either of them, there were others.

Keisha was a student in the Kennedy School's one-year master of public administration program. It was designed to burnish public administrators who were at a point in their careers where they were ready to level up. They would come to Harvard, acquire some interesting ideas, and go back to continue their work with an Ivy League imprimatur. Frankly, it was a cash cow for Harvard, since, almost without exception, the tuition fees were paid in full by the students' employers. But these were not people of Pamela's age, fresh out of college and without any experience. These students were serious professionals living real lives.

That's part of what attracted me to Keisha when I met her. She was born into an impoverished family in rural Mississippi but had spent most of her life in Los Angeles and now worked for the city. She was a South Central girl in her midthirties. I learned that she knew more than a couple of real gangsters. She proudly wore her hair in long braids before it became a trend. She had very dark skin and a voluptuous, Marilyn Monroe–like figure. Her voice was a sultry cat's purr. Keisha had a real life in L.A., including a long-term partner who would definitely have been a Gouster had he grown up in Chicago in the '50s. Despite our different backgrounds, we shared something important in common: I well understood the part of her that stayed connected to a sketchy, rough, and occasionally dangerous community even though she had a prestigious job and career; and she understood the part of me that was drawn to the ghetto streets of Boston to surreptitiously seek thrills and fellowship. She had enrolled in the class that Tom and I were co-teaching called Public Policy in Divided Societies.

We began seeing each other outside of class, and soon enough I would start paying her visits in her dorm room at the Episcopal Divinity School off Brattle Street near Harvard Square, where she was staying for the year. Keisha and I were not restrained in our activities. I can only imagine what the other women in the dorm, most of whom were divinity students, thought of the sounds coming out of that room. Not that I cared. I was often greeted with a knowing smile when passing one of her dorm mates on my way in or out. Keisha liked to party, and she introduced me to cocaine (which came to her via the US mail in periodic "care packages" from back home). We'd do a few bumps up in her room, sometimes off each other's behinds, but I didn't really care about the blow. Keisha's backside was far more appealing to me than the drugs were.

Only a handful of other black women were in the MPA program, and Keisha befriended one of them who was herself carrying on an affair with another married faculty member. The four of us would occasionally get together for drinks after work, and I'd half-joke with my fellow teacher about what would happen if our wives ever found out. I had by then doubled down on leading a secretive life. I didn't mention to any of them that there was yet another woman I needed to keep our secret from, as well.

WHEN I WAS GROWING UP, my mother had never been a big consumer of alcohol. She couldn't tolerate more than a drink or two in one sitting. But that all changed after I left home to move in with Charlene. Her drinking became more frequent. It started with her affection for Champale, a malt liquor designed to taste like champagne. Auntie Eloise would sip real champagne while Mama would guzzle her Champale. She progressed from there to bourbon, brother Adlert's drink of choice. Old Grand-Dad (100 proof) was her standard, though Old Taylor or Wild Turkey would do in a pinch. One Thanksgiving after I had started at Harvard, I went home to Chicago for a visit. There was a party at the home of Rose Duncan, a family friend from the Bethel AME Church's literary guild, which Aunt Eloise oversaw. It was rumored that Adlert and Rose had a thing going on. Everyone was hanging out, laughing, playing cards, and having a good time.

My mother started drinking. She got a little tipsy. And then she got

sloppy drunk. Soon she was so inebriated that she was mumbling inco-
herently to herself. I realized that we had to get her home. She was
barely conscious and unable to walk unaided, so a few other guys from
the party and I had to practically carry her downstairs. We managed to
pour her into someone's car, but then came the real challenge: We had to
get her up to her apartment, which was on the second floor. Each of us
grabbed a leg or an arm as we tried to hoist her up the stairs. We pushed
and pulled, with my mother mumbling the whole time, her dress riding
up over her waist. None of the other men said anything about it, but it
was horribly awkward, and I was humiliated. Everyone now knew that
my mother was a drunk.

Even after that incident, Mama's drinking didn't slow. One day when
I was back in Cambridge, she called me and told me she was thinking
about retiring. By then she had split from her fourth husband, the "country" boy, Mack. She was living alone in a small apartment owned by her
cousin Carey. Carey's mother, Nunna, had been the Great Aunt who
took in my mother at age twelve, after her mother, my grandmother Nettye, passed away. Mama was paying below-market rent on that apartment.
She was in a position, if she kept working, to be self-sufficient. She had
a civil service job as a receptionist with the Veterans Administration, a
gig that came with a pension and other retirement benefits. But she was
only in her late fifties, and the minimum retirement age for government
workers was sixty-two. If she retired before sixty-two, she'd get far fewer
benefits and a minuscule payout on the pension.

I tried explaining the situation, telling her that retiring just then was
a bad idea. First, she needed the money and the benefits. All she had to
do was stick it out for a few more years, and she'd be able to retire in
comfort on her pension. Second, there was the issue of her lifestyle. Her
job gave much-needed structure to her life. I told her, speaking frankly,
that the last thing she needed was to wake up at eight in the morning
and realize she didn't have to get out of bed if she didn't feel like it. She
needed something to do with herself, I observed. I told her I feared that,

if she didn't have to be at work by nine o'clock five days a week, she would drink around the clock to fill the void.

But she said she was tired of working. She intended to retire and take a lump-sum payment in lieu of a pension, and that was that. The payment would turn out to be a few tens of thousands of dollars, not nearly enough to live on for the rest of her life. What did she intend to do once the money ran out? How was the rent going to get paid? How was she going to afford groceries?

"God takes care of babies and fools," she told me.

I knew what that meant. It meant that she expected me to provide for her from then on. That made me angry. I did not mind helping my mother out with expenses, but this was different. It was as though she was daring me to say no when she knew that I couldn't. It would bring shame on me, she calculated. And she knew that I knew this, which gave her a decisive advantage in this game we were playing! After all, what kind of son refuses to help his mother, especially when he's got a fancy Ivy League job and a consulting gig on the side? As Tom Schelling would have seen instantly, this was a classic case of the Samaritan's dilemma, the game in which a person does not try hard enough to avoid some bad outcome because a sympathetic bystander exists who, she knows, cannot credibly commit to withholding his assistance. As I saw it, Mama was playing me, a guy who thought of himself as the consummate Player. In fact, she was rolling over and giving up, and she was coercing me into helping her do it. I resented her for making me an enabler of her choice to live in bad faith.

I called Lee Lee to talk about it. My sister responded with a characteristic plea for sympathy: "Don't judge Mama. She's just trying to find happiness, and you know what a hard life she's had. She's got a hole in her heart. You know that she's the sweetest person you'll ever meet. Doesn't that count for something? Mama loves us."

"Fuck that," I said. "When you love somebody, you are willing to endure pain and sacrifice on behalf of their growth and their development. That's what love means. True love is action, not sentiment. It's a lot more than a bunch of mournfully recited words."

Yes, Mama had sacrificed for us, and I did not doubt that she loved us. But putting me in this position did not feel like an act of love at all. It felt sneaky and underhanded. If she needed a little help to make ends meet, even if it were more than a little, I would have gladly given it to her. But she wasn't incapacitated. She was perfectly capable of taking care of herself, and she was choosing not to do so. That I could not respect. And I could not respect her attempt to exploit my desire not to be seen as a bad son. I may have never felt more like my father.

PAMELA MAY HAVE STARTED TO SUSPECT I was involved with another woman. She didn't know who Keisha was, but she started to ask questions. I would get irritated. We would fight. But, despite my growing indifference to the intellectual side of our relationship, I was not ready to relinquish Pamela. My pride and sense of self were still somehow entangled with her: I was the kind of man who was so impressive that even a young woman like her would be happy to live as my mistress. As long as she was sleeping up there in our penthouse every night, I could still tell myself that that was true. I wanted to keep her in place, so I planned something that would help maintain my stature and status in her mind.

I had recently impressed newly appointed Supreme Court Justice Antonin Scalia. I first met him at the Judicial Conference of the DC Circuit Court of Appeals in 1985, a year before his high-court appointment. He was in the audience during a debate I had on affirmative action with the Harvard Law professor Larry Tribe. Tribe was singing the praises of Harvard Law's efforts to bring in black faculty and pointed to, as the triumphant results of the policy, their recent hiring of two legal scholars, Randall Kennedy and Christopher Edley Jr., both of whom are black. I happened to be friends with both Randy and Chris. They were my peers at Harvard, and they were (and are) indeed brilliant legal minds. But I had a point to make.

"Well, there are two mutually exclusive and collectively exhaustive possibilities here," I said. "Either you think Kennedy and Edley are absolutely first-rate, as I believe they are, in which case you should have hired them even without an affirmative action policy—you would not have discriminated against them due to their race, I hope. Or you actually think they're not first-rate and they would not have been hired without affirmative action, in which case you're patronizing them with your beneficent decision to include them within your club nonetheless. So which is it?"

I had trapped one of the premier legal thinkers of my generation. It was like David and Goliath, for there is no appealing response to that question. Scalia, an affirmative action skeptic if there ever was one, had a good laugh with me about it when the panel concluded. It happened that his great friend, fellow DC Circuit Court judge, and future Supreme Court colleague, Ruth Bader Ginsburg was organizing a conference at the Hebrew University of Jerusalem, and Scalia recommended that she invite me. I decided that I would take Pamela with me and show her the kind of globe-hopping elite, the kind of major league Player, I really was. We'd spend two days at the conference and then another three taking in the Holy Land. I would take her down to the south of the country to Eilat, and tour the ancient ruins at Avdat in the Negev Desert. We would snorkel and float in the sea and, I was determined, make love on the beach.

By then my nomination for the under secretary position had become public. When I walked into the conference in Jerusalem, anyone who knew me knew I was up for a big public-facing job. And here I was once more with Pamela on my arm. Even those who had no idea who I was could probably have guessed that this young woman was not my wife. The political theorist Michael Walzer, my colleague from my year at the Institute for Advanced Study in Princeton, was there to speak as well, and he furrowed his brow a bit when I introduced him to my date.

After the conference, we departed for Eilat. The drive from Jerusalem requires passing through the Negev, a huge desert one can traverse for miles without seeing any sign of civilization other than the road. It has an otherworldly feel to it, especially in the spring, when colorful wildflowers, shimmering mirages, and grassy fields dot the landscape. During this drive, we got into an argument about one thing or another, and she demanded to be let out of the car. I was angry, so I pulled over, and she actually did get out and start walking. Where she intended to go, I had no idea. There was nothing around but sand and road. Finally, I persuaded her to get back in and we made up, but incidents like this were becoming more and more frequent.

Once in Eilat, we made our way to an empty stretch of beach on the Gulf of Aqaba and pulled over. I grabbed a blanket, and we snuck down away from the road. With the sun high in the sky, it was like an improvised sauna underneath that blanket. After a few minutes we were naked and going at it, when we heard a voice yell, "What are you doing down there?" I poked my head out and saw two men in Israeli Defense Force uniforms standing by their car on the road, close enough to see that something was going on but too far away to tell exactly what.

"We're tourists! We're here to enjoy the beach," I yelled back. The two men spoke to each other for a moment.

"Okay," one said, "Just be careful." I promised that we would, and they drove off, leaving us to our business. Like almost anyone else who saw Pamela and me together at that time, they might not have known exactly what was going on, but it was probably easy enough for them to guess. What they couldn't guess was that they had stumbled into the fulfillment of a fantasy that I had dreamed up and then made real. A beautiful woman, an exotic beach on the other side of a great ocean, and me, the transcontinental jet-setter who made it all happen. To such lengths

was I willing to go to in order to get what I wanted, and I wouldn't be
denied anything.

IN THE COURSE OF TALKING with Bill Kristol about my role as under
secretary, he had told me to expect a vetting process. I had no worries
about a routine background check. On paper, everything was above-
board. My divorce from Charlene was finalized, I was married to Linda,
and I had nothing to worry about in my financial records. After years of
delinquency, I had finally settled up on back child support obligations to
Alden's mother. There was the matter of that arrest for auto theft back
in Chicago, but I had been a minor, and I hadn't been in trouble with
the law since then, so my court record had been expunged. There was
my penchant for marijuana, but in order to catch me at that, someone
would have to search my house or have me followed, and I doubted they
would go that far.

One day, though, I got a call at my office from Pamela. Two FBI officers had shown up at the apartment wanting to know more about this
property that had my name on the lease. They asked Pamela who she
was and what she was doing there. I'm not sure what she told them, but
I knew this wasn't a good sign. Not long after, these same agents set up a
meeting with me at my office at the Kennedy School during which they
asked me a handful of innocuous questions. Bill had told me to expect
this interview, so I wasn't alarmed at their presence. But I could guess
what was coming. They finally got around to asking about the apartment. I had no wish to find out what happens when you lie to the FBI,
so I acknowledged to them that I was indeed paying for the apartment
and that Pamela was living there. It was perfectly legal. Still, I knew
legality wasn't the issue. A cabinet nominee with a secret apartment and
a secret girlfriend would not fly in Reagan's White House, and it would
especially not fly with my would-be boss, William Bennett, who would

go on to author the bestselling *The Book of Virtues* and was the administration's most ardent champion (publicly, anyway) of "family values."

I racked my brain for any explanation that was remotely plausible, aside from the real one, but there was nothing to be done. I was sunk. It had honestly never occurred to me that anyone would have discovered Pamela, but then I was not worried about what anybody else thought. I had paraded Pamela around town in Boston, brought her to events in my workplace, introduced her to colleagues, and flown her halfway around the world to a prestigious international conference. I not only allowed the unofficial world to make contact with the official world, I knocked down the wall between them with a sledgehammer, and disorder ensued. Did I not think there would be consequences? Of course I didn't. I was a Master of the Universe, after all. Who could sit in judgment of me?

Well, I found out who: the FBI, and pretty soon Bill Kristol and William Bennett. Since I had already been announced as Bennett's preferred candidate, I knew that my withdrawal would lead to some embarrassment for him, and I was sorry for that. Wanting to spare everyone as much awkwardness as possible, I called Bill Kristol before he had a chance to call me. I told him that I wasn't ready to leave academia after all. Bill was perplexed. I had seemed so gung ho, and now all of a sudden I was bowing out. He didn't understand, and all I could offer him were weak apologies.

Fourteen

That was it. The call was in. There was nothing else to do about it. Even if I changed my mind, I couldn't very well call Bill Kristol back and tell him, "Just kidding, I still want the job." I had talked to Linda about withdrawing before I did it, and she was relieved. She was opposed to the Reagan administration on political grounds, and my employment there would have meant more events where her presence would be expected. Between work and Pamela, I didn't set aside all that much time for Linda. We were together, but we were living separate lives. With me living and working in DC and her remaining in Boston, physical distance would only have exacerbated the emotional distance that had already come between us.

I didn't, of course, tell Linda that I was withdrawing because the FBI had found my love nest and interviewed my twenty-three-year-old girlfriend. And in fact, that was not my only reason. While the federal agents no doubt saw what was going on, they never asked either Pamela or me about the exact nature of our relationship. Surely, I wouldn't have been the only man in Washington with a mistress. There were other potential roadblocks that I had cleared without causing too much concern to Kristol or Bennett. I had been delinquent in my student loan repayments from graduate school, and someone in MIT's administration leaked that information to the press. I got things straightened out quickly and paid the money back. Another journalist had gone to Chicago to research my past and found Alden. There was an interview with him in the paper. He was then sixteen years old, and I had not had any contact with him since he was an infant. When he and Janice were informed that I was up for a job in Reagan's White House, the reporter wrote that Alden turned to his mother and asked, "Mom, does that mean I'm going to grow up to be a Republican?" I was angry about the story, but I had to give Alden credit: it was a great line, and I deserved his sarcastic barb.

It was all too easy to imagine a Democratic senator waving those clippings in the air during a confirmation hearing and noting the apparent hypocrisy in a conservative bureaucrat, an advocate for fiscal responsibility and family values, with unpaid debts and an unacknowledged son born out of wedlock. Still, Kristol and Bennett stood by me.

Though I never told anyone at the time, I was just as relieved as Linda that I had withdrawn. The truth was I felt unprepared to embark on the life of a government bureaucrat. In academia, I understood the work, the personality types, the culture, and the rules, both written and unwritten. I felt at home in a university setting. I had begun my professional life as a theoretical economist set on becoming the black Paul Samuelson. When that didn't work out, I transformed myself into a fire-breathing social critic. I knew how to play those roles. But I had no idea how to navigate political life in Washington. As a black Republican, I would have a target on my back at all times. Everything I did and said would be scrutinized and held up for public consumption. Maybe tens of thousands of people total had ever read my magazine essays, perhaps a couple hundred thousand may have read the handful of op-ed pieces I'd written for daily papers. Now I'd have an audience of millions that I would have to relate to differently. I couldn't whip myself into a righteous fury and let loose in front of the news cameras. I would have to answer to Bennett, and he would have to answer to Reagan. And those millions of people wouldn't be readers of a magazine or a newspaper; they would be the people to whom I was ultimately responsible, the American public. I did not have a handle on what such a role would require of me.

That is the cover story. And it was true, so far as it went. The real story was also true. If I took a job in Washington, I would have to stop fucking around. I'd have to stop visiting the projects to score weed and to play chess with probable criminals. I certainly couldn't pick up prostitutes off the street. Maybe a seasoned Washington pro knew how to get away with such things, but I didn't. Despite being a prominent Harvard professor with something of a public profile, I wasn't exactly a household name. But in Washington, even relatively obscure political appointees are local celebrities. If I was spotted only once in the wrong place with the wrong person, I'd end up causing a scandal. I wasn't ready to give up the freedom to do whatever I wanted whenever I wanted with whomever I wanted, to step down from the throne to which I was entitled as a Master of the Universe, to put Uncle Adlert's paisley smoking jacket back in the closet.

MY WITHDRAWAL, THEN, was not without its consolations. But ironically, my putative cause for the withdrawal—Pamela—was no longer one of them. After returning from Israel, our relationship continued its downward trajectory. We were fighting all the time now, and what I took to be her indolence was a constant source of irritation. Here I was supporting her financially so that she could pursue her dreams, I thought, and all she did was sit around smoking her way through our stash. If Pamela had been a distraction from my boredom with my everyday existence, she was now becoming just another hassle. The novelty had worn off.

Two days after my phone call to Bill, I was about to enter the apartment building to see Pamela again and mildly dreading the experience, when someone called my name. I turned around and saw Mario, the tailor and clothing designer whose corner shop was located on the building's first floor. He was a jovial Italian, in his midforties, I'd say, with a winning smile. As politely as he could, he informed me that some weeks ago my "wife" had purchased a couple of his dresses and said that I would pay the bill, which amounted to $600. This was news to me. Pamela had never said anything about buying new dresses. Apparently, she just assumed she could do whatever she wanted, and I would foot the bill. I apologized to Mario, insisted that he take what cash I had on me, and promised to pay the rest as soon as I could get to an ATM.

When I got upstairs, I was angry. Who was Pamela to go around spending the money I earned without so much as asking? She was no one, just some privileged college kid sitting around with her hand out who didn't know or care what it took to make her own money. Mario's bill was the last straw. I wanted to be through with the whole thing. I confronted Pamela immediately, yelling at her that we were done. I wanted her out. She yelled right back and said she wasn't going anywhere. She then retreated to the rooftop terrace and planted herself there. I became enraged, bellowing for her to get out, but she refused. I then did something I knew, even then, I should not have done. I grabbed her by the shoulders and physically moved her toward the stairs. She tried resisting, but I persisted in forcing her step by step through the apartment and out the front door, which I slammed shut as soon as I got her across the threshold. I stomped into the bedroom, grabbed a few handfuls of her clothes, and threw them out the door into the hallway, telling her to leave and not to come back. It must have been humiliating for her, but I wanted to humiliate her, to make her feel my contempt.

We continued screaming at each other through the door until a voice from the bottom of the stairwell called up. Two police officers were standing below. Apparently, a neighbor, alarmed by the intensity of our argument, had called the cops. Pamela went downstairs. I waited, wondering what she was telling them.

An officer then knocked on the door and asked me to come downstairs. The four of us—the two cops, Pamela, and me—discussed what had happened. Since my name was on the lease, the officers said it would be best if Pamela found somewhere else to stay. Since she didn't know anyone in Boston well enough to ask them for such a favor, the policemen said they would take her to a women's shelter for the night while she decided what to do next. They asked me to go back upstairs, which I did, thinking that would be the end of it.

The adrenaline from the argument was wearing off, and I realized that I had lost control. I did not strike Pamela, but I'd put my hands on her. The fact that first the FBI and then the local police had been alerted to the existence of the relationship was perhaps a sign that things with Pamela had reached their nadir. There was no way to heal our relationship after this, and, frankly, I didn't want to. It was over. The idea that I had considered leaving Linda for that girl now seemed insane. What had I been thinking? Whatever difficulties I was going through with my wife, I didn't want to leave her. I waited until I was sure the police were long gone, then I locked up the apartment and headed home, back to my other life.

IT'S THE DAY FOLLOWING THE BLOWUP at my South End apartment, a Friday, and Linda's sister Rhonda is visiting. It's a lovely summer day, and the three of us are hanging out, planning what we're going to do with the afternoon. The phone rings, I pick it up, and Harvard's general counsel introduces himself. He tells me that his office has just received a call from the Boston police. As a courtesy, they have notified Harvard that a warrant has been issued for my arrest on assault charges relating to an altercation with Pamela Foster, and if I do not present myself at a police station by nine o'clock the following Monday morning for booking, officers will be dispatched to arrest me.

I have no earthly idea what is going on. Yes, Pamela and I did argue. And yes, I did put my hands on her. But I did not hit her or attempt to harm her physically. Nothing I did could have caused injury, and at no point did she tell me I was hurting her. So what is this about? I don't know, but I do know that I am now in deep, deep trouble. I suppose I should be grateful. If a judge really has issued a warrant, the cops could walk into one of my lectures, arrest me in front of my students, and then march me across the Harvard campus in cuffs. Instead, I'm being allowed to surrender of my own volition and avoid public humiliation. At least for now.

By the time I hang up with the general counsel, my heart is racing. Whatever happens next, I know I finally have to tell Linda what's been going on. I call her away from Rhonda, sit her down, and tell her about Pamela Foster. I don't tell her much, only what I think I must. But it is enough to make her clench her fists, set her jaw, and glare at me. Occasionally she interjects, asking for clarification on some detail or another, but I hedge and speak in vague terms. When it's over, we agree that I should call Christopher Edley, the Harvard Law professor, for advice about what to do next. Chris had been Linda's classmate at Swarthmore. He and I are friendly enough that I figure he'll take my call even though it's a weekend. And he does, telling me he'll contact a lawyer named Martin Gideonse on my behalf. Marty Gideonse, with the able assistance of an up-and-coming black associate named Charles Ogletree, runs the Harvard Law School's criminal law clinic. He's a veteran navigator of Boston's local court scene.

Marty doesn't know me from Adam, but he agrees to meet with me at once on Christopher's recommendation. I soon learn that this is characteristic of Marty Gideonse. He has a well-earned reputation as a big-hearted mensch. Whatever I have done, I'm now in dire straits and need someone to guide me through a confusing, potentially life-altering process. Knowing this, Marty shows up to help. We meet that Saturday at his office, and he asks for the whole story about Pamela. I tell him everything. When I finish, he looks at me very seriously and asks, "Have you told your wife all of this?" I say that of course I haven't. I've told her only what I think she needs to know.

"Tell her everything," he says, "and tell her now. She needs to know.

She doesn't deserve to be blindsided by anything that will be coming out later. And you can assume that it's all going to come out."

I know Marty is right, and I'm a little ashamed that it's taken the urging of a virtual stranger to make me fully confess to Linda. However I may have rationalized my infidelity, I can no longer justify keeping her in the dark when my affair with Pamela is about to become a matter of public record. She knew that a lot of stuff was going on, and that had been enough to keep our relationship in a state of détente for years. But I can no longer pretend that her knowledge that I was—that I am—unfaithful constitutes permission to keep from her the full reality of the Pamela affair. The barrier between my official and unofficial lives is about to crumble for both of us. I can no longer rely on our tacit common knowledge of my double life to substitute for an explicit account of this particular transgression.

After the meeting with Marty, I drive back home. Rhonda is already gone, her visit cut short. I sit down with Linda, and this time I tell her everything about my relationship with Pamela. I tell her about the correspondence and our rendezvous at The Hay-Adams. I tell her about flying Pamela to Boston and meeting her in New York. I tell her about taking Pamela to the W. E. B. Du Bois Lectures. (But does she already know about that one?) I tell her about the apartment in the South End with my name on the lease, about the terrace and the gazebo. I tell her about Israel. Finally, I tell her about the altercation and the police.

Linda listens to all of this silently, betraying nothing of how she feels. That I will have to imagine. With all of it in the open, Linda begins to coolly strategize. "What are the next steps?" she asks. We begin creating a list of tasks that must be accomplished, people who must be notified, expenses that may be incurred. This is Linda's way of dealing with a crisis, even one in which she is the victim: stay calm, get proactive, meet it head on, find some way of getting your arms around it. I don't have the courage to ask her what she is thinking and feeling at this moment, but I can see that she cannot stand the notion of adopting a passive, self-pitying posture.

Whatever the fallout, legal and otherwise, Linda has decided that her feelings about it will keep. Would I have maintained the same steadiness if our roles had been reversed? The idea that Linda would ever do what I had done never crosses my mind.

MARTY GIDEONSE STOOD BESIDE ME at the arraignment, where I pleaded "not guilty" on charges of, among other things, "assault with a deadly weapon." The weapon was allegedly a "shod foot," with which Pamela said that I stomped on her. No such thing happened, but then I could see that the charge was not the only thing amiss. Pamela showed up to court wearing a neck brace, though I cannot understand how she would have incurred any injury to her neck. The situation would have been comical, fit for a Tom Wolfe novel, if it was not so gravely serious. I had mistreated her, that much I could not deny. I was cruel. I did not have to eject her from the apartment in the way I did, knowing she had nowhere to go. I could have simply told her that it was over and it was time for us to go our separate ways. Despite the falseness of the charges, I was largely responsible for the events that had brought me to the court-house that day. But the fact was that I did not harm her physically.

I was released on my own recognizance to await trial, but there was much more than waiting to do. Tom Schelling and Graham Allison, dean of the Kennedy School, had called me in for a meeting to discuss how we would handle the story. The news had gone public. The wire services picked it up. "Harvard professor pleads innocent to assault" ran the UPI headline. My recent withdrawal from the White House position had not yet been made public, ensuring that this assault charge would be a national story. "Professor Accused of Assault Won't Seek No. 2 Education Job," reported the *Los Angeles Times*. Harvard and the Kennedy

School didn't see this as a mere lover's quarrel. For them, it was a public relations nightmare.

Allison was rattled. He sat behind his desk reeling off questions: "What are we going to do? What are we going to tell the press? Can he continue to teach? What's our strategy? What does the short run look like here? And what about two months out? Six months out?"

Finally, Tom stopped him cold.

"Glenn," he asked, "how is Linda? How is she handling this?" It struck me that Tom was thinking beyond Allison's crisis management mode. I was touched that for him, even at a moment like this, the personal took priority over the professional.

I said that, with her fists balled up, she had accepted what I had done and was now determined to move forward. With Linda's feelings acknowledged, Tom allowed the meeting to proceed. Perhaps he thought that Linda would have left me on the spot or kicked me out of our condo, telling me that if I liked my little apartment and its gazebo so much, I should go live there instead. (The *Herald*'s story carried a photo of the "love nest" where the encounter between Pamela and me occurred.) But Linda didn't do that. In fact, I knew she wouldn't. I knew that she was going to stick it out, pick through the wreckage of the disaster I had caused, and salvage what she could.

It was now all out in the open. Everyone knew—or thought they knew—what I had done. At home, Linda and I were barely on speaking terms. At Harvard, I knew that almost anybody who passed by me was thinking, "There's that conservative black guy who beat up his twenty-three-year-old girlfriend." I was angry that my actions had been blown out of proportion, but now that I had to face up to what I actually had done, I felt nothing but shame. The sense of accomplishment and the surging masculine bravado I had derived from possessing Pamela had curdled into a rotten feeling in the pit of my stomach. The South End apartment, once a monument to my sexual conquests, had become unbearable to think about.

There was even this omen from the gods: When I was finally able to return to the apartment to pack up my things, I discovered that Pamela had been there before me, and she'd been busy. She had taken a pair of scissors and methodically cut up every piece of clothing that I kept in the place, including my uncle Adlert's paisley smoking jacket, which now lay in ribbons strewn like entrails about the kitchen floor.

That week was Harvard's commencement. I had to retrieve some papers from my office at the Kennedy School. The last thing I wanted was to get roped into a conversation, so I hustled in, hoping no one would see me. In order to get where I was going, I had to pass by the outdoor graduation ceremony for the Kennedy School's master in public administration program. I should have been sitting in one of those seats, looking on as these newly minted MPAs received their diplomas. Instead, I shielded my face and walked by as quickly as I could. But as I passed, I happened to glance up at the stage, and there I saw Keisha looking back at me, and next to her was Ron Ferguson, my old friend from MIT who was teaching a course in the program. God only knows what they were thinking. I couldn't bring myself to acknowledge them, so I picked up my pace and walked on.

There was nowhere I could go to seek comfort, and being alone just led me to dwell on my misery. I had caused this. I was the problem. And I couldn't very well escape from myself. The evening the story broke in the *Boston Herald*, I got a motel room with Keisha. Now that she had graduated, she would be heading back to Los Angeles. I would have liked to take her out to a nice dinner to celebrate her achievement and to say goodbye. We were both adults. We knew our relationship wasn't going to last after she left Cambridge. She deserved better than a furtive meeting in an anonymous motel room, but such was my notoriety that it would have been impossible for me to dine out alone, much less with yet another woman who was not my wife. Lady K, as I called her, didn't press me about it—she understood what I was going through.

Late that night, I drew myself a bath, got in, and picked up the day's copy of the *Herald*. Marty had told me what was in the story, but I hadn't yet read it myself. Just a week earlier, I believed I had been in control of my life. I decided where I went and when, who I slept with and how, what I said and did. If one life was not enough, I could live two. Now, I thought, I controlled nothing. I was at the mercy of Pamela, my wife, my lawyer, the courts, my colleagues, and now the press. I had called my father earlier in order to reach him before he read about me in the papers. "You keep up like this and they'll have nothing to do with you," he told me. "It won't matter how smart you are. It won't matter how many degrees you have."

Sitting naked in the bath, I read the alleged facts of my case in cold, hard print, my father's rebuke ringing in my ears, and I wept.

AS THE TRIAL DATE APPROACHED, friends reached out privately to convey their support. None did so publicly, and I wouldn't have wanted them to. I had already brought enough shame on myself and my wife; I didn't need any more collateral damage on my conscience. When I ran into Edith Stokey, she hugged me and told me I would be okay. That was good enough for me. Harvard was taking a wait-and-see approach. I wasn't teaching over the summer, so there was no immediate need to take any action. But if I was convicted of a violent crime, they would almost certainly void my tenure agreement and fire me. Even if I received no jail time, a conviction would mean my academic career was over for good.

In the meantime, Marty Gideonse went to work. I could see why he was in charge of teaching law students how to become effective criminal defense lawyers. His dedication to my case went well beyond filing motions and crafting strategy. He was there for me both as legal counsel and as a friend. And Charles Ogletree helped prepare me for a possible deposition. Marty would walk me through the next steps in the procedure, and then we would talk about how I was handling things emotionally (not well). He would try to steady me. I couldn't honestly talk with

Linda about how I was feeling. Even if she hadn't been so angry with me, after all I'd done to her it would have been wrong to burden her with my feelings of guilt and shame. So Marty stepped into the breach. If he ever got bored with the law, he would have made for an outstanding therapist or priest!

Then something strange happened. Pamela, who had moved back with her mother in Pittsburgh, simply stopped cooperating with the prosecutor. She told the court she wouldn't testify. Without the participation of the victim, the state no longer had any way to pursue the case. By that summer's end, all of the charges were dropped. There was still the possibility that she might sue in civil court. Marty reached out to Pamela's mother, who was handling her legal affairs, proposing a settlement to agree not to sue. But she said no. They didn't want any money, and they didn't want to sue. According to Marty, Pamela's mother had convinced her daughter that it was better to get away from the entire mess as quickly as possible and to move on with her life. If she stayed mired in a criminal trial and then a civil trial, it would come to define her. She was still very young, and she could get past it. I have no way of knowing what Pamela's mother was thinking, but I believe she hadn't wanted her daughter to be defined by her victimization. In any case, this was a pure windfall for me. I was avoiding further legal and financial sanction in this affair. But I'd like to believe that, even if her mother's perspective hadn't benefited me directly, I would still have admired it for its wisdom.

That I would not, after all, have to face criminal charges for what had happened was certainly a relief. But the damage to my reputation had been done. My marriage and my sense of self had been shaken to their foundations. To be sure, the prospect of a trial had been terrifying. But at least a criminal trial eventually ends. From where I was sitting, I could not see any end to the chaos I had created in my life, and in Linda's life. When I told Marty that, with the legal issues nullified, Linda was still staying with me, he said, "You're one lucky dude. It's a good thing we don't get what we deserve in this life. A lot of guys I've worked with who put themselves in this kind of situation, they end up in a motel room with a hooker and a bottle of cheap gin. And you've still got your wife!"

He couldn't have known how close to the mark he was. I did have my wife, but barely. We floated past each other like ghosts, discussing only the most basic elements of our lives: bills, groceries, errands. And, while I was treated civilly at the Kennedy School, I knew that at least some of my colleagues had to have believed that I did what the papers said I did, no matter what kind of front they put up when we encountered each other in the halls. The narrative became twisted. In the mind of the public, my withdrawal from the White House job merged and combined with the assault charges, making it seem as though I had taken myself out of consideration because I had been accused of a crime.

I moved about in a state of nebulous uncertainty, always wondering if the person I was talking to—a colleague, a student, a convenience store cashier—secretly regarded me as an abusive monster. I had doubts of my own. I knew I was not an abuser of women, but I was certainly not a Master of the Universe any longer. In truth, I had never been one, had I? I wasn't even the master of myself. The affairs and conquests now, under the glare of the official world's searchlight, looked like the sordid dalliances of an entitled pig. I did not feel like an entitled pig but, forced to see my actions from outside of myself, I could not fully disavow what I took to be the world's view of me.

If Aunt Eloise had never known me, if I was just another name in the headlines, would she have read my story in the paper, clucked her tongue, and thought to herself, "God help him, there's one who's really crossed over to the other side of the line"? Would my father agree with her? Entertaining that thought was unbearable to me, precisely because it was only too plausible.

Fifteen

Not long after the end of the Pamela Foster affair, I traveled to Lisbon, Portugal, to meet with an international group of scholars working on a report about how South Africa might make a peaceful transition away from apartheid. Chaired by the noted sociologist Peter Berger and funded by the Anglo American Corporation of South Africa, the group included specialists on the economics, politics, and history of that country, as well as some thoughtful observers like me who brought an outsider's perspective to the deliberations. Another outsider was the Lutheran minister and theologian Richard John Neuhaus, who would soon, and amidst some fanfare, convert—he might well have said "revert"—to Catholicism. In the 1960s, Richard had been the pastor at St. John the Evangelist Church, a predominantly black and Hispanic congregation in a low-income Brooklyn neighborhood. His cerebral, passionate sermons had argued for the civil rights cause of that day and against the Vietnam War. He became nationally prominent when, along with the Jesuit priest Daniel Berrigan and Rabbi Abraham Joshua Heschel, he founded the antiwar organization Clergy and Laymen Concerned about Vietnam. He had also marched for the civil rights of black Americans alongside Martin Luther King Jr., which impressed me greatly.

But Richard was impressive for many other reasons. He had recently launched a small think tank in New York City called the Center for Religion and Society, and he had just published a much-discussed book, *The Naked Public Square*, a trenchant critique of radical secularism in American public life. I wasn't particularly religious at the time but, having read my essays in the *New Republic*, *Commentary*, and the *Public Interest*, Richard could see that at the core of my arguments was an implicit moral critique. My declaration of war against "the enemy within" was, he thought, a call to black America to seek higher ground. Perceiving a spiritual subtext there, he invited me to participate in seminars at his center, where issues of social inequality, ethics, and public policy were discussed. It was through these encounters that we became friends.

Peter Berger, himself a Lutheran layman, had written extensively about the sociology of religion. He and Richard were good friends, and they had collaborated on other projects in the past. South Africa's system of racial segregation and its brutal repression of its black population were under enormous international pressure to change, and that inevitable change would come with the risk of bloody retribution from black South Africans who had endured many decades of subordination. This was a tinderbox if there ever was one. Mindful of the stakes involved, Harry Oppenheimer, the head of the Anglo American Corporation and one of South Africa's leading industrialists, with the help of his assistant Bobby Godsell, had recruited Berger to pull together our study group and to produce a report, the first draft of which we were gathered in Lisbon to discuss.

My personal troubles went unmentioned in our formal sessions. However, as Richard and I conversed privately over dinner one evening after a day of discussion and debate, he asked me how I was holding up. The truth was that I was a mess. I was trying to pick up the pieces, but they kept slipping through my fingers. Perhaps being so far from home imbued me with a sense of license, and in frustration I let loose. I complained to him, who I had assumed would be a sympathetic listener, about the press's depiction of me as a hypocrite. Newspapers in Boston and Chicago had gone back to investigate my past and dug up whatever dirt they could find. They were portraying me, unfairly I felt, as a feckless libertine who nevertheless prescribed Victorian morals for the "black underclass." I was struggling privately with the fallout from my behavior, and now the press was using me to sell papers. He listened to my spiel in silence.

"You know," I finally blurted out, "Martin Luther King wasn't faithful to his wife, either. And yet, nobody thought that diminished the force of his public arguments for civil rights. Those two things are incommensurate! Likewise, what I did was wrong. I know that. It was terrible. But there's private life and there's the public sphere. Judge my public arguments on their merit, and you'll see they're right, no matter what I've done in my personal life. Frankly, I can't see what one has to do with the other. I'm a social critic. I never claimed to be a saint."

This was not the right thing to say to Richard John Neuhaus. He slapped the table with his hand and thundered at me: "Don't you ever, ever say that! That's just plain wrong! King's infidelity was a profound moral misstep on his part. And it hurt the movement. He was less effective as a public leader because of his private misdeeds. Now, if you deign to stand up and to tell people how to live, then you have a responsibility to live decently yourself. Otherwise, you make a mockery of the very ideal of public morality. You're either a moral leader or you're not. Now you choose."

I conceded to Richard that he was probably right, and we moved on. In truth, I didn't buy it. My actions had been profoundly irresponsible and had wounded those around me—that I could not deny. But at the time I was unaffected by Richard's righteous anger. What did my bad behavior have to do with two-thirds of black children being born out of wedlock? What did it have to do with violent crime in black communities? Nothing at all, as far as I was concerned. My critical analysis of the social maladies afflicting my people remained unchanged, and if they could not be refuted by data or argument, they damn sure couldn't be refuted by pointing to my personal shortcomings. As if to prove Richard's point, I thought all these things despite having fathered an illegitimate son of my own, and despite having survived the criminal charge of assaulting my mistress.

I didn't say anything like that in public, of course. If I had, who would have listened? Amidst the many challenges confronting the Roman Catholic Church, Richard John Neuhaus would later face questions concerning his own moral leadership. He, too, would have to make choices, and it is not entirely clear that he always made the right ones.

BACK IN 1981, over the Christmas holiday when I was still at the University of Michigan, the economics building caught fire and burned to the ground. No one was hurt, but the fire consumed almost everything on the premises, including the contents of my office. My books, my papers, my notes, mementos, the photos I kept on my desk, the desk itself—the fire took all of it. The only things recovered from my office were two charred cubes that had formerly been my file cabinets.

The university established a temporary home for the economics department in a wing of the medical complex that was just then being refurbished. They set up some makeshift offices with empty bookshelves, file cabinets, and desks. Resting on each desk was a stack of blank, white paper tablets and some cups full of paper clips and pens. When I sat down at the desk reserved for me and tried to get back to work, I found I could make no headway at all. I was paralyzed by the loss of my things. I didn't know where to begin. Without my books and photocopied journal articles to reference or the notes that contained a record of my thinking, I was totally at sea. I sat there in my antiseptic new office for months, staring at barren shelves and empty drawers, accomplishing little, my mind churning but unable to gain traction on any of the problems I had been working on before the fire. It took Tom Schelling's call from Harvard to rescue me from my doldrums.

I felt that same sense of loss and aimlessness following my arrest. I searched for a solid idea to grab hold of, but I touched only air. I was empty and numb, my mind a void. My affairs with Keisha and Pamela were over, the criminal charges were dropped, the threat of a civil suit was gone, and Harvard had opted to allow me to return to teaching in the fall. Yet I had not recovered. Not even close. The disaster was ongoing. The formal inquiries regarding my relationship with Pamela may have ended, but the wounds the scandal had inflicted continued to fester. My relationship with Linda remained frosty. She was clearly in pain, but I could not console her. I had no idea what to say to her beyond apologizing yet again. Nor could I reach out to anyone else I knew for comfort. I had hurt people. The suffering I was enduring, I knew, I had brought on myself, and in the most unsympathetic way possible. Acknowledging that I was responsible for this state of affairs did nothing to mitigate the shame and despair I felt. The plain fact was that I would have to deal with it—or fail to deal with it—largely on my own.

My "solution" to this quandary was to seek out the only thing I knew that could reliably make me feel good. At night, after another day of failing to communicate with Linda, I would go out to my haunts in Boston's black neighborhoods. Sometimes I'd come around for a game of chess if I knew where one could be had, or I'd hang out and have a drink at a bar or go out in search of women. This was the sort of behavior that had gotten me in trouble in the first place, I knew, but I felt that it was all I had. Things had gotten as bad as they could get, I figured, and I looked on my situation with a fatalistic resignation. Whatever was going to happen was going to happen. I could no longer navigate the official world, not even at home. I had made a shambles of the respectable side of my life. That part of me hardly seemed inhabitable anymore, which left me with only the street for respite.

One night, I was hanging out at a club. In my late thirties now, I was getting to the point where I was almost too old to be there—if you're the oldest person in the club, then you're in the wrong place! But I just needed to be out somewhere and around people. I noticed a pretty, provocatively dressed, full-bodied woman alone at the bar. She seemed like she wouldn't mind a friend, so I approached her and started a conversation. Soon it became clear that she was a working girl. I had no problem with that. When she suggested that we go for a ride somewhere, I was game.

IN MY CAR, SHE ASKS IF I EVER GET HIGH. I say sure I do. I like to smoke weed, after all. So she says we should go to her place. Why not a quick smoke before getting down to business, I think. That sounds fun.

She directs me to her building, a run-down tenement about a half-mile from the club. The vestibule and staircase are crowded with people, some murmuring to one another, some others shouting down the stairwell, and some just sitting around doing nothing. We work our way past them and up three flights of stairs to her apartment. She takes me to her bedroom and then asks for fifty dollars.

"Fifty dollars?" I ask. "For what?"

"For the drugs," she says.

Fifty dollars is pretty steep for some weed in 1987, but if she's including the sex, I guess it all adds up. I give her the money and she disappears into another room. When she reemerges, she's holding a small packet made from a folded scrap of newsprint. She opens it, and I see some little white crystals. I ask her what it is, and she tells me it's cocaine. I had done coke with Keisha, but that was powder. I have no idea what this stuff is.

"I thought you snorted cocaine," I say. "What do we do with this?"

"We smoke it," she says.

She takes out a bag from beside her bed and removes a plastic soda bottle into which she had burned two holes using the tip of a cigarette. She takes out some tin foil, a sewing needle, a straw, and a lighter. She covers the mouth of the soda bottle with the tin foil, then stipples the foil with holes using the sewing needle. She then lights a cigarette, takes a few drags, and taps some ash over the foil, creating a filter over the holes.

She sticks the straw into one of the holes on the side of the bottle then sprinkles some of the cocaine crystals over the top of the ash. She picks up the bottle such that her thumb covers the other hole, then brings the straw up to her mouth, flicks the lighter, holds it to the crystals, and sucks. Pale smoke seeps into the bottle. When it's full, she slides her thumb off the hole and sips the smoke through the straw. She holds it in and then exhales a faint cloud.

"Your turn," she says.

I follow suit.

As I exhale that first hit, I feel like someone has plugged my brain directly into a wall socket. Warmth spreads throughout my body, my heart begins to race, and the ambient sense of unease that had hovered in the background of my perceptions ever since I received the call from Harvard's general counsel disintegrates. My attention is focused solely on this room, this woman, myself, and the plastic bottle in my hand. There is no past pursuing me and no future looming before me, only the euphoria of a present that seems endless.

After a few minutes, though, the glow begins to fade, and I feel myself reentering time's stream. The woman and I each take another hit. The feeling is less pronounced now, less surprising, but no less pleasurable. The woman calls to the next room, and another woman enters. They are sisters, it turns out, and she takes a pull off the plastic bottle. I briefly consider suggesting a threesome. But having sex would mean I'd have to stop smoking, and this new drug is far too interesting to put down now.

I am by now aware that I'm smoking crack. And I am of course aware of the horrible toll that crack and freebase cocaine are exacting from black urban neighborhoods, including the one where I'm currently holed up. Families destroyed, once functional communities sent pinwheeling into chaos and violence seemingly overnight, discarded vials crunching underfoot, vacant stares from dazed addicts, the horror stories go on and on. I had never understood how this drug could take hold of a person and make him do terrible things he would not otherwise do. But now I see. Because it turns out that smoking crack feels really, really good. So good, in fact, that as I take another hit—the last hit that my fifty dollars has bought me—I can't name any other experience that compares, and I can't think of anything I'd rather do at that moment than to smoke more.

I check my watch. About a half hour has passed since I first entered the woman's bedroom.

AFTER SMOKING CRACK THAT FIRST TIME, whenever I would go out for the evening, practically fleeing from my home rather than deal with the tension there, I'd always search out that woman. I would stop into the clubs and bars where I knew she could probably be found. I would cruise by the patches of sidewalk where prostitutes gathered to ply their trade. I wasn't searching for the woman, though. I was searching for what she could get me: another hit. And often enough, I found it. I would pick her up and sometimes we would go back to her apartment to smoke, but I did not feel safe there. The other residents and whoever else was hanging around started to recognize me. I did not want to be known by these people, because they saw exactly what I was there to do. Many of them were there to do the same, and I felt it was only a matter of time before one of them sized up my clothes and my shoes and my watch and decided that, with the flick of a switchblade or the flash of a gun, I would make a perfectly serviceable human ATM.

So the woman started to take me around to the places where she would procure the crack. Sometimes she would buy it from street dealers who hung around certain corners and in certain doorways. She would hand over whatever money I had given her, and the dealer would produce a small baggie. A few times we went to her friends' apartments. At one of these, I watched with fascination as several young women stood in the kitchen using baking soda and boiling water to process a massive pile of powdered cocaine into crack. There were also drug dens where you could buy and use crack in one place, at least until your money ran out, which would happen quickly. The woman seemed to know every-body who ran these places, and we could walk in, make the buy, and then head off somewhere else to use.

Whoever had the drugs in these places ran the show. Crack was all anyone there cared about, all they wanted, and often if a woman was out of crack and out of cash, she would resort to selling her body for next to nothing just to stay high. When I first set foot in a crack house, I was frightened and a little disgusted. This was a far cry from passing a joint around in the upstairs room at Aunt Eloise's. Spectral figures clutching stemlike glass pipes sat hunched on the floor or on ragged furniture. Whenever I had to enter such a place, I made my visit short.

Things went on this way with the woman for weeks. I would search her out, pick her up, and we would get high. I thought of it as a mere variation in my nocturnal activities, just a little twist on my regular routine. If getting out of the condo allowed me physical distance from my problems, crack got me far enough out of my head to leave behind the depression and despair that settled over me when I was sober. With the fall semester now upon me, I knew expectations were high. I had embarrassed myself and the Kennedy School, and the only way to begin coming back from that was to show that I was undiminished by the Pamela Foster episode, to produce excellent work, and to teach with control and mastery over my subject.

I did not know if I was up for the challenge. I did know the drug use wasn't helping, but it was the only thing that stymied my depression. The previous months had been consumed by legal strategizing and exis-tential despair. Now, when I sat down to take notes on some political or social issue, my thoughts unerringly drifted back to the mess I had made. Unable to make progress on any real work, I kept returning to the thought that I was at the beginning of a steep decline from which I would not be able to return. The more entrenched this thinking became, the more I was unable to focus, the closer I perceived myself inching toward the point of no return. The enemy without—the press, my legal troubles, the management of my public profile—had been, for the time being, held at bay. Yet the effort had so depleted me that I was now as vulnerable as ever to the enemy within.

But while I was high, I didn't have to worry about any of that. Crack's effects were predictable and reliable. You go up fast, you come down fast, you take another hit and start all over. Crack has a rhythm to it that's just as much a part of the experience as the high itself. The only trouble was running out. When there were no more drugs and I had spent all the cash I had on me, I'd crash. Whatever anxieties the drugs suppressed came flooding back in, with the added "bonus" of a deep physical desire to get high again, along with the shame of knowing that what I was doing was beyond disreputable. Once the high wore off, I would drive home, enter the condo without waking Linda, who would have gone to bed hours earlier, and drink alcohol to try to wind down and quell the jitters that crack left in its wake. Eventually, when my body and brain had hit the point of exhaustion, I would fall into a restless sleep.

ONE NIGHT I PICKED UP THE WOMAN, and she directed me to a building where she said drugs could be found. I gave her $100. She told me to wait in the car, that she would be back in a few minutes. I saw her disappear through the front door. Ten minutes went by, then a half-hour, and then an hour, with no sign of the woman. This presented me with a dilemma. I could go in after her, but I did not know what awaited me on the other side of the door. Finally, I drove off empty-handed. I never saw her again.

By the time the woman disappeared, I had been ferrying her around Boston long enough to figure out how to get crack myself. There were the street dealers who skulked around on the corners, Dominican guys hanging out on Tremont Street, right on the fringe of the South End, or on Columbus Avenue, running down toward Jamaica Plain. And there were other stretches in Roxbury, Dorchester, and Mattapan where these guys could be found. They were there all hours of the night and day. If you wanted crack at 1:30 p.m. on a Sunday or 6 a.m. on a Tuesday, you could get it there. Once I knew how to spot the dealers, I would pull up, roll down my window, and hand them $20 or maybe more. They would pull a bag or two from beneath their tongue, or from inside their sock, or from a fold in their knit cap, hand it off to me, and I would be on my way.

Because I had relied on the woman to procure crack for me, and because once she procured it, we would use it together, I only ever got high while I was out at night. Now that I was buying it myself, I could use whenever and wherever I could find the space and the time. As my options opened up, what had been an interesting addition to my nocturnal repertoire soon became an obsession. That fall I was teaching only one class, and my duties were light. Ten other faculty members and I were co-teaching a large, required course for first-year students of the master in public policy program at the Kennedy School. Each of us would lecture once per semester, and we would all run our own weekly discussion section. This meant almost every week, all I had to do was be present for the lecture and then to lead my section. Besides grading papers, which wasn't all that arduous, and preparing the one lecture I would have to give that semester, all I had to worry about were office hours and the occasional faculty meeting.

Harvard was just a few minutes away from one of the spots where I would regularly buy. If I had a two o'clock meeting that would get out at three o'clock, and I knew that Linda would be attending an event at Tufts that would keep her out of the house until seven o'clock, I could leave the condo at 1:15, get cash at an ATM, drive to Jamaica Plain, buy the drugs, and get back to Harvard in plenty of time to gather my things from my office and make it to the two o'clock meeting. If the meeting ended on time, I could be home by 3:15 with almost four hours to myself to luxuriate in my own living room and get high. The smell of crack doesn't linger, and even if Linda had noticed a strange odor, she wouldn't have known what it was. Usually, though, I used it alone in my car.

If my colleagues knew something was wrong, they never said anything about it. I would cancel the occasional office hours session or class meeting, but none of the other faculty were aware of what I was doing. In my mind, nothing was wrong. I just liked getting high, that's all. If I had to cancel class once or twice, I could chalk it up to the ongoing stress I was experiencing from the Pamela Foster affair and my struggle to get work done. To all appearances, I was quietly rallying from a bad summer.

Linda may have noticed that I was gone more frequently at night, and all through the fall the tension between us persisted. Sometimes she would head to bed, and I would tell her that I planned to stay up for a while and listen to some records on the stereo. Once I was confident that she was asleep, I would slip out to buy more drugs and smoke them in my car or in the garage at home. I would leave the stereo on. If Linda happened to come down while I was out and mentioned it the next morning, I would simply tell her I went out to buy a snack and forgot to take the record off. Maybe she believed I really was out buying a bag of chips at two o'clock in the morning and maybe not. She was past the point of asking too many questions.

After a while, I realized that I could get more drugs for my dollar if I simply processed the powdered cocaine into crack myself. It's a simple procedure. All you need, besides the cocaine, is a lighter, water, baking soda, some Q-Tips, high-proof alcohol, a ceramic mug, and a piece of cheesecloth or an old T-shirt. Mix equal parts cocaine and baking soda in the mug (more baking soda than coke is fine but not vice versa) and pour a little water in to dissolve them completely. Then dip a Q-Tip or two into the high-proof alcohol, light it, and hold it under the mug. After a few moments, the water will boil. Quickly pour more room-temperature water over the boiling water. This will cause the baking soda–cocaine compound to crystallize and precipitate to the bottom of the mug. Take the piece of T-shirt, hold it tight over the top of the mug, then filter the water through it. You'll be left with a small, wet pile of crystals. Once the crack dries, it can be smoked. The key for me was always to make sure I had all the cooking supplies stocked up before I bought the coke. Once I had the drugs in hand, I would itch to start the process and get smoking as quickly as possible. I also didn't want to have to walk into a grocery store and see the look on the cashier's face as she rang up baking soda, tin foil, and a jug of water.

I had the process down, but I found I would need better cocaine than what I could buy on the street. Cooking crack filters out any impurities in the product. When I tried it with coke from the street, often there would be almost nothing left to smoke after I cooked it. Those Dominicans on Tremont sold stuff that, in an effort to increase their profits, they cut and cut again, until there were hardly any real drugs in the little bags of white powder they were handing off. They didn't care if a disappointed customer came back or not. Cocaine was so popular in the 1980s that there would always be another new customer who heard Tremont was the place to buy. This ready supply of new customers disincentivized the dealers from selling a better product than their competitors across town. So what if people were getting ripped off? What were they going to do, complain to the Better Business Bureau?

As an economist, I understood that to get a better-quality product, I needed dealers who wanted repeat customers and thus had an interest in selling the purest cocaine they could find. And I located one, living in a nice corner apartment with big bay windows and a brick stairwell. He didn't operate on the street. He relied on a network of regular customers who were willing to pay a premium for better drugs. These were the type of people who, like me, would take their business elsewhere if the quality dipped. While it wasn't as convenient as driving by and doing the trans-action out of my car window, it was worth the trouble. I could get more crack from $50 of his coke than I could from $100 of those other guys'.

Now that I had the right supplier and I knew how to make my drug of choice myself, I could do it anywhere. I kept the necessary materials in my car, where I would cook and smoke the crack if I didn't have enough time alone at home. Often, I was driving around Boston in what was essentially a makeshift mobile drug lab.

Occasionally, if I felt like I wanted more space than my car could offer, I would rent a motel room. There I would cook up the drugs and smoke them at my leisure. I would bring some beer or liquor and watch pornography I had rented on the way. I found that autoeroticism only increased the pleasure I could derive from the crack, and those two practices—smoking and masturbation—soon became bound up with each other. Like crack itself, the combination of sexual spectacle and powerful drugs crystallized into a compound that, once I tasted it, became my preferred mode of consumption. Whatever pleasure I used to derive from the ego trip of seduction was now displaced by ecstasy on demand, enjoyed in the privacy of a sordid motel room, with no other parties present to distract me from the only thing I then cared about.

The problem was, as ever, the comedown. Sitting alone in my car and staring at my homemade crack pipe as the high wore off was bleak. Sobering up and surveying the stack of orange VHS cases, the lurid scene playing out on the TV, the mess of my cooking area, the empty bottles, and the ashes, it was impossible not to reflect on how depraved this part of my life had become. If I had hit my daily ATM withdrawal limit of $300, I would have to force myself to clean the mess and go home. But if I had any cash left or could get my hands on more, there was no question. I was going to go out, buy a bag, and head straight back to the motel.

ALL THAT FALL, I KEPT UP THE ROUTINE. If I wasn't smoking crack, I was looking at my watch, wondering how long it would be until I could get free of whatever tedious obligation ensnared me and go out to smoke again. Crack wasn't a distraction from my life. The opposite was the case. I was barely sleeping or eating, grabbing just enough rest to enable myself to get up and start the process of subterfuge, copping, and using all over again. There was no doubt in my mind that Linda thought I was having another affair and, in a way, I was. Better that she thought it was another woman with whom I was enthralled than that she knew the truth.

Amazingly, despite this exhausting merry-go-round, I somehow managed to perform the role of Glenn Loury, academic economist and social critic. After the Pamela Foster affair, I had serious doubts as to whether I'd ever receive another invitation to speak anywhere publicly again. So when I got a call asking me to come to the University of California, Davis, to deliver a lecture (entitled "On the Profitability of Interruptible Supply," about the strategic use of oil embargoes), I was elated. If I was still legitimate in my peers' eyes, I could cling to legitimacy in my own.

The night before my flight out to Sacramento, I cooked up a batch to take with me. Before I entered the airport, I slid it into my shoe, beneath the sole of my foot. Even if airport security pulled me aside, I knew they wouldn't check there. Who could imagine being asked to take your shoes off at the airport? I boarded the plane without incident. At Davis, I delivered a successful lecture, attended the dinner afterward, and the next day I headed back home. I still had the crack with me, wanting to save it as a reward for a job well done. Aboard the plane, I went to the bathroom, locked the door, removed the crack from my shoe, unscrewed the smoke detector on the ceiling, and lit up at thirty thousand feet.

Not long after, I had a conference to attend in Florida. I had an 8:00 a.m. flight, so at 5:00 a.m., I kissed Linda goodbye and drove directly to Tremont Street to buy a small stash to take with me. All those unscheduled evening hours after the panels and the cocktail receptions and the dinners would need to be filled, so I bought three bags off a Dominican guy leaning in a doorway and tucked them into my sock. I had parked my car a couple blocks away, and as I reached out to grab the door handle, I heard, "Kick it in! Crack or cash! I don't care which! I don't want to have to shoot you."

I turned to see a skinny, desperate looking man standing a few feet away from me. He had his hand inside his jacket and looked to be clutching something. It might have been a gun. Then again, he might have been bluffing. For a moment I considered calling his bluff by refusing him, and then I remembered that I had three bags. I bent over, pulled one of them out of my sock and threw it at his feet. The man stooped to retrieve it, and I got in the car and sped away. As I made my way toward the airport, I thought about how clever I was to get out of that situation with most of my stash. It did not occur to me to think about how clever I had been to get myself into that situation to begin with.

Close calls abounded that fall. One weekend afternoon, Linda and I were hanging out at home, and I felt the urge to get high. I excused myself, telling her that I had forgotten there was something I had to take care of at work. Smoking in my car in broad daylight wasn't an option, so I headed into my office at the Kennedy School. The place would be empty on a late-semester weekend afternoon, and if Linda called my office looking for me, I'd be right there to answer.

I shoved my gear and a towel I kept in my car into my attaché case and went in. Sure enough, no one was around. I entered my office and stuffed the towel around the bottom of the door to ensure that, if anybody did happen by, they wouldn't see my light on. I proceeded to smoke. The place was dead silent. I must have been concentrating on setting up my next round, because by the time I heard the footsteps echoing through the hallway, they were almost at my door. When I noticed them, I froze. The footsteps stopped for a moment, and I heard a knock. I held my breath. Someone was standing right outside my office, not ten feet from where I was sitting, with all the incriminating evidence strewn across the desk in front of me. Whoever they were, they must have heard me. I waited.

After a moment, I heard a key slide into the lock of the door next to mine. That was Tom Schelling's office. He was on the other side of the wall, and he knew (or thought he knew) that I was in. Then my office phone rang. I let it go, not daring even to move. Through the wall, I heard the rattle of Tom's phone being set back into its receiver. Just a few months ago, running into Tom on a weekend afternoon when it was just the two of us would have been a delight. He was a mentor to me, practically a father figure. I couldn't name anyone I admired more. A pipe, a lighter, and a bag of crack were sitting on my desk, a faint cloud of smoke hung in the air, and I was high as a kite. Under no circumstances could I allow Tom any proof that I was there.

Through the wall, I heard Tom puttering around his office, shuffling through papers and books. With the pipe sitting right in front of me, the temptation to take another hit was overwhelming, but I couldn't risk it. Couldn't he just finish his business and leave? Who went into the office on a weekend, anyway? Suppose he imagined that I was in here and in some sort of distress that was preventing me from answering the phone. Suppose he called security and they came and open my door. What would I do then?

After forty-five minutes or so, the shuffling stopped, and I heard his door open and close. His footsteps receded down the hall. When I was sure he was gone, I finished off the rest of the crack, packed up, and got out of there as quickly as I could.

Richard John Neuhaus had told me you're either a moral leader or you're not. I had to choose. I didn't know if I had yet made such a choice, or even how it could be made. But if you had asked me to choose between living as I would have others live and my next hit, I could have told you in a second which of those alternatives I would take.

Sixteen

I n my sober moments that fall, I had been playing around with an
idea that grew out of my conversations with Albert Hirschman at
the Institute for Advanced Study in Princeton two years earlier. It
seemed simple at first, hardly worth dwelling on. In order to communicate effectively in public, we often must speak indirectly. Everyone knows
this. Everyone does it. There are certain speech acts that one cannot
utter overtly in public without risking social opprobrium or worse. The
specific views that draw sanction when openly expressed are historically
contingent, shifting and changing with the social and political development of a given society. To cite an extreme example, openly declaring
the supremacy of the white race was a pretty ordinary thing to do in the
American South of the 1850s. By 1987, you could ruin your entire life
by saying such a thing in public.

It's probably a good thing that a belief so noxious is now considered
so wrongheaded that it's largely kept out of public discourse. But there
are people who still believe it, even if they won't risk the consequences
of saying so out loud. And there are other, far more common, far less
abhorrent positions that, were they stated openly, would put the speaker's reputation and social standing at risk. As I came to reflect on this
fact, its direct implication became clear to me. If one wants to speak

publicly, whether in the political sphere or in ordinary conversation, a certain amount of self-censorship is often required.

For example, a politician wishing to convey to his white constituency that he is against affirmative action would not say, "Too many unqualified black students attend our universities," even if that is what he and his constituents all believe. Why not? Because, even if it could be demonstrated that, as a matter of fact, there really are too many unqualified black college students, saying so in those terms sounds racist. The politician and his constituents may hold racist views or they may not. Whatever the case, none of them wants to be *perceived* as a racist. So the politician might say something like, "I believe admission to our nation's top universities should be merit based." This sounds almost meaningless on its surface but signals to the constituents that the politician is on the same page as they are when it comes to affirmative action, while allowing all parties to plausibly deny that their views have anything at all to do with racism, whether that is actually the case or not.

Most Americans, even those with minimal political awareness, will understand what is being communicated in the latter statement. What interested me was not so much *what* such statements mean but *how* they convey meaning, and what conditions have to be met for speakers to navigate two conflicting imperatives: to give voice to ideas that some find disreputable, but to do so in such a manner as to remain reputable themselves. The more I thought about the interplay of communication and public perception, the more complicated even seemingly ordinary public statements and conversations appeared. It occurred to me that in such a situation, which is our ever-present situation, there is no such thing as truly free speech.

I started paying attention when I heard public figures engaging in this sort of balancing act. The examples quickly became too numerous to keep track of. We were in the early stages then of what came to be known as the political correctness debates, when not only ideas but the language used to describe ideas could become a source of major, partisan political disputes. Whatever one thought about black people, using the term *Negro* to describe them (us) was now considered not simply old-fashioned but evidence that the speaker harbored prejudiced views. (Never mind that *Negro*—with a capital N—originally became common parlance as a more dignified alternative to terms like *colored*. Plus ça change.) The political left had come to regard using PC terminology as a meaningful act in itself, while the right thought that demands to implement PC terminology were merely a veiled attempt to censor their substantive views.

With all this in mind, I began crafting the beginnings of a theory of self-censorship and political correctness. I hadn't written any of it down in formal prose. I took notes here and there, outlining loosely connected observations, analyses of pertinent examples, and theoretical lines of argument. This was different from anything I had ever worked on; it was more sociolinguistics than economics. Though my approach was influenced by the insights of game theory, this was not shaping up to be a technical economics paper. Nor did it have the makings of a magazine piece. It was too theoretical and abstract for that. It was indebted to the sui generis work of economists like Tom Schelling and Albert Hirschman, and to the writings of the great sociologist Erving Goffman, all of whom were deeply attuned to the delicate entanglement of individual psychology, strategy, and group behavior. I knew I was onto something interesting.

Near the end of the semester, my turn came to present a lecture in the course I was co-teaching. Perhaps if I had not been spending so much of my time either high or trying to find ways to get high, I would have cobbled my notes together into a piece of prose fit for recitation before the class. As it turned out, my lack of preparation actually stood me in good stead. I stepped up to the lectern at the front of a hall full of students and a row filled with distinguished colleagues like Robert Reich (who would go on to become secretary of labor under Bill Clinton) and the brilliant public policy analyst, Mark Kleiman. At the start of the lecture, I would glance down at my notes once in a while. But as I continued to talk, I realized I didn't need notes at all. In that moment there seemed to be no barrier between my brain and my tongue, and in talking through the ideas I had been mulling over, it became apparent, even as I was speaking, that I actually had a fully formed argument. It was rigorously thought out, as I had been working on it for months, but also spontaneous, as I had never before actually articulated the argument aloud in a sustained fashion.

The novelty of the argument must have come through, because when I concluded, the roof came off the place. The entire hall applauded enthusiastically. Afterward, my co-teachers gushed about the lecture, telling me how brilliant it was, that this was something I absolutely had to write up and publish. I felt both pride and relief. Even as one part of my double life was consuming the other, I was still able to dazzle. Perhaps I just needed to find the right balance between getting high and pursuing my intellectual interests.

A few days later, I got arrested. Again.

———

I WAS CRUISING THROUGH THE SOUTH END in the early evening, high and looking to get higher. I had a little cocaine, but I still had some money in my pocket, so I was looking around for more. My car was sitting on the side of the road when I saw the police cruiser pull up behind me. This was not good. But I told myself maybe they were just pulling over for some unrelated reason. I acted as though nothing was wrong and pulled back onto the road, hoping they'd just let me drive away.

When the cruiser's lights began flashing, I knew I was in trouble. As I pulled over to the side of the road, I leaned back and tried to hide the coke and marijuana I had on me in the back seat. I was driving a late-model Saab and was reasonably well dressed. Maybe my glasses would lend me a studious enough air that the cops would let me go without asking too many questions.

When one of the officers approached the window, he asked why I had been parked at the side of the road in the first place. If I said "no reason" or "none of your business," the encounter could have turned hostile. So I told him something that sounded plausible enough but not so bad that he would want to waste his time bringing me in and dealing with the paperwork.

"I'm just looking for some girls," I said.

My gambit failed. I stood by the side of the road, watching as he rooted around my car. When he moved to the back seat, I knew I was sunk. He came up with the drugs and my homemade pipe in his hand. Part of me clung to the hope that he might let me go. Obviously, I wasn't a dealer or a gangster. And the amount of drugs I had on me was very small.

After he and his partner conferred, they radioed into the station to let them know who they had. Then they put the cuffs on me, read me my rights, and put me in the back of the squad car. On the way to the station, one of them joked that he didn't know what was more dangerous, the girls or the crack. We were in the midst of two epidemics, after all: crack and AIDS. I supposed he was trying to be my "buddy," buttering me up so that I would make things easier on him, because then I would be less likely to resist. That was almost as insulting as the cuffs.

After I was booked, I called Marty. While he was on his way to get me out, I sat in a cell in the back of the police station, growing increasingly nervous. The crack I had smoked and the adrenaline from the arrest were both wearing off, and panic overtook me. I was, however temporarily, *behind bars*. There was no way to avoid what was coming, nor would I be able to avoid telling Linda about how I had ended up in this mess. I would have to come clean with her, a prospect I dreaded nearly as much as I feared the legal consequences of having been caught with a controlled substance.

A COUPLE OF DAYS AFTER THE ARREST, the story broke. Once again, my name was in the Boston papers and, again, the story got picked up nationally. I had been lying to the police when I said that I was looking for women, but the cops leaked that I'd made that statement and the news services reported it as the truth. So now, in the eyes of the public, I had probably beaten up my mistress, then I had gotten busted with a car full of drugs while trying to solicit sex. My colleagues could eventually excuse an affair with a younger woman as a misstep, but this was some-thing else. Robert Reich was quoted in one of the stories. When asked if he had any idea that I was using drugs, he said that as far as he knew, nobody had any idea. Recalling the lecture on self-censorship that he'd witnessed just a couple of days before my arrest, he said, "I had never seen Glenn so brilliant and lucid." I hoped he didn't think my performance was chemically enhanced—I was stone sober!

Still, I knew this revelation would have everyone who knew me thinking back on any interaction we had in the months since I had started using. "Glenn and I had that long talk a few months back. Had he been high?" "I saw a little sweat on Glenn's brow when I ran into him on the quad back in September. Sure, it was a warm day. But maybe he was high." The truth is that none of my colleagues ever saw me under the influence of crack. I never attended meetings or taught while I was smoking. If I had been high, they would have known something was off right then and there. There would have been no need for speculation.

Calls started coming in from friends. If they had been concerned about my mental state after the Pamela Foster affair, now they were really alarmed. The Glenn Loury they knew did not seem like the kind of guy who could have two run-ins with the police in the space of seven months, and for such sordid offenses. But then the Glenn Loury they knew didn't spend his time hanging out in neighborhoods they didn't even like to drive through. The Glenn Loury they knew flew around the world delivering invited lectures at prestigious universities and sat on advisory boards and worked as a sought-after consultant. He didn't prowl around Mattapan looking to buy hard drugs off the hoodlums on the corner, at the risk of being robbed, or worse.

I tried to avoid contact with other people as much as possible, but I had to talk to Marty Gideonse. He was again acting as my legal representation, and again he was as much a sympathetic sounding board as he was a lawyer. He was extremely worried, not so much that I would end up in prison but that I would self-destruct. I told him that I would be okay, that I would straighten out. Marty had gotten the court to agree to let me go through a drug deferral program in lieu of a more punitive sentence. If I could complete some number of hours of counseling, the court would consider the matter closed. If I got caught with drugs again or stopped attending my counseling sessions, I'd be going to jail.

That was a good deal for an addict. But the way I saw it, I wasn't an addict. I just liked getting high. There were plenty of respectable people I knew who drank alcohol to excess on a daily basis, and none of them had to go through the infantilizing process I was now enduring. It just happened that my drug of choice was illegal. I broke the law, granted. I knew there would have to be consequences. But addiction counseling? That was for drunks, junkies, and crackheads. I was a respected Harvard professor. I would go to the sessions to remain a free man, but not because I thought I needed them.

In the state of Massachusetts, if you received three traffic tickets for moving violations within a twelve-month period, you had to attend a six-hour driver's education class to avoid having your license suspended. I had been ordered to attend that class more than once. The instructors attempt to get to the root of the problem, to encourage the "students" to think about the behavior and habits of mind that lead to reckless driving. But I didn't think of myself as a bad driver, and I doubt anybody else in the class truly thought of themselves as bad drivers, either. It was just a hoop you had to jump through to continue going about your business. That was exactly how I thought about my drug counseling sessions, too.

The lessons the counselor tried to impart may have applied to addicts. Not being an addict, I thought, I had little or nothing to learn from them. I just had to be present and feign engagement in order to ensure the counselor didn't report back to the courts that I had skipped out on my obligation.

And so, notwithstanding the enormous risk I was taking, I continued using. I continued sneaking around, buying crack, and smoking it whenever I could get away for long enough to enjoy it. Even if I could not admit to myself that I had a problem, I could not ignore the obvious fact that this behavior was now crazier than ever. The sane thing to do would be to stop, if only because the courts would not have mercy on me if I was caught again. I told myself that I would stop, told myself that I just wanted one more hit. But to no avail. If I woke up in the morning and resolved not to use that day, I found that I was thinking about crack by noon. And once I started thinking about it, I started planning how I would go about getting it.

One evening, I blew off my scheduled counseling session and bought some cocaine instead. Later that night, I went down to our garage on the lower level of the condo. I sat in the dark in the back seat of my car smoking. Suddenly, as I was holding the lighter to the pipe, Linda appeared in the entryway. She must have seen the lighter's flame hovering in the blackness of the garage. She fell to her knees and began banging her fist on the floor and sobbing. "Oh God! Our life is over! This is the end!"

When I had made my way home after my arrest and sat Linda down for yet another confession, she saw how close to the edge I was. With her head in her hands, she told me that if I did not stop using, it would destroy us. She didn't want the marriage to end. She wanted things between us to be good, to be solid. Hadn't we once been in sync with each other? For her, agreeing to the court-ordered outpatient treatment was a step in the right direction. I'm not sure whether she truly believed it would help me or not. But every time I left the house to attend my drug treatment sessions, she could point to some concrete measure that was being taken toward the reestablishment of something like normality. It allowed her to believe that I was getting better.

Around this time, a friend told her, "Glenn's precocious. If other guys have their midlife crises in their forties, Glenn's going to have his in his thirties." A crisis begins and ends, and perhaps believing that I was going through a phase—an extreme phase, but a phase nonetheless—convinced Linda there was a natural expiration date on this behavior. Seeing me hunched over in the dark, hiding away from her in the home we made together, punctured her illusions and destroyed whatever ideas she had about my supposed sobriety. My problem was much worse than I had let on. Left unchecked, it might never end, short of my demise. Addiction was alien to Linda's pragmatism and self-discipline. This was a problem she could not truly comprehend, and it was rapidly consuming the life we had built.

I rushed over and tried to console her.

"No, it's okay, baby. It's going to be fine. I'm going to stop," I told her. In that moment, I may have even believed it myself.

EVEN AFTER GETTING CAUGHT BY LINDA, I continued using. I did not know how to stop. And I was once again robbed at gunpoint, this time while I was looking to buy some marijuana. I approached a couple guys on the sidewalk, who told me to follow them down an alley. As we turned off the street, I saw an older black man sitting on a front stoop. He gave me a nod as I passed by. The alley opened up into a lot, in which an old Volkswagen bus sat up on cinder blocks. It looked like it was serving as someone's home. One of the guys stood between me and the street and the other one climbed into the bus, supposedly to get the weed. After a moment, the roof hatch of the bus popped open, and the guy emerged holding an enormous gun that looked like it could put a hole in a brick wall. He cocked the weapon, and I could hear metal click on metal.

"Kick it in, you punk-ass bitch!"

He was pointing the gun at the ground, not at me. At least not yet. My wallet was in my back pocket, but I had slid the money I intended to spend on the weed into my sock. I took the cash out of my sock and threw it on the ground. Had the guy demanded my wallet, which contained several hundred dollars more, I surely would have kicked that in, as well. But I wasn't going to hang around and see if they wanted anything else. As I passed by the second man, he slapped me on the back of the head.

"If you come back here with the cops," he said, "we'll find you and blow your fucking head off."

As I walked briskly away from that scene, I passed the older man still sitting on the stoop. He just looked at me and nodded his head again, knowingly, as though he had seen this routine play out a dozen times before, which I reckon he probably had.

That was the second time I had my life threatened over drugs. But not even that stopped me. I went on like this for weeks, continuing my routine of copping, cooking, and smoking, all while hiding from Linda, avoiding my friends and colleagues, and hoping I wouldn't get busted again.

The breaking point finally came at ten o'clock on a Saturday morning in mid-January. I was sitting in my car in a Burger King parking lot. I had been out all night smoking crack. I tried to pull out cash from an ATM to buy more, but I had reached my daily withdrawal limit, which didn't reset until noon. With no more drugs and no way to get any, I was coming down. In the gray morning light, my nerves shot, I was no longer able to hold my disgust for myself at bay. The constant need for drugs, the constant lack of sleep, the exhausting cycle of getting high, coming down, and concealing all of it was breaking me. Guilt and shame seeped into me—this was the blind alley into which all my cleverness had led me. Yet the need for another hit was as strong as it had ever been. If I could have gotten my hands on a twenty-dollar bill, I knew I would have taken it straight to the nearest dealer. My mind was just clear enough to recognize that as the thought of an insane person. Not having anything more than some loose change in my pocket, I went to the payphone by the Burger King and called Linda.

"Baby, I didn't make it," is how I opened the conversation. I told her I just could not stop. I needed help. I didn't know what was going on anymore or what I was doing. She begged me to call the clinic where I had been attending my outpatient counseling sessions and tell them what I had told her. I didn't want to, but I had no choice. Maybe, she said, they could offer me some guidance. Maybe I could set up an appointment for the following Monday.

Whoever picked up the phone at the Appleton Outpatient Clinic was adamant. After consulting my file, she insisted: I was to come in right then. "Do not go home. Do not make any stops. If you're able to drive, hang up the phone, get in your car, and come directly here. Someone will be waiting for you out front."

I thought about going home to sleep it off. But then I would have to lie to Linda about what the person at the clinic had said, and I just did not have the energy to fabricate yet another story. Besides, I knew that I'd use again, given the opportunity. So I hung up the phone, got in my car, and drove to the clinic.

THE APPLETON OUTPATIENT CLINIC was housed in McLean Hospital. Even before my contact with Appleton, I knew of McLean by reputation. It was and is a state-of-the-art center for the treatment and study of mental illness. When I presented myself to the orderly waiting for me, he brought me inside. One of Appleton's counselors strongly suggested that I submit myself for inpatient treatment, a program where I would formally agree to allow them to keep me on a locked ward for several weeks while I detoxed and began an intensive recovery regimen. I would have to sign a waiver agreeing that they could hold me there even if I later tried to leave. If you walk out of here today, they told me, you're going to be using again in no time. I was in no state to disagree with their analysis. I signed the papers and submitted myself to the care of the institution.

In my first days at McLean, I was kept mostly in isolation, fed well, humored by the staff, and given physical examinations. I was allowed no contact with anyone from outside the hospital, including Linda, though she knew what was happening. She had apparently dropped off some clean clothes for me. I talked with counselors and therapists who lectured about the neurochemical processes that occurred in my brain when I smoked crack and explained what was happening now that I had abruptly stopped. Knowing what was going on inside of me at the molecular level would have been interesting if I had been in the frame of mind to appreciate the information, but it did little to quell the ravenous cravings I felt. My body was urging me to get up, walk it out the front door, and get it down to Tremont Street where it would find those Dominican guys and the only thing that would give it relief.

Once the first waves of withdrawal passed, the tension eased a little, and I was able to consider my situation. I was now in a mental hospital and would remain here for at least the next month. I would be monitored by hospital staff and attend several addiction counseling sessions a day, most of them in a group setting, and all of them overseen by a professional whose job it was to help ensure that I never smoke crack again. The Appleton House was nice enough, all things considered. But I wouldn't say that it was comfortable. The fluorescent lighting and tiled floors and locked exits served as constant reminders that this was not a vacation spot. I may not have been in jail, but neither was I free to go.

Most of my time would be spent among my fellow patients. I would learn that McLean charged $500 per day for their inpatient treatment, which was covered by my insurance. There were businessmen whose financial success had enabled their habits, suburban housewives whose glass of wine with dinner had become a bottle or two, an heir to a famous Canadian liquor fortune who bragged constantly about his daddy's cars and homes and insisted that the rules didn't apply to him. There were others who I imagined qualified for free care. Some clearly had nothing or less when they walked (or were wheeled) through McLean's doors. Some patients stumbled around like automata, their eyes sunken, their moods unpredictable, and their figures skeletal.

Spoiled rich kid or drug-addled zombie or Harvard professor, in the eyes of the hospital staff, we were all the same. It didn't matter that I had a similar educational pedigree as some of the doctors treating me. Any attempt I made to relate to them on that level was politely but firmly rebuffed. This wasn't the kind of hospital you ended up in by happenstance, maybe because you slipped on some ice and broke your arm and needed to get patched up. At bottom, the same thing had brought all of us patients here, and it wasn't an accident. It was a fact about us. We were all addicts.

ONCE MY HEAD CLEARED, my days at McLean were saturated by boredom and punctuated by flashes of indignation. I was still in denial about the truth of my condition. Whatever I said to the staff during our counseling sessions, I didn't believe that I belonged there. The bland food, the narrow bed, the loads of dirty and clean laundry Linda would ferry between our house and the hospital, the endless therapy sessions, all of them were just more hoops to jump through, more boxes to check so that I could go home and get on with my life. Whatever the staff may have thought, I wasn't like these other patients. Maybe they had some real problems to deal with. Maybe they drank vodka in secret or popped pills because they didn't have any other way to fill their days. Well, I had plenty to do. The drugs were a hindrance, no doubt, and so was all this therapy. In my idleness, I began theorizing about my own situation and offering my analyses of the incentive structures of the institution during counseling sessions. But whenever I began unspooling one of these arguments, the counselor would invariably shut me down. "You've got too much going on in your head. Keep the focus on yourself. Try being still." It seemed to me that being still and talking about myself was pretty much all I was doing.

Even as I was bored and annoyed by what I took to be the platitudes and navel-gazing of therapy, I was also afraid. I thought about smoking crack every single day, and I was terrified that, if I was let out, I would go straight back to Tremont Street. While I chafed at the constraints on my freedom, I had to acknowledge that I was not wholly in control of myself. Uncle Moonie kicked heroin cold turkey. He didn't need counseling. He gritted his teeth and pushed through it. I thought of my father. With his superhuman willpower and icy determination, he would never have gotten himself into this situation in the first place. But if he had, if he somehow had slipped up, he would have seen it as his duty to fix the problem himself. Somehow, I knew that I would not be able to demonstrate the same resolve. I needed help, even if I didn't want to admit it.

I did eventually find ways to fill the hours between counseling sessions, dispiriting meals, and sleep. The communal room in the place had a piano. Linda was a dedicated pianist, and we had a small Steinway upright in our home. I would sometimes sit on the bench and plunk around. My attempt to learn the saxophone back in Michigan was a failure, but I found I had a knack for the piano. Although I'd never taken lessons, I could pick up the chord changes in new tunes pretty easily. I got good enough that I could eventually play with some finesse and feel for the instrument. So I would sit in the communal room and play the handful of songs I knew, voicing the melody in my right hand and blocking out chords with my left. I was at least good enough that no one begged me to stop!

I also had visitors, who were permitted on weekends and during a two-hour window after dinner, three nights during the week. Marty Gideonse, good man that he was, would stop in to see me from time to time. Occasionally, he would have something to tell me involving legal matters, but mostly he just wanted to make sure I was doing okay.

I confided in him that I didn't know if my marriage would survive this latest debacle. He had joked about guys who get caught cheating with their mistresses ending up drunk and alone in seedy motel rooms. Now he saw that I had gotten myself someplace worse. He had been right: I was lucky to have a woman like Linda, who would stand by me through all this. She wouldn't leave me while I was in such a delicate state. She loved me despite what I had done. She called or visited almost every day. But after I kicked the habit, after I was released and showed myself to be stable, would love be enough? Or would she want to wash her hands of me? I just didn't know.

After Linda, my most frequent visitor was Tom Schelling. He would drop by every week without fail to fill me in on what was going on at Harvard, to tell me about what he was working on, or just to talk. Tom happened to be running a small program at the Kennedy School dedicated to the study of smoking behavior, so he was fascinated by even the little details I would feed him about addiction treatments and the inner workings of McLean. Tom wanted to make sure I knew he was there for me, that he wasn't writing me off. He was a true friend, but I also suspected that he was once again blaming himself for my predicament. He felt that he had inadvertently put me in a tough position when I first came to Harvard and could not navigate my dual roles in economics and Afro-American Studies. Maybe if he had never persuaded me to come to Harvard, I wouldn't have started off down the path that led me to a locked psych ward. The idea that Tom was in any way responsible for my predicament was absurd, of course. If he had been able to look at the situation objectively, he would have seen that. But he cared about me, a lot, and I could tell he couldn't quite shake the feeling that he was somehow at fault.

Perhaps he also felt that, if things had worked out differently, he might have ended up in a place like McLean himself. Tom was a drinker. That was well known. At the Kennedy School, he would habitually have two beers with his lunch. He made no effort to disguise it. He would sit there in the restaurant, happily chatting away with his lunchtime companions, sipping his drinks the whole time. This was true throughout the year, except for the month of January. In January, as he made sure everyone knew, Thomas Schelling would abstain from alcohol entirely. I don't think anyone knew for sure why he did this: Was it to demonstrate to others that he didn't *need* to drink, or to demonstrate that to himself? It was one of those things people knew about but also knew not to ask too much about.

During one of his visits, Tom confided something to me. One night, years before I came to Harvard, he had one too many and got behind the wheel. He was driving erratically, and the police got involved. It wasn't the first time. While he was vague about the details, it was serious enough that he had been arrested. Had it come out in public that this renowned economist, a pillar of Harvard's intellectual community and an advisor to the military on matters of the highest sensitivity, had been picked up for drunk driving, it could have badly damaged him. He knew he had lost control that night, and that someone could have gotten injured or worse. But it never came out. I'm not sure why, and Tom never explained. I suspected that, through some series of backstage machinations, Harvard had made sure the story didn't get into the papers. My own misbehavior was so egregious that no such cover was available to me.

My crack cocaine binges and Tom's driving under the influence were hardly equivalent offenses. Mine seemed much worse. But I appreciated that Tom wanted me to know I was not alone, that he understood what I was going through. Though Tom was a staunch atheist, I could still imagine him looking at me sitting there, my life balancing on a knife's edge, and thinking to himself, "There but for the grace of God go I." But if God's grace or fate or mere happenstance had kept Tom out of trouble, it was of no help to me just then. For the time being, I wasn't going anywhere.

Seventeen

I spent five weeks in McLean that winter and into the spring of 1988. I went to the counseling sessions, jumped through the hoops, and eventually I began to feel more confident in my sobriety. I had not stopped thinking about using, but the cravings were less frequent and less powerful. It was time, really time, to get back to my life and to start rebuilding what I could. After the counselors at McLean agreed that I was stable enough to leave inpatient treatment, I checked myself into what they called a three-quarter house: an old building on the hospital's grounds that had been converted into a group home. It was an arrangement halfway between a halfway house and home. Residents were free to come and go, but we were all required to attend a daily 6:00 p.m. check-in meeting where we would share our feelings and whatever challenges we were facing. Seven others were living there. All of us were former Appleton patients. We had our own rooms, but we were encouraged to spend time around each other in the communal living area and kitchen whenever we weren't sleeping or out at work. Of course, it was strictly forbidden to bring any kind of addictive substance onto the premises.

Things started out well enough. I relished having most of my freedom back. Slowly, I started to reconnect with friends and turn my attention back to work. But after about three weeks, I relapsed. One afternoon,

I made my way down to one of my old corners and copped. There was no inciting incident. I just realized that it was something I could do, so when those familiar cravings came, I did it. The next day during our group meeting, as my fellow residents went around the room, I felt awful. These meetings required trust and honesty from all involved. People were baring their souls, talking about parts of their life that even some of their closest friends didn't know about, divulging how tormented they were by the decisions they had made. Listening to all that and knowing that I had broken the house's most important rule was too much. When my turn came to speak, I fessed up, admitting that I had gone out and gotten high. As soon as I finished talking, one of the people who ran the place told me to pack my things and leave immediately.

I didn't take it personally. The people in charge of the house had to protect the sobriety of the residents. We were all as fragile as could be. Anything or nothing could trigger a relapse. If another resident even suspected that I was using, it could make them want to go out and get high, too. We were all still addicts, and an addict's mind could seize on any rationalization for going back to his drug of choice. If the thought "I could go get high" creeps into an addict's mind, it can easily become "I should go get high," and soon enough, before he even realizes what's happening, he's on his way out the door. What I didn't tell anyone was just how irresponsibly I had acted. The night before that final meeting, I had stuffed a towel under my door and smoked crack inside the facility. If another resident had caught a whiff of it, they could easily have been triggered and gone right back to using themselves. It was a terrible thing to have done, a betrayal of the trust these people had put in me. The shame was too much. I couldn't admit to it.

What was I doing to myself? Why was I doing it? And how could I stop? The truth of the matter was, I had no idea. Awash in self-contempt, I began, for the first time since my drug arrest, to ponder these questions seriously. The handwriting on the wall was becoming harder and harder to ignore. I was worse off than I thought—much worse. I was an addict, plain and simple, and my drug of choice was notoriously hard to shake and as easy to buy as fast food. Even after a month-long hospital stint, I still couldn't trust myself not to use it. I came to see that regarding the treatment regimen at McLean as a long, complicated set of formalities was a monumental mistake. Sure, I chafed at their insistence that my degrees and accomplishments meant nothing, that, despite my intelligence, I was just like all the other patients there. But it was becoming clear that, if I could not stay sober, that brain power did me little good. It could even be a hindrance, as a stranger had told me one night after hearing me share at an AA meeting. He said that my intelligence might mean I was more in need of help than the average person, because the same abilities that enabled me to solve complex equations could be used to rationalize getting high again. I'd never thought about it quite that way before. I finally had to admit to myself, in the wake of the relapse, that I needed help; that I needed protection from myself; that I couldn't think or talk my way out of the mess I'd gotten myself into. My dad's tale about Adlert's visit on the night of my birth began to haunt me: "Brilliance without discipline is just not good enough." I came to see that pride and a lack of discipline had been my worst enemies.

My insurance plan gave me sixty days of inpatient treatment, and I still had just over three weeks left. I went back to the inpatient clinic at McLean and told them everything. They readmitted me and began the detox process all over again. Linda took the news stoically. We had resumed conjugal visitations after my move to the three-quarter house, and we had rekindled the tenderness and warmth that had cooled over the last year. But my relapse put a damper on all that. It seemed I was back to square one in the recovery process. Once again, the narrow beds, boring group sessions, and Linda shuttling laundry to and fro. Once again, affluent addicts and semicomatose lifers. Once again, collective confessionals modeled on Alcoholics Anonymous meetings. This time it was different, though. This time I was paying attention. This time, I told myself, I'd do it right. I sensed that I might not get another shot. I was a hair's breadth away from permanent residency on the other side of the line.

I also had a new reason to straighten myself out: Linda was pregnant! Despite all that had been happening in the last years, we had been trying without success to have a child. Linda had fibroids, which made it difficult for her to conceive. But she had corrective surgery, and in the few weeks that I was out of the Appleton Clinic at McLean something clicked. She was joyous, and I was happy, too. But contemplating the birth of my child also gave me a jolt of anxiety. If I could not stop using drugs, I would be worse than useless as a father and partner. I wanted to get clean for myself, Linda, and our unborn child, and the due date served as a hard deadline, which added pressure to my recovery. My record as a father had thus far been less than sterling. I was estranged from my daughters, Lisa and Tamara. I checked in with them regularly but saw them infrequently. They had been skeptical of Linda at first, but she hung in there and continued to reach out to them. With time, she won them over. Auntie Eloise had warned me to shower my girls with love and affection, even from a distance. I loved them intensely, but I knew I wasn't showing it enough, and now I had my hands full with recovery. Alden was still a blank space in my life. I'd had no contact with him at all, and I made no effort to get in touch. I knew nothing about the kind of man he was becoming. This time, I told myself, things would be different. I was determined to be present for this child.

The people who ran McLean would occasionally invite religious leaders to participate in group sessions. A priest, minister, or rabbi would encourage us patients to speak about spiritual issues that may have been troubling us. The second step in the recovery program of Alcoholics Anonymous involves believing in a "higher power," which can restore you to sanity, and the third step involves deciding to turn yourself over to the care of that higher power. AA is purposefully vague about what higher power means. It needn't be religious, though many people think of it that way. I had always had trouble with the concept. Religion had never held much sway over me, despite attending the Bethel AME Church in Chicago when I was young. I suppose I believed in some kind of God, but because of my aunt Eloise's role in various church activities, I'd seen enough of their inner workings to know that, often enough, their leaders were some of the biggest sinners and most blatant hypocrites you'd ever meet.

One day near the end of my first stretch at McLean, a couple of weeks before Easter, Sarah, a woman from the Charles Street AME Church, came in to lead the group. Afterward, I confessed to her my reservations about the spiritual dimension of recovery. I could not see my way to committing to organized religion after witnessing so much corruption. If these were God's disciples, what did that say about Him? Sarah was very patient with me, meeting my frustration with sympathy and trying to answer my unanswerable questions. Finally, she asked me to pray with her. She opened her Bible, and we read Psalm 23 together:

> *The Lord is my shepherd; I shall not want.*
> *He maketh me to lie down in green pastures: he leadeth me beside the*
>   *still waters.*
> *He restoreth my soul: he leadeth me in the paths of righteousness for his*
>   *name's sake.*
> *Yea, though I walk through the valley of the shadow of death, I will fear no*
>   *evil: for thou art with me; thy rod and thy staff they comfort me.*
> *Thou preparest a table before me in the presence of mine enemies: thou*
>   *anointest my head with oil; my cup runneth over.*
> *Surely goodness and mercy shall follow me all the days of my life: and I will*
>   *dwell in the house of the Lord forever.*

I had heard and read these words many times as a child. I knew them by heart, but I had not thought about them in years. Moreover, I never considered them as being addressed to me, personally, which is what Sarah urged me to do as we bowed our heads and prayed. I found, much to my surprise, that I was moved. If ever there was a valley of the shadow of death, I was in it. And I was afraid. Afraid of relapsing, afraid that I would lose everything that was good in my life, afraid of failing my unborn child. The psalm proposed something I desperately wanted to believe but had not been able to articulate: that I am not alone. By insisting on seeing myself as a man above my condition—distinguished by my intelligence and accomplishments from the junkies and drunks that surrounded me, separated by my Ivy League legitimacy from the black people in the projects with whom I had associated, and yet grounded by my black authenticity in a way that my academic colleagues never could be—I thought of myself as singular. And in that singularity, I felt pride. And in that pride, I came to cherish my secrets, to identify with my uniqueness, my apartness, my aloneness. Addiction only amplified a state of isolation that I had conditioned myself not only to accept but to prize.

It was no longer working for me. Something had to change. But simply not using drugs was not enough, nor was that even possible without admitting that I could not pull myself back from the brink under my own power. The words of the psalm, through their beauty and wisdom, drove home to me that my isolation was not such a good thing after all, and that I was not as alone as I thought. I read them, for the first time, not as a set of metaphorical propositions about God, but as a personal message meant for Glenn Cartman Loury. The poem's "I" was *me*, literally. This way of thinking was a startling revelation. I did not know at the time what to do with this insight, but I knew I could not brush it aside.

I was released from McLean just before Easter, and I suggested to Linda that we go over to the Charles Street AME Church on Sunday. Sarah had invited us. I wasn't quite sure why I wanted to go, except that I had felt something when I prayed with her. If there ever was a time to go to church, it was Easter Sunday. I was not yet resurrected, but I was trying to get there. Linda and I slipped into the church and found seats in a back pew. I sat quietly, absorbing the cascading sounds of the music, and the words of the sermon. As it all washed over me, I felt as though

I was back in the church of my youth. Memories of adults testifying, and of the organ swelling behind the choir's harmonies, all of it came flooding back to me. As the pastor preached his sermon, with his voice rising and falling as he dilated on the miracle of Christ's resurrection, something touched me that I had not felt in a long time, that perhaps I had never felt. Tears welled up in my eyes. I had not expected to be so moved by the service. I was walking through the valley of the shadow of death. It seemed a miracle that I was still alive. I could have gotten myself beaten or killed a hundred times over. I could have overdosed sitting in my own car or been stabbed in the neck in a crack house. I could have been infected with a deadly venereal disease. That none of this happened, that I was now sitting in a church pew, sober, with my wife at my side and a healthy baby in her belly, seemed beyond improbable. I could not account for it. Certainly, it was more than I deserved. I came to that service in the spirit of curiosity, not hoping to find revelation. Yet something was revealed there that, in the power it had over me, left me feeling confused and in awe.

When the service ended, with these thoughts swirling in my mind, I bolted from the church without so much as thanking Sarah for the invitation. I didn't talk to Linda about what I was feeling. I couldn't put it into words. But my wife could see that something had happened. In the days following Easter, the feeling that a significant event had occurred in that church didn't go away. I could find no explanation that would account for it. Some higher power, I felt, had left its mark on me. Even so, I subsequently relapsed.

IN JUNE 1988, I departed the grounds of McLean Psychiatric Hospital in Belmont for the last time. Chastened by my quick relapse after moving into the three-quarter house in April, I left not knowing if my fragile sobriety would hold. To use or not to use? That was my existential question.

I entered a halfway house in Boston. The Hamilton Recovery Home, which sits on Mount Ida Road, just above the Fields Corner station of the Red Line T, is in the working-class neighborhood of Dorchester. The facility itself is in a house that had formerly been a family residence of pretty good size, six bedrooms or so. It had been converted into a place where men came to stop drinking, and it was run by a guy named Bob Brown. Bob was of Irish ethnicity, born Catholic but a fervent convert to evangelical Christianity. He had been a Boston cop and a drunk. He was sent to prison on corruption charges, and he sobered up while inside. When he got out, he could not return to the police force, so he decided to devote his life to helping other men stop drinking. He founded this halfway house, and as the years went by it became a highly respected therapeutic community. He was well thought of by the folks counseling me at McLean. They said that Bob Brown was helping men get sober and regain the lives they had lost to drugs and alcohol. So I took up residence there.

Bob was a tough taskmaster. When I came into the house, I had arranged with a private lab to get a blood test periodically to verify that I had no cocaine in my system. Bob informed Linda and me that my days of arranging such things were over. He didn't believe in testing. He'd know intuitively if I was using, he informed me; and if I used, he was going to throw me out. "We don't need a test. We don't need to get a certificate from somebody. You just worry about getting to your meetings and not using cocaine again. I'll worry about running this house."

I thought I would need my car to get back and forth to work, but Bob declared that I didn't need a car. He asked Linda to take my keys. If I had to get somewhere, I could use public transportation, just like everyone else in the house. "What you actually need, Professor Loury, is to become acquainted with the T," he said. He did allow me to keep a bicycle at the house, and I rode it up to Cambridge when I wanted to go to my office, weather permitting. The rules of the house stated that residents were required to be there from Sunday evening until Saturday afternoon. Once you had passed an initiation period, you were permitted to go home and visit your family—if you had a place to go and people there to receive you—from noon on Saturday until 6:00 p.m. Sunday. You were required to be back in time for the Sunday evening meeting. Missing that meeting could get you thrown out.

At some point, Bob turned to Linda and said, "When this guy starts coming home, I want you to promise me something: You won't have sex with him until I let you know that it's okay. I don't want him running home to mama, being made to feel all good while forgetting about the fact that he has one job and one job only, and that is not to use." Linda was about three months pregnant at the time, and here was this guy telling her not to have sex with me. And she was nodding yes! "No problem. I can do that," she said. I resented this. I had no car, no control, and now Bob was forcing a vow of celibacy on me. But I swallowed whatever reservations I had. "Okay Bob, what's next?"

Soon I was getting up every morning at six o'clock. I would get myself ready for the day, and then go to my office at Harvard where I'd stay all day and try to work, and then return to the house in time for the mandatory six o'clock sessions that Bob presided over. Later, most evenings, I'd go out to an AA meeting. At first, my bunk was in a room I shared with two other men, one of whom had just been released from Walpole State Prison, where he was rumored to have served eight years for attempted murder. He was a menacing-looking light-brown–skinned black man with sunken, beady eyes and a weathered face. He never smiled, seldom spoke, and perpetually wore a masklike glower, as though he was ready to fight. I avoided interacting with him as much as possible, fearing that if I so much as inadvertently bumped up against him in the hallway, he'd try to kill me.

My other bunkmate was a screwball white kid named Randy who, when he was out on the street, would shoot up a mixture of heroin and cocaine called a speedball. He was a sweet guy in his early twenties who smiled constantly and emitted a silly giggle whenever he was amused by the antics of other men in the house. I liked him. Two years after leaving the house, I was devastated to learn that Randy had been found dead in an alley somewhere in South Boston, a needle hanging out of his arm.

After six weeks or so I graduated to a better room on the second floor in the front of the house, which I shared with only one other roommate. He snored incessantly. I went without a good night's sleep for days until it dawned on me that I could just buy a pair of earplugs. That was life in this halfway house, the foundation of my recovery. We went to work—or to look for work—every morning, and we went to an AA meeting every night. You came back to the house at 5:30 p.m. for the slop they passed off as dinner and then sat through the mandatory in-house meeting at six o'clock. You got to go home on Saturday afternoon and spend twenty-four hours or so with your family if you were lucky enough to have one. But you had to be back in time for the evening house meeting on Sunday. It was recovery 24/7/365.

The rules in the house dictated that you meet once a week with your counselor to check in. Mine was a nice guy named Jack, a former resident of the house who had come back to mentor other men and help them get sober. Aiding other addicts was one of AA's Twelve Steps. Jack had once been in the same spot that I was in. He and other peer counselors could tell you the ins and outs of the program, how you get to your meetings, what to do with your cravings, how to make the best use of your sponsor, and so forth.

Bob had the habit of sitting in these meetings from time to time, to observe, quietly, in the back of the room, what was going on between a counselor and the resident. He sat in a meeting with me and Jack one day. I told Jack I was doing fine. "I'm better than fine," I chirped. "Here are the AA meetings that I'm going to." I then told him about how on Monday nights I'd go over to Saint Anselm Catholic Church, on Wednesday nights I'd go to the Lutheran parish, on Fridays I'd go over to the IBEW union hall, and so on. I told Jack that I was working the steps and that everything was looking up. I'd read much of the recovery book, and, despite past errors, I had truly become a "Friend of Bill." I felt good making this report, as though I had it all down. I'd memorized all twelve of the steps, and I began to recite them as proof of my dedication to the program.

As I went on about my progress, Bob spoke up. "Jack," he said, "this guy is snowing you. He's telling you what you want to hear. He's lost in a cloud of professor-speak. He hasn't said one real thing about his real feelings since I've been sitting in this room. If you don't break through, we're going to lose him."

Then, Bob Brown turned to me and said, sarcasm dripping from his voice, the following words: "Alright, Professor Loury, since you're such a *clever fellow*, answer me this: What were you doing out there in the streets of Boston, showing your ass just like a nigger from the projects?"

This white man called me, Dr. Glenn Cartman Loury, the N-word. It was not okay for him to say that to me, I think. How dare he talk to me like this? I should pack up my stuff and go rather than subject myself to the taunts of this racist. I don't have to be here. I'm not in jail. There is no court order.

But Bob Brown, in his own inimitable fashion, accomplished his goal, which was to get my attention. I faced a moment of truth, because, while I was furious about how he spoke to me, I was also keenly aware that I didn't know the answer to his question. What *was* I doing out there? I didn't have a clue. I didn't know how I ended up in those places where I was hanging out, behaving in the self-destructive and humiliating way that I was behaving. But I knew that I didn't want to go back to the aimless, fruitless, futile way of living that I had just barely been able to pull myself out of. And I knew that I was afraid of relapsing again.

I don't now remember what I said to Bob at that moment. I probably said nothing at all. I probably seethed and looked at him fiercely. He held my gaze. If it had been anyone else, I might have considered hitting him, but that thought never crossed my mind. He stood six foot five and probably weighed around three hundred pounds. Fighting was not exactly the way to handle the situation. Perhaps I subconsciously realized that, having so ruined myself, I had arrived at the point where I didn't have the standing to voice my indignation. I must have recognized somewhere deep down that Bob's question needed answering, not to satisfy him, but to satisfy me. I sucked it up and decided to stay at Hamilton Recovery Home.

Bob was a crude, crass guy from South Boston. He was probably a little close-minded and a little bigoted, though I don't believe he harbored any hatred for black people. Profane and rough around the edges as he was, he was a kind of minister who selflessly devoted his life to helping others. Whatever anger I felt toward him in that counseling session turned into admiration in the weeks that followed. There were guys hanging around that house who had completed the program years and decades earlier and still returned to volunteer. They kept coming back because they were dedicated to Bob and saw in his personal mission to help others get sober a reason to stay sober themselves.

I stayed in that halfway house from early June 1988 until just before Thanksgiving. Technically you're supposed to stay there for six months, but, with Bob's blessing, I left after five months and change because Linda's due date was approaching. The other guys in the house razzed me about it, joking that the college professor had graduated early. I was ready to go. I still experienced cravings, as I would for years to come, but I had learned to recognize what triggered them and how to deal with them. If I passed one of the old corners where I used to cop, I'd get an itch to go back, but I could now acknowledge it and put it aside. Whenever I had too much time on my hands, the cravings would return, so I learned to fill the time with books or work or meditation. If I was alone in the evening and craving a hit, I'd try to find a basketball game on TV and concentrate on that. Just before I entered the halfway house, my Celtics went down to the Pistons in the Eastern Conference Finals. I then had to watch as the Celtics' archnemesis, the L.A. Lakers, went on to defeat the Pistons, seizing the NBA championship title for the second consecutive year. Still, it was better than using cocaine.

I also began studying the Bible, memorizing long passages in order to put my mind to work on something other than thinking about using. My experience at the Charles Street AME Church was still with me, and I felt the need to delve deeper into whatever it was I had felt. Bob Brown, a Bible-thumping, born-again evangelist, encouraged me in this.

On the day I left the halfway house, Bob told me, in so many words, that he was proud of me. I was touched by that. The thought that this big, tough, profane, working-class Irishman thought well of me made me feel proud in turn. But Bob also admonished me to keep working the program. I was not done, he said. This was the end of the beginning, not the beginning of the end.

ON JANUARY 3, 1989, my son Glenn was born. Linda suggested that we name him after me. I had my misgivings. I wasn't sure that, after all I had done, giving him my name was any kind of honor. My father had chosen to change the spelling of our last name to free himself from the father who had so badly failed him. Would this perfect, innocent child someday feel the same way about me? But Linda insisted, saying, "I can't think of anyone I would rather name my son after." I had put this wonderful woman through hell. I had deceived her and betrayed her and lied to her. Still, she refused to give up on me. Humbled by Linda's love, I agreed that our firstborn would be called Glenn Cartman Loury II.

Where a year earlier I had spent my nights prowling around Roxbury, Dorchester, and Mattapan, cooking crack in my car or wallowing in cheap motel rooms, I now spent them holding my infant son in my arms, pacing his room to lull him back to sleep, and then returning to lie down beside the woman I loved. None of it, I thought, should have been possible. After a year of fitful recovery, Glenn II brought joy into my life where before there had been only fear and addiction. He even made me glad to see Mama again when she made the trip to Boston to meet her grandson. Once, while I was in McLean, she had called me, and when I picked up the phone, I could tell she was drunk. I was so angry with her. There I was, trying my best to sober up, confined to a mental institution, and there she was, slurring her words and rambling. But when she arrived in Boston and laid eyes on Glenn II, she was absolutely infatuated. She was a doting, chirping grandmother. She fussed over him and sang lullabies to him in that beautiful voice of hers. For the first time in a long time, her presence was a delight.

Even with a newborn to care for, both Linda and I knew I could not afford to neglect my recovery. I attended AA meetings a few times a week. The contrast was stark. Our home was full of the joy of new life; the AA meetings were litanies of degradation and horror held in church basements choked with cigarette smoke and the smell of bad coffee. Still, it was necessary for me to attend, to support others who were struggling to remain sober, and to reaffirm my own sobriety.

When it would come my turn to speak at these meetings, I sometimes found that unexpected things came out of my mouth. At one of them, I spoke out loud something that I had never told anyone. Back before the Pamela Foster incident, Linda had gotten pregnant. She got far enough along that we told our friends about it, and they were all very happy for us. But then she miscarried. It was painful, both physically and emotionally. We later learned about Linda's fibroid condition and the need for her to have a myomectomy, a surgery to remove the fibroid. She was devastated by the double blow of the miscarriage and the bad news from the doctors. Linda badly wanted a child, and so, I told her and everyone else, did I.

Outpourings of sympathy came from friends and family. Every day, it seemed, someone would ask me, "How is Linda? And how do you feel? Are you doing okay?" I would tell them about how devastating it all was. When the subject came up, I would lower my voice and affect a pained expression and say that I was struggling through it.

But that was a cover story. It was the story I knew that I, in my role as loving husband and aspiring father, was expected to tell. The real story is that I felt relieved when Linda miscarried. I had not wanted another child. A baby would mean I would have to curtail my affairs and flings. I knew what having an infant in the house was like, and it would be almost impossible to continue to exercise my right as a Master of the Universe to seduce any woman I could, whenever I wanted to. I was so enamored of my own entitlement that I was secretly pleased that it could continue unimpeded.

One of the cardinal rules of AA is that no one is to render moral judgment on anyone else sharing at a meeting, no matter how reprehensibly they've acted. So no one told me I was a bad person, no one told me I should be ashamed of myself, no one told me how selfish I was. They just reiterated that the most important thing was not to drink, or in my case, not to smoke crack. I understood the utility of the rule. If people feel they'll be judged for their actions, they'll be inclined not to share them, even if they want desperately to unburden themselves. The addict will then keep his shameful secret to himself, and it will continue to feed the self-loathing, which, for many addicts, is at the source of addiction. "Secrets make you sick," is the way they put it in the recovery community. AA meetings provide a place where these secrets can be shared, in the hope that unburdening can take the place of drinking.

No doubt this is a necessary process. It was necessary for me. But at the same time, I was finding AA's monomaniacal focus on sobriety to the exclusion of all other values to be unsatisfying. My life as an addict not only became unmanageable, it became undignified. AA could help keep me sober, but it could not provide a foundation on which to rebuild the moral structures I had demolished. Sobriety was necessary but insufficient for that reconstruction. I came to believe that, for such a daunting project, I would need more sturdy materials.

Eighteen

Sometime in the early 1980s, shortly after arriving at Harvard, I came into contact with Ray Hammond and his wife Gloria White-Hammond. They were black physicians who had been undergraduates together at Harvard in the '70s. By the time we met they'd launched successful medical careers, but they were also actively involved in community outreach work, helping black students at Harvard and MIT to develop the techniques and habits of mind that would empower them to achieve academic success. Collaborating with another black couple—a Harvard-trained psychologist named Jeff Howard and his wife, Anita—Ray and Gloria cofounded an education consultancy called the Efficacy Institute, which focused on raising black students' performance by helping them to identify and overcome some of the psychological scars of American racism.

The Hammonds were both devout Christians, and the pastoral aspect of the consultancy appealed to Ray and Gloria more than the money did. When Jeff Howard started to build up the business, it became clear to the Hammonds that they would have to spend more time pitching their seminars to potential clients and less time developing the spiritual lives of their students. In the end, they left the business behind entirely, opting instead to found a new church. Gloria quit her job as a pediatrician to devote herself full-time to the project. And Ray chose to work as an emergency room doctor on Cape Cod, packing a week's worth of shifts into grueling three-day marathons so as to make time for this new endeavor.

Linda and I came to have great respect for the Hammonds. They were highly educated, extremely intelligent professionals who could easily have used their skills to make a lot of money and live very comfortable lives in one of Boston's tony suburbs. Instead, they lived in the ghetto, on one of the very same streets where I used to go looking for hookers. They lived there because that was what they could now afford, but mainly because they wanted to live among the people they were trying to help. That community needed ministering to, and ministry was the work to which they had been called. The Hammonds took risks on behalf of their beliefs. Linda and I admired them for it. These devout Christians weren't the kind of hucksters who had soured me on religion back in Chicago. No one could doubt their sincere dedication to serving God and to fostering the uplift of His people.

We became founding members of the Hammonds' fledgling church, launched under the auspices of the African Methodist Episcopal denomination for which, as coincidence would have it, they had chosen the name Bethel. "Beth El"—Hebrew for "House of God"—had also been the name of my home church back in Chicago. Linda and I started attending Bible studies in their living room, where Ray would sit with a small group of us, teasing out the meaning of a given passage and encouraging us to learn the books of that sacred text inside and out. They would also hold Sunday services in their home for the eighteen or so of us who constituted their initial flock. The church's membership quickly ballooned. Services moved to the recreation room of a local nursing home, and then to the gym of the Mattahunt Community School, and later to the gym of the Parkside Christian Academy. I would show up early to help set up the metal folding chairs that served as makeshift pews and stay late to help pack them up again. This ritual soon took on a significance for me comparable to that of my formal recovery in AA. The unfolding, arranging, and folding of chairs, alongside the other faithful volunteers, provided spiritual nourishment. It was all so simple and egoless. The point was not to be the best at the task of setting up chairs, a legend in that field, but simply to get the work done so that worship could commence. No advanced degree was required. It was a small act, but it felt good to work with other like-minded worshippers toward something larger than myself.

The services themselves were ecstatic affairs, often both tearful and joyous. The flock would bang out a steady rhythm on tambourines, with a cacophony of voices crying out from every corner of the room in spontaneous exaltation. When the choir's song rises, when the preacher shouts out a fiery and inspiring sermon, when a room full of people is swept up in a fever of devotion, praising God Almighty without restraint, anyone present who can allow himself to suspend his doubts, even for a moment, becomes part of a whole. When I closed my eyes and sang the familiar hymns, or shouted "Amen!" alongside fellow worshippers, the boundary between self and other fell away. My cries of "Hallelujah," "Thank you Jesus," and "Glory to God" were the same cries ringing from the mouths of my brothers and sisters standing beside me, and were indistinguishable from cries that had rung out for generation upon generation in spaces just like those I stood in each Sunday. Just as the "I" of Psalm 23 was me, I was also every reader of the psalm, every prayerful soul on bended knees, every singer of the songs echoing from the rafters of a middle school gymnasium which then, in the presence of God, stood transformed by the power of our devotion into a holy cathedral.

In those moments, I came to believe that Jesus Christ died for my sins. I believed that He had been resurrected from the dead and had ascended to heaven. I believed that, in so doing, Christ had established the means by which I, Glenn Cartman Loury, could enter into a direct relationship with the creator of the universe. I walked out of church feeling like a fallen man with a cleansed heart, a man who was grateful for his wife and son, grateful for his sobriety. I found solace in the study of the Bible, in the solitude of prayer, and in those rapturous worship services that I experienced among the faithful.

Pastor Ray Hammond knew that, as a newly sober man, newly returned to the church, and with a new child, I could benefit from one-on-one counseling. If I was disturbed by thoughts of my double life or felt the desire to use or even had a dream in which I was thrown back into my life of prowling the projects at night, I would consult Ray, and he would take me to a Bible passage that helped me make sense of it. (Thus: "No temptation has seized you except what is common to man. And God is faithful; He will not let you be tempted beyond what you can bear.") I was deeply moved that Ray took a personal interest in my spiritual development. He gathered me under his wing and mentored me in my newfound walk with Christ.

Soon I began supplementing the meditation techniques I learned in rehab with prayer. But I found simply closing my eyes and praying to be a strangely difficult thing to do. You're supposed to commune with the Lord. How do you figure out what to say to Him? Ray provided a template that aided me. The mnemonic device was ACTS (as in the Book of Acts): Adoration, Confession, Thanksgiving, and Supplication. Acknowledge His greatness. Tell Him your secrets. Express gratitude for His mercy. And petition Him for His heavenly grace. This formula for how to talk to God worked for me like a charm. Praise God Almighty! But, was God actually listening?

While alone, I felt prayer to be a comfort, but Ray would sometimes break up the congregation during Bible study to engage in group prayer. Groups of five or so would circle up, and we would take turns leading the prayer, citing scripture from memory, and speaking with as much eloquence as possible. Now, I spoke publicly for a living, so I probably had a leg up on the others. But Linda and I both felt uncomfortable leading prayer. We felt put on the spot. We had to be ready to pray at a moment's notice, even if we weren't feeling particularly prayerful. We'd have to muster up all we could and offer something that would provoke an enthusiastic "Amen" from the group. We both felt that there was a little too much performance in this ritual; it felt inauthentic. Still, Ray asked it of us, so we did it.

How does a rational man, a man otherwise devoted to the most worldly of disciplines, stand for such a thing? How could I surrender my reason—however temporarily—to that which requires faith above all? These questions turned over in my mind once the echoes died down, the worship services concluded, and the chairs were stacked in their place. How could I believe in the literal truth of Christ's crucifixion, resurrection, and ascension? How could I believe that I could find salvation only through His love? At the time I did not know. But I did know that what I felt at church was real. I did know that my life had been transformed, and it seemed plausible enough to me that this transformation was living proof of God's grace. I knew that, at this church, Linda and I were in the right place.

I also knew that the Hammonds were unlike Bob Brown in pretty much every way except the one that counted most: They all changed people's lives for the better. They had certainly changed mine. A guy named Ronnie often came to the men's ministry that Ray would convene once a week in the evening. There we would talk about matters of faith particular to us as men, husbands, fathers, and sons. Ronnie had lived a hard life. He had struggled with addiction and unemployment. His mother was a star member of the Hammonds' church, and she insisted that Ronnie attend, hoping that the Hammonds' support network would help him find stability and sobriety. He was a handyman, so Linda and I would sometimes hire him to fix things around the house or put on a new coat of paint in a room. We got to know each other better, and I watched Ronnie's life change under the influence of the Hammonds. He straightened out, turned away from the lure of the streets, and devoted himself to Bible study and work. He found meaning in his life where before he could find none. In this, he was not alone. I came to see that, despite our different stations in life, Ronnie and I had a lot in common. I enjoyed his company. Linda and I would invite him for dinner on occasion. This, I came to see, was how the church could reclaim a fallen community—one soul at a time.

When the time came, we chose to baptize Glenn II in the Hammond's church. He was the first child to be born into the flock, and we took it as an honor. The Hammonds had done so much for us, and especially for me, as I was still in need of all the help I could get.

THE HAMMONDS' CHURCH OFFERED MORE than just religion, though. The flock was maybe 95 percent black. Of those, perhaps half were middle-class professionals like Linda and me: doctors, lawyers, teachers, small businessmen, and so on. But the other half were working-class folks. These were people like those whom Linda and I had grown up around. They were pragmatic and grounded. Some of them struggled to make rent every month. Most of the black faculty members Linda and I encountered at Harvard and Tufts reminded me of the snooty "brothers" at Northwestern. They had comfortable upbringings. If they hadn't ended up in academia, they'd have high-paying white-collar jobs somewhere else. I enjoyed talking to some of these people, but there was a whiff of the "Negro Cognoscenti" about many of them.

One of the things that initially drew me to the housing projects of Roxbury, Dorchester, and Mattapan was kinship with working-class black folks. That kinship had led me down a dark path. But Linda and I both felt connected to black people who shared our upbringing, and the Hammonds' church provided us with a group of friends around whom we felt at home, with whom we shared an understanding and a culture. Some of the men had stories to tell about life before finding Christ, stories every bit as harrowing as my own. I took great comfort from this.

But there were aspects of church life that did make Linda and me feel uncomfortable. While we were both believers, we were still creatures of reason. Diligent scholar that she was, Linda began researching the history of the Old Testament and the Gospels on her own. She was fascinated by the way the books of the Bible we have today were pieced together over the course of millennia from works by various authors in a multitude of places writing under their own particular sets of historical and cultural pressures. She would have liked to introduce these matters in Bible study, but there was no place in the Hammonds' living room for that sort of scholarly exegesis. When she went to Sunday school at her Episcopalian church as a child, any deep questions she might have raised about, say, contradictions in the varied accounts of Jesus's life provided in the Gospels had been shut down. She was told to take the words of the book literally and unquestioningly, and this offended her blossoming young intellect.

The Book of Acts states that when you become a believer—when you pray and seek and ask and petition God—you will be imbued with the power of the Holy Spirit. (Matthew 7:7 expresses this: "Ask and it will be given to you; seek and you will find; knock and the door will be opened to you.") This power, the church taught, can allow one to do supernatural things. The Hammonds' congregation had a Pentecostal and charismatic flavor to it that emphasized reason-defying miracles, even though the denomination was in the African Methodist Episcopal tradition. AME congregants are known among black churches to be relatively highfalutin, bourgeois, and maybe a bit snobby—there's not much tambourine banging or falling out in the aisles at the average AME church. They're typically more staid than their black Baptist counterparts. But the Hammonds taught that the promises made in Acts were to be taken literally. If one seeks baptism in the Holy Spirit, the Spirit will come upon you and will expand your powers to spread the faith, to witness, to preach, to speak in tongues and to interpret the speaking in tongues, to prophesy, and to heal the sick.

One member of the church, Chris Gray, had been fighting breast cancer for some time, and soon it became clear that she was losing. We watched her diminish—week to week, month to month—before our very eyes. She was going through treatment, but it wasn't working. The doctors could not stop the progress of the disease. Chris was dying. Everyone in the church knew what was going on, and I thought that most people felt the way Linda and I did. We were devastated. All the sophistication of modern medicine could do little for Chris, so we tried to reconcile ourselves to the inevitable. We prayed for her, of course, but both of us believed that if the treatments weren't working, it was only a matter of time.

One Sunday during services in the Mattahunt Community School's gym, Ray Hammond asked us to pray over Chris Gray, to pray for God to heal her. The flock had scores of members by now. All of us closed our eyes and extended our hands toward her. A rumbling of prayer began over in a corner somewhere. "Lord, come into our midst at this moment, oh God, Jesus please, we know that anything is possible for you, we know that when the doctors fail, when the medical technology runs out, when all the therapies have run their course, even then, Lord God, you can still do something. You can make miracles happen, Father. We are believing this promise. In the name of Jesus, we pray!" Shouts of assent, hallelujahs and amens, rose from the crowd amidst more prayers extolling the power of God to do what science plainly could not do: save the life of this woman. As they prayed, tears welled up in the eyes of the people gathered, moved by their belief, their conviction, their certainty, if it be His will, that God would reach into this woman's body and pluck out the cancer that was devouring her.

I was as moved as anyone by this display of holy devotion and fellowship. And I was just as crushed by the thought of Chris's impending demise. And yet, as Linda and I drove back home after the service, we admitted to each other that we were incredulous about supernatural healing. These people really believed that a miracle would save this woman, when the fact of the matter was that those cancer cells were going to continue multiplying until there was nothing left of poor Chris. Prayer is one thing, but many of these people were *convinced* that God could heal her, that through their faith and the power of the Holy Spirit, they could successfully petition God to make it so. To Linda and me, this was not a reasonable expectation. Instead, we saw it as something much less noble: false hope. We thought it was an effort on the part of the church members to make themselves feel better rather than to face a terrible truth. Needless to say, we kept such errant thoughts to ourselves.

I wish we had been wrong, of course. Chris Gray passed away not long thereafter.

In other words, there were limits to how far my belief in Christianity would take me. My fellow congregants knew that I was a relative new-comer to the faith, and I assume most of them knew who I was and what the last two years of my life had been like. They read the newspaper just like everyone else. In the Hammonds' church, full acceptance into the religious communion was not something that happened automatically. It was the fruit of one's spiritual growth and maturation, something that had to be arrived at gradually, so my development as a Christian was a matter of some concern. One Sunday, as I was stacking chairs after the service with a crew of other worshippers, one of them, sister Arlene, asked if I might not be ready to take the next step in my walk: baptism in the Holy Spirit. I had already begun talking with Ray about the formal baptism that occurs with symbolic immersion in a baptismal pool, but this needed to be complemented by a more robust spiritual commitment. The other members of the crew agreed that now was as good a time as any for me to petition the Spirit to receive the powers promised to believers in the Book of Acts. I agreed, but I was apprehensive because I knew that such baptism in the Spirit was supposed to be evidenced by some kind of sign, like speaking in tongues. Not only had I never spoken in tongues, I strongly suspected that when others did, they might have been putting on a bit of a show. Linda and I had often said as much to one another after an especially animated service.

But it was too late now to state my reservations; they had already begun praying for God to reach His hand down and touch me, to empower me with the gifts of the Holy Spirit. Clearly, I was a worthy vessel. Would He not, at this very moment, intercede? Would He not show His majestic self to us? In Jesus's name!

I sat there with my head bowed and my eyes closed, the hands of my brothers and sisters resting gently on my head and shoulders, all of them praying fervently that the Spirit take hold of me. They prayed and prayed. And prayed. And prayed. Sister Arlene even began to pray in tongues. After a while, things started to get awkward. I felt no different than I had before all these prayers began, but they showed no signs of stopping. They had made up their minds. They were *going* to witness a baptismal miracle, even if they had to stand there all day. Something had to give. Finally, not knowing what else to do, I opened my mouth and babbled gibberish for maybe ten seconds in a forced effort to speak in tongues. I felt incredibly silly doing it, but it seemed to me at the time that I had no choice! The others rejoiced. They embraced me and congratulated me and welcomed me into the faith. I was glad they were happy, but I was just as glad to hop in my car and get out of there, as I pondered exactly how I would tell Linda about my "encounter" with the Holy Spirit.

EVEN AFTER "SPEAKING IN TONGUES," for my baptism to be complete, I would have to go through a formal ceremony in which I would be sub-merged into a pool and reemerge spiritually reborn into the faith. The Dorchester Temple Baptist Church had a tub in its cathedral designed especially for this purpose, so one Sunday afternoon the Bethel flock convened there to witness the event. I was much more committed to this ritual than I was to the impromptu laying on of hands. It was a mean-ingful event to me, one that signified another step I had taken away from the darkness of addiction and deceit and into the light of faith and family.

I wanted important people in my life to be there with me as I took this step, so I invited Tom Schelling to the service. Tom didn't have a religious bone in his body. I'm pretty sure he thought the entire thing was nonsense. But he also knew it was important to me. The church had been instrumental in helping me stay sober, so Tom wanted to offer a show of support. When he arrived that Sunday, he came not with Corrine, his wife of some forty years, but with a woman named Alice Coleman.

Some weeks earlier, word had gotten around the Kennedy School that Tom had left Corrine. I was flabbergasted. In all our conversations, he had never let on that his marriage was in trouble. But then Tom had always held his cards close to the vest. He hardly ever let on to anyone about anything. If there was some sort of scandal brewing, or if Tom was distressed, I wanted to be there for him. Since he didn't tell me himself that things were over between him and Corrine, I didn't feel that I could call him up and ask. Instead, I went to Edith Stokey, the hub through which all official and unofficial information passed at the Kennedy School. She revealed to me that Tom had been miserable for many years. Corrine was, had always been, a very difficult person, she said. He had wanted to leave her for some time, but he hadn't had the courage to do it.

It also turned out that Tom had been living something of a double life himself. Alice resided in Washington, DC, and for decades she and Tom had been conducting a long-distance affair. When I learned this, the scales fell from my eyes. Tom was a member of the National Academy of Sciences, which is headquartered in DC, as were branches of the defense establishment with which Tom was involved. He was seldom around on Fridays. Everyone knew he went down there almost every weekend on some kind of business or another. Now it became clear that, while he likely did have much to do in DC, he was also going there to see Alice. When I met with him and Graham Allison, the Kennedy School dean, to talk about how we would handle the Pamela Foster affair, Tom had asked me if Pamela and I were in love. I told him I thought we had been, but by then I wasn't so sure. His question now took on a different significance, and I wondered whether he had been mulling over his own situation: What kind of sacrifice are you willing to make for someone you love?

Tom reached his own conclusion. The four sons he had with Corinne were by now all grown and living lives of their own. Alice had also been married when she and Tom encountered one another, and her children were also fully grown. Corinne herself was a longtime staffer at the American Academy of Arts and Sciences, which was housed in Cambridge. She was well known as a professional in her own right. She and Tom had been together since their graduate school days at Harvard in the 1940s, so their breakup made waves. Still, as Edith told it, this was all for the best. Corrine was devastated, but Tom was happy, and as Edith saw it, he deserved to be happy.

One night, Tom invited Linda and me and little Glenn II over for dinner at the apartment he was now sharing with Alice on Massachusetts Avenue, close to Central Square. He wanted us to spend some time with her. The place was sparsely furnished and anonymous looking—their dining room setting was hardly bigger than a card table. But it didn't seem to matter to either of them. They were clearly in love. After decades of waiting, they finally got what they wanted. In another year, Tom and Alice would depart Boston. Tom took a position at the University of Maryland, and the two of them bought a little house they loved in Bethesda, Maryland, just over the District of Columbia city line. In years to come, Linda and I would visit them there from time to time.

AFTER A TUMULTUOUS COUPLE OF YEARS, two very public scandals, and my struggle with addiction, I was finally easing back into normalcy in 1989. But I now felt a little uncomfortable around my Kennedy School colleagues. The faculty, staff, and administration were all supportive of my recovery, and they even accepted my newfound religion. Still, I couldn't help but feel that they now viewed me through the lens of my troubles. I also had to figure out what kind of work I was going to do. I certainly couldn't return immediately to opining about matters of race and public morality. Until I could show that I truly had changed my ways, I wouldn't have any standing from which to speak. What was I to do?

Luckily, MIT reached out and offered me a year-long visiting scholar's position. I was due a semester's sabbatical leave from Harvard, and MIT came up with funds for the other half of my academic year's salary. The economics department there thought it would be best, given how recent the scandals had been, if I refrained from teaching and focused solely on research. That suited me fine. I could spend some time away from the Kennedy School, but I wouldn't have to relocate, allowing me to remain with Linda and Glenn II and maintain my routine of AA meetings and church activities. In the fall of 1989, I set up shop in a humble basement office in MIT's economics department. There I'd spend eight to ten hours a day with my notepad, journals, and books, reimmersing myself in economic theory.

It was a slightly odd existence. I was dwelling underground, my head full of equations. I was not required to do much more than attend the odd talk or seminar. I spent my time working on some interesting problems. One was a paper on nonrenewable resources that I labored over for months. The end result was abstruse, even for me, and so complicated that it would need substantial streamlining if it was to ever appear in print. The paper, "Tacit Collusion in a Dynamic Duopoly with Indivisible Production and Cumulative Capacity Constraints," still sits, unpublished, in my office file cabinet. (But you can find a PDF online!)

Another problem I was working on was blackjack. I had taken a few trips to Atlantic City recently with Lee Lee's husband, Wesley, who went there at the invitation of some of his business contacts. (He was her fourth—and last—husband. Two brief and unhappy marriages had followed Trey.) He was a funny guy with idiosyncratic interests. He had a fascinating and successful career as a self-employed metals trader. He was 100 percent legitimate, but his work sometimes put him in contact with people who weren't; hence, Atlantic City. He invited me to come along on some of these trips, and we'd play blackjack at the casinos.

Technically, gambling is forbidden by AA, but I'd never had a problem with it. While Wes and I were having fun at the tables, it occurred to me that, given blackjack's simplicity, there must be a way to calculate an optimal playing strategy. There are rules of thumb in blackjack, but had they been rigorously theorized? I decided to test it out by putting to work some of game theory's backward induction techniques.

When I got back to MIT, I taught myself some elementary BASIC computer programming and set out to write the code that would allow me to calculate exactly when to stay, when to hit, when to split, when to double down, and so on (all the while finessing the card-counting issue by assuming an infinite deck). I had managed to make some headway on the problem, and I thought Tom would get a kick out of it. When I next visited him at his office, I told him about this clever program I was designing. He listened attentively, smiling all the while. When I was finished, he walked over to his shelf, pulled down a book, and showed me that someone had already solved this exact problem about a decade earlier, and without the artificial "infinite deck" assumption. So much for blackjack!

I wasn't blazing any new trails in terms of technical economics down there in the basement, but I was getting my sea legs back. It felt good to reconnect with my first love and not to worry about what public stand I would take on whatever battle in the culture war was riling people up that week. My neocon and magazine friends had not abandoned me—I was still invited to attend publication board meetings for the *Public Interest* and I knew the *New Republic* would have been receptive had I wanted to write something for them. The enemy within the black community was still going strong; there was much to do and say. But diving back into social criticism didn't hold the same appeal for me that it once did. I was starting to think that it might be time to get out of the race game.

THAT SAME YEAR, a strange coincidence occurred. Eugene Fodor, the violinist who had performed at the state dinner at the White House I attended with Linda years earlier, and whose virtuosity that night had made quite an impression on us, was arrested in Martha's Vineyard. He was charged with breaking and entering and possession of narcotics. As it turned out, he had been struggling with cocaine addiction for years and would continue to struggle for years thereafter. Reading the news, I couldn't help but think, "There but for the grace of God go I." And this time I meant it.

WHEN I RETURNED TO THE KENNEDY SCHOOL in the fall of 1990, my spiritual commitment to Christianity was as strong as ever. I was again co-teaching a big, required course on ethics. The reading list included many classic texts. We'd read Aristotle and Kant and contemporary figures like John Rawls. Each of these writers had their own way of approaching humans' attempt to understand their relation to the Good. But now that Christianity had become so important in my life, I couldn't help but notice that virtually none of the readings had anything to say about spirituality. That was understandable—few if any of my colleagues were religious, and many were atheists. Still, I thought, if it was our job to train future makers and analysts of public policy, and perhaps a few future political leaders, wouldn't it behoove us to consider what the rich history of religious ethics might have to contribute?

I had recently come across a book that made me consider what Christian ethics might look like in practice: Charles Colson's *Born Again*. Colson's name isn't the first that comes to mind when one thinks of ethics, unless it's by way of a negative example. He was one of Richard Nixon's dirty tricksters, and he had gone to federal prison after pleading guilty to conspiracy charges relating to the cover-up of the Watergate burglaries. That was only one of many capers Colson got up to in the White House.

By the time he went to prison, he was widely known as a key participant in one of the most corrupt administrations in American history.

Just before he went in, though, he had a spiritual awakening of his own. He was born again into evangelical Christianity, and he spent his time in prison rehabilitating himself and ministering to his fellow inmates. His 1975 book recounts his conversion and his attempt to grapple with the criminal, degraded life he had been living before he found God. While in prison, his beliefs led him to become interested in prison reform, and he subsequently founded the Prison Fellowship Ministries, an organization that performs outreach to incarcerated individuals and their families, and advocates on their behalf. I recognized myself in elements of Colson's story. Here was another Master of the Universe, a man who had been driven by nothing but the desire to seize and maintain power. His entire existence revolved around his own selfish pursuits, which he prioritized above all, including the law. Maybe I hadn't engaged in anything so serious as a conspiracy to cover up a political crime, but in my hubris, and in my dedication to my own gratification above all other concerns, I had been more like him than not. And I thought, if Christianity had led someone as notorious as Charles Colson to a life of value and meaning, couldn't others benefit from hearing his story?

I photocopied fifteen pages from Colson's book and distributed them to the mailboxes of my co-teachers in the course, along with a memo. The memo argued that we ought to consider the role of belief and religion in the course. No particular religion, I said—it would have been inappropriate to proselytize in the classroom, and I had no wish to do so. I wasn't interested in spreading the Good News so much as I was in asking how substantive spiritual beliefs could find a place alongside formal ethical calculation. That was a serious question, I thought, because knowing the right thing to do and actually doing what's right in the face of temptation are two very different things. The ethicists we were reading addressed themselves mainly to the former problem, but I knew from personal experience that one's religious conviction could powerfully facilitate one's dealing with the latter problem. Furthermore, as my friend Richard John Neuhaus never tired of pointing out, any religious person in the United States must find a way to square their spiritual convictions with the secular nature of public life, especially if that person is to go about the work of policymaking and governance. Thus, raising questions about the importance of religious conviction in a required ethics course at the John F. Kennedy School of Government seemed to me like a valid avenue of critical inquiry as well as a practical concern to bring to the attention of my fellow teachers and our students.

From what I could gather, my colleagues were less than enthusiastic about my memo and the excerpt from *Born Again*. They were willing to forgive and forget when it came to my transgressions. Whatever our political differences, they liked me as a person and were relieved to see me back on my feet. But Nixon was another thing entirely. They loathed him and probably would until the day they died. To them, his surrogate Charles Colson was nearly as bad. Nor did they appreciate my attempt to bring religion into the course. One day a colleague came to my office, closed the door behind him, and assured me that I was a better man than Colson would ever be, so there was no need to worry myself about these questions.

My well-meaning colleague missed the point entirely. This wasn't about whether I, Glenn Loury, was a good person or not. It was about reflecting on the nature of ethical commitment. Luckily, not all was lost. Occasionally, other faculty would quietly thank me for attempting to introduce religion into conversations at the Kennedy School. It was not something they felt they could talk about openly, given the rigorously secular nature of the institution. Over the course of the semester, some students would confess to me that they, too, were believers. Every so often, we would gather in my office to talk of spiritual matters and even to bow our heads together in prayer. They longed to hang a decent drapery of faith to clothe the religion and democracy of Neuhaus's "Naked Public Square."

At some point in the academic year, I began to feel uncomfortable at the Kennedy School. This was not due to my openly religious views. Nor did I feel that I was being ostracized because of my run-ins with the law. To the contrary, I felt that everyone was going out of their way to be nice to me. The distinguished political scientist Robert Putnam, who had by now taken up the responsibilities of dean, assured me I could stay there just as long as I wanted. Many people never left once they got there. Where, after all, do you go after Harvard? The welcoming atmosphere at the Kennedy School that had been such a relief after the debacle of my first two years in Cambridge was now having a paradoxical effect on me. I had messed up badly, and there were no evident consequences for me at the Kennedy School. Maybe there should have been. But everyone was so *nice* to me, I began to feel as though I was living off the largesse of the institution rather than earning my keep. Had I become a charity case, someone who was perceived to need a protective environment, lest I go off the rails again?

I didn't want that. My hypertrophied sense of pride had been deflated, and that was probably a good thing. But as my self-respect returned over the course of my recovery, I began to worry that I was being coddled. I wanted to earn my position, not rest on my laurels. But I began to suspect that I was drifting.

IT IS THE SPRING OF 1991, and I smoke crack again. I know this is a bad idea even as I go to one of my old corners to cop. But a question is nagging at me. I have overcome my addiction to the drug. Getting high is now definitely a part of my past. But, what was it about crack that had seduced me? Was it really so good that I was ready to throw my life away over it? I want to know. So one evening, as Linda and Glenn II sleep, I sneak down to the garage and light up. As the drug hits my system, I feel the familiar high overtake me. The rush comes on, as always, and the euphoria. But this time the intensity of the experience is attenuated.

I can tell I am high, but it is a hollow feeling. I sit there in my car, considering the effect the drug is having on me. Is *this* what had compelled me to put myself through that interminable cycle of shame and desperation? Is *this* what I had chosen over my wife's love and companionship? I feel the drug moving through me, but it is nothing at all to me now. The primary feeling it evokes in me is shame.

When I am finished, I throw the pipe in the garbage bin. This will be the last time I ever touch crack cocaine.

ONE OF TOM SCHELLING'S MANY ingenious contributions to economics and social theory was to conceptualize what he termed "the problem of self-command." In this body of work, he deploys game theoretic models in order to understand how conflicting imperatives within a single individual can be understood, and how those conflicts can be resolved through "self-binding strategies." For example, a habitual smoker desires a cigarette. Knowing that cigarettes are bad for his health, expensive, and detrimental in any number of other ways, he also desires not to have a cigarette, and in fact never to smoke a cigarette again. Tom theorizes the problem by treating the individual not as one, but as two different agents involved in a zero-sum game with one another. In order for the nonsmoker to gain the upper hand, he must deploy strategies that the smoker cannot counter. These may be as simple as throwing away any cigarettes and ashtrays in the house to close off access, or as complex as telling his wife to leave him if she catches him smoking or paying the clerk at the corner store in advance not to sell him cigarettes. In order to win the game, the nonsmoker must, like Odysseus lashing himself to the mast, commit to a self-binding strategy that the smoker cannot undo. His intellectual investment in this problem of self-command was why, friendship aside, Tom was so interested in my experience at McLean, where I had voluntarily committed myself to the care of the institution in order to stop smoking crack. His work on the problem of self-command is one of the many contributions to game theory that would result in his being awarded the Nobel Memorial Prize in Economic Science—alongside the Israeli American mathematical economist Robert Aumann—in 2005.

My initial self-binding strategy had, after a couple false starts, resulted in a win. The Glenn Loury who wanted to quit crack for good vanquished the Glenn Loury who would have spent every penny he had on the drug. I believed I had out-thought that other Glenn Loury, that enemy within. And while I never did go back to hard drugs, neither did I reflect on an emergent pattern in the various games I had been playing throughout my life, one in which a game I seemed on the verge of winning would get away from me at the last minute. I thought I had a winning strategy when I "borrowed" that car for prom night back in Chicago, and I ended up in cuffs. I thought I had solved the problem of the economist versus the black economist when I arrived at Harvard, and soon enough I choked. I was a Master of the Universe until I wasn't, and my entire life came crashing down around me. The pattern should have been clear: my strategic calculations had a tendency to exclude some rather significant externalities.

In looking back and rendering the story of my life in prose, the flaws in those seemingly well-made strategies can appear so obvious as to be embarrassing. I believed that recommitting myself to Christianity and giving myself over to God would cement my triumph over the enemy within. But, as would become clear soon enough, even with a commitment to a faith that transcends reason, in the end, one cannot escape the logic of the game. As long as life goes on, the contest for self-command continues. There's no escaping it. In convincing myself that I was finally complete, finished with the game, and was no longer set against myself, I had, unknowingly, ceded ground in a conflict within which I was still enmeshed. The problem of self-regard, it turns out, becomes most insidious just when one thinks one has put it to rest.

Nineteen

I stay quiet about my growing misgivings about Harvard, telling only Linda that I'm starting to feel like I need a change from the Kennedy School. It would be hard to explain this to anyone else. You're comfortable, well liked, and well paid; you carry the imprimatur of one of the world's most prestigious universities, and this makes you want to *leave*? Trying to break it down to a stranger, to explain how important my sense of *honor* is to me, would require introducing them to my father, and telling them my entire life story. For the time being, I content myself with tinkering around with economics and writing the odd essay and book review. I don't put out any feelers, not wanting it to get back to Harvard that I'm thinking of leaving. They'll just offer me more money, I think, which will make it even more difficult to quit. I'm not trying to leverage a better deal for myself. I want a new challenge and a fresh start.

One day, by sheer coincidence, that new challenge comes calling. It speaks in the voice of Laurence Kotlikoff, the chair of economics at Boston University. Larry's name is known to me—I've seen his work in the economics journals—but I've never met him. Boston University's economics department has, frankly, a middling reputation. It's not exactly a force in the field, so I'm a little wary. But as Larry talks about his vision for that department, I grow intrigued. He's made it his mission to transform the place into a powerhouse, and he thinks I can help make that happen. I'll learn later that, along with some serious economics chops, Larry has considerable skill in negotiating the byzantine administrative networks that control the purse strings at Boston University. He has managed to make an end run around the layers of deans and associate provosts that normally stand between department chairs and the funding they desire, appealing directly to the university's swashbuckling president, John Silber, whose unbridled ambition is to convert BU from a "streetcar college in Boston" into one of New England's great universities. Larry is happy to help him. His pitch to Silber boils down to this: give me enough money and together we can create one of the best economics departments in the country.

It turns out that Larry and Silber are two of a kind: rambunctious change agents full of out-of-the-box ideas and ready to stir things up. Through some combination of reason, flattery, and cajoling, Larry has sold his vision to Silber, and now the two of them are working their way through a wish list of some of the nation's top economists, calling them up and pitching them hard on BU with lavish salaries, generous research budgets, and a posh, newly remodeled office space. When I sit down with them in Silber's office one day, it's clear that they're serious. It's an extremely appealing offer: ample research funding and sabbatical leave, a university professor title that would allow me to teach essentially whatever material I want, and a *doubling* of my current salary. And I wouldn't even have to move, which is a major benefit considering Linda's position at Tufts. Moreover, the offer comes with a housing subsidy (a mortgage with a below-market interest rate), enabling Linda and me to successfully bid on a four-bedroom split-level colonial with a finished basement, set on a half-acre lot with a lush garden in the back, that we'd already been looking at in the Boston suburb of Milton. The house is not very far, as it happens, from the Jamaica Plain neighborhood where the Parkside Christian Academy is located. Having outgrown the gym at the community school, the Hammonds' church, Bethel AME, is now holding services there.

I stand now on the right side of the line with my wife and young son. Soon Linda will give birth to our second son, Nehemiah. Family, recovery, and religion have quelled my need to seek thrills by running the streets, or to find satisfaction by wading into the culture war. After two semesters sitting in that MIT basement office thinking of nothing but economic theory, my desire to return to technical work has been reawakened. I have ideas that I want to pursue. I have something to prove. Joining this up-and-coming department as a star recruit would signal to the Bob Solows of the world that I want back in as a serious Player in the big-league economics research game. I tender my resignation at Harvard, pack up my office, and move it across the Charles River to BU. I was lost, and now I'm found.

BY MY SECOND YEAR at my new institutional home, I was on a hot streak. I had reinvested myself in the application of economic theory to issues of inequality, social capital, discrimination, and affirmative action, and the effort was paying off. In 1993, I published three papers in the *American Economic Review*, one of the leading journals in the field. Two more papers of mine appeared in top journals in 1994. I was even more productive in my first years at BU than I had been as a newly minted scholar at Northwestern and Michigan in the 1970s. I was elected as a Fellow of the Econometric Society in 1994, a high honor for a theoretically oriented economist.

Four of those recent publications were the fruit of collaboration with Stephen Coate, a younger colleague of mine at the Kennedy School. I began discussing research ideas with Steve before my leave year at MIT. Our most influential paper was entitled, "Will Affirmative-Action Policies Eliminate Negative Stereotypes?" It caused a bit of controversy when it appeared in the *AER* in 1993, although that was certainly not our intent. In fact, we specifically avoided arguing for or against racial preference policies in that essay. Instead, we focused on the interactions between an employer's information and a worker's incentives when there is pressure from the government to equalize hiring rates for different racial groups. Such pressure is what we meant by affirmative action, and an employer's belief about the skill level of the typical worker belonging to a racial group is what we called the employer's stereotype about that group. In our theory, an employer's decision about hiring a worker depends on his group stereotypes, and on what he knows about individual applicants. We analyzed how affirmative action affects this decision calculus. If employers believe that one group of workers is on average less skilled than the other, and if they are compelled by the government to hire from the two groups at the same rate, then they will use a less exacting hiring standard for workers in the disadvantaged group in order to comply with the government's mandate.

We argued in the paper that this could be problematic if the goal is to eliminate negative stereotypes, because the hiring standards of employers ultimately determine workers' incentives to acquire skills. A costly investment in skills only pays off if it increases the chance for a worker to get hired. Workers who think that they will be hired even if they do not become skilled will have less of an incentive to make that investment. This was our key insight: that under an affirmative action policy, employers' beliefs and workers' incentives mutually determine one another. As a result, government pressure on employers to equalize hiring outcomes can have the unintended consequence of creating the very inequality between racial groups it was designed to remedy, since making it easier for a certain group of workers to get hired can undercut their incentives to acquire skills. As a result, employers' belief that a less exacting standard for hiring workers in a disadvantaged group is necessary for parity can become a self-fulfilling prophecy. Affirmative action can backfire, leading to what we called a patronizing equilibrium.

Employers think achieving racial parity requires setting a lower bar for "disadvantaged" applicants. Yet, by lowering the bar, they reduce the incentive for workers in the favored group to acquire skills, thereby reinforcing their disadvantaged status!

Our paper was a theoretical exercise, to be sure, but one that was (and remains) highly relevant to the real world. After all, if we tell one group of undergraduate students that to be admitted to law school they must have an A– grade point average and must score above the 90th percentile on the admissions test, while telling another group of students that a B grade point average and a 70th percentile test score performance will suffice, then we shouldn't be surprised to see better academic performance on average from the students who face the more demanding admissions standard.

I had long harbored a visceral skepticism toward racially preferential selection policies, despite having benefited from them myself. I had been admitted to Northwestern in 1970 through a special initiative designed to seek out black students. At MIT's economics PhD program in the early 1970s three slots were reserved in each cohort specifically for applicants of color, of which I was one. Once admitted to MIT, I received funding from a Ford Foundation program designed to lighten the financial burden of grad school for African American students. So why was I dubious about programs that had proven so helpful to me?

In my view, affirmative action had worked for me because I had the talent and work ethic to make good on the bet that a special investment in me would pay off. Those programs got me in the door, but they would have been little help to me if I had been unable to meet and exceed the standards of those institutions. As Marcus Alexis had warned me, although MIT may have been especially receptive to black applicants, once I got there, they weren't going to take it easy on me just because I was black. I'd have to prove my worth, and I did. Nobody could question whether I deserved my position there or anywhere thereafter—all they had to do was to look at the rigor and depth of thought on display in my work.

But racial preferences didn't work that well for everyone. Consider the case of Clarence Thomas. He, too, was an uncommonly gifted student. He, too, was a beneficiary of affirmative action. And he, too, excelled in one of the top graduate programs in his field, Yale Law School. He had the goods. But he came to feel that his Yale diploma was hardly worth the paper it was printed on. As an "affirmative action hire," many suspected that he lacked the jurisprudential skills to justify his prominence, that he had coasted through Yale as a charity case, and that he was little more than a black mascot conservatives could trot out to neutralize any accusations of racism that came their way. Never mind that he was eminently qualified for the positions he held. Being black and conservative, he felt that the specter of affirmative action gave liberals an excuse to delegitimize him.

Conversely, my Harvard appointment as full professor with tenure at age thirty-three, before my research program had matured and with parallel responsibilities in two very different fields, was also a case of my career trajectory being altered by affirmative action. Did I have the talent and work ethic to make good on Harvard's bet? I cannot know what others thought, but I know I was less than certain about that. I know I choked, and I know paralyzing doubts almost got the better of me. I know that those doubts caused me to reject Bob Solow and Peter Diamond's overtures for me to come "home" to MIT, that they led me to embrace Tom Schelling's idea of crossing over to the Kennedy School, and, ultimately, to me throwing myself headlong into the culture war issues on race, inequality, and social justice. In all this, the question remained: Had I actually been helped or hindered? That question was foremost in my mind when in the early 1990s I undertook to write that paper with Coate about affirmative action and negative stereotypes.

I WAS THINKING ABOUT THESE same issues as I watched my friend Clarence Thomas go through the now-notorious confirmation hearings that followed his appointment by George H. W. Bush to the Supreme Court. Anita Hill's accusations notwithstanding, I definitely saw the merit in Thomas's sense that he was enduring a "high-tech lynching." It was not just his character but also his accomplishments that were put on trial, accomplishments that were assailed, with grim irony, by the very liberals who championed the affirmative action policies that had given him an opportunity to succeed. The sheer hypocrisy of it all was mind-boggling. For political liberals, affirmative action was said to have "leveled the playing field," and it was taken to be a racist act even to ask whether its beneficiaries were as capable as nonbeneficiaries. Unless, of course, the black beneficiary held the wrong political views, in which case affirmative action then became clear evidence that he wasn't qualified. This tendentious and selective application of the concerns about affirmative action was a clear example of the patronizing equilibrium effect that Coate and I had sought to formally analyze.

At the time I thought that, if affirmative action policies at the university level could result in questions about the competence of as distinguished and established a figure as Clarence Thomas (or Glenn Loury!), then we needed to ask if such policies were worth preserving in their present form. After all, they were never meant to be permanent. The idea at the outset was that affirmative action would serve as a corrective measure to counteract ingrained discriminatory practices. Once the first generations of African Americans who benefited from affirmative action could acquire college degrees, gain a toehold in the labor market, accumulate wealth and social capital, and pass it on to their children, the logic went, we could begin to phase it out, as it would become unnecessary. But if what Stephen Coate and I theorized was true, then the policy could lock in racial stereotypes, and we would have to seriously reconsider the viability of the project as then construed. If affirmative action inadvertently ended up perpetuating the very stereotypes it was meant to help dismantle, it would be a futile endeavor. It would need to be rethought. My goal was not to argue for the wholesale destruction of affirmative action. Clearly, I thought at the time, it needed to exist in some form. But in the course of our careful and rigorous analysis, Stephen Coate and I had identified some not implausible circumstances in which its present form was suboptimal.

In the summer of 1992, I presented an early version of this paper at a conference at Stanford's center for mathematical economics that was run by an imposing figure named Mordecai Kurz. It caused a commotion. During the Q & A session, hands shot up around the room, and I caught some heat from my fellow economists. The argument was rather technical in its details, but I had made my point. One hand that didn't shoot up, though, was that of Donald Brown. Don was a well-published mathematical economist, and an African American, who was then a senior figure in Stanford's economics department. When I was in grad school back in the 1970s, his star was on the rise. He was at Yale then, just a few hours via Amtrak from Cambridge. The Black Graduate Economics Association at MIT, of which I was then president, invited him to come give a lecture, and he declined. Don didn't want to be brought to MIT as a "black economist," he wanted to be appreciated as an economist, full stop. He didn't think much of the idea that we economists who happened to be black might be sequestering ourselves from the rest of the profession. We black students were all outraged by this at the time. How dare he refuse an invitation on these grounds? Didn't he know that we blacks had to stick together?

In time, I came to admire him for his stance. It was principled. He was no conservative. He simply believed that for black economists to be taken seriously, they needed to meet the same standards as everybody else. In this, he may well have been following David Blackwell's example. Blackwell, a black man, had established himself as an excellent statistician first and foremost. As the years went on and I made a name for myself after graduate school, Don and I became friends. In 1977, shortly after I had finished my studies at MIT, Don invited me to present parts of my thesis at the annual meetings of the American Mathematical Society. Even though I became a Reaganite just a few years later, that didn't interfere with the mutual respect between us.

And yet, despite my conservatism, two decades after I began my studies at MIT, I was still trying to walk both paths—to be both an outstanding economist-who-happened-to-be-black, and to be a black economist promoting the uplifting of his people. And, while Don might not have liked the idea of speaking before the Black Graduate Economics Association at MIT in the 1970s, he was still black himself. As such, he read my paper with Coate as an attack on affirmative action, and this displeased him, especially when some of his more conservative colleagues in that room took such pleasure from my presentation. Actually, I didn't see it that way. I believed my critique of racially preferential policies could ultimately benefit black Americans. If affirmative action wasn't working, if it didn't eliminate negative racial stereotypes but instead exacerbated them, then we needed to find another path.

But on that occasion at Stanford in 1992, Don was pissed. He was seething at the thought that I would use our chosen field of study, economic theory, to rationalize the dismantling of affirmative action. He let me know as much after the session concluded, insinuating that I was betraying black people, under the cover of technical analysis, in the name of some conservative political line. I took that as an insult. Don was a brilliant guy. I knew that he could understand the equations and the theoretical models. Why couldn't he see, as an economist-who-happened-to-be-black, that there was more to this vexing issue than simple racial politics?

I found that the paper drew similar reactions from other black economists. I was messing with a cherished institution in black life. Talking about affirmative action with a black American can be a little like talking about Israel with a Jewish American. Just as an otherwise liberal Jew can take a surprisingly hardline stance on the Israel-Palestine issue, even some conservative African Americans buckle down and shake their heads if you question affirmative action. In such matters, the call of the tribe can ring out louder even than political ideology or, indeed, than reason itself. I considered the paper's publication in the *American Economic Review* to be a triumph (its subsequent reception, with thousands of citations and with its main arguments referenced in textbooks, has fully justified this). But, clearly, I had gone against the tribe. And this left me wondering how far I could push the envelope before I would find myself an outcast among my own people.

IN THE SPRING OF 1993, *The 700 Club* came calling. Word of my rise and fall and rise, my recovery and Christianity and newly thriving family life, had become well known in conservative circles. And there were few more conservative institutions in American life than the Christian Broadcast Network, its flagship show *The 700 Club*, and the show's long-time host Pat Robertson. The producers wanted to do a segment about my most recent transformation, and they wanted to capture me in my element. So one lovely afternoon, a camera crew came to our home in Milton to visit with the Lourys. They shot footage of Linda and me sitting on our back porch as Glenn II and Nehemiah scrambled around our sprawling backyard with Clifford, our black Labrador. You couldn't imagine a more idyllic scene. And indeed, taking it in through the eyes of the crew allowed me to see that, after so many years of uncertainty, Linda and I had settled into family life. I was now, finally, living the kind of life I prescribed for others but had previously chosen not to adopt myself.

Watching the boys grow, being present for them in a way that I was not for Lisa or Tamara or Alden, caused me to reflect on my own past. Not just the recent past, but my youth and all the experiences that made me who I was. Around this time I published an essay in *Commentary* in which I told the story of my friendship with Woody and of that Black Panthers meeting that almost came between us. It was a meditation on the dialectical relation between race and individual identity, one in which I had occasion to reflect on the ways that my own racial self-understanding could, if I allowed it, limit my young sons' growth. In that essay, Woody's story ends with the conclusion of the Black Panthers meeting. I noted that we had fallen out of touch, and that I assumed Woody, with his fair complexion and relatively minor black ancestry, was now living somewhere as a white man. But I did not recount the actual circumstances that led to our friendship's end, which came years later. I had not spoken about that with anyone.

There is the cover story and there is the real story.

The cover story is that when I returned to Chicago to join the Northwestern University faculty in 1976, I reconnected not only with my family but with Woody and Elvie, his wife. They were doing great. Woody had his law degree and was working as a corporate lawyer for McDonald's, while Elvie was working part time at an office in the Loop. They had a couple of kids, they were prospering, and they lived in a nice apartment in a high-rise on North Avenue, not far from my Lincoln Park bachelor pad.

Back in my hometown, I got to hang with my old friends again, my oldest friends, in fact. When we were able, we got together, listened to records, sparked up a joint or two, and had a few drinks—we'd all moved on from Boone's Farm by then. It was exciting to see that we were all coming up in the world, that our lives were changing for the better, that we were growing into the people we had hoped we'd one day become. We were all the children of working-class families. Now Woody and Elvie had white-collar jobs. I was a professor. We had come up together, and now we got to celebrate our success together.

That is the cover story. And it's true, so far as it goes. But there is also the real story.

Woody's job was grueling. He spent long, long days driving from site to site in the Chicago suburbs. Elvie got off work at three o'clock, and sometimes I offered to pick her up and give her a ride home so she wouldn't have to take public transportation while Woody had the car. Why not? We were friends.

These drives became a semiregular event. I'd pick her up, we'd talk for the duration of the ride, and I'd say goodbye. But over time, our talk grew flirtatious. And when we weren't talking, I heard my heart race in the silences as I stole glances at her while she sat in the passenger seat. One day, as I was driving her home, I put my hand on Elvie's thigh. She didn't remove it. We looked at each other, and we didn't have to say a word.

We began an intense, passionate affair. We would make love anywhere: on the living room floor, on the desk in Woody's home office, anywhere two bodies could cram themselves. There was no plan here, no future. The things that ought to have stopped us—Woody's feelings, the marriage, the friendship, the risk of getting caught—only made the affair that much more thrilling. We didn't want to get caught, but knowing that we *might* get caught imparted a transgressive edge to the sex.

At some point, Woody grew suspicious. His schedule was like clockwork, so I knew when not to be at his apartment. Maybe Elvie or I let something slip. Maybe she mentioned my name a little too often. More likely, we all knew each other so well that he was simply able to sense that something was off.

One evening, Elvie came over to my place. Before we even made it halfway up the stairs, we were all over each other, pulling off each other's clothes, our breath quickening. Suddenly, there was a loud knock at the front door. We both froze. We could hear Woody shouting outside. My car was parked out front. Elvie had her own car by now, and it was parked in a lot around the corner. He certainly could have spotted it from the street. "Glenn! Elvie! I know you're in there! Open the goddamn door!" We said nothing, not even daring to move. Then Woody showed that he meant business. He kicked in the narrow window beside the front door, sending shattered glass skittering across the entranceway. After that, silence. We waited. Once we were pretty sure he was gone, Elvie got up, put on the clothes I had torn off her, and left.

I don't know what happened when she got home, but a few days later,

I was summoned to their apartment. Woody's father was present, maybe to provide emotional support to Woody, maybe to take the grandkids to his place if necessary, or maybe, if things got heated, to prevent Woody from grabbing a kitchen knife and going after his best friend. I had seen Woody wrestle in high school. I didn't much like my chances against him if things got physical. And he was as hot-blooded just then as he ever was. Now his anger was turned on me and Elvie. He meant to get the truth out of us. He told us he knew there was something going on, but he wanted to hear us admit it.

I heard my mother's words echo in my head: "If caught, deny everything." Elvie and I both told him there was nothing going on, that he was imagining things, that we would never betray him. As we denied and denied, Woody grew angrier and angrier, and pretty soon the three of us were shouting over each other. His father interceded, telling everyone to be quiet unless he gave them permission to talk. We went on like that for a while, but Elvie and I stuck to our cover stories. We said we had done nothing, and Woody believed nothing we said.

I betrayed Woody once at the Black Panther meeting, and our friendship survived. As I left his apartment that evening, I knew it wouldn't survive this. Elvie and I humiliated him, and we did it to serve our own desires. Later I would get an inkling of Elvie's reasons. After their marriage broke up, Elvie came out of the closet as a lesbian. Evidently her affair with me was only one part of a larger reckoning with her sexuality. As for why I did it, I had no earthly idea. As a budding Master of the Universe, I wanted to do it, so I did.

As for Woody, I would hear nothing more from him for many years, until, in 1996, Ira Glass produced a segment based on my *Commentary* essay for his lauded radio show, *This American Life*. He tracked Woody down. He was by then working as a lawyer in the Chicago public defender's office. Glass reported that behind Woody's desk hung a poster printed by the Black Panthers that read "Eldridge Cleaver for President." It turned out that Woody had no idea I was any kind of public figure, that

I was a writer, or that I had gone through any of my late-1980s ordeals. And I had clearly misjudged him. Far from choosing to pass, he had elected to proclaim his blackness as loudly as ever. When Glass asked if my betrayal of him at the Black Panther meeting back in 1970 ended the friendship, Woody told him it hadn't. Ironically enough, he hadn't given that event all that much thought after the fact and was surprised that it was such a pivotal event in my life. No, something else had ended the friendship, but he declined to tell Glass what it was. The loyalty Woody felt to his race endured. My loyalty to him had not.

CHARLES COLSON MUST HAVE RECEIVED word I had tried to teach his book at Harvard. If I was in his shoes, I might have gotten a kick out of the idea of a bunch of liberal Ivy League professors who hated my guts feeling compelled to read my work. Because, while Colson had turned away from crime and selfishness and toward religion and service, he was still very much a conservative. Prison Fellowship Ministries had grown by leaps and bounds after Colson was released. Part of its success came from his ability to appeal to networks of Christian conservative donors who were taken with Colson's story of spiritual redemption and his advocacy for Christian values in public life.

Colson had invited me to join Prison Fellowship Ministries' board of directors, which is how I found myself standing at a podium in an auditorium in Colorado Springs, with a few hundred people in front of me and a twenty-foot projected image of myself behind me. I had been asked to give my testimony, to talk about how I had been lost but, through the power and love of Jesus Christ, was now found. My speech was one of the culminating events of a conference that Colson had put together to discuss religion, public life, and the work of Prison Fellowship Ministries.

I knew what I was going to say when I got up there, and really, I had only to speak from the heart. My presence at the event and my role in the organization meant that I now occupied a new place in American conservatism. Due to my affiliation with the modes of analysis and thought published in places like the *Public Interest*, I was thought of, and thought of myself, as a neoconservative. But, whatever the private beliefs of other neocons, they were usually silent on matters of religion and spirituality. Most of them had a background in social and political science, and aside from the odd personal essay, if they ever did engage religious matters, it was by way of thinking about the role of religious institutions as tools for the implementation of social policy.

I was also a social scientist, of course, and I too saw the value of utilizing religious institutions as adjuncts to policy. But my public proclamations of belief and my new involvement with conservative religious ventures, like Prison Fellowship Ministries and Richard John Neuhaus's new magazine, *First Things*, meant that I now occupied a slightly different political vector from that of other neocons. I didn't think, as much of the religious right did, that Christian doctrine should dictate public policy. But neither did I think that religious thought should be kept out of policy debates entirely. The very reason I circulated those excerpts from *Born Again* to my Harvard colleagues was to encourage them to think about the way that faith might inform—though not determine—policy.

After all, what would Christianity mean without good works, "to walk, even as He walked" (1 John 2:6)? What would public policy mean if not serving the public good? Charles Colson was doing good works with Prison Fellowship Ministries, spending his time and energy offering counsel to those most in need and, indeed, often abandoned by society. In redirecting his donors' wealth to the aid of those who had nothing, whose prospects upon release were dicey, and who were so often despised and scapegoated, Colson was, in my view, doing God's work. While I believed that crime needed to be punished and that the most dangerous offenders needed to be locked up, it was hard to square America's apathetic approach to prisoner rehabilitation with its use of prison as a catchall solution to crime. If people emerged from prison no better than

they were when they went in (and sometimes worse), with no sense
of purpose or real possibility of improvement upon release, then what
were prisons for? Recidivism, I thought, was a policy failure as much
as it was a failure of the individual, one that the government seemed
to have no interest in correcting. Colson was stepping into the breach
and doing with private enterprise what the government could or would
not do. That mission was both Christian and conservative, and so I was
happy to be affiliated with it, despite that, standing there at the podium
in Colorado Springs, I could not bring myself to turn around and face
that twenty-foot version of Glenn Loury, the born-again Christian hero,
that loomed over the crowd.

JUNE 1993 MARKED LINDA'S AND MY ten-year wedding anniversary. I
spent a long time contemplating what that meant. We had gone through
so much, I had put her through so much, and yet here we were, truly
happy together, perhaps for the first time. I did not know that I deserved
such happiness, only that I felt it, and that it could only have come by
way of Linda's grace and that of God's. She was the reason I spent my
evenings playing in the living room with my two beautiful sons and
cracking jokes with the woman I loved instead of skulking around the
ghetto looking for another hit, another empty sexual liaison. She knew
it. I knew it. But I wanted her to know that I knew.

So after surveying the rows of anniversary cards at a stationery shop
and finding them all too saccharine and insincere, I sat down and wrote
her a letter myself. I reflected on my own initial ambivalence about our
relationship. I had not expected it to last forever, but now I could not
imagine life without her. I enumerated the things that made me love
her, and I thanked her for all she had done for me:

> I cherish you and the children beyond any saying. I thank you for
> what you have given, genuinely and from the depths of my soul.

It is my prayer that we may, as they say, "grow old together" for the next half-century. I look forward to the changes which will surely be many, and not all easy, through which we shall have to go together as our marriage continues to mature. I think now with pleasure of the joys *and* sorrows which we shall share as we watch our children grow to adulthood. May God grant us an extended middle age, and a long life thereafter. May our journey together always be such as to keep each of us interested, grounded, entertained and motivated to achieve our individual potentials. May I learn to love you in ways I have not yet thought of. May my touch always be tender and warm to you. May you find in this relationship, now and in the years ahead, what I know I have found—peace, joy, contentment, happiness, challenge, humor and of course, a burning, unquenchable thirst for more.

It took ten years for me to understand how important Linda was to me. Perhaps that was simply how long it took for me to figure out what I wanted out of life and that I couldn't get it alone. To live the life I wanted, I could not live only for myself. At nearly forty-five years of age, I was finally getting it.

Twenty

As the 1990s progressed, something changed. Or perhaps I had changed. A decade-plus into my life as a public intellectual, despite my rather scandalous fall from grace in the 1980s, I was still championing the same causes I always had, leveling the same critiques of the present civil rights establishment that I always had. And why not? The problems of the black inner cities were as bad or worse than they had ever been. The self-satisfied bureaucrats and hustlers and politicians who arrogated to themselves the right to speak on behalf of black folks were just as full of it as they had ever been.

But, whereas once my moral critiques of race politics and policy had placed me center stage in public debates, I began to notice that, more and more, I was becoming a bit player, one who was trotted out when a little "authenticity" was needed to fill out a panel or argue against some policy or another. What I opposed was clear enough. What was I for?

Still, I may well have continued living happily as a religious neocon firebrand had it not been for the publication of three books: Charles Murray and Richard Herrnstein's *The Bell Curve*, Dinesh D'Souza's *The End of Racism*, and Abigail and Stephan Thernstrom's *America in Black and White*. These books and the circumstances surrounding their publications exacerbated whatever lingering tensions I felt between my blackness and my politics, and quickly, within a matter of a few years, made those tensions untenable.

The Bell Curve was published in 1994 with the support of the market-oriented, conservative think tank the American Enterprise Institute (AEI), where Charles Murray was a fellow. Even before its official release, it became one of the most controversial works of social science ever published in the United States, and three decades later it remains so. The book makes claims about the crucial importance of cognitive ability in determining life outcomes, and the extent to which genetic inheritance causes observed differences in performance on IQ tests. It weights these genetic factors very heavily, suggesting that attempts to bring various lagging groups in the US up to speed have failed because those groups are intrinsically incapable of performing at the highest levels due to their low average levels of intelligence. According to Murray and Herrnstein, African Americans constituted one of the lowest performing groups. This implies that the epidemic of black underperformance we were then experiencing may be a permanent and ineradicable feature of the American social landscape. It wouldn't matter what kind of programs and what forms of affirmative action you implemented, it was the fate of black Americans, due to a low average level of cognitive ability, to remain at the bottom of the heap.

Murray had a background in political science, not cognitive psychology. To make *The Bell Curve*'s case about genetics and IQ, Murray relied on Herrnstein, an elite, if controversial, quantitatively oriented psychologist at Harvard. However, Herrnstein died just before the book's publication. When the time came for Murray to back his claims up in public, he no longer had the man who built much of the scientific case for their arguments at his side.

Nevertheless, AEI knew that they had an epochal book on their hands, and they went about promoting it assiduously. They celebrated its release with a conference in Washington, DC. They must have poured at least $100,000 into this event. I attended in my capacity as a member of AEI's

academic advisory board. Scores of others came, and experts were flown
in from around the country to talk about the book. Presumably those
experts had a chance to read *The Bell Curve*, and presumably they were
already more or less sympathetic to its point of view. Whatever the case,
the book received very little pushback at that conference.

Once *The Bell Curve* made its way out to the public, the mood was
quite different. Controversy over the book's claims about race and IQ
erupted, and it quickly became a monumental bestseller. In magazines
and newspapers, on TV and the radio, Murray was pilloried as a racist
and a eugenicist by anyone even vaguely left-of-center and by more than
a few who were right-of-center. But largely the mood on the right was
one of triumph. As the months rolled on and economists and psycho-
metricians and sociologists began analyzing Murray and Herrnstein's
data and evaluating the statistical techniques they had used to reach
their conclusion, criticisms started piling up in just about every technical journal you could name. Experts took issue not only with the book's
policy recommendations and its implications but also with its methods.
Many of these critiques, which were real and substantial, came from top
researchers who found the empirical analysis lacking. But rather than
respond to the substance of the critiques, Murray blew them off, writing in *Commentary* that the tenured liberals in academia *had* to reject his
findings. If they didn't, their entire world would collapse.

This did not strike me as an adequate response at all. Linda and several other social scientists wrote replies to Murray's *Commentary* piece,
taking him to task both for what they saw as the book's flawed method-
ology and his nonresponse to the steadily accumulating body of critical
scholarship. I had plenty to say, as well. Murray had written a book that,
if its argument held water, could reconfigure the way we think about
racial inequality in America. He was making extraordinary claims, and
so I felt he ought to go to extraordinary lengths to defend them. I had
relationships with *Commentary*'s editors, Norman Podhoretz and Neal
Kozodoy. I'd published a few essays and reviews with them, so I figured

they would be receptive to a nuanced essay from me that was fair but critical of Murray. I didn't think he was a racist. In fact, we were friendly with each other. Years earlier, I had spent the night at his apartment in DC when I was in town and needed a place to stay. I sat up playing chess with Murray and his journalist friend, Charles Krauthammer, that evening (I beat them both, for the record). I admired Murray's earlier book *Losing Ground*, a prescient critique of welfare policy. But this IQ stuff was a different kettle of fish entirely.

To my surprise, Neal wrote back saying that *Commentary* wasn't interested in jumping on the anti–*Bell Curve* bandwagon. It was clear that they thought of Charles as one of their guys, and they were closing ranks to defend him. I responded to Neal, writing that they were more than happy to have me contribute when they spent months attacking Jesse Jackson for making allegedly antisemitic comments. If they came for the Jews, I wrote, you'd expect me to step up and say something. Well, as I saw it then, Murray was, in effect, coming for the blacks, and now *Commentary* had no interest in anything I had to say about it. What was that about?

I never received a response from Neal Kozodoy.

After being rejected by *Commentary*, I went to AEI president Christopher DeMuth and requested that the organization fund a follow-up conference on *The Bell Curve*. Now that the experts had had a chance to examine the data, a real public debate about the viability of its arguments was in order. If my colleagues in the social sciences couldn't coax a real response out of Murray, maybe AEI could. But DeMuth refused. He said that Murray was tired of talking about *The Bell Curve*—Murray wanted to move on. There would be no further discussion about it at AEI.

I was outraged by this response. I had a lot of respect for Charles Murray. I liked Charles Murray. But critics were saying his analysis of the data was fatally flawed. He therefore had a responsibility to answer the charges, because the consequences of such an argument as his could have an incalculable impact on our society. And now he was saying he wouldn't face the critics best equipped to challenge him *because he didn't feel like it?* The meaning of this was clear to me. AEI was doing exactly what Murray had accused his critics of doing: playing a political game rather than searching out the truth. Maybe I was naive to think that they would host an event that could undermine the credibility of a book they had already poured serious money into promoting. But if Murray and AEI wanted to make claims as consequential as these, they ought to be willing to defend them. My academic colleagues deserved better, I thought. African Americans deserved better.

The animus I felt toward *The Bell Curve* didn't end there. In the rotating column I wrote for the *New Republic*—"Hard Questions"—I would, for years, take potshots at the book and at Murray. I mocked what I took to be his lack of technical facility. It was all a bit snooty on my part. But the entire incident stuck in my craw in a way that couldn't be reduced to the argument and certainly not to Charles Murray as a person. True, I didn't like that he had ducked the critiques. But the reaction I received from conservative outlets when I registered reservations about *The Bell Curve* bothered me even more. It forced me to question what I was doing and where I was going in my post-recovery political life. The questions nagged at me. They wouldn't go away.

WHATEVER MY FEELINGS IN 1994, decades have now passed since the publication of *The Bell Curve*. If time has not borne out all of its claims (I think the jury's still out on some of them), what is now apparent is that many of the criticisms Murray received then, and is still receiving to this day, are wrongheaded and unfair. I was not at fault to insist that he face his critics more squarely. But in my tacit assent to the idea that his or any other investigation into connections between genetics, intelligence, and race is a priori racist, I was just plain wrong. These are legitimate questions and we're only beginning to grapple with them. Murray's book, whatever its flaws, will one day be viewed as an early entry in an important body of research. Since *The Bell Curve*, Murray has published many more books, several of which are profoundly incisive works that ask questions few are willing to contemplate out loud. We need more such iconoclastic provocations. We should not simply brush them aside, nor should we write off their authors.

IN 1991, I PARTICIPATED IN A DEBATE on William F. Buckley's TV show, *Firing Line*. The resolution was "that freedom of thought is in danger on American campuses." I was arguing the affirmative position alongside John Silber, Dinesh D'Souza, and Buckley himself. D'Souza had earned his spot at that table alongside the three of us largely on the strength of his new book, *Illiberal Education*, which, as the debate moderator, my *New Republic* editor Michael Kinsley, noted, could have served as the text for the entire debate.

I liked D'Souza's book. It seemed to me that political correctness was indeed running amok on campuses, that harmless idioms and figures of speech were being dubiously cited by campus activists as evidence of entrenched racism and sexism, that classic texts in any number of fields were being pushed off syllabi at the behest of left-wing culture warriors, and that matters of public morality were being ceded to a handful of noisy relativists who seemed to hold all values (save their own) in contempt. *Illiberal Education*, while perhaps a little shaky on the facts, voiced similar concerns. It wasn't just us staid old professors who had complaints (my God, was I really past forty?); plenty of students objected to this state of affairs, as well. D'Souza was a bit nervous at the debate, lacking the self-assurance of some of his opponents, like the literary theorists Stanley Fish and Catharine Stimpson. But for someone who was by far the least experienced debater on the stage, I thought he acquitted himself reasonably well.

In 1991, I regarded D'Souza as a fledgling ally. His next book made me rethink things. In 1995, he published *The End of Racism*, a purportedly devastating critique of liberal racial politics. When I perused my copy, I was shocked to find a profoundly dishonest book, one that mangled the history of slavery, arguing for instance that, because a handful of free blacks owned slaves in the nineteenth century, slavery could not have been a racist institution. The book described African Americans living in inner cities as though they were barbarians, all of whom existed in a state of squalid, crime-ridden ignorance. As I turned the pages and the list of offenses grew, I could not comprehend how anyone with even a passing familiarity with American history and culture could believe any of it, much less write a whole book in that register.

And what was worse, many conservatives *lauded* D'Souza! I guess I could understand that to a point. *The End of Racism* was, at its core, a critique of liberal welfare and civil rights policies. I, too, was a critic of these policies. But the mode of argument he employed and the flippant, irreverent, and inflammatory language he used to describe African Americans whom he should have regarded as his countrymen ought to have placed the book beyond the pale. I saw no desire in that book to improve the lives of the black people living in the inner cities, or to help America deal with its age-old civic dilemmas of race. I saw only contempt and condemnation.

I'm not sure what Bill Kristol expected when he asked me to review *The End of Racism* for his magazine, the *Weekly Standard*. D'Souza was a conservative, I was a conservative. We were both affiliated with the American Enterprise Institute. I suspect Bill Kristol thought I'd have mostly positive things to say. I did not. The review I sent in was, if not exactly scathing in its tone, then unqualified in its judgment. As a work of social criticism, *The End of Racism* was worth little, in my opinion. Any worthwhile arguments found in it were borrowed from superior thinkers, like the great iconoclastic economist Thomas Sowell. D'Souza did not so much argue that American culture was in a state of crisis—a sentiment to which I would have readily agreed—as he freighted all the failings he perceived in the country onto the backs of black Americans, who he saw as constituting a different society entirely from the larger, presumably white culture it existed alongside of. To Kristol's credit, he published my review anyway.

Regardless of the problems in some black communities in the United States, we were (and are) one nation, indivisible. "Their" problems are our problems, the problems of America writ large. Conceiving of all Americans as belonging to the same social totality need not entail taking a permissive attitude toward the very real "social pathologies" (as I would have said at the time) that afflicted so many black communities. But neither could we shrug our shoulders and cast "them" (the unassimilable ghetto blacks) out because they had become inconvenient.

D'Souza and I no longer occupied the same side of the debate. That was both figuratively and literally true, as we were now often pitted against each other in public forums. I found the position he represented to be intolerable. AEI employed D'Souza as a fellow, and under Chris DeMuth's leadership they were, as I saw it, once again promoting a book that was taking an irresponsible position on race. At least Murray and Herrnstein were intellectually respectable figures who harbored, I thought and still think, no racial animus. I didn't know if the same could be said for D'Souza. I felt *The End of Racism* was not only an embarrassment to AEI but to conservatism in general.

I decided that I wouldn't stand for it. Neither would Bob Woodson. He was an adjunct fellow at AEI at the time. Bob has never been able to tolerate anyone condescending to black people—his belief in the competence and value of black Americans is bone-deep. He and I agreed that we could no longer be affiliated with the American Enterprise Institute. Bob doesn't do anything quietly, so we called a press conference at the offices of his National Center for Neighborhood Enterprise in Washington, DC, announcing our resignation and explaining our reasons. *The End of Racism* was garnering headlines everywhere, so two prominent black AEI affiliates quitting their positions over the book was big news. We found our names cropping up in newspapers around the country. The *Wall Street Journal* put the story on the front page, along with a cameo illustration of Bob and me. I worried that Dinesh D'Souza's race—a brown man, an immigrant from India—would lend him unearned authority to address the race question in America. The public had to know that he was in no way the representative of conservatives "of color."

THE THIRD INCIDENT WAS by far the most painful of the three. For years, my friends Abigail and Stephan Thernstrom had been working on a book about race relations in the twentieth century. It was to be a sprawling admixture of social science, narrative, and social criticism. I had a sense of the Thernstroms' basic positions. I knew they were sharp critics of the Civil Rights Movement's latter-day incarnation. But so was I. I also knew they harbored no racial animus. They were great and loyal friends to Linda and me, practically family. They had given Glenn II a stuffed lobster as a gift, and it was a beloved toy that he insisted on dragging with him wherever he went. He called it Abby. Seeing him clutching it as he slept was a reminder of how much love there was between the Lourys and the Thernstroms.

The trouble began in the summer of 1996. One evening, Linda and I hosted a barbecue at our place. The Thernstroms came, as did the sociologist Alan Wolfe and his wife Jytte Klausen, a political scientist at Brandeis University. Alan was a fellow university professor at BU. He and I had team-taught a great books course about political theory, underwritten by a grant we had secured from the John Templeton Foundation. It was a beautiful evening, the kids and the dog were running around in the yard, and the six of us adults sat out on our screened porch talking politics after the meal.

Abby and I began to get into a bit of a dispute. She sounded pessimistic about the race situation. She seemed to suggest that troubled black communities might be beyond hope. If they wanted better lives for themselves, it was their problem. I couldn't get on board with that. "Look," I said, "I know the liberals are fucked up. But that doesn't mean we shouldn't care about what goes on in the ghettos. We can't write them off. We need to stay engaged. So what if we don't know what the solution to the problem is. We should keep at it. And if the next solution doesn't work? Well, we just have to try again."

Abby wasn't the only neocon who had lately developed this fatalistic attitude toward the urban crisis. I had found myself in similar arguments with Norman Podhoretz and Midge Decter, and I said much the same thing to them. Neoconservatism, I told Norman, was supposed to be a response to the limitations of the liberal approach to the urban crisis. But that doesn't mean that, when the going gets tough, you throw up your hands and say, "Well, it's *their* problem now." That's not to say I didn't occasionally feel despair, but I thought that, increasingly, the conservative response to any problems having to do with race was moral condemnation and diffidence, without any plausible alternatives.

Abigail seemed surprised by my insistence that conservatives needed to become more proactive on the race front. As the argument continued, things grew heated. Nothing got resolved. I just couldn't buy the idea that it was enough to criticize the liberal approach to the urban crisis without a competing policy proposal, and Abigail was perplexed that I thought anything more could be done. Things cooled down eventually, the party broke up, and everyone went home. But it was clear that everyone present was going to think about what had been said for a long time.

The following year, just before the publication of the Thernstroms' *America in Black and White,* Jack Beatty, a senior editor at the *Atlantic,* got in touch to see if I might be interested in reviewing it for the magazine. I said that I would. I hadn't yet read it, but I knew Abigail and Stephan well enough to anticipate their view of race in America. The book was a densely footnoted, sweeping, and impressive narrative on the trials and tribulation of African-descended people in the United States, from emancipation to the present day. It was, at bottom, a critique of over a century of liberal race policy and civil rights reform, an indictment of America's chosen course on the race question. It drew on mountains of historical and statistical research on income levels, education, crime, birth rates, and any number of other categories for black and white Americans, painting a dire picture of failure for what the Thernstroms called "the figment of the pigment," their sarcastic reference to the persistence of race-conscious law and policy.

When I received *America in Black and White* and started reading it, I found it dispiriting. During a long car trip, Linda drove while I sat in the passenger seat reading and taking notes for the review. I would read passages aloud to her and then formulate my rebuttals, and I found myself getting angry with the Thernstroms. The examples and data seemed cherry-picked and tendentious to me. I was not buying the narrative, and the more I read, the more I felt I had to use my review to say something, friendship or no.

Over the course of five thousand words, I took a scalpel to *America in Black and White*. It was an evisceration, and one that I can now, looking back, hardly call dispassionate. The review was, in some sense, a continuation of that back-porch argument we'd had the previous summer. But I'd had time now to really think about what I wanted to say. Near the beginning of the piece, I wrote that the Thernstroms' conservatism was "no sin." But further down, I wrote the following:

Being right about liberals' having been wrong is an accomplishment, to be sure, but it is no longer good enough. Many among the black intellectual and political elites are confused, angry, and scared. They lash out unreasonably, they play the race card with abandon, and they long for the moral simplicity of an earlier time. This may be deplorable, but under the circumstances it is understandable. Harder to understand is why so many serious students of the race problem in this country are content to start and end their discussion with a demonstration of the fact that racial liberals are confused, angry, and scared. Fixation on this point distorts one's ethical and scientific judgment. It is bad for the soul. This is a sin—one that is committed over and over again in this book. As a result, despite the many fine qualities the authors bring to the execution of their task, they have in my view failed to produce a work worthy of [Gunnar] Myrdal's mantle, to guide our public discourse on racial matters into the twenty-first century.

My review that followed was a point-by-point rebuttal of the Thernstroms' major claims. A reader who knew nothing of my relationship to the book's authors could be forgiven for thinking I had something against them. I didn't, at least not personally. I still considered them friends. But *America in Black and White* represented a viewpoint that had, I felt, led conservatives down the path to apathy and, at times, to a kind of smug satisfaction at the failures of the policies they abhorred. Never mind that real people were suffering as a result of those failures. I ran the review past Linda before sending it in. She gave it her enthusiastic endorsement.

I knew the review would bother the Thernstroms, but I didn't know how deeply it would wound them. It wasn't just that I had criticized them. It was that I did so in the pages of the *Atlantic*, possibly the most high-profile organ of liberal opinion in the country. I can imagine that it might have seemed like I was airing dirty laundry in public. Here I was, a black conservative turning around to my (former?) liberal adversaries and lending my credibility to their cause against that of my friends. But, at some level, I didn't care that it hurt their feelings. My discomfort with their positions on race had been building for some time. When a white man named Charles Stuart blamed the 1989 murder of his pregnant wife on a black would-be robber in Roxbury, police went door-to-door in that neighborhood harassing seemingly every black man they could find. The truth came out later: Stuart had shot his wife himself and invented the robbery whole cloth. Even after that revelation, the Thernstroms defended the police dragnet, saying that it was a reasonable measure, given the crime rate in the community. They were rationalizing the police reliance on one of the worst racial stereotypes. That pissed me off, and it was only one of many such offensive statements.

After the review came out, Alan Wolfe told me he had had coffee with the Thernstroms. They couldn't understand why I had done what I did. "He's black," Alan told them. "Of course he's going to advocate for his people." He understood where I was coming from. The Thernstroms did not. One day, I received a letter from Abigail taking me to task for the review. She called it "intellectually dishonest and morally reprehensible." I wrote back saying I was sorry she felt that way, but that I had needed to say what I said. I never heard back from her, and I never spoke with either Abigail or Stephan Thernstrom again.

Perhaps in writing the review, I was being disloyal to my friends. In the past, they had defended me in public even when it put their reputations at risk, and I had done the same for them. But how far could I take my personal loyalty to the Thernstroms before it stretched other, equally important commitments to a breaking point? I had to make a choice between loyalty to my friends and loyalty to my own beliefs. I believe Abigail interpreted my choice as a lack of nerve, as though I didn't have the stomach to do and say what was necessary in the race debate. If that's what she thought, so be it. I regretted losing the Thernstroms as friends, but remaining silent was just not an option.

DESPITE THESE BREAKS with the conservative mainstream, I still considered myself to be a conservative, albeit increasingly a critic—not an enemy—within. More and more conservatives championed what they saw as "colorblind" policies, which sought to remove race from public consideration. While that may have been, in some ways, a worthy ideal, America has never been colorblind. The idea that we could make it so by fiat was sheer fantasy. The dubious and cringeworthy stock phrase "I don't see color" increasingly became a conservative substitute for a considered position on one of the most important issues in American history.

And even if it was possible to have one, would I really *want* a color-blind society? My blackness was important to me. It was also important for my conservative allies, though they were loath to acknowledge it. Ironically, it seemed I was sometimes called upon to lend the credibility of my color to the conservative side of an argument whose stated purpose was to nullify the significance of color. That was incoherent at best. After all, if color really didn't matter, if conservatives truly were colorblind, why bother asking me to weigh in? Any intelligent white guy who knew a thing or two about racial issues would have done just as well. That is, if color didn't matter.

But it did matter. It mattered just as much to the conservatives who said it didn't as it did to me, who never tried to deny the importance of race in contemporary American life. The attempt to take race-conscious policies off the books at the federal and state levels could lead to irresolvable tensions both in terms of the ideological premises of the proposed laws and the lived contradictions of those of us who were involved. (How, for example, can the government effectively enforce antidiscrimination laws without taking account of the racial identity of a firm's employees?) I thought many of these race-conscious policies took the wrong tack, that some of them needed to be rolled back. But that didn't mean we should pretend to ignore the existence of race.

Case in point: in 1996, Ward Connerly, a wealthy black conservative businessman and a regent of the University of California, had thrown his weight behind Proposition 209, an antidiscrimination ballot initiative that would have, among other things, made race-consciousness in college admissions illegal in the state of California. This had been a longtime goal, and it was one with which I had much sympathy. Behind the scenes, Justice Clarence Thomas had helped to assemble a project called the Center for New Black Leadership. He was an informal booster, someone who opened doors and ensured that the camera crews would show up at our press conferences. This was a group of prominent African Americans who would advocate for conservative positions on a number of matters of public concern. The board included Phyllis Berry Myers, who had worked with Thomas at the Equal Employment Opportunity Commission and testified on his behalf at his Supreme Court confirmation hearings. Shelby Steele and Arianna Huffington were also involved. I was asked to join as chairman, and I happily accepted.

There was a raft of issues that I thought the Center project could engage, like criminal justice, welfare, and education. But Thomas and many of the board members were gung ho on seeing Proposition 209 enacted. This was a chance to actually make change, to bring about the effective end of race-conscious affirmative action in a state of some thirty-one million people with hundreds of thousands of students enrolled in public universities.

To call Proposition 209 controversial was an understatement. It was national news, and, politically, it was a street fight. No matter which side won, everyone was going to get banged up. As conservative blacks, we had so many important issues where we could use our influence to move the needle. I worried that immediately getting involved in an issue that hot could alienate the very (black) people who could make useful allies in the future. This was affirmative action, their cherished institution. We were tugging on a delicate, central thread in African American life and culture, and we couldn't be sure what would unravel along with it.

One afternoon, I visited Clarence Thomas in his chambers at the Supreme Court and expressed my misgivings. Backing 209 was a risky move, I offered, one I wasn't sure those involved with the Center project should make this early in its existence. Thomas was not pleased with this response. As he saw it, it was now or never. If we didn't take this opportunity, who knows if we would ever get another chance. Now, he wanted to know, where did I really stand? I tried again to explain what I saw as the complexity of the issue, but he wasn't interested in what he must have regarded as my lack of resolve. The meeting came to an abrupt end not long after, and I walked out of his chambers knowing that I would have to resign as chairman of the group. It was clear that the Center for New Black Leadership was going to get involved in the California election with or without my consent, and I couldn't effectively lead it in a state of ambivalence.

In November 1996, Proposition 209 was duly enacted into law by California's voters. It remains on the books to this day.

IT SEEMED TO ME THAT I was being instructed by my conservative colleagues not to think, and to choose sides between my political affiliations and my race, my tribe. I felt compromised. But then, I began to think, wasn't that the deal I had implicitly struck all along? Had I really become the "pathetic black mascot of the right," as Martin Kilson had called me all those years ago? What would Uncle Moonie have thought of my political affiliations? I began to wonder in earnest: Just who had I become?

These thoughts had not troubled me much back in the 1980s. But I had done a lot of things in the '80s that hadn't troubled me at the time, and that I now looked back on with a shudder. The enemy within me shared many qualities with the enemy within the black community. Both had a problem with drugs, and both had a problem with family life. I had forced the enemy within me into retreat, and I had many allies in the battle. I had a job with generous paid leave, so I never had to worry about keeping the lights on. I had a wife who had stuck it out and supported me instead of leaving me to struggle on my own. I had a religious community who saw it as their responsibility to help me walk the righteous path. Had I been short even one of those allies, I could not be sure that I would not have fallen back into addiction, or worse.

How many poor black folks living in the inner cities, suffering from the social pathology that plagued those communities, had even one or two of those resources at their disposal? How many of *them* had allies against the enemy within? I knew better than anyone that almost everyone needs help to pull themselves out of dire conditions, often a lot of help. I had lived for years with a sense of myself as a fallen man. Now, sitting on high and wagging my finger at those living lives I did not approve of, I veered dangerously close to outright hypocrisy. I still believed in the essence of my moral critique. The out-of-wedlock birth rate, the violent crime, the lackadaisical approach to education, these were serious failings within the community. But were not those troubles partially perpetuated by a sense of alienation and hopelessness, by spiritual voids that could be filled neither by government programs nor by spontaneously generated "personal responsibility"?

I saw myself as a truth-teller, a black conservative saying the things that liberals didn't want to hear. But more and more, I found that many of my fellow conservatives didn't want to hear what a recovering Glenn Loury had to say, either. These poor blacks are my people, I thought. When the music stops, everyone has somewhere to go, whether it be Ireland or Italy or Israel or wherever else, an ancestral homeland to which they can retreat, if only in their mind and in their soul, to find succor and to honor the memory of their forebears. Where could I go? America was my home and that of my people. The black South Side was where I went in my mind's eye when I reflected on what made me who I am. And however badly I wanted it to change, I could not disavow it. Nor, I now found, could I go along with those who would.

Twenty-One

After spending years growing more and more uncomfortable with my position within conservative circles, it seemed I had finally fallen out of them almost entirely. The negative reviews of D'Souza and the Thernstroms, the break with AEI, and, increasingly, the critical pieces I was publishing taking the right to task about this or that made things more or less official. I still had conservative friends, of course, and in many ways, I *was* still conservative. My views about economics and the virtues of markets hadn't changed. I still had doubts about affirmative action and concerns about the bad incentives of welfare. And while inner city crime rates were falling around the country, violent disorder in black communities was still very much a problem that concerned me, and its victims were still almost exclusively black. But I came to think that conservatives were willing to throw the baby out with the bathwater, to ignore or to demonize black people in desperate circumstances without wanting to be bothered with the messiness of actually trying to solve the problem.

Although I had once declared that I was "getting out of the race game," I now found myself being drawn back toward explicit questions of race, but with a new emphasis. I had an idea. When Boston University president John Silber hired me as a university professor, I was one of a cadre of high-profile figures he brought into the fold. There were the writers Elie Wiesel, Derek Walcott, and Saul Bellow, the philosopher Roger Scruton, the poet and critic Geoffrey Hill, the physicist Eugene Stanley, and my political scientist friend Alan Wolfe, among many others. Silber expected that, creative and intellectually promiscuous as we all were, we would make good use of the freedom our positions afforded us. And we, in turn, would help to make BU—and Silber by extension—the envy of every university on the East Coast.

So I proposed to Silber that I create something I would call the Institute on Race and Social Division. It would be interdisciplinary in nature, global in perspective, a home base where I could invite world-class thinkers across the humanities and social sciences to spend some time working on whatever they liked and attending seminars and talks with one another. I'd provide funding for recent PhD recipients focusing on matters germane to the Institute to come work on their projects. And we'd host a series of academic seminars and big public lectures.

I was inspired in this initiative by my year at the Institute for Advanced Study in Princeton, where I had the opportunity to spend time with the likes of Michael Walzer and Albert Hirschman. That enriching experience had changed the way I thought about so many things. Given the resources at my disposal, I envisioned creating a place where others could have a similar experience. And best of all, I would be at the center of things, soaking it all in, getting the benefit of all the brilliant minds that I could gather together to think through the very problems I had spent my public and academic career grappling with. Also, I thought that I needed to open up my thinking a little bit, to dislodge myself from the confines of America's discourse on race and see what I could glean from the rest of the world.

By 1997, the Institute was up and running. We had a suite of eight offices on the fifth floor of a converted apartment building on Commonwealth Avenue, which was occupied by half a dozen or so postdoctoral fellows at any given time. We also had a conference room where our seminars would be held. I hired a wonderful woman named Sherry DuPont as my administrative assistant. She was a fellow member of the Hammonds' church, as it happened, and she quickly became my right-hand woman. A member of the Bethel choir with a stunning singing voice, she also ran day-to-day operations at the Institute with total efficiency and great attention to detail. She picked out the furniture and conference table, she picked out the art for the walls and the curtains for the windows, and she made sure that everything was up to her exacting specifications. I quickly took a liking to Sherry. Being such a stalwart part of the church, working with her was a little like working with family. In due course, I would learn that she had attended Howard University on a music scholarship but had to drop out before finishing. In her thirties, she went back to school at Trinity College in Hartford, Connecticut, to finish her BA. Her lifelong dream, one she was still working toward, was to attend law school.

Within a couple years, the Institute on Race and Social Division was booming. We brought in many talented younger scholars, such as political scientists Steven Teles and Melissa Nobles, historian Mia Bay, philosopher Jorge Garcia, and economists Kerwin Charles and Roland Fryer, who enlivened the place with their new ideas and energy. We invited an impressive string of speakers to give lectures and attend events. The great Indian economist Amartya Sen, the British philosopher and critic John Gray, the French sociologist Loïc Wacquant, American social science luminaries such as Gary Becker, Cass Sunstein, Charles Tilly, James Heckman, and many other distinguished guest lecturers all came to speak at the Institute. As director, I had the honor of introducing each of them to the audience of hundreds that would invariably turn out for our events. I also had the great privilege of hosting many of them at cocktail receptions and dinner parties in the house near the BU campus that the family and I had moved into specifically for that purpose, the cost of which was substantially underwritten by the university.

Even though I was now thinking more about race than I ever had, I still thought of myself as being out of the race game. Because, for me, what went on at IRSD wasn't a game. It wasn't totally insulated from the culture wars and partisan race debates—nothing truly could be—but at the Institute on Race and Social Division we studied the race problem as serious scholars, not as political partisans or pundits. For my part, I continued to publish economic theory, often with collaborators around the Institute and in BU's revitalized economics department. I was no longer quite at home among the conservatives. Instead, I had created a new home for myself.

SOME YEARS EARLIER, Linda, the kids, and I had taken a trip back to Chicago. Tamara was graduating from law school at the University of Illinois, and we wanted to celebrate with her. By now, Lisa and Tamara had fully accepted Linda as a part of our family, and they both adored their little brothers. Their feelings about me were more conflicted. Our relationship had been damaged by my prolonged absence from their lives. They would come to visit us in Boston fairly regularly, but that wasn't a substitute for the years and the distance. Finishing law school was a major milestone in Tammy's life. I wanted to show up to honor her achievement.

We were all hanging out the day before the party, when Lisa and Tammy suddenly grew very serious. "While you're here, there's someone we'd like you to call," Tammy said. She handed me a scrap of paper. "This is Alden's number."

When I heard his name, I froze. I had not gazed upon Alden's face since he was a baby, and I'd made no attempt to get in touch with him or to check in. I wasn't even sure that my daughters knew he existed. As it turned out, Tammy informed me, Alden had attended the University of Illinois at Champaign-Urbana as an undergraduate and then dropped out. After a few years of working as a DJ and pursuing some other ventures, he managed to work his way back in. That was where Tamara had stumbled across him. They had both been attending the school, she as a law student and he as a returning undergrad. A black man about her age with the last name "Loury." That spelling. Thanks to my dad, there were only a handful of us on Earth with that name. And thanks to Janice Brazan, Alden had been given my last name, not hers. Tammy knew immediately that she and Alden must be related.

I gathered that once Tammy confirmed Alden's identity, she and Lisa began building a relationship with him that they concealed from me. He was their half-brother. He was family. They wanted to know him. Evidently, he felt the same about them. Now I was standing before my daughters, both of them looking at me expectantly as I held my eldest son's phone number in my hand. They wanted me to call right then and there.

I was trapped. This was plainly an act of coercion on their part. How could I stand there and tell them no? To do so would have been beyond cowardly. I mildly resented their maneuver. Hadn't my mother's attempt to coerce me into supporting her financially angered me all those years ago? But this, I had to admit, was necessary coercion on their part, and it was for a righteous cause: forcing me to live in good faith. If I had told them I would do it later or once I returned to Boston, they could not be sure I would follow through. *I* couldn't even be sure I would follow through. I had spent decades avoiding Alden already, decades in denial, all the while knowing that if I had wanted to get in touch, it would have been easy. I felt shame wash over me. This was what it took to finally get me to face my firstborn son, an act of benevolent subterfuge on the part of my daughters.

Linda knew about Alden; I told her about him before we got married. I had to, because my overdue child support payments had caught up with me shortly after moving from Michigan to Harvard. Nevertheless, now I felt as though something hidden had been exposed. My tacit refusal to acknowledge my son was an open secret in the family. I eventually did pay the back child support, though not without prompting. But that was all there was to our "relationship."

I dialed the number, and he picked up. I told him this was his father speaking. When he replied he sounded tentative, unsure of himself. I couldn't blame him. However much Tammy and Lisa may have prepared him for this phone call, it had to have been at least as surreal for him as it was for me.

We agreed that we would meet the next day, before Tammy's party. As I saw him approaching, his face snapped into focus. I could see the echoes of my features, the faint traces of that infant's face I had last seen in 1969 visible even now in the man walking toward me. It was him. Once the truth of his identity sank in, my first thought was how much courage it must have taken for him just to show up. To agree, after all these years, to meet the father who had abandoned him, to agree to hear him out, that took enormous courage. Would I have been able to summon the strength to do the same in his place? I could no longer repress my shame over what I had done (and what I'd not done). I had shirked my responsibility to Alden, and in doing so, I had betrayed him and his mother. Nor could I fail to recognize my own hypocrisy. Hadn't I spent years lecturing about "the crisis of the black family"? I thought again of my father claiming Lee Lee as his own. What would he think, I wondered, if he could witness this reunion scene. I shuddered at the thought.

I suggested to Alden that we take a walk. We wandered around the neighborhood for about an hour, our talk halting, each of us trying to figure out where to begin a conversation that should have started decades ago. But what do you say? Pastor Hammond had taught me how to speak to God, but I was at a loss now when it came to my own son. Perhaps this was a time for prayer. I might well have proposed this if it hadn't seemed so unctuously self-serving. For his part, Alden was passive, quiet even, though I did not get the sense that he was a quiet person by nature (he was still my child, after all). He didn't evince any anger but rather a sense of wonder. He must have spent years imagining what he'd say to me should the opportunity arise, maybe even envisioning a moment like this one. I could only guess at what was going through his mind.

Despite the awkwardness, we agreed our reunion was a good thing. We'd put one foot in front of the other, take it slow, and with time we'd come to know each other. Tammy's party was about to start, so we parted ways. I now had Alden's phone number. I'll be in touch, I told him. And I meant it.

And yet, years would go by before I exchanged words with him again.

———

BY THE END OF THE DECADE, the Institute on Race and Social Division was really on a roll. There was a sense that I had not only broken with the right on matters of policy but also aligned myself with the liberals. I did little to discourage this. In fact, it felt good. There were very few black conservative public intellectuals of note in America. In the 1980s and '90s, you probably could have fit us all comfortably in someone's living room. Most of the black intelligentsia ranged from the center-left to the far left. Those were the people who gave it to me the worst during my years as a proud Reaganite. They criticized me on television and in print, inveighed against me, and called me—if not explicitly, then in spirit—an Uncle Tom and a grifter who was shilling for the racist right. Nothing made me more furious than the accusation of "disloyalty," the idea that because I was willing to call out the obvious failures of black leadership, I was somehow betraying black people writ large. My colleagues in economics had always been receptive to my technical work, but when it came to matters of culture and politics, it was hardly even a decision for the Negro Cognoscenti: for most observers, I was obviously beneath contempt.

But now I sensed that my very public resignation from AEI, my indignation at *The Bell Curve*, and my subsequent criticisms of the right on race matters was casting me in a more favorable light with mainstream black public figures. "Finally," you could almost hear them say, "he's come around." They started to invite me to their panels and their cocktail parties. When I gave a lecture, they would show up, and not just to hector me from the audience during the Q & A. In 1999, I was invited by the American Economic Association to speak at a conference in Austin, Texas, organized by the Association's Committee on the Status of Minority Groups in the Economics Profession. I delivered a lecture entitled "The Superficial Morality of Colorblindness," making it very clear that I stood against the prevailing attitude among conservatives on that question. As soon as I finished, I heard the voice of the Howard University economist Bill Spriggs shout out, "Welcome home, Glenn!" I didn't mind hearing that. Not at all.

Perhaps it was this sense that I was back home where I belonged that led Henry Louis "Skip" Gates Jr. to invite me to deliver Harvard's W. E. B. Du Bois Lectures for the year 2000. Gates was the most prominent black academic in America, known not only for the quantity and quality of his research but as a kind of promoter of African American history and culture. His scholarly bona fides—a mountain of publications and an endowed chair at Harvard—lent an air of authority to his public statements about race, and his undeniable skill as a communicator ensured that he was called upon often to fill that role.

Under Gates's management, the W. E. B. Du Bois Lectures had by this time become one of the most prestigious academic speaking engagements in the country. I leapt at the opportunity to deliver them. And I had been working on some ideas ambitious enough to meet the demands of the moment. I had been developing a theory of racial inequality, one that took seriously the notion that blackness remains a real social impediment, while rejecting the notion that we can adequately explain racial inequality by making recourse to normative ideas about moral error, individual prejudice, and de jure discrimination. Racist beliefs and behaviors are no doubt ugly, I thought, but their ugliness cannot account for the way that racial inequality persists in predictable and established patterns. Blackness carries with it a social stigma, and people with dark skin, in general, receive less fair treatment in America than those with light skin. You could look to figures on discrimination in housing, bank loans, and other areas and find that this is the case.

The concept of racism was too imprecise to have any real power to explain how this stigma could perpetuate itself. "Racism" connotes a kind of irrationality, a mistaken and illogical preference on the part of the racist about who deserves fair and just treatment, about who is worthy of respect and trust. But it seemed to me that stigma could be more readily explained as both a *rational response* to a set of social circumstances and the *cause* of those circumstances. Imagine the case of the stereotypical New York City cab driver who does not want to stop for young black men because he fears being robbed. He believes picking up a young black man to be less wise than picking up, say, an old white lady, because he believes that young black men are, on the whole, more likely to rob him than old white ladies. Now let's also say that, as a statistical matter, the cabbie is correct. No matter how unlikely he is to be robbed by a young black man, he is still *more* likely to be robbed by one than by an old white lady. Cabbies then rarely choose to pick up young black men.

But when this happens, young black men who are simply looking to hail a taxi will notice that it's almost impossible to get one to stop. They'll then find some other means to get where they're going and eventually stop bothering to even try to hail a cab. As a result, cabbies who engage in biased profiling will have incentivized law-abiding riders to take themselves out of the pool of potential fares *and also increased the likelihood that any young black man looking for a ride will be a robber*, as only robbers will be left. In that case, the cabbie will be acting rationally when he sees one of them trying to flag him down and keeps driving. Through this rational behavior, he will also have brought into being the very state of affairs to which he is reacting. The color of the potential fare's skin has nothing to do with their propensity to rob—dark skin doesn't explain why young men rob cabbies—and yet it will have become a somewhat reliable indicator of a fare's intent to do just that.

What we call stigma, then, is best described as a social process. The central idea around which my W. E. B. Du Bois Lectures turned was that stigma consists of "biased social cognition." Biased because it prefers one group to another; social because it plays out in a complex field of interactions among many people; and cognition because it inheres in the thought processes that motivate social actors. I use the cabbie example for its familiarity, but in the lectures, I showed that biased social cognition can go a long way to explaining any number of forms of racial inequality, and without relying on the idea that such inequality is necessarily the result of racial animus or malice. Ordinary people and institutions can respond to incentives in totally rational ways that actually create and perpetuate the very stigmas they are responding to.

I had the argument for this series of three lectures mapped out in my head, in my notes, and in shorter talks I had been giving. The matter of getting everything organized and ready for public consumption, though, was another thing. As the date approached, I was scrambling, laboring over my phrasing, wanting to get every single word nailed down. My argument functioned like a Swiss watch—each part meshed with every other. Each lecture had to be perfectly articulated in order to do justice to the logic of the whole, and so writing everything out required intense concentration. My tendency to procrastinate over high-pressure projects was not helping. I had waited until the last minute to finish conference papers before, but at meetings like that, I would be speaking before maybe fifteen people, and fifty at the absolute most. A certain amount of looseness was acceptable. I would be speaking before about a hundred people at the W. E. B. Du Bois Lectures, many of them top experts and prominent figures, with the cameras rolling to boot. They would be expecting a major statement, and I couldn't disappoint them. Mere hours before I was to step up to the podium, I was still writing that evening's lecture. I finished with just enough time to throw on a suit and get out the door.

Skip Gates hosted a dinner at his beautiful home the evening after that first lecture. Larry Summers, who was about to finish serving as Bill Clinton's Treasury Secretary and would soon be named president of Harvard University, suggested to me that in my lecture I had described something like a bank run on black people. That had never occurred to me, but Larry was right! A bank run happens when people come to believe that their bank is going to run out of money. Believing their savings to be at risk, they all, in a totally rational fashion, attempt to withdraw it at the same time. But when everyone tries to withdraw all their funds at the same time, the bank actually *does* run out of money, which *does* put the savings of anyone who didn't make it to the bank in time at risk. A shared belief about some state of affairs, regardless of whether or not it is unavoidably true, brings that state of affairs into being.

Dinner concluded around eleven at night, after which I went home, got what sleep I could, and then got up bright and early because, of course, I hadn't finished the second lecture, either. Again, I was writing up to the very last minute. I went and delivered the talk, attended a dinner at a restaurant, went home, slept for a few hours, woke up bright and early, *finished writing the third lecture*, delivered it, attended the reception afterward, and then went home and collapsed into bed. To any future deliverers of the W. E. B. Du Bois Lectures, a word of advice: do not procrastinate.

Despite nearly sabotaging them myself, the talks were a huge success. They got an enthusiastic reception in the room and in the dinner conversations afterward. Lindsay Waters, the editor of Harvard University Press, got in touch soon after to suggest that the lectures might make a good book. The next year it was published under the title *The Anatomy of Racial Inequality.*

NOT LONG AFTER THE LECTURES, the MacArthur Foundation invited me to advise them on their grant-making strategy. I would attend a series of meetings to that end, along with eight or ten other invitees. The Foundation had sent us the names of the other participants. They wanted to ensure that each of us knew something about the others, so they asked everyone to submit a portfolio that we felt best represented our work, and all of us would be given copies of the lot of them.

The package that arrived for me was pretty hefty. I wanted to make sure that I fully absorbed all this material, so the weekend before the meeting, I drove up to the summer home in New Hampshire that Linda and I had bought. I intended to do nothing more than read over the material at a leisurely pace and relax.

One of the portfolios came from a woman named Laura Washington, the publisher of the *Chicago Reporter*, a legendary periodical focused on politics and culture. In it was a selection of articles that conveyed her editorial sensibilities and those of the paper. As I leafed through the photocopied sheets, my eyes stopped on a title: "Fatherhood, Ready or Not—'I'm pregnant, and it's yours.'" The byline read "Alden Loury."

The piece tells the story of the birth of Alden's daughter Amirah, my granddaughter. Alden had split up with a long-term girlfriend, but a few weeks after the breakup, she informed him that she was pregnant. Alden faced a crisis. He could not be with Amirah's mother—they were simply not compatible—but he could not bear the idea of his daughter growing up without a father. Without naming me, he told of his own fatherless upbringing, of our first meeting, of my subsequent silence, and of his determination to be present for his daughter in a way that I had not been for him. After listing the lengths he'd gone to in order to be present for Amirah, he ended with the line, "Still, every day I work to be a better father than I have been—and a better father than I ever had."

As I read Alden's writing, I went cold inside. The sensation of shame was excruciating. I had a granddaughter. How could I not know that? What had I done? I felt such admiration for Alden, both for his determination to raise Amirah and for his beautifully crafted prose. He was a good man, a gifted man. Like my own dad, Alden knew what it meant to struggle, and he was gritting his teeth and pushing forward with everything he had. His grandfather would be so proud of him. I, too, felt a strange sense of pride, although I knew I could take no credit for what Alden was making of himself. That credit, I realized, was owed to Janice Brazan. I sat there alone at the kitchen table, still clutching the article, and I wept.

Once I composed myself, I grabbed my address book and immediately dialed Alden's number. No one picked up. But in the days that followed, I tried again and again until I finally reached him. "I read your piece," I told him. "My God, I don't know what to say. How can I begin to apologize?" I asked him if we could try again, and to my great relief, he said we could. Alden would have had every right to tell me to go to hell, but he had the grace to grant me another chance. Maybe I couldn't ever make things right, but I could do my best. I was resolved: I would not blow it this time. I would not choke.

The MacArthur Foundation meetings began a few days later. At the opening cocktail reception, I scanned the room and quickly found Laura Washington. There weren't many black women there; she was easy to spot. Our eyes met, and in an instant I knew that she knew everything. I walked over and introduced myself. Within minutes we were locked in a hug.

Alden, who had been working as a journalist for the *Chicago Reporter* for some time, apparently told Laura that I had gotten in touch after reading his article. Coincidence or fate or God provided her with the chance to send a message through that portfolio that everyone at the meeting would read, but that only I would truly understand.

My son was hurting. I had hurt him. But still, after all these years, it was not too late. It only occurred to me later that Laura must have asked Alden's permission to include his piece in the portfolio. She wouldn't have taken such a delicate personal matter into her own hands. I was more grateful to her than I would ever be able to say.

This time I made good on my word to Alden. I started calling him regularly, and soon he was calling me. We had a lifetime to catch up on.

He only knew of me what he read in the papers, and a lot of that was not very flattering. I knew virtually nothing about him. Little by little, over years and decades, our lives became entwined again. When he got married, Linda and I flew out for the wedding. I was worried about seeing his mother, but she assured me that she was glad I came. In 2004, I happened to be in Chicago for a conference when Alden's wife Adrienne went into labor. The hospital was only a few blocks from the hotel where I was staying, so I hoofed it over in time to welcome my granddaughter Alexis into the world. I was so happy just to be there, and so happy that Alden and his family were happy that I was there. Looking down at Alexis, I felt a sense of pride that I knew I had not earned. It was God's grace, yet again. Still, I was there because Alden was my son, and now, finally, I was his father.

THE PUBLICATION OF *The Anatomy of Racial Inequality* put to rest any remaining doubts about where I now stood. It was a sophisticated work of social theory, but any educated reader could understand it if they read it closely. It was also pretty clearly a work of progressive thought. Accordingly, it received very good reviews in places like the *New York Times* and got thoroughly scorched in a number of right-wing publications. The conservatives not only didn't like the book on its merits, they were annoyed with me for breaking with them. But I didn't care. I knew the book was good, and I believed it would stand the test of time.

I also experienced something that truly showed me I was "back home." After the September 11 attacks, Skip Gates and Cornel West convened a conference of black academics to consider what to do in the wake of this catastrophe and the war that was certain to follow. The keynote speaker was Jesse Jackson, a man who I had attacked in print on more than one occasion. I was a bit nervous to meet him. In one of those attack pieces, I had misquoted him, and I subsequently had to apologize. It was an embarrassing mistake. I spotted him talking with Skip Gates and some others, and I approached. I told him I wished I hadn't written what I did. He didn't really respond. But during his presentation, he made a point of saying, "To say that Glenn Loury isn't black because he disagrees with me, well that's just stupid. We can't afford to leave brilliant minds like that by the wayside."

There were murmurs of assent. It felt *good*. Warmth bloomed in my chest. Bill Spriggs had welcomed me home, but now, I thought, I truly *felt* like I was home, embraced by my black peers and kinsmen, by the Negro Cognoscenti. Once again, I was a member of the tribe in good standing.

Around the same time, I received an invitation to speak at the University of Illinois Chicago. The man who invited me was Stanley Fish, one of my opponents in that *Firing Line* debate on political correctness I had participated in years before. While we were adversaries onstage, we got along famously after the taping. Despite not buying a word of his postmodern theorizing, I thought Stanley was brilliant, witty, and interesting. He was dean of the humanities at UIC, and when *The Anatomy of Racial Inequality* came out, he asked me to give a university-wide lecture. This was the biggest audience I would ever have in my hometown, so I invited my uncle Alfred to attend. Adlert had died years earlier, but I at least wanted Alfred to see what his nephew had accomplished; I wanted to show off a little in front of this man who meant so much to me. Alfred was apparently receptive to the idea, because he brought eight of his sons with him.

We all attended the reception together, which was hosted by the distinguished economic historian Deirdre McCloskey at her stylish loft apartment in Printers Row, in the South Loop. Watching my proudly working-class uncle mixing with a room full of refined academics was hilarious. Caterers passed out canapes. Alfred popped one in his mouth without looking at it and immediately spat it back into his hand: "Ugh! What is this?" When someone told him it was raw tuna, he looked appalled. "Y'all got any pork back there?"

Alfred was in his late seventies, but every bit of his charisma and charm was intact. Deirdre was absolutely smitten with him. She didn't know anything about his life or his twenty-two children by four women or his idiosyncratic beliefs. All she saw was a tall, handsome man with a magnetic personality and a beautiful smile. Alfred didn't know anything about Deirdre either, other than that she had a really nice apartment. They were openly flirting with each other, and at some point I felt like I had to tell him what everybody else in the room knew: Deirdre was a trans woman. It was no secret. She had just published a book about her transition. A piece of information like that mattered to a guy like Alfred. I have no idea what was going through his head when I told him, but he was clearly shaken. Talk about culture shock.

Later in the evening, it was Alfred's turn to take me aside. He wanted me to know that he was not very happy with the lecture I had delivered, nor with the way I was comporting myself among my white colleagues. Alfred didn't read the kind of magazines and journals where I published when I was a neoconservative, nor those where I was publishing now. But he could tell from my talk that I wasn't a radical of any stripe. He didn't like the way I was glad-handing with the white administrators and senior faculty, didn't like the equanimity with which I met respectful criticism from white people who raised their hands during the Q & A. Where was the fire? Where was the oppositional spirit? Didn't I know that the white man still had his boot on our necks?

"Who are you?" he asked. "What are you trying to achieve? We could only send one of us out to MIT and Harvard, to that world. We sent you. And now I don't see anything of us in what you do. Don't you realize that we are a people apart here in America, that we're in a fight to the death. And now, professor, it seems like you've joined the other side."

I stood there as Alfred berated me, angrily thinking that I should just tell him off. I didn't escape the South Side; I transcended it. What did Alfred understand of my life? I'd traveled all over the world speaking before different kinds of people, meeting different kinds of people, trying to make my mark. I'd lectured in India and Australia and Korea and

South Africa. I'd shaken hands with the president of the United States and with the pope. I felt at that moment that Alfred's vision was very small, that he lived a narrow existence, and now he was trying to grab my ankle, pull me down, and cram me back into it with him.

In *A Portrait of the Artist as a Young Man*, James Joyce has Stephen Dedalus say, about Irish nationalism, "When the soul of a man is born in this country there are nets flung at it to hold it back from flight. You talk to me of nationality, language, religion. I shall try to fly by those nets." I thought I understood exactly what Joyce meant. One had not only to escape one's origin but to use the very fetters that held one in place as the means to achieve freedom. Ralph Ellison, author of that great American novel *Invisible Man*, would have agreed. And that was precisely what I had been trying to do: get free. Alfred seemed to be telling me that freedom could only come at the price of my "authenticity." I wanted that authenticity, but not if it meant sacrificing all that I had worked to become. It also seemed to me that true authenticity must run deeper than some outdated notion of white oppression. I wouldn't be defined by the folks who stood against me, no matter who they were, no matter if it was "whitey" or my own uncle.

Beneath all the anger, though, I also felt a deep sadness. Here was a man I had grown up trying to emulate. For a formative period in my life, Alfred, like his older brother, Adlert, was all I believed a man should be. I could never truly extinguish my desire for his approval. Now that he had withdrawn it, I felt I had lost something I could not replace. My black colleagues may have been telling me that I was home, but now I knew the truth of the matter: I would have to forge my own path forward, that I could never go home again.

Twenty-Two

In the fall of 2000, big things were afoot for my assistant Sherry DuPont. Despite having transitioned to a twenty-hour work week, she was keeping things at the Institute on Race and Social Division running smoothly, presiding over the day-to-day scheduling and operations with a sure hand. We had hired an assistant administrator, a woman named Bobbie Patrick, to help her out. Nonetheless, if anybody—myself included—had a question about what was going on, when it was happening, how it would be paid for, or whom to contact about some issue, Sherry was the woman to see.

She was also hot on the heels of her dreams. She had been admitted the previous spring into Boston University's law school, and she was doing great. I'd see her hustling around campus in her bib overalls, her hair pulled back and her book bag trailing behind her. I'd walk by a campus café and see her through the window, pencil in hand, concentrating hard on some legal tome. And her efforts were being recognized by her peers. In her second semester, she made law review. I was sure nothing could stop Sherry. I was so proud of her.

But in the spring of 2001, she fell ill. She contracted a virus that attacked her heart, and the doctors couldn't stop it. The only solution was a transplant, and she did not have much time. All summer, Linda and I worried over her, wondering when she would receive word that a suitable heart was available. It never came. By early fall 2001, Sherry DuPont was dead.

Sherry's death devastated me. I couldn't process it. We worked side by side every day. I watched her grow and admired her drive and determination. When she made something good happen for herself, I felt like something good had happened to *me*. This woman who had had a false start or two was finally coming into her own. She had her entire life ahead of her and every reason to be optimistic. She lived an exemplary Christian life, had a family that loved and supported her, and had been ensconced within a big circle of friends. Maybe nobody deserves a fate like Sherry's, but she certainly deserved better, I thought.

Sherry was a pillar of the Hammonds' church. She was so beloved, had so many friends and family coming in from out of town to pay their respects, that they had to move the funeral service to a larger venue, the St. Paul AME Church in Central Square in Cambridge. Her mother flew in from New Orleans. I had never met her, but she knew I was an important person in Sherry's life. When someone pointed her out to me, I approached her to offer what condolences I could. I told her mother how much Linda and I loved Sherry, what a wonderful person she was, and how we were struggling with the tragedy of her death.

"Don't worry," Sherry's mother said, "she's with Jesus now. He loved her more and took her unto himself." She seemed almost serene, not at all the picture of a grieving mother.

I was taken aback for a moment. But then, I thought, I can only imagine what she's going through. The pain must be unbearable, and she's trying to deal with it the only way she knows how. If, God forbid, something like that happened to one of my children, I'm not sure how I would deal with it. I mumbled something in response and took my leave.

The pews were filled when Pastor Ray Hammond stepped up to the front of the cathedral to deliver his sermon. This was not some street preacher. Ray Hammond was an educated man, a doctor, a man of science. Surely, he would be able to understand and convey the reality of the situation in the course of paying tribute to Sherry's life. But as he spoke, the same sentiment that animated Sherry's mother's comments came from Ray Hammond's mouth. "We have not come here to mourn the death of Sherry DuPont," he said, "but to celebrate her everlasting life." He stood up there praising Jesus, and he sounded almost excited for Sherry, as though she had simply embarked on a long trip. As his sermon wound down and as the spirit of the Lord seized the assembly in that sanctuary, an almost joyous atmosphere emanated from the other mourners. They broke out in song as they filtered past the casket that held Sherry's body, repeating the refrain, "God's not dead. He's still alive," and closing with, "I can feel Him all over me!"

Now, perhaps Jesus was alive, and perhaps Sherry had gone to join him. A couple of years ago, I might have agreed without giving it much further thought. But in the preceding months I began to experience doubts about the literal truth of Christ's resurrection. I began to waver in my faith, bothered by a creeping sense that His teachings may not be the last word on this life. Sherry had in fact been taken, and she had been taken *from us*, I thought. When I walked into IRSD on Monday morning, she would not be there to greet me. When I attended church on Sundays—which I had been doing less and less frequently—I would not hear her soaring voice rising from the ranks of the choir. When I walked by the campus café, I would not see her head poking out from behind a stack of books. She was not on some eternal holiday with Jesus, I thought. She had been struck down by a freak illness, and as a consequence, I would never see my friend again, and neither would any of these people. My heart was broken. I had come there to mourn, to experience the pain of this tragic loss and to commune with others who shared my pain. Now I couldn't do that.

I sat there in my seat seething, enraged at what I saw as the delusions of these people singing and dancing while our friend lay there cold in her casket at the age of thirty-nine. I had agreed to deliver a eulogy, but

I did not deliver the one I had prepared. Instead, I rushed out some perfunctory remarks, practically in tears, and then sat back down. I imagine others thought I was stricken with grief, but they could not have known the anger I felt toward them. They were cowards. I couldn't bear to be around them anymore. I grabbed Linda and got out of there as soon as I could. When we got home, I reached for my Nietzsche and lost myself in *Beyond Good and Evil*.

Was this what it was all about, all this Bible study and prayer and meditation on the life of Jesus Christ, our savior? Did it just boil down to turning our heads toward the eternal so we would not have to face the trials of the temporal? He died for our sins, but did that mean that we were absolved from our suffering by the promise of redemption? If so, then a Christian life lived in this way amounted to bad faith, I thought, a denial of our responsibility to face up to the reality of our situation— namely, that there is an abyss into which one can fall, and it goes all the way down. It occurred to me, as I perused the writings of my favorite German philosopher, that this denial was not the righteous path, it was the self-righteous path, and I started to feel I could no longer walk it.

Not long after, I found myself in New York. I decided to call on my friend, Father Richard John Neuhaus. I was still struggling with Sherry's death, still furious with my coreligionists, and still questioning whether I would come out the other side of my crisis with my faith as a Christian intact. Richard was living in a kind of monastery on the Lower East Side of Manhattan, though he was not a monk himself. It was a spartan existence. His room was up a drafty flight of stairs. It had little more than a bed, a couple of chairs, a desk, a table, and a bookshelf in it.

By then I was drinking socially again. Cocaine was in the past. I never had a problem with alcohol alone and never would. I saw nothing wrong with having a scotch or two in the evening or sharing a bottle of wine with Linda over dinner, despite AA's absolute prohibition on any drinking at all. So Richard and I sat there in his room, a bottle of whiskey between us, and I poured out the story of Sherry DuPont. I recounted my friendship with Sherry, my wavering faith, and the funeral that I feared had marked the end of my life as a Christian. And as I told the story, my perplexity and anger all the while evident, Richard began to chuckle softly. I thought back to Tom Schelling's laughter when I told him of my insecurities at Harvard. I persisted, but he kept chuckling, and finally I stopped and glared at him and asked just what was so funny about this tragedy and the terrible crisis of faith it had provoked. Was it a joke to him?

"You think you're the only one?" he asked with a grin. "Christ Himself, on the way to His crucifixion, cries out to God to relieve Him of the sacrifice He must make. Ultimately, He hands Himself over to his fate, but He had His doubts along the way. Read Augustine. This arduous path is what you choose as a person of faith. There's belief within that doubt of yours, and still more doubt within the belief that's within that doubt. It's a never-ending struggle. Did you think it was going to be easy?"

Perhaps at some level, I did think it would be easy. God was a solution to the problems I had made for myself. If I could put myself in His hands, read my Bible, and follow its teachings, that would sort out life's messiness and ambiguity. My life needed saving, and the church saved it. Now that I was standing on my own two feet, belief had become less of a necessity and more of a comfortable routine. While I would often return to the words of the Bible, the truth was that God occupied fewer and fewer of my thoughts. In the early days of my conversion, I believed that I believed. But I began to wonder whether that belief in belief had itself been nothing more than a coping mechanism, a cover story, a temporary, pragmatic solution to an insoluble existential dilemma.

Richard's counsel gave me the fortitude to press on for a while longer. But as I continued to search my belief, I found only doubt at its center with nothing deeper concealed within. Gradually, I fell away from the faith entirely. After Sherry DuPont's funeral, it would be many years before I would attend church services again.

THERE IS THE COVER STORY and there is the real story.

The crisis of faith I experienced following the death of Sherry DuPont was authentic. My anger and my doubts and my waning belief in salvation through Christ were authentic. But there was something else happening around this time that aided and abetted my exit from the church.

One day at IRSD, I noticed that I had an appointment on my calendar for a meeting with someone named Ajume Wingo. He was a philosopher, and he had sent ahead some of his work for me to read. It was fascinating but a little esoteric. At the time, he was writing in the subfield of aesthetics, studying African masks. "African Art and the Aesthetics of Hiding and Revealing" was one of his papers, which had been published in the *British Journal of Aesthetics*. I liked his work, but it wasn't the sort of thing that we did at IRSD. I wasn't sure what this person wanted, but I had no objection to meeting him.

The man who arrived at my office stood about six foot two. He was built like a linebacker, with dark skin, a round face, and an enormous smile. He spoke in heavily accented but grammatically precise English with a resonant baritone. Ajume, I learned, was from Cameroon and a member of the Nso Royal Family. He carried himself with a regal bearing. He had studied philosophy in his homeland before coming to the United States to obtain degrees at Berkeley and the University of Wisconsin–Madison. After some preliminary chitchat, he simply asked if he could be a fellow at IRSD. This was not the normal application procedure. It would have been easy to send him packing, telling him to wait and submit a formal application just like everyone else. But there was something about him. He was very smart and very serious about his work. More than that, though, his personality and his sheer presence won me over. I found I just couldn't turn him away.

In a way, I fell in love with Ajume Wingo. Not in the romantic sense,

of course. But I found that I was irresistibly drawn to him. He was physically imposing and inarguably charismatic. He exuded confidence and
carried himself through the world like someone who was accustomed
to getting his way. He was a "man's man" who could talk philosophy
all day, then turn around and dance the night away. Uncle Alfred was
unimpressed by my circle of academic friends, but I could imagine him
being fascinated by Ajume Wingo. The guy was African royalty. That
would have been catnip to Alfred.

Ajume and I began hanging out a lot. He was fun, and he fed my ego
constantly. He took to calling me Shey Glenn, *shey* being an Nso royal
honorific. When we were both in Genoa, Italy, for a philosophy conference, he introduced me before my talk by declaring, "We are in the
presence of greatness." Whenever we talked, he would defer to me and
treat me as though I was the final authority on all matters. He would tell
me that back home in Cameroon, a man of my great accomplishments,
standing, and resources would have several wives, not just the one.

There was a club in Boston that Ajume liked to go to on Tuesday
nights. Instead of rock or hip-hop or whatever they normally played, the
DJs would spin music from all over West and Central Africa. It seemed
like half of Boston's African immigrant population must have been in
attendance on a weekly basis, and Ajume started bringing me along with
him. We wouldn't go out every week, but often enough. The music was
incredible, and so was the dancing, and so were the women.

At the club, Ajume would introduce me to some of his female friends.
There was Camille, an acquaintance of Ajume's. There was Grace,
from the town of Ho in the Lake Volta region of Ghana. There was
Lana. There was Tanya, a law student at Harvard. Slowly, by degrees, I
found myself drawn back into a life of late nights and secret rendezvous.
Through Ajume's connections in Boston's African community, I found
myself in contact with irresistible women who often regarded me with
the same deference that Ajume did. Was I not a man of great accomplish-

ment, standing, and at least some wealth? Did I not deserve the rewards and attention that were naturally due to such a man?

Despite his role as a facilitator, Ajume did not lure me back into a life of infidelity. Not hardly. I didn't need his help to yield to temptation. I had been primed for it my entire life. Not all of these relationships were sexual—Tanya was very careful to draw the line—but even one of them would have been enough. These women weren't only beautiful; they were also *interesting*. They led fascinating, often challenging lives. They spoke languages I'd never heard of, carried with them traditions about which I could not learn enough, and sometimes cooked outrageously delicious food. I was drawn to them, and they were drawn to me. Once I found myself in their world, I was not eager to leave it.

The real story. When my infidelity started up again, I had still been a somewhat regular presence on Sunday mornings at the Hammonds' church. It soon became difficult to endure the tension between the life of Christian virtue I was now clinging to only tenuously and the familiar life of infidelity and sexual indulgence. I would make excuses not to go to church or not to take up a leadership role in initiatives that Roy and Gloria had asked me to spearhead, like teaching a Sunday school class for new members. By the time Sherry DuPont's funeral came around, I was good and ready to leave the church. The spectacle I had witnessed, atrocious as I found it, allowed me to take the last step on a path I was already walking. What my friend Father Neuhaus did not know was that the Christian ethic had become a constraint that was no longer sufficient to bind me.

Ajume wasn't some nefarious influence on my life. He was a true friend to me and my family. He became very fond of Glenn II and Nehemiah, and he was a welcome presence at our house. At least for the most part. I suspected that Linda grew a bit weary of him, especially as she began to notice that when I was out late, it seemed almost always to be that I was hanging out with Ajume. That was true sometimes, but not always.

Around 2000, I was working with a particularly brilliant graduate student in economics who had come to Boston to participate in a summer program we ran at the Institute. We had come up with a good idea for a paper we could cowrite, so the two of us went to my summer home in New Hampshire for a couple of days to hunker down and work on it. We spent a weekend sketching out equations, taking long hikes in the woods to talk through ideas, and sharing meals. It wasn't the sort of thing I did with every grad student, but this kid was very special. He was an extraordinary talent, and because he came up hard and had more than a few stumbling blocks in his path, I felt a kind of kinship with him. Linda and I both did. He had great respect for Linda, both as a person and as an economist. During his time in Boston, we practically adopted him, having him over for dinner and even letting him crash at our house for a couple days when he was having trouble finding a place to live.

I needed to drop something off with Camille, one of the women Ajume had introduced me to, so on our way back to Boston, I decided to stop at her apartment. I told my young grad student that it wouldn't take long, I just wanted to say hello to a friend. As soon as Camille let us in, it must have been obvious that we were more than friends, not only from the way we were talking to each other, but from the framed photograph of me that sat on the coffee table.

In some sense, this was madness. My grad student friend and I had not known each other for long, and yet I was pulling back the curtain and showing him my newly revived double life. This must have put him in a terribly awkward position. Linda had been just as kind to him as I had, and now I was revealing that I was almost certainly cheating on her. I had a secret, and now he had a secret, one he never asked to carry. But I wanted him to know. I saw something of myself in this talented young scholar, and I wanted him to see that there was more to me than Glenn Loury, academic economist and social critic. I was a deeper guy than that, more complicated than that. Perhaps I also imagined, given that his background was not so dissimilar from my own, that he grew up in the same world of men that I grew up in, one that regarded a mistress as a notch in your belt, not evidence of moral turpitude. In a perverse way, I think I believed revealing my relationship with Camille would make him see me as I once again wanted to be seen, as Glenn Loury, past and present Master of the Universe.

Years later, after the grad student received his degree and embarked on a stellar career of his own, he said to me, "I never understood what you got out of those relationships." I cannot deny that his bemusement spoke well of him. I didn't really answer his question at the time, but there was an answer: Nothing could define me. I wasn't reducible to "economist" or "Christian" or "black man" or even "husband" or "father." I was those things, certainly. But I was much more than that. This was my life. I was only going to get one shot at it, and if I saw a way to broaden my experience, to enlarge my world, I was going to take it. This pursuit of experience often led me to do things I could not morally justify. Once, on a solo trip to Africa to deliver some lectures, I took a detour to visit Grace, who had moved back to Ghana. She introduced me to her friends and family and showed me what life was like in Ho. We toured the cities of Accra and Kumasi. I carry what I learned and saw on that trip with me to this day. In a small way, it changed me. My lifestyle was not admirable. It could lead me to do shameful things—things that wounded innocent people. I knew this. But shame was a price I was willing to pay.

It was impossible to communicate, just then, the complexity of my feelings. I knew that Linda's were as complicated as my own, and sometimes I would catch hints of that complexity. During the Monica Lewinsky scandal in the late 1990s, for example, Hillary Clinton could find no quarter. The right had always loathed her, and they now mocked her for any number of reasons: for allowing herself to be humiliated, for serving as a bad example to young women, for being too subservient, for being too domineering, for being too ambitious, for being unable to satisfy her husband, and so on. But some liberal feminists also took Hillary to task. In their view, she should have left Bill as soon as she found out he had been unfaithful. To do less than that was to tacitly condone male sexual impunity and to send a retrograde message to women that it was their duty to "stand by their man," no matter what he did. By staying with him, these women argued, she was striking a blow against feminism.

Linda hated what the Republicans were saying, but she couldn't stand that these supposed feminists would go on television and talk like that. Obviously, she thought what Bill Clinton had done was wrong. But she often said these feminist pundits didn't really know about the married life of the Clintons. They were standing in judgment of something they knew nothing about. Marriage wasn't easy. Hillary was doing what she deemed best for herself and her family, and any judgment should end there. I, of course, was in no position to offer anything other than affirmation of whatever my wife might have said about the Lewinsky affair. Linda's views were consistent with her own actions regarding my past affairs. But, I asked myself, could those views change?

DESPITE MY INFIDELITIES, I was still invested in being a father to Glenn II and Nehemiah. When they were old enough, I began taking them each on little father-son trips. Maybe we'd go for a weekend in Montreal in the summertime, or take the train down to New York to see the big city. Linda and I were part of a parents' group we called STARS: Seeking Tomorrow through Achievement, Responsibility, and Service. There were six or seven families in the group, including that of my MIT buddy Ron Ferguson and his wife Helen. We were all middle-class professionals, all of us at least friendly toward Christianity, and all of us were black. Mostly it was about forming a good peer group for our kids and providing them with stimulating experiences. We'd go to the children's museum or the science museum or the symphony together. We'd do a little homeschooling, like cooking up science projects for the kids to do.

It's not easy to keep an eight-year-old interested in an intellectually challenging task, and all of us parents would try to outdo each other in the cleverness of our activity designs. This triggered Linda's fierce competitive drive, and her creativity. She created interactive logic puzzles for the kids to figure out, and she was especially adept at finding ways to get them thinking about art. She taught a little lesson about the Spanish Civil War and had the kids running over to an image of Picasso's *Guernica*, all of them jumping around and pointing out details. She taught them about perspective and the vanishing point, revealing to them the techniques behind European realism such that they actually understood and became excited by it. Then she introduced them to the Impressionists.

We wanted to make sure Glenn II and Nehemiah experienced as much of the world as they could. When I was invited to give a talk overseas, if Linda's schedule permitted it and the boys weren't in school, we'd all go as a family. In Europe, we'd take the kids on the train and zip around the continent, showing them whatever sights we could. We took them to London and Paris, to Rome and Athens, to Vienna and Prague. On one occasion, when I was invited to a seminar in Austria, we all went, along with Linda's mother, and the Salzburg Global Seminar organizers put us up in a castle. Literally. There were thirty-foot tapestries on the walls and marble, gold, and crystal everywhere you looked. We had our own apartment in the place all to ourselves.

Linda and I had both had to learn how to refashion ourselves from working-class city kids into the kind of people who wouldn't get nervous when they saw more than one fork at their dinner setting. We wanted Glenn II and Nehemiah to feel as though they were at home in the world, wherever they might find themselves. I had the benefit of Pentti Kouri, who put me through high culture boot camp back at MIT. But my kids were growing up in a big house in a cosmopolitan environment, where talking about Monet and listening to classical music was simply part of the atmosphere. They would get good educations, attend good schools, read challenging books, and interact with all manner of people without, Linda and I both hoped, the sense that doing so was in some way antithetical to their blackness. I wanted my kids to listen to Mahler and listen to John Coltrane and feel, unselfconsciously, that both belonged to them equally. By now I felt they both belonged to me, but coming to that understanding was not an easy process. I did not want my kids to hear the admonishments of my uncle Alfred in their heads whenever they found themselves enjoying something he would have deemed "too white." And yet I wanted my kids to know that, while Uncle Alfred's world was nothing like their own, he and the Chicago South Side neighborhoods that he inhabited were also part of their inheritance.

My life and Linda's would also be part of that inheritance, something they would have to learn how to reckon with in order to understand where they came from. I was past fifty now, and still I was trying to come to grips with my own past. Would it take Lisa, Tamara, Alden, Glenn II, and Nehemiah that long?

Twenty-Three

In 2003, during a routine examination, a doctor found a lump in Linda's breast. She hadn't been feeling ill. As far as either of us knew, up until that point everything was fine with her. But there it was. A lump. Neither of us was sure what it meant, but we both knew what it might mean. The doctors acted quickly to remove it along with some adjacent lymph nodes, and Linda went through a course of radiation. She completed the radiation, and the tests came back clean. We hoped that would be the end of it.

But one morning, not too long after she got her strength back, Linda was playing tennis with a friend and found herself short of breath. She took a break but was unable to recover, and we took her back to the hospital. When the scans came back, the doctors discovered that the cancer—that's what it was; Linda was not one to resort to euphemisms—had spread. There were nodules in the pleura of her left lung. A more aggressive course of treatment was called for.

Linda's oncologist, Dr. Rochelle Scheib, recommended both radiation and chemotherapy. Soon Linda was receiving massive doses of drugs with names longer than my arm. Chemo essentially acts as a poison that attempts to kill off the cancer chemically. But this also requires poisoning the host body, and the side effects of treatment could sometimes seem as bad as the disease. While her first round of radiation left Linda feeling fatigued, the combination of radiation and chemotherapy sapped her strength almost entirely. Linda was a lifelong athlete who took pride in her physical fitness, but the treatment rendered her unable to exercise much beyond taking short walks. The doctors put a shunt into her arm that would allow her to receive the drugs without having to stick her anew with an IV every day, and the port would occasionally get infected, which meant more treatment and more drugs. She developed edema and had to wear compression sleeves and massage her arm constantly to prevent fluid from building up in her extremities. She lost much of her hair and took to wearing stylish wigs with artfully tied head scarves that camouflaged her baldness.

Dr. Scheib was outstanding, exactly what both Linda and I needed. She was comforting but realistic—she did not traffic in false hope or superficial cheeriness. Linda would have had it no other way. Her straight talk was reassuring even when the news was not as good as we'd hoped. She was also tied in with the active research community revolving around Harvard and the Dana-Farber Cancer Institute in Boston, where new therapies were constantly being explored. In the midst of a challenge like this, when a loved one is being subjected to medical treatments of a complexity and sophistication that a nonspecialist cannot truly understand, you have nothing to go on but your doctor's word and manner. Linda and I were both experts in a technical field—we both knew you couldn't just sit a layperson down and explain economics to them over the course of an hour. Now we were the laypeople. We had to put our trust—and Linda's life—in the hands of an expert. We could not really *know* whether Dr. Scheib's analysis and recommendations were sound, but we came to *believe* her. When she showed us the scans, we would see the tumors shrink and shrink and then grow and then shrink again. For all the pain, we thought the outlook was reasonably positive. It was going to be a long road, we knew, but there was no reason to believe that

Linda could not beat cancer. We put thoughts of the worst-case scenario out of our minds.

AMIDST ALL OF THIS, I took another new job, this time at Brown University. My move was due in part to a falling-out I had had with BU's John Silber and in part to the initiative of Brown's relatively new president, Ruth Simmons. By the fall of 2001, I had started to chafe a bit around Boston University. I wanted to take the Institute on Race and Social Division to the next level by recruiting affiliated scholars who could hold regular faculty appointments in the social science departments at BU while raising an endowment for that work from alumni benefactors whom Silber had been cultivating for many years. When I proposed that IRSD be featured in the university's fundraising campaigns, Silber, who by then had elevated himself to the superordinate position of chancellor, told me in so many words that he thought I was getting too big for my britches. I was deeply offended by his disdainful manner. The fact was that my track record of successes at IRSD since its founding in 1997 was one of the very best things happening at BU in those years. Everyone was saying so. To be dismissed out of hand was infuriating to me. After some thought, I decided in the fall of 2002, about a year after Sherry's death, to shutter IRSD and return to the economics department full time.

At about the same time, I read in the *New York Times* about the efforts that Ruth Simmons, the first African American president of an Ivy League institution, was making to diversify Brown's faculty. The economics department there was quite respectable. I knew a few of their economists by reputation. So, after enjoying a long-overdue sabbatical leave from teaching duties at BU, I let it be known through the grapevine that I would be interested in entertaining an offer from Brown. It took a while to materialize, but by the spring of 2005 an attractive offer was in hand. My sense of honor thus restored, I happily accepted. I took up my new duties at Brown that fall.

Brown has a reputation as the most liberal of the Ivies. Considering my much-touted return "home" to the black left, I fit right in there. The only problem was Brown's location: Providence, Rhode Island, about an hour and a half by car at rush hour, south from Boston. It would have been a trying commute to undertake four times a week, especially in the winter. So Linda and I agreed that I would rent a place in Providence and stay over there Monday through Wednesday nights when classes were in session. This was a common solution to "the two-body problem," in which married academics have jobs at institutions in different cities. Being away from Linda and the boys left me with a sense of nagging remorse—the fact that I was coming to enjoy my time away from them only made it worse. But, knowing me as she did, she insisted that I take the position. She could see that I badly needed a fresh start. We would find a way to make it work.

Once I settled in at Brown, I found myself drawn to a new problem: incarceration. I had begun thinking about the mass incarceration issue years before, when developing the W. E. B. Du Bois Lectures. Crime rates in the United States skyrocketed in the 1970s and remained high throughout the '80s. The nation's political response to this crime boom was to launch a corresponding prison boom. "Tough on crime" was a phrase that resonated mostly with conservative Republicans in the 1960s, but by the time we reached the mid-'80s, hardly any candidate running in an urban area—Democrat or Republican—could win an election without promising in one way or another to make criminals pay. This payment often came in the form of harsher, longer prison sentences, three-strikes laws that doled out decades-long or life sentences for repeat offenders (and not always violent offenders), and mandatory minimums that prevented judges from using discretion in their sentencing. It was not uncommon to see campaigns where each candidate tried to outdo the other when it came to punishing lawbreakers, each swearing they would crack down harder than the other on criminals. It seemed to me that, with this prison buildup, we were balancing our cultural budgets on the backs of some of the least advantaged of our fellow citizens, many of whom were black men. This, I thought, was bad social policy and wretched social ethics.

Perhaps this had been a necessary solution to the crime problem when it was running rampant in the cities, threatening to throw places like Detroit and New York into a state of civil disorder. That was the kind of thing I might have argued back in 1984. But by 1994, when Bill Clinton signed into law a now-notorious bill that imposed tougher federal sentencing guidelines and funded increases in the number of local police on the streets of America's cities, crime rates were already plummeting. They would continue to fall throughout the 1990s and into the 2000s, when they ended up at levels comparable to those of the early 1970s. Yet, despite this historic deflation in crime, when I began to study mass incarceration more Americans were in prison than ever, with around 2.25 million behind bars in state and federal prisons or local jails on a given day in the year 2005. That is a staggering number, even in a nation of 300 million. I was stunned to learn that the United States had 5 percent of the world's total population and 25 percent of its prisoners.

These prisoners were disproportionately male, and they were disproportionately black. We could cite any number of factors contributing to this sorry state of affairs: Yes, black men were more often convicted of violent crimes; but black men were also more likely to be arrested on drug charges (despite being no more likely than whites to use drugs). Yes, black men were more likely to leave high school without a degree; but black men also held less wealth, were less likely to be employed, and so on. Looking at the figures, it seemed to me that, on balance, America's incarceration policies posed grave questions about crime but, more fundamentally, about freedom. How could we truthfully call America the land of the free, I wondered, when our attitude toward so many of our citizens was to lock 'em up and throw away the key? How could we look at the huge numbers of black men languishing in our prisons, I asked, and honestly say that we were living in a racially just society?

I decided to launch a course at Brown on the subject of mass incarceration. It was a public policy course, not an economics course, though I drew on many quantitative studies in the criminology literature. Mainly, though, I was interested in the interaction between our carceral policies and the political foundations of the American nation itself. In my first semester offering the course, I lucked into a spectacular group of undergraduates. Any professor with a couple decades of teaching experience will be able to recall a handful of classes where, through some mystery of interpersonal chemistry, method of instruction, and subject matter, everything just clicks. In those rare classes, the seminar discussions are simply electric, and the students flock to office hours brimming with questions. My fall 2006 offering of Race, Crime, and Punishment in America was one of those semesters for me. I was really on top of my game as a lecturer, and the students were right there with me. Incarceration was a relatively new topic for me, more sociology and politics than economics. But we forged ahead, and every week it felt like my students and I were breaking new ground, discovering new ideas, and putting each other to the test. I grew to be very fond of them—Ariel Werner, Rakim Brooks, Trevor Stutz, Dan McCombie, Andrew Marantz, and Nathaniel Lepp, among others—and we developed lasting relationships.

One factor making the semester special was the presence of a transfer student named Andres Idarraga, who had himself spent years in prison. He was a second-generation American who got caught up in gangs, guns, and drugs and ended up getting busted. When he was released, he decided to remake his life. After a year at the University of Rhode Island, he applied to Brown and was admitted. His written work revealed a brilliant student with some rough edges, and his brooding presence transformed our classroom. Andres was exactly the kind of case that I found troubling when I thought about the consequences of mass incarceration. His crimes notwithstanding, he quite clearly was not a piece of human refuse fit to be warehoused in a dank cell for decades. Rather, he was an uncommonly gifted human being who had managed, through sheer intelligence and drive, to set himself back on track. What about the prisoners who didn't possess Andres's gifts but who nevertheless had the potential to become productive, law-abiding citizens? As things stood, when they got out of prison, despite having paid their debt to society, their records would make it very difficult for them to attain any kind of success. As a nation, we knew how to punish people, how to make them pay the debt we determined that they owed society. But we seemed to care little and to know even less about what happened to them once that debt was paid. The television show *60 Minutes* did a segment on Andres, who went on to Yale Law School after graduation. Correspondent Morley Safer interviewed me at Brown, and I used the opportunity to decry the monumental failures of America's criminal justice system.

The sociologist Bruce Western was a major influence on my thinking about incarceration around this time. His new monograph, *Punishment and Inequality in America*, received a lot of positive attention, and we soon became collaborators. We cultivated the habit of meeting for a beer or two on Saturday afternoons when we were both in Boston, at Murphy's, a public house not far from Bruce's lovely brownstone in Brookline. I got to know his wife, Jo, and their three wonderful daughters. Over pints at Murphy's, we would talk about race, incarceration, social policy, and pretty much everything else: our families, our lives, and our ambitions. Bruce became one of my closest friends, and that closeness led us to spur each other forward in our thinking. Soon we launched several public projects meant to call attention to the problem, and to formulate a critique of America's—as I would have said then—hypocritical and inhumane carceral policies. We became a tag team of sorts, convening forums that were meant to provoke discussions among our peers on what we saw as this most pressing ethical problem.

I went all in on incarceration. I did feel it to be a pressing issue, and, in some measure, a moral stain on the social fabric of the United States.

I also knew the tone of outrage I often struck resonated with that cohort of black intellectuals into whose good graces I had only recently been welcomed back. Indeed, there was no *blacker* project than criticizing America's prisons, through whose gates so many African American men were passing. It was a cause that united black radicals and black centrists, the kind of thing, I told myself, that any thinking black person would perceive to be a problem on its face. I had now fashioned myself into a voice of alarm and protest, and this only elevated me in the eyes of my new peers and, to be honest, in my own eyes, too.

BY EARLY 2007, the tests on Linda's liver began to concern Dr. Scheib. After another scan, she discovered a nodule. There followed more radiation, more chemotherapy, more tests, more appointments, and more adjustments to Linda's treatment plan. Slowly, the hope that Linda would ever be cancer-free faded away. Conversations about remission were displaced by talk about managing illness and maintaining quality of life. Returning after yet another appointment, Linda looked at me and said, "I may not know when I'm going to die, but I'm pretty sure I know what I will die from."

I supported Linda as best I knew how, but I just couldn't wrap my mind around what she was going through. The toll the cancer and the treatments were taking on her were visible to anyone. She was clearly a sick woman. Still, she insisted on retaining whatever normalcy she could. She continued to teach, work on papers, and attend faculty meetings at Tufts. I couldn't comprehend how she could sit at her desk and scribble out lecture notes all the while knowing that, in a very real sense, there was a deadly enemy within her. I couldn't tell her about my befuddlement. Neither could I simply ask her how all this made her feel. If Linda wanted to maintain the normal rhythms of our life, I wasn't going to disrupt things by dumping my own incomprehension and existential anxieties on her. But I couldn't keep it all to myself. During one appointment, I found myself alone with Dr. Scheib, and I asked her how a person could continue to live while this sword of Damocles dangled over her head. She replied, "You had a stroke once, didn't you?" It was true. I had a minor stroke in 2000 while sitting in my office at IRSD. Luckily, Sherry DuPont was there, and she took me to a doctor immediately. I recovered quickly and, other than the loss of some peripheral vision, there were no lasting effects. Yes, I told Dr. Scheib, I had suffered a stroke. "Well," she said, "how do you know you're not going to have another one?" I said I supposed I didn't know, but I also didn't sit around wondering if I might. "Maybe you should wonder," she said.

This was perhaps her way of telling me that I had my own health issues and that I should monitor them. Good advice from a good doctor. But I think she meant something more. She was reminding me that every one of us is hovering over the abyss. Linda did not know when her end would come, and neither did I. But it would come for me, just as surely as it would for Linda. I simply had the luxury of not dwelling on it. For all my troubled thoughts about Linda's condition, about the day-to-day ups and downs, the endless blood tests and chemo sessions, I rarely thought about what I was choosing to do with my own limited time on the planet. Indeed, I was living as though I was something more than a human being constrained to enjoy but one life on this Earth. Whenever I was not working, I divided my worldly existence between caring for Linda and worrying over her condition, and pursuing my liaisons and affairs. Was that really how I should have been spending my time?

Had I tried to achieve any kind of perspective on my own actions, I might have identified an unsettling parallel between my way of going about things and that of those Christians whose behavior at Sherry DuPont's funeral had so enraged me. In my own way, I too was denying the reality of death, of Linda's eventual death, not by turning away from the world but by immersing myself too deeply in it. Before Linda's illness took hold, I could tell myself a story about living the most expansive life I could. Afterward, and in the face of what was looming before us, I should have been able to see these affairs for what they were: sheer distraction, their own kind of turning-away, their own brand of cowardice.

Though Glenn II didn't know about my affairs, he felt my absence. I spent half the week in Providence, and as a consequence I began to lose track of little things in my sons' lives. Linda would fill me in on the details of their schoolwork and social lives, but it was a poor substitute for being there myself. Nehemiah may have missed me, but as he grew older he became harder to read. He was like Linda in that way. If he was having trouble, he preferred to deal with it himself. Glenn, on the other hand, had no qualms about making his dissatisfaction known. One day, after I arrived home from my weekly trip to Providence, he let me know, in his way, that my presence was missed.

"What's the name of my math teacher?" he asked. "What's my English teacher's name?"

I didn't know.

An argument ensued. Glenn told me I was shirking my duties as a member of the family, and I replied that I had to work to keep food on the table.

"Where are you? You're missing in action! Why are you always out somewhere else?"

He was unrelenting. And finally, without thinking, I blurted out the truth.

"Because I'm bored," I said.

That was it. At home, puttering around the house, attending to the minutiae of domestic life, I would become restless. When the family wound down at night and headed for bed, I'd find myself itching to get up, go out, and find some action. I couldn't do that back in Boston. But in Providence, with most of my responsibilities off in another state, I could do as I wished.

Glenn was appalled.

"Fuck you. You're bored? With your family? Fuck you."

That show of disrespect made me angry. But hadn't I, in so many words, said the same thing to him? In pursuing relationships with other women, or simply in going out and losing myself in what my solo evenings had to offer, I got a rush of excitement I simply couldn't get at home. I felt I needed the thrill and risk of seduction. Without that, what was I? Just a middle-aged professor who spends his days tapping out articles and sketching out equations and lecturing to students. I was more than that, and I needed to prove it to myself. But I could no longer ignore the collateral damage my search inflicted on those who should have been closest to me. Weren't they what made me more than what I was?

SOON AFTER I MOVED TO BROWN, just as I began to immerse myself in the literature on mass incarceration, I received an invitation to deliver the Tanner Lectures on Human Values, for 2007, at Stanford. Initially I thought I'd speak about affirmative action. But it occurred to me that this could be an opportunity to develop and present a more systematic critique of mass incarceration to a wider audience, via another high-profile series of talks. The forum was prestigious enough, and the subject was certainly weighty enough. Moreover, I had all along been contending that human values—that is, America's vision of human values—were precisely what was so problematic when it came to mass incarceration. So, despite my concern that, as an economist, I might fail to muster a level of philosophical profundity requisite to the occasion, I enthusiastically accepted the invitation.

The series of two talks were to include formal responses from scholars whom I would help to choose. One person I really wanted to invite was the theoretical sociologist Loïc Wacquant, a protégé of the immensely influential and pioneering thinker Pierre Bourdieu. Loïc, an expert on prisons and incarceration, had long been frustrated by other social theorists' inattention to what he saw as one of the most pressing problems of modern society. When I reached out to him, he told me that, though he would be teaching in Paris at the time of the lectures, he would take a long red-eye flight in order to make it to Stanford in time to attend and respond. I was honored that he thought this occasion was worth the trouble.

In the talks, I wanted to drive home that, while I was engaged in a social scientific analysis of race and mass incarceration, I was keen to underline some questions that the social sciences were ill-prepared to address, but that were no less important for that fact. Our prisons had, it seemed to me, become little more than human warehouses where the people we labeled thugs and criminals could be stored, in often deplorable conditions. Though these people had done bad things, sometimes terrible things, they were also just that: people. How should they be valued? "It should be clear," I said, "that social science has no answers for the question of what weight to put on a 'thug's' well-being, or on that of his wife or his daughter and son. Nor can science tell us how much additional cost borne by the offending class can be justified so as to obtain a given increment in security of life and property—or in peace of mind—for the rest of us." These were problems social science could describe but could not solve. That did not, I thought, relieve us, as citizens of the United States, of the responsibility of solving them through political deliberation. Simple cost-benefit analyses of incarceration could not do the job. A moral accounting was required.

Over the course of the two lectures, I laid out the problem and engaged in just such an accounting. My key idea was to distinguish personal responsibility of the individual offenders from the social responsibilities of the state. Criminals needed to be held accountable, but that should not be our only moral accounting. The argument connected. One person in attendance was the philosopher Joshua Cohen, a former student of John Rawls and the editor of *Boston Review*. The *Boston Review* magazine had a book imprint with MIT Press, and Josh thought enough of the lectures to publish them there, along with three of the commentaries, under the title *Race, Incarceration, and American Values*.

Josh and I became fast friends, and he invited me to record a conversation with him on something called *Bloggingheads*. This was an innovative web-based platform developed by the journalists Robert Wright and Mickey Kaus, who had met at the *New Republic* in the 1990s, back around the time when I was still writing for the magazine. One day, Bob realized that he could simulate the appearance of an online, face-to-face conversation between two people in two different places simply by having them each talk on the phone while recording video and audio of themselves, and then splicing everything together after the fact. I say "simply," but at the time the kind of technology we now use to regularly speak to each other on the web was in its infancy. There was nothing simple about it.

Pretty soon, Bob and Mickey were hosting all kinds of discussions between journalists, scientists, philosophers, and pretty much any two interesting people who had something to say to each other. My conversation with Josh was fun and it was a success, and soon Bob invited me to start inviting people on myself. One of my earliest conversations was with a young black linguist named John McWhorter, who had lately made a name for himself by publishing a book called *Losing the Race* and later resigning from his tenured position at UC Berkeley to join the Manhattan Institute, a conservative New York–based think tank. I put the screws to John in that conversation, trying to figure out why this brilliant young black intellectual was so gung ho on positions that sounded suspiciously right wing to me (and I was in a position to know). He held his own, though, and while I did not say so at the time, I secretly thought he may have been more often right than wrong.

IN 2008, LINDA AND I WERE IN BARCELONA. She had been invited to a conference to deliver a lecture about her work on social capital, and I tagged along. One afternoon, we sat in a square watching the people go by. Linda tried to get me to stop turning away and to face her. She knew about the affairs. After all that had come before, she recognized the signs: the absences, the thin excuses, the vague alibis. What about that letter I had written to her marking our tenth wedding anniversary? We had now been married a quarter century. Did those professions of faithfulness and love mean less now than they had then? What happened? She did not even mention what was most obvious to both of us: her cancer. And yet I could not, even then, bring myself to give her a straight answer. I performed contrition and begged forgiveness, but with both of us knowing what each knew about the other, I doubted the performance had much effect.

NOT TOO LONG AFTER the Barcelona trip, doctors found that the cancer had spread to Linda's brain. Surgery was impossible. She was already cycling through a number of experimental treatments, each of them with their own set of side effects. Nobody said it out loud, but we both could feel it: Linda was running out of time.

One day, she went to an appointment with Dr. Scheib. She was gone for a while, longer than usual, and I began to worry. I went down to see if her car was in the garage and saw it instead sitting in the driveway. When I went out, I found her behind the wheel, her head down, bawling uncontrollably. I slid into the passenger seat and sat silently beside her as she wept. Linda was not given to self-pity. If she had a problem, she didn't wallow. She made a plan and tried to fix it. She was a doer. But there was no fixing this. Between her sobs, she choked out a few words: "I don't want to die." I put my arms around her, told her I loved her, and said that we would get through this together. But we both knew how it would end.

Some years earlier, I started a family tradition. I'd rent a big house in the mountains or on the seashore for a week and gather the whole family there for an annual reunion. Lisa and Tamara and their young children would come and join Linda, Glenn II, Nehemiah, and me. Eventually,

Alden and his family would join in. We'd spend the week hanging out, going to the beach or the pool, bowling, playing cards, watching movies, and just enjoying each other's company. By the time Linda's illness advanced, though, it was clear that she would not be able to make the trip. She was now dependent on a walker and wheelchair. Just getting her up and down the stairs in our home was a task. She was too frail.

Still, Linda wanted to get out of town for a bit. She loved the Maine coast, so I rented a small house up there where she and I and Glenn and Nehemiah could spend a quiet weekend together and take in the sea air. I called my daughters to tell them about the change of plans, and Lisa got extremely upset.

"You're excluding us," she said.

"I'm not excluding you," I said. "Linda just wants some time alone with her children before it's too late."

She replied with a cutting remark, I replied with one in turn, and the call ended with both of us in a foul mood. I wanted Lisa and Tamara to see Linda. *I* wanted to see Lisa and Tamara, and I knew that Linda did, too. They were welcome to visit us anytime. But Linda also wanted time alone with her sons, and there was no way I was going to deny her that. When we returned, I called my daughters and asked them to please come and visit. Linda was dying, we didn't know how many opportunities there would be. Tamara got on a plane and spent a few wonderful days with us in Boston. Lisa, still fuming, refused.

Later, Lisa and I had a heart-to-heart. I wanted to understand what our argument was really about, because it wasn't about whether Lisa was going to visit us in Maine or in Boston. She didn't begrudge Linda time alone with her kids. There was something else bothering her.

"Daddy," she said, "we were just beginning to feel like we were part of your real family. Then you told us not to come. I felt like we were being excluded, and at a critical moment. I know she's Glenn and Nehemiah's mother. But she's our stepmother, and we love her, too."

My "real family." Lisa wasn't trying to hurt me, but the phrase stung all the more for its honesty. I had tried to heal the wounds my absence inflicted on Lisa and Tamara, and the fact that they had so much love for Linda and the boys was evidence that the attempt had at least partially succeeded. Of course Lisa and Tamara were my real family. But the attempt to bind us all together into a whole was proving even more difficult than I had expected.

IN THE WAKE OF *Race, Incarceration, and American Values*, speaking invitations poured in. My "partner in crime," Bruce Western, and I took the show on the road, bouncing from event to event, university to university, continent to continent. We spoke all over Europe. In Australia, whence Bruce originally hailed, we had a ball wandering the streets of Sydney, occasionally ducking around a corner to take a few puffs on a joint. The work we were doing could not have been more serious, but in some ways we were like kids, each of us goading the other. These were the years before the publication of Michelle Alexander's bestseller *The New Jim Crow*, which brought even more heightened attention to race and mass incarceration. If anyone anywhere wanted to talk about black men and prisons, it seemed, I would get a phone call about it. And Bruce and I kept stoking the fire, putting together projects about race and incarceration for the American Academy of Arts and Sciences and the National Academy of Sciences, and coediting a special issue of the journal *Daedalus* focusing on the topic.

My role was clear: I was to get onstage and rain down righteous fury on the evils of incarceration in America. I was to inveigh against my country's outrageous treatment of black men and to rage against the hypocrisies of the so-called justice system. It was a role I reveled in, as it allowed me to whip myself up into a frenzy of high-flown rhetoric and to whip up my audience in turn. The lectern became my pulpit, and I transmuted the preacher's fire-and-brimstone exhortations into sermons on the moral decrepitude of my country's failures, dressed up in the respectable language of the social sciences.

These performances—for that's what they were—left me feeling exhilarated, enamored of my own abilities on the stage, and intoxicated by the affirmation of the crowd. But late at night, when the adrenaline wore off and there was no one around to shake my hand, slap me on the back, and thank me for my "truth-telling," I began to question just what it was I was doing up there. I loved the high I got from speaking in this way and receiving the adoration of these strangers, the nods of affirmation I received from other African Americans who encouraged me to keep going out there and telling the truth. But was I doing this because I was a truth-teller or because I loved the feelings I got from playing the role of the truth-teller? In the midst of all the fervor, the crowd's approval began to take the place of a serious evaluation of my own premises. True, I thought, we were locking up too many people. But when anyone asked—or when I dared to ask myself—just what those young men had done to get themselves in trouble with the law in the first place, I brushed the question aside. Punishment was on one side of the ledger, but crime was on the other. In concerning myself only with the former, I began to think, I could not perform the genuine act of moral accounting I was claiming to undertake. There was a kind of intellectual dishonesty implicit in my righteous crusade against the over-incarceration of black men.

To complete the accounting, to balance the books, I would have to sacrifice something: that feeling of righteousness that I had come to love and to which I had, in some sense, become addicted. That feeling came to bolster my own certitude in my "authenticity," my blackness. I was carrying the flag for my black brothers, metaphorically raising my fist in solidarity. And I was met with solidarity in return. That felt good. But the doubts I began to feel, my niggling distrust of my own performance, was a different kind of authenticity, one that embodied a fuller, less passionate, less readily galvanizing analysis of what was really going on between the city streets, the courtroom, and the jailhouse. To engage in that kind of sober, balanced reflection, I would have to admit that my own play for authenticity, dependent as it was on the affirmation of the crowd, was perhaps not as authentic as it felt in the moment.

Twenty-Four

By 2010, the day-to-day reality of Linda's condition was a part of every decision we made. That fall, I had a sabbatical from Brown, and Columbia University asked if I'd like to spend the 2010–2011 academic year as a visiting professor. I had misgivings. Providence wasn't so far from Boston, but New York was a trek. Something could happen, and it would take me some time to get home. But Linda insisted I accept the position. She would not hear of anyone—neither me nor Glenn II nor Nehemiah—turning down any opportunity because of her. She told me to stay in Manhattan four days out of the week, just as I had been doing in Providence while at Brown, and to come home for long weekends.

"But you need me," I told her.

"What are you going to do for me here? There's nothing to be done," she said.

"I can hold your hand," I offered.

"You go do what you need to do," she said. "You can hold my hand on Friday, Saturday, and Sunday."

Besides, she would have her eldest son around. Glenn II had enrolled at Haverford College in 2007, but he was having some trouble. He decided to take a year off to figure things out, so he was staying at home with us in Boston. I was conflicted. On one hand, I thought he needed to get his education and complete his degree. On the other hand, as Linda's capacities continued to diminish, he was a great help and a comfort. And even though Linda felt the same way I did about Glenn's education, I also knew that she treasured every moment she could spend with him.

Glenn had already been present for one of Linda's health scares. That summer, I was in England delivering some lectures at the University of East Anglia. Linda had developed diabetes as a result of the treatments, and she went into shock. Glenn called me in a panic, worried that she was going to die, but he got her to an emergency room. I had to cut my trip short and return home.

Glenn and Nehemiah were each handling the illness in their own ways. If Glenn was feeling something, he would express it. He wanted to be involved in decisions, to be kept abreast of whatever was happening with Linda. You never had to wonder whether he was happy or frustrated or sad or angry—he'd let you know. That was his way of dealing with an impossible situation over which nobody had any real control. Nehemiah, though, became more withdrawn. He would be entering his third year at Columbia in September 2011, majoring in astrophysics, and he poured himself into his studies. I understood that he was taking school seriously, and I was glad to see it, but there were times when a little arm-twisting was required to get him to come visit with us. It was understandable. He was trying to manage being away from home, beginning this challenging new phase in his life, and dealing with his mom's terminal illness. The two of them, mother and son, had always been so close. He was having trouble facing up to her imminent demise. I don't know that there would have been a good way to handle it.

In February 2011, Linda began having some cognitive difficulties. She was slurring her speech and experiencing trouble with her memory. There was swelling in her brain, the result of the tumor. Though the doctors couldn't remove it, they could operate in other areas to relieve some of the cognitive symptoms. But Linda was still teaching. It was an undergraduate course in microeconomics that she had taught for many

years—she probably could have done it in her sleep. She opted to schedule the surgery over spring break in order to minimize the amount of
time she would have to spend out of the classroom. Linda loved teaching,
and she was not going to let the cancer deprive her of that joy any more
than was absolutely necessary.

As that semester wound down, we knew there was not very much
time left at all. By late May, Linda was more or less bedridden. I had a
knee issue, so after I wrapped things up at Columbia, I came home and
underwent knee replacement surgery. We made quite a pair. Linda and
I spent the early summer of 2011 laid up in bed together watching Red
Sox games and police procedurals on TV as Glenn tended to us, shopped,
took care of the house, walked our new dog, McCoy (our beloved Clifford had died some years earlier), cooked us meals, and brought us ice for
our respective aches and pains. I spent a lot of time sitting at the edge of
the bed and rubbing Linda's feet. I joked that our sex life may not be that
great, but I'd become a terror from the knee down. That made her laugh.

By the end of summer, the tumor in Linda's liver had grown to nearly
the size of a baseball, and the one in her brain continued to expand, as
well. We had a therapist come in to work with Linda on speech and
cognitive issues, but after some weeks, the health insurance company
balked at paying for sessions. When I got on the phone and demanded to
know why, I was told, in so many words, that they didn't see the point,
since Linda's prognosis gave her only a couple of months. I became very,
very angry. The point was not how long she had to live but that she be
allowed to live with dignity, to express herself and communicate with
the people she loved. I didn't give a damn if it was for another five years
or just one more day. Perhaps I was naive or overwhelmed by my emotions, but I could not believe they had the nerve to try to withhold care
on those grounds.

Still, the prognosis was what it was. Near the end of summer, Linda
made the decision to stop treatment and go into hospice care. There was
nothing further to do, and having so little time left, Linda wanted to

spend it as comfortably as possible. A hospice nurse came into our home to administer care, and we decided to take Linda off her IV drip—her body could no longer process the fluids. When I told Glenn about this decision, he became upset.

"So we're just giving up?" Glenn asked.

"No, we're not giving up," I said. "We're being prepared. We're facing reality. She's going to die."

Linda tried to maintain her humor through all of it. The boys would read to her from the mystery novels she loved, watch TV with her, or just sit and be with her. Some years earlier, Richard John Neuhaus was diagnosed with an aggressive form of cancer that he thought would kill him. He survived, but in the intervening period, when he believed he was facing death, he wrote *As I Lay Dying*, a book about the experience of preparing yourself for the end of life. I read this book to Linda in bed, and we both took solace from its wisdom. As he had for me on so many occasions before, Father Neuhaus offered counsel in a time of crisis.

Downstairs, away from Linda's hearing, I began making funeral arrangements. I knew her wishes. I asked Ray and Gloria Hammond to come over to offer some advice. In their pastoral work, they had to assist in many funerals, so I asked them to recommend a black-owned funeral home. We also had to discuss what kind of service Linda would receive. Her faith had waned around the same time as mine. Glenn was respectful but adamant that there be no singing and dancing, no celebrating God's promise of everlasting life, and no one laying hands on Linda's body. He was right to insist; it was not what Linda wanted. The Hammonds readily agreed. They only wanted to honor this woman they had known for so long.

As September rolled around, we knew it was coming time. Tamara came up to help oversee things and lend a hand. Linda's lifelong friend, Elizabeth Holman, practically moved in. I implored Nehemiah to come home from college as soon as possible. But he resisted. He would tell me about all the studying he had to do and the exams he had to take.

We would keep him apprised of Linda's condition constantly, but he continued to delay. This was not out of indifference. It was precisely the opposite. Linda's ordeal had been very, very hard on Nehemiah. Taciturn by nature, he did not have a ready outlet for his emotions, but I knew they were there. He was struggling and unable to voice his anguish, so he pushed it away.

One night, the phone rang at around one o'clock. It was Alyson, Nehemiah's girlfriend. He was drunk, raving, crying, and incoherent. I could hear him. This was not like Nehemiah, and Alyson was frightened. I told her to put him on the phone, but he was alternately weeping and babbling. It was impossible to talk to him. She took the phone back, and in the background I heard him cry out: "It's my mom! It's my mom!" He had tried to hold it back, tried to control it, and now it was all coming out.

The next afternoon, out on my daily walk, I called him, figuring he'd have sobered up enough to listen: "You need to get your butt back here *now*." Forty-eight hours later, he was back. He was still trying to sequester himself from the pain, staying in his room and burying himself in his schoolwork. I would periodically retrieve him and bring him in to spend time with Linda, and then he would return to his books. He was trying his best. All of us were.

THE NIGHT BEFORE LINDA DIED, I had a dilemma. Linda was asleep, and her body was fighting for every breath. Her chest rattled and moans escaped her throat. I laid there next to her, a pair of earplugs in my hand, my mind whirring over what to do. I was exhausted. I needed to sleep. But Linda's breathing made it impossible.

I could put in my earplugs. That would dampen the sound enough to allow me to drift off. But something was preventing me from doing it. Horrible as they were, I knew these were some of the last sounds that Linda would make. They were evidence of her pain. She couldn't do anything to make herself more comfortable, and I had already administered a maximum dosage of pain medication. But I could make myself more comfortable. At the time, something about that seemed terribly wrong. I would be literally stopping my ears to keep out the sounds of Linda's suffering. It seemed inhumane, somehow.

This is silly, I thought. If I told Linda about this, she'd look at me like I was crazy and tell me to put the earplugs in and get some sleep. It's not like it would be hurting her. And I needed to get some rest—tomorrow would be another trying day. Still, I couldn't shake the thought that there was some moral issue at play, that the earplugs were just another instance of a choice I had been making all along: not to stare reality in the face, but to turn away. This was real. It was happening. Perhaps I owed it to Linda to suffer along with her, even if she would not know it.

Eventually, exhaustion got the better of me. I put in the earplugs. Nevertheless, guilty and anxious as I felt, I didn't sleep a wink.

LINDA IS LAYING PROPPED UP IN BED. Her eyes are closed. Nehemiah is in the bed on one side of her, Glenn on the other. I sit at the foot of the bed rubbing her feet. McCoy is curled up on the floor, wanting to get as close to Linda as he can. He is our dog, but he prefers her to everyone else. Glenn is reading aloud from the novel *Skinny Dip* by Carl Hiaasen, one of Linda's favorite writers. When the boys were younger, Linda used to love reading aloud to them from the pulpy mysteries she favored. It feels like the most natural thing in the world. It is hard to know whether Linda is awake or asleep, whether she can hear Glenn's voice or not.

In the September evening, the sun is still out and light fills the room. There is no sound save Glenn's voice, the occasional rustle of the sheets, McCoy's murmurs, and Linda's shallow breath. When she slumps over, we realize her breathing has stopped. Glenn cries out: "Oh, no!" I run downstairs to get the hospice nurse who sits in the living room. He puts a stethoscope to her chest, looks at me, and tells me what I already know. She's gone.

Dr. Scheib arrives soon after the nurse breaks the news. She just happened to have scheduled a visit for right about now. She sits with us and offers what comfort she can. Then, when the nurse produces a death certificate, she fills it out and signs it.

I go downstairs and begin the strange, almost bureaucratic work of contacting those who need to be contacted to let them know that Linda has died. Over and over, the words pass my lips. "Linda died tonight. Linda died tonight." Over and over, I tap out the words into email text fields. No one who hears the news will find it surprising. As I say the words over and over, they lose their meaning. They are mere shapes and sounds that in no way reflect what has happened, the disappearance of the life that was present upstairs in our bedroom an hour earlier. I call my family and Linda's family. I call a handful of close friends. I write to Linda's department chair.

After a while, the morticians come to take Linda's body away. I force myself to watch as they place it in a black bag, carry it downstairs, secure it on a gurney, and load it into the back of the hearse. As I'm standing outside watching this, I see one of our neighbors down the block. She's out walking her dog. When she realizes what she's seeing, she stops and calls out, "I am so sorry." She starts crying, crosses the street, and wraps me up in a hug.

THERE WERE A THOUSAND THINGS TO DO after Linda died. Some of them I attended to right away. Some of them I still haven't been able to bring myself to do. After a few weeks passed and I steadied myself, Glenn II and I went to pack up Linda's office at Tufts. Everyone at the university had been so thoughtful in the wake of her death. The economics department sent a wonderful letter paying tribute to her as an economist, a teacher, and a colleague. They organized a memorial gathering. They also continued to pay Linda's salary for the 2011–2012 academic year, more as a show of respect to her than anything.

As I stood in Linda's office, I considered the things she kept close to her, the things that she thought would represent her to anyone who walked in or that reminded her of who she was. There were pictures of Glenn II and Nehemiah and me. Her degrees hung framed on the wall. The books she found most profound and useful were close at hand on her shelves. Something was displayed prominently in her bookcase that I recognized but had not seen in a long time. It was the letter I wrote her on our tenth anniversary. She had it framed. I wondered how often she read over it, whether it reminded her of my true feelings for her. I wondered how often she looked at it with love and how often with bitterness. It represented, in equal measure, how deep our love was and how often I had failed to do it justice. I did not share my thoughts with our son. I silently put that framed letter in the box of things to save.

I also found a self-help book in her library. It was about learning to forgive those who have wronged you. As I leafed through the pages, I saw that Linda, ever the diligent scholar, had underlined passages and scribbled notes to herself in the margins. Many of those notes clearly referenced things I had done. She made a study of forgiving me. Perhaps that's what it took to live with me. I had to be treated as a miniature research project. She could not control me; at times, I could barely control myself. Nor did she want to control. She wanted peace. Peace with me and peace with herself. I would not grant her that, not nearly as much as I should have. It struck me that she would not have purchased such a book, much less read it so closely, if she had not felt her ability to forgive on her own was lacking. She wanted to forgive but, at some point, worried she could not. So she took action, wrote out a plan that would bring her closer to the person she wanted to become. She spent a lifetime in that pursuit. I was a part of it. Our children were a part of it. Her work and her students were a part of it. Now that the pursuit had ended, I could only hope that she knew how far she had gotten. I knew I had a long way to go. I placed the book in the box beside the letter.

Twenty-Five

I 'll spend the rest of my life thinking about Linda, her death, and what I found in her office. The markings in that self-help book gave me a glimpse of what she was going through—of what I put her through—and how she tried to deal with it. How she dealt with that struggle, the conclusions she drew from her reading and introspection, I can only speculate. While I knew her almost as well as I knew myself, there was a part of her that was inaccessible to me and will remain so forever.

Shortly after Linda's death, Tamara experienced another tragedy. Her husband, Tony, died unexpectedly. He was a good man, a supportive husband, and a wonderful father. My heart broke for my daughter. I knew how it felt to lose a spouse, but Linda and I had over thirty years together. Tamara and Tony were just getting started. Our grief brought Tamara and me closer together. We consoled each other as best we could, sharing our feelings and our memories. Our exchanges were probing and candid. It was as though I was talking with her—really talking—for the first time. During one of our long conversations, the topic of my infidelity came up. Tamara didn't know everything, but she knew enough.

"I always wondered," she said, "why Linda didn't do something about it. She could have fought for your attention, greeting you at the front door wearing nothing but Saran Wrap. Or she could have kicked you out of the house, forcing you to choose between her and the other women. Anything. I don't understand how she could be so passive about it."

To be honest, I didn't understand it either. Linda never issued an ultimatum, never threatened to leave me, never acted as though she was in competition with any of the other women. Why was she so passive about my infidelity when she was so proactive in every other area of her life? I could speculate, but now I would never know for sure. A disconcerting thought crossed my mind. I alone bore responsibility for my actions, of course. But since Linda never forced the issue, did I interpret her relative passivity as a kind of tacit permission? It wasn't permission, exactly, and yet she suffered the consequences without trying to make me share in the pain I caused her. If she had forced the issue, would I have stopped? I wanted to say that I would have, but that was the grief talking. Now that she was gone—really gone—I would have done anything to bring her back. But at the time, I truly don't know how I would have reacted, whether I would have heeded her if she drew the line, or if I would have crossed it, as I had done so many times in my life.

After the funeral, Nehemiah returned to Columbia, and Glenn II and I continued living together in our house in Brookline. But the place was far too big for just the two of us and McCoy. With Linda gone and with my job in Providence, there was no reason to stay. Linda and I built that home together, and Glenn and I spent months taking it apart, boxing up our belongings, deciding what we could part with. I spent a long time going through Linda's possessions during the packing process. I picked up and considered every article of her clothing, every piece of her jewelry, every memento, book, and scrap of paper, some of which I still have today.

Glenn, McCoy, and I moved into a three-bedroom condo in Providence. It was close quarters. Living together allowed Glenn and me to mourn together, to reminisce about Linda and talk about how we were each dealing with her loss. But privacy was hard to come by, and I was frustrated that Glenn continued to delay his education. There were other undercurrents of tension. A couple years earlier, Glenn had come out of the closet as a gay man. Linda and I both heard him and accepted him. He was my son. I loved him no matter what. His boyfriend Rob was welcome at our home and our family gatherings.

Still, there was an uneasiness between us when it came to his sexuality. He knew that the conservative company I kept for so long was often, in the best of cases, disapproving of the idea of open homosexuality. And he knew what the rest of our family was like. When I told my father that Glenn came out of the closet, he said, "You're trying to tell me Glenn's gay?" "No," I said, "I'm not *trying* to tell you. I'm telling you! And yes, he's gay!" My father reacted skeptically, telling me that it was my problem to deal with, not his. He acted as though I was weak for accepting Glenn's sexuality, and he seemed angry that I hadn't done anything about it. What he would have had me do, I have no idea.

I felt I had to tell Glenn about my conversation with his grandfather. Glenn put on an air of indifference. He was not surprised. Familial rejection was a common story in the world he was starting to inhabit. But I suspected that, deep down, Everett's dismissive attitude hurt him. Glenn II grew up observing the way the men in our family carried themselves, with their pride in their masculinity and their swagger. Though he never knew Adlert, he heard enough stories about him to figure out what kind of man he was. Of Alfred and his progeny, Glenn had direct experience. At Linda's funeral, Rob sat in the front row with Glenn, Nehemiah, Alyson, and me. Rob was Glenn's partner, so that was where he belonged. But when Alfred's sons filed by to express their condolences, Glenn detected mockery in their faces.

I wondered whether Glenn wondered how much of that discomfort with homosexuality I harbored within myself. He knew that I looked up to Alfred and Adlert as a young man, that I at times strove to emulate them. Did I, he may have wondered, also absorb the knee-jerk homophobia that was so common to the South Side? My love for and acceptance of Glenn never wavered for an instant. Rationally, I knew there was no difference between my sons' feelings for their respective partners. But there was a part of me that struggled to understand what he was going through, and sometimes I came up short in ways that I did not when I contemplated Nehemiah's relationship with Alyson.

Glenn's openness about his sexuality led me to think hard about the friendships I had with men in my own life. I brought Ajume onboard at the Institute for Race and Social Division partly on the strength of his scholarship but partly because I admired him specifically as a man. Spending time with this man's man, I felt, imparted some of his own masculinity to me. One day, Ajume came to visit the family at our summer place in New Hampshire. We ended up, somewhat by accident, taking a twenty-mile hike through a mountainous forest. We walked ten miles uphill, stopped to have a Coke, and then turned back around and walked the ten miles back. It was exhausting, but keeping pace with a physical specimen like Ajume made me feel like I was every bit the man he was, and I loved it. I was attracted to him because, in his presence, I felt like what I imagined it felt to be him. I could not call this erotic, but it was something more than friendly.

At the time, I could not have put what I felt into even those vague terms. Nor could I have understood that my faint uneasiness with Glenn's sexuality might have more to do with me than it did with him. There is nothing shameful about the way I felt about Ajume. Nor was there anything wrong with the close relationship that I enjoyed with my friend Chuck while working at R. R. Donnelley, the Chicago printing plant, decades earlier. Indeed, I reveled in putting myself into competition with other men in those South Side pool halls precisely because it allowed me to feel fulfilled in my masculinity. Before I could allay whatever anxieties my son had about my perception of him, I would first have to reckon with how I felt about myself.

BUT WHAT DID I REALLY KNOW about myself? No observer watching me stand up there on the stage raging against the carceral state could have doubted my commitment to my cause. But beneath that apparently uncompromising dedication was a deep ambivalence about the project on which I had spent the previous five years. I was a man of the left who had spoken out against the war in Iraq, who had condemned the irresponsible bankers who caused the financial crisis of 2008, and who occasionally had some nice things to say about Barack Obama, our first black president.

My ties to the right were all but severed, a perception I solidified in 2012 following the death of James Q. Wilson, the father of "broken windows" policing and a perennial target of progressive criminal justice reformers. Less than a month after he passed away, in the pages of Josh Cohen's *Boston Review*, I wrote that I had nothing but contempt for his so-called achievements in the realm of public policy and social theory. I ended the piece unequivocally:

> With all due respect to the influence of his writings on bureaucracy, policing, and social policy, I'm just not buying the hagiographies that appeared in the likes of the *Wall Street Journal*, *Los Angeles Times*, and *Boston Globe* after his passing. For my money, he died with an awful lot to answer for.

Anyone reading the piece could be forgiven for thinking that I was actually *glad* he was dead.

I was not glad. I had my disagreements with Jim, especially when it came to his beliefs about the genetic basis for criminal behavior. But those beliefs did not capture all that he was. He was a conservative intellectual icon for half a century. He was a groundbreaking and influential figure in the study of American government. I knew him rather well. He was often involved in one project or another at the Kennedy School. When Bruce Western and I proposed a big study of mass incarceration to the National Academy of Sciences, Jim was chairman of the committee that approved it and he didn't object, despite the fact that he clearly disagreed with our analysis and premises. Moreover, as I admitted in the obituary, he was a kind, generous, and open-minded man. This was true generally, but it was also true of his dealings with me personally. Jim Wilson was a friend to me. We coedited a book together. I'd met his lovely wife, Roberta, and had dined on more than one occasion in his home. We had taken different paths, true enough. In saying that, in effect, he had blood on his hands, I was not honoring what he had at one time meant to me, nor was I expressing what I truly thought about the magnitude of his accomplishments. In time, I came to regret what I wrote about him.

So why did I write it? Because I knew that's what someone who espoused the kinds of things I espoused in public ought to say. Because I knew that, in writing as I did, I would receive yet another chorus of amens from my fellow travelers. Because that was what the Glenn Loury I had become was now expected to say. Bruce had encouraged me to go public with the piece after I'd shown him an early draft. He had no sympathy for Jim Wilson's position at all. The obituary was of a piece with all of the other work Bruce and I were doing, and in that sense it, too, was charged with the energy and enthusiasm of our friendship. But the obituary was not the act of bold truth-telling it pretended to be. Rather, it was the work of a guilty conscience. I thought I had to decide between fealty to a friend and fealty to principle, that one had to be sacrificed for the other.

I had put myself in this situation before, when I reviewed the Thernstroms' *America in Black and White* in 1997. Forced to choose between loyalty to friends and loyalty to my beliefs, I chose the latter. In that case, I felt I couldn't be silent, and I have no regrets about what I did. But the Jim Wilson obituary was different. Abby Thernstrom let me know what she thought of my review; she was more than capable of defending herself. Jim Wilson was dead; he couldn't speak up for himself. The obituary put the moral emphasis in the wrong place, demonizing a man

I knew to be honorable in the service of a cause whose main attraction was, by then, merely the accolades it brought me.

Those accolades began to exert less of a hold on me. By 2012, the warmth I felt after my "homecoming" had cooled. Being a black liberal no longer felt as important as it once had. This waning enthusiasm was sped along by my changing views on the administration of our first black president, Barack Obama. The election of a black president was an achievement, but it belonged to the American populace, not to Obama himself. That we could progress from a nation that harbored a virtual apartheid regime within its borders to one with a black president within my lifetime was remarkable. But the figurehead chosen to carry the torch of racial progress to the pinnacle of the American political system was, in my mind, little more than a political operator, albeit a gifted one. I did not doubt that Barack Obama was intelligent, but his self-presentation as an icon of American blackness struck me as absurd. He had no real ties to the history of black people in this country. If you took his Kenyan father (who he never really knew) out of the equation, I could see nothing of the African American experience in his life. I couldn't accept the idea that he represented, in his very being, the ascension of black Americans from slavery to full citizenship to prosperity. His endless touting of his ties to Chicago, with the implication that he was a product of the very same South Side that made me, only drove home that, while he understood how to convey "authenticity" to the American public at large, there was almost nothing real about the persona that he presented for the TV cameras. My uncle Moonie, I was quite sure, would have been singularly unmoved by Barack Hussein Obama's act.

Years before Obama's election, my friend the political scientist Robert Putnam organized the Saguaro Seminar, an ongoing project focused on civic engagement, and I was invited to participate. He pulled together massive funding to support dozens of experts and meetings in different cities over the course of a couple years. Barack Obama, then still an Illinois state senator, came to one of these sessions. There was a sense that he was headed for bigger things, and he had a reputation as a bit of an intellectual. But when he spoke in that seminar, he said almost nothing of value. I wasn't impressed. Now, it's likely that, with his political ambitions, he knew that anything he said even in a private environment like that would be on the record. If he took a position on a topic in that room, it could come back to bite him later. But my first impression of Barack Obama was that he was more concerned with tailoring his image than anything else, and that impression did not change during the course of his presidential campaigns and, indeed, his presidency.

Things could get awkward. Most people around me simply assumed that I shared in the elation that took hold following his election. I would never deny the historical import of Obama's presidency, but the sense of triumph that surrounded his ascent was made by liberals to carry more symbolic value than it could bear. I didn't disagree with everything he did and stood for, but what he was made to represent—the culmination of black political self-determination—felt empty to me. All of that "our time has come" rhetoric left me cold. What struggle did he have to overcome to get where he was? An absent father was no doubt a difficult thing to deal with, but his life was one of prep schools and elite universities and the political fast track. I don't think that one must undergo hardship in order to lay claim to their blackness, but the dissonance between Obama's claim to represent "the black experience" and his actual life experience was just too grating for me to ignore. My childhood friend Woody was "blacker" than Obama, as far as I was concerned.

Put it this way. During Obama's first campaign, a brilliant black student of mine at Brown approached me after class one day and asked, in all seriousness, "Is Obama a pimp?"

"Excuse me?" I replied.

"Is he a pimp? Because he's mind-fucking all of us."

He said it, not me!

ABOUT THE SAME TIME Jim Wilson passed away, the death of someone else became a cause célèbre. During an altercation in a Sanford, Florida, housing development, George Zimmerman pulled out a gun and shot a young man named Trayvon Martin to death. Though a jury later affirmed that Zimmerman had shot Martin in self-defense, the killing of a young, unarmed black man kicked off waves of protests. People marched in the streets, angry at what they perceived as the police's mis-handling of the case, some of them brandishing cans of Arizona Iced Tea and bags of Skittles, the snacks that Martin had left the house to buy at a convenience store at the time of the incident. Players for the Miami Heat, including LeBron James, wore hoodies during a pregame warm-up to demonstrate their solidarity, and pretty soon the killing of Trayvon Martin became a national issue. His death and even his name became a litmus test. It was obvious, wasn't it? Zimmerman was a gun-toting murderer who prowled the streets hunting for black people, aided and abetted ex post facto by a racist police force who worked overtime to cover up his crime and to portray him as a victim. If you couldn't agree with that, then you were on the wrong side of history.

Well, I found that I couldn't agree with that narrative. The entire affair seemed like just so much opportunism, if not on the part of the protestors, then on the part of those who gave them license. The Trayvon Martin case attracted a familiar class of hangers-on who used it to gin up the notion that, really, little had changed since the bad old days of Jim Crow. In the process, they saw their stars rise and their faces appear on TVs across the country. According to the likes of the attorney Ben-jamin Crump and the formerly disgraced but more recently rehabilitated Reverend Al Sharpton, the boot was still on our necks. Even Obama himself, normally a master equivocator, made clear where he stood (or where he wanted to be seen as standing) when he said, from the White House briefing room, "If I had a son, he'd look like Trayvon."

The entire thing roiled me. Bob Wright had given me my own show on *Bloggingheads*, called *The Glenn Show*, where I had carte blanche to invite whomever I wanted and to say whatever I wanted. My conversa-tions with John McWhorter became a regular (and quite popular) feature of *The Glenn Show*. We were the self-described "Black Guys at *Blogging-heads*," who regularly discussed race matters. Naturally we talked about the Trayvon Martin case a lot. And as we talked, I found it difficult to toe the line. John certainly wasn't toeing it. To ask honest questions about the police's handling of the case was one thing. To treat Trayvon Martin's death as some kind of epochal civil rights event on a par with the lynching of Emmett Till was another thing altogether.

But I was still Glenn Loury, a fierce critic of racial injustice and foe of mass incarceration. So when media outlets called for a quote or to invite me to speak about Trayvon Martin, I knew what they expected of me. I gave them every reason to expect it. I spent years giving lectures, writing articles, and publishing books that affirmed the existence of entrenched racial inequality and proposed remedies to eliminate it. I had wanted to come home, to feel the embrace of my people. I felt it all right, and now it was beginning to suffocate me. When I received yet another request to go on the radio in order, I assumed, to bemoan grave injustices of America's racial regime, I had to ask myself just what I was representing. Had I become just another spokesman for the Negro Cognoscenti?

IN 2013, BROWN UNIVERSITY invited New York City police commissioner Ray Kelly to give a lecture. Kelly had presided over a massive expansion of stop-and-frisk police tactics, along with a host of other surveillance measures. (As it happened, Jim Wilson was one of the primary thinkers whose work led to the development of stop-and-frisk.) I was at the time very skeptical of these strategies. Under Kelly's leadership, black men and teenagers in New York City were being stopped on the street and searched under the thinnest of pretexts. Often people who were doing nothing but minding their own business were subjected to humiliating encounters with officers who were on fishing expeditions, hoping to find drugs or weapons. I had actually been detained by the NYPD in

Harlem in 2010 while working as a visiting professor at Columbia, for the pretextual offense of "riding a bicycle on the sidewalk."

Regardless of my feelings about his policies, I wanted to hear what Kelly had to say. He was an extremely powerful figure at the forefront of a controversial new development in policing. I wanted to hear his justification for these tactics come out of his own mouth. There was plenty I wanted to say back to him, too. And I had a prime spot near the front of the stage, so I was pretty sure I'd be able to ask a question when it came time for the Q & A.

Kelly took the stage, but before he could get a word out, students in the audience began shouting him down. "Racism is not up for debate!" "No Justice! No Peace! No Racist Police!" "We're asking you to stop frisking people!" The interruptions were met with scattered cheers from around the hall. Marion Orr, the political science professor who had invited Kelly and who introduced him, asked the crowd to settle down and to wait for the Q & A, but the disruptions continued. After some fifteen minutes of this, it was clear that Kelly wouldn't be allowed to speak, so he turned around and went back home to New York.

I was stunned. I'd attended plenty of raucous, contentious lectures before, where members of the audience were clearly unhappy with the speaker. Hell, I'd even been the guy they were mad at! But whoever the speaker was, he was there to make his case, and he needed to be heard out. Then, when the time came, whoever had the microphone could tell him just how wrong he was and why. To shout down the speaker, to prevent him from presenting his argument, and to replace reasoned discourse with mob tactics was not what we did in the university. If someone there was so sure he was right and Kelly was wrong, he should raise his hand, take the mic, and explain to everyone there exactly why they should take his side rather than the other guy's.

I had always prized the university as a place where even unpopular ideas could be examined and debated without fear of repression. Even abominable ideas needed to be analyzed and subjected to examination rather than passed over in silence or repressed entirely. How else could we be sure that we could understand these ideas? How could we know they were so bad unless we engaged with them ourselves? This line of thinking is hardly original to me. It's straight out of John Stuart Mill's *On Liberty*. The free exchange of ideas is one of the foundations of the modern university, indeed of modern democratic society. Without that exchange, it seemed doubtful that we could have either.

The students and local residents at that event were now interfering with the process of free inquiry and rational debate. Even though I thought it was awful behavior, in a way, I could understand it. They were only responding to the political environment around them, which was increasingly one that prized protest as an inherently moral act. They were young and fired up. But clearly the faculty and administration would have to take action against their disruptive behavior. No matter how impassioned these young people were, they could not be allowed to impede the process of free inquiry. There needed to be consequences.

Brown's president, Christina Paxson, immediately issued a statement condemning the protestors' actions and reaffirming the university's commitment to the free exchange of ideas. But when the university investigated the protestors, they were given a slap on the wrist and sent on their way. No real consequences followed. And worse, the university produced a navel-gazing report which concluded that, while perhaps the protestors should not have disrupted Kelly's lecture, the university should have taken into consideration that Kelly's presence at Brown had the potential to "harm" students who had experienced trauma that might have been triggered by exposure to frightening ideas like Kelly's. In essence, the university was apologizing for doing exactly what it was supposed to do: expose its students to ideas and teach them how to formulate ideas of their own in response!

A precedent was set. At universities around the country, when a controversial, almost always conservative figure was invited to give a lecture, they would sometimes find themselves met by protestors who saw it as their mission to make sure the event never took place. Activists and some members of the media referred to these tactics with the rather genteel term *deplatforming*. A more honest term would have been *censorship*.

What disturbed me more than the protests was the divided response of the faculty. Most professors knew that censoring speakers debased the university's mission. Some of them, including me, spoke out and said as much. But protests like the one at Brown also received support from people who ought to have known better. They saw themselves as the standard-bearers of a movement, one so convinced of its moral mandate that it had no need to consider anyone's ideas but its own. One of the student organizers was even honored at the Department of Africana Studies' subsequent commencement exercise for her "leadership" in this sorry affair.

AMERICA'S MAINSTREAM NARRATIVES about race were shifting in two directions. One direction was toward mass incarceration, which had been a relatively obscure issue, one that only activists and academics paid much attention to. By the 2010s, it came to occupy more and more of the national discourse on race. One reason for this was Michelle Alexander's book *The New Jim Crow*. In it, she drew a direct line from the abolition of slavery to the development of the convict lease system, which allowed states to sell prison labor to private entities. She argued that the modern prison system, which was disproportionately populated by black men, was nothing more than a new plantation, that many laws were designed and enforced in order to provide a steady supply of coerced, mostly black labor, and that prisons in general were mechanisms that largely existed to control America's black population. This was abetted by the clause of the Thirteenth Amendment that prohibited involuntary servitude "except as a punishment for crime whereof the party shall have been duly convicted."

I found Alexander's argument unconvincing. Yes, the prison system was badly in need of reform, but the idea that it primarily functioned as a tool to suppress African Americans was wildly overstated. Alexander had little to say in her book about violent crime, for instance, and its many black victims. Her analysis was overly simplistic. That, of course, was its appeal. In this account, the Thirteenth Amendment didn't abolish slavery, it actually re-enshrined it in the US Constitution. Therefore, the critics said, the entire notion that the Civil War, the passage of the Thirteenth, Fourteenth, and Fifteenth Amendments, and Reconstruction ended black enslavement was nothing but a jingoistic myth meant to paper over a malignant historical reality: nothing had changed since the nineteenth century.

I was a critic of mass incarceration, but this was absurd on its face. If pressed, promoters of the New Jim Crow narrative would admit that, well, yes, there was the Civil Rights Movement, and, no, black people weren't literally enslaved. Still, the notion that we had made little progress since the end of Reconstruction in 1877 became a startlingly common line of argument. That I couldn't abide. We were the freest, wealthiest population of black people on the face of the planet. To say that, because our prisons needed reforming, we might as well still be in chains was tantamount to sneering in the faces of the generations of African Americans who fought and sometimes died for the rights we enjoyed.

The New Jim Crow narrative took a complex issue—prisons—and moved an overly simplistic version of it to the center of national racial discourse. The other new thread in the racial narrative did the same: the cops. New attention to police killings of unarmed black men gave rise to a social media hashtag that, by the time the 2014 riots in Ferguson, Missouri, following the death of Michael Brown, had coalesced into a decentralized movement called Black Lives Matter. The premise of the movement/slogan was that black lives did not matter, not to the police and not to those who either implicitly or explicitly supported them.

With Black Lives Matter garnering headlines and with the slogan becoming ubiquitous not only at marches and protests but in the windows of houses and storefronts, on bumper stickers, and practically anywhere those three words could fit, some thought that a true movement was coalescing. In 2015, the radio host Christopher Lydon invited me onto his show to discuss Black Lives Matter and the supposed plague of police violence that was claiming the lives of black men. Chris was an old friend. He and his other guest, the historian Peniel Joseph, waxed ecstatic about the Black Lives Matter initiative, talking about it as though it was the next Civil Rights Movement. They apparently expected me to join in, but I responded coolly. Were we really so sure that Mike Brown had been gunned down in cold blood? The facts were not yet in. And what had this loose affiliation of activists done to justify laying claim to the mantle of the Civil Rights Movement? Chris and Peniel seemed especially thrilled that BLM's most prominent activists were queer women, but I failed to see why their sexual identity had anything to do with what they were trying to accomplish.

Neither could I understand the idea that Black Lives Matter was in any way comparable to the Civil Rights Movement. And I certainly couldn't understand the way the BLM movement lionized the victims of these shootings as though they were civil rights heroes. "Michael Brown was no Rosa Parks," I wrote in the pages of the *Boston Review.* Clearly, the expectation was that, as a black intellectual concerned with matters of racial justice, I would be all in with BLM. But I knew that the central issue that had galvanized the movement was not so clear-cut at all. Yes, black men were killed by police at disproportionately higher rates than white men. But far, far fewer black men than white men were killed by police in total. And what were the circumstances surrounding these killings? Whenever I tried to broach the issue, I was given the same rebuttals: Don't you know it's open season on black people? Don't you know the cops are looking for any excuse to put a bullet in us? Can't you see we're in a fight for our lives here? Don't you know they think we're all thugs?

I knew what they were talking about. I saw it all the time in Chicago in the 1950s and '60s. But this was not Chicago in the 1950s and '60s. I certainly didn't want to see anybody shot by the police, but why couldn't I raise perfectly reasonable questions about the frequency of encounters between black men and police, about the crime rates in black neighborhoods, and about the rates at which black people were killing each other? If black lives mattered, why didn't Black Lives Matter want to talk about those issues? It seemed to me that the activists concerned with preserving black life and well-being ought to worry about what was going on within black communities at least as much as they worried about the cops.

If Black Lives Matter had just been one way of thinking about race and politics, I wouldn't have been that worried about it. But the slogan had become a litmus test. If you weren't for Black Lives Matter, then you must think black lives *don't* matter. Even if you wanted to criticize BLM, you would have to preface the critique with a disclaimer in order to be heard: "Of course I agree that black lives matter, *but . . .*" This was the new face of "black authenticity." A slogan. A bumper sticker. A checkbox. Beyond the basic semantic meaning of the phrase, a sentiment with which practically anyone would agree, "Black Lives Matter" seemed to signify little. And yet, as a correct-thinking black person, I was expected to go along with the movement and praise them unthinkingly.

I found that I couldn't, and I started saying so. I said so on my *Blogginheads* show, in print, and to whomever asked. As a consequence, I saw much of the goodwill I had accrued with my co-racialists in the course of the past fifteen years slowly drain away. If my progressive critiques of colorblindness and racial stigma and mass incarceration had brought me back home, back into the good graces of the tribe, my rejection of the New Jim Crow and BLM had cast me out into the wilderness again. I wasn't a social reject—I still had plenty of friends—but there was a sense that I could no longer be relied upon to say "the right thing." "The right thing" was that all black people in the United States lived under a regime of systemic racism, that we were beset by the machinations of white supremacy at every turn. To be black was to live under constant threat; any black person in the country who didn't fear for her life every time she walked out the front door had merely internalized the racism that was woven into the very fabric of social life in America.

I wasn't having it. Of course we had problems. Of course racism still existed. Of course there was unfairness. But to regard those unfortunate facts of modern life as the very essence of blackness was to profoundly misconstrue what it meant to live free. Black American identity was forged in an attempt to overcome racism and to achieve the incompletely realized ideals of the nation that made us. To cling to the very prejudice that we were always meant to transcend, to make it the sine qua non of black selfhood, was a horrific error. Never mind that regarding the residual unfairness of American race thinking as an all-encompassing white supremacy was sheer hyperbole. Unfairness needn't define us. It didn't define me, not when Uncle Alfred suggested that it should, and certainly not now that "systemic racism" had become the catch-all definition of everything having to do with blackness.

Giving voice to these thoughts continued to put me on the outs with the correct-thinking elite circles in which I traveled. I suppose I should have felt despair. But I didn't. I felt unburdened. For years I dined out on mass incarceration, reaping the rewards of advocating for an intellectual position that, I now realized, only took half the problem into account. We had been locking up too many people for too long, and too many of them were black. But if mass incarceration was unjust, then so too was the fact that so many law-abiding black people residing in high-crime areas had to live with the violence and disorder caused by a handful of their unruly neighbors. There was no place for that glaring fact in the critique I had been offering.

The rush I got from the performance of righteous fury was no longer enough to compensate for the hollow feeling that overtook me when I stepped back behind the curtain. What began as a sincere attempt to understand a real political problem had somehow curdled, almost without me realizing it, into bad faith. Once I accepted that continuing on that path would require me to align myself with political and moral positions I just could not stomach, I became able to let go of the work that had brought me so much success and had caused me so much turmoil.

Once I did let go, I found plenty of other people who were receptive to my ideas, and those people tended to be conservatives. Even though I had spent the last fifteen years or so condemning their ideas and their politics, I found that many of them were more than happy to hear me returning to many of the themes I had set aside in my days on the left: the state of the black family, the black victims of violent crime, and the necessity of building social capital within black communities. It's not that I ever stopped worrying or thinking about these problems—I certainly didn't think they were solved—but in devoting my efforts to writing and speaking about racial inequality and mass incarceration, I had let them fall by the wayside. Perhaps I believed that, with crime rates falling across the nation, these problems would finally work themselves out.

They didn't. And as I found myself unable to follow the left where it was headed, I had to acknowledge that my social critique and my disposition were better suited to the right. That acknowledgment, I knew, meant that I would now find myself opposed to many of the allies I had made in my time as one of the Negro Cognoscenti. So be it. Bill Spriggs had welcomed me back home to the black left. But I could not go home again. I was a conservative, and in truth I suspected that's what I always had been.

When I considered where my latter-day thinking over the preceding decade had led me, it began to feel almost alien. Who was that guy up there ranting with righteous indignation? The problems that troubled me all those years ago hadn't gone away just because I had largely stopped attending to them. They were still there. The enemy within black America was still there. Evidently, the enemy within me was still there, too.

Twenty-Six

I n the years following Linda's death, I dated a little here and there,
but I didn't find a real connection with anybody. In my youth and
into middle age, I had fooled myself into thinking that I was the
consummate Player, a Master of the Universe. Well into my sixties now,
those days were behind me. My life was full. Full of work, full of friends,
full of children and grandchildren. But still, I wanted more.

Thirteen or fourteen months after Linda died, Glenn, Nehemiah, and
I flew out to Riverside, California, to visit Lee Lee and her husband,
Wesley. On the way back, we stopped in Houston where a handful of
Uncle Alfred's progeny had settled, among whom were my cousins,
Tanya and Ernestine. They were living together at Tanya's sprawling
place. My cousin Tanya reminded me in so many ways of Aunt Eloise,
with her regal bearing, refined tastes, and dogged ambition. She had done
well for herself in Houston, where she moved after earning a doctorate in
pharmacology at the University of Michigan. Her older sister Ernestine
had been struggling in her life until Tanya took her in, just as Aunt Eloise
had taken in my mother, and helped her get back on her feet. Ernestine
was working at a sandwich shop, and one afternoon Tanya took me to
visit her there. While we were sitting at a table chatting over pastrami
on rye, one of her friends happened in and sat down. We introduced

ourselves, talked for a bit, and the woman left. Then one of Ernestine's friends came in. And then another. Quite a coincidence, I thought, all these attractive, single friends of Tanya's and Ernestine's just happening into this sandwich shop at the same time on the same day.

The sisters had apparently made it their mission to set up their eligible bachelor cousin with one of their girlfriends. I was Tanya's project now, and she was not going to stop until she successfully played matchmaker and claimed her bragging rights. There was no point in fighting it. I was in her sights and Tanya was going to have her way. So a few years later, when she called me up and asked if she could pass my number along to someone, I said sure. Why not?

The woman was one of Tanya's oldest friends, LaJuan. We talked on the phone a few times. I liked her. She was smart and witty. I knew from Tanya that she had a reputation in their group of friends as a news junkie with sharp elbows when it came to political arguments. LaJuan had survived a rough upbringing and a tumultuous family life. No one handed her anything on a platter, but she pulled herself together nonetheless and made a success of her life. I respected that. She didn't finish her BA, but she was a compulsive autodidact, a voracious reader with expansive tastes. The copies of the *New Yorker* and the *Atlantic* that sat out on her coffee table weren't just for show—she actually read them. I really enjoyed talking to her. We started calling each other more frequently.

I happened to be spending the academic year at Stanford, and it just so happened that in early 2016 LaJuan and her sister were planning to take a holiday in San Francisco. Yet another remarkable coincidence, I thought. LaJuan and I made plans to have lunch at a Napa Valley restaurant. I took an Uber from my apartment in Menlo Park to her hotel in San Francisco. We had sent each other pictures, so I knew what she looked like, but when she stepped off the elevator, I was struck by the sight of this beautiful, shapely woman. This was going to be an exciting afternoon. We said hello and hugged, and then she looked back over her shoulder: "Oh, there's my sister!" I knew her sister, Trischelle, was accompanying her on the trip but hadn't realized she'd be joining us for this lunch. Oh, well. Apparently, there would be a chaperone.

The three of us took their rental car to the restaurant, and we had a nice afternoon. LaJuan was every bit as bubbly and clever in person as she had been on the phone. After a few hours, it was time to part ways. LaJuan was driving, and I was riding in the passenger seat beside her. I could not take my eyes off her. A bit of her thigh was exposed where her skirt was riding up, and it took all my self-control not to reach over and rest my hand on it. That would have been too forward. Also, Trish could have seen me from her perch in the back seat. When LaJuan pulled over to drop me off at my apartment, I wanted to do something to let her know what an impression she had made on me. Since the thigh was, unfortunately, out of the question, I took her hand in mine and lowered my head to kiss it.

I found out later that this was a winning move. The next month, LaJuan invited me to come visit her in Houston. Gentleman that I am, I told her that I would stay with Tanya. My first night in town, LaJuan took me to one of her favorite spots, a club with live music and a dance floor. She loved to dance, so we got out there on the floor and worked up a good sweat moving to the beat. After a few drinks and some hors d'oeuvres, we decided to move on. I swear I had every intention of going back to my cousin Tanya's place that night, but I ended up at LaJuan's. The next afternoon, we met Tanya for lunch. "What happened to you last night, Glenn?" she asked. LaJuan and I smiled and shrugged. "Oh, I see." Tanya must have known those bragging rights were within her grasp.

After that, I knew we'd be seeing much more of each other. LaJuan made another trip to visit me at Stanford. When my term ended there, I went off to deliver a talk in Oxford—the Lee Lecture in Political Science and Government at All Souls College. LaJuan was in Tel Aviv at the time—her work as a cybersecurity consultant took her all over the globe. We talked over Skype one evening, she in Israel and me in England, and we both felt like we were on top of the world. All that summer we engaged in marathon Skype sessions, whether we were at home or abroad. Though we were apart from each other physically, we were always connected to each other, whether we were texting or calling or Skyping. I could not get enough of lovely LaJuan. Much to my delight, she seemed to share the feeling. There was no question: we were in love.

We made trips to visit each other over the course of 2016. At the end of the year, I had some lectures to deliver in India, at the Delhi School of Economics, and I had a friend in Kolkata who invited me to visit should I ever be in that neck of the woods. It was near Christmas, and I wanted to spend the holiday with LaJuan, so I invited her to come with me. We could turn it into a vacation. I delivered the lectures in Delhi and introduced LaJuan to my economist friends, Rajiv Sethi and his sister, my former student, Rohini Somanathan. We toured New Delhi, got down to see the Taj Mahal, and had a blast.

In Kolkata, we stayed at the Oberoi Grand, an over-the-top, colonial-era palace that had been turned into a hotel. There was a front gate and employees in uniform, luxurious rooms, and a stunning grand lobby. I'm somewhat embarrassed to say that I was a little nervous about introducing LaJuan around in my academic circles. I remembered how wrenching those evenings with Charlene had been back in the 1970s at MIT, how excluded she had felt as the only one in the room with no knowledge of economics. But I needn't have worried. LaJuan was her bold, charming self, and she won everyone over. In Delhi, Rajiv and Rohini were absolutely taken with her. In Kolkata, Ayesha Pervez, a former student of mine at Brown, said, "What are you guys waiting for? Get married!" LaJuan protested that we'd known each other for barely a year. Ayesha just glared at me: "Marry her, you fool."

After that incredible vacation, I had to go back to Providence and LaJuan had to go back to Houston. But I didn't want to be away from her. Notwithstanding Ayesha's prompting, I wasn't quite ready to propose marriage. But I knew I was in love with this woman, and, with my seventieth birthday right around the corner, I didn't want to waste any time. So I suggested that we move in together. I knew it was a big ask, but she agreed. She didn't want to waste any time, either. Her job allowed her to work remotely, and she would have to shift around some clients, but she could make it work to come to Providence. It would take a lot of preparation for her to pack up her life and move it across the country, and I was anxiously counting down the months.

Before the move, though, LaJuan had to oversee her daughter Lauren's wedding. I flew out to Houston for the big day. At the reception, LaJuan and I chatted with the other guests. We told one of them that LaJuan would soon be moving out to Providence to live with me. "Ah, so you're getting married?" he asked, innocently. Instantly, LaJuan grew uncomfortable. It was an obvious, perfectly natural question. We weren't kids, after all. We each knew what we wanted out of a partner, and we found it. But neither of us had seriously broached the topic of marriage.

My God, I thought. What's wrong with me? I'm asking this woman to uproot her life, and I haven't offered her anything in the way of commitment. Now she's been embarrassed, and all because I didn't take a moment to really think about what I was asking her to do. I was ashamed that it took a stranger's question to make me realize how thoughtless I'd been. I needed to put some skin in the game, too. It was the right thing to do, and I had finally reached a point in my life where I wanted to do the right thing.

LaJuan was set to come out to Providence for another visit in July, so in June I started shopping for a ring. I found one online and put the order in, but she was arriving very soon. As the date approached, I was sweating bullets, praying this ring on which I had dropped thousands and thousands of dollars would make it in time. It was supposed to arrive in a FedEx locker. Every day I would check the locker, and every day it was empty. Finally, two days before LaJuan was scheduled to land in Providence, the ring showed up.

I made reservations at a high-end steakhouse and let them know I was going to propose there. They got things all set up for me. I popped the question. LaJuan said yes, and the staff showered us with rose petals and opened the champagne. The neighboring tables applauded. It was like something out of the movies. But that was the kind of gesture that felt appropriate for such a propitious moment, something big and bold. I wanted people to know how proud I was that this beautiful, intelligent, vivacious, passionate woman was going to be my wife.

LAJUAN AND I HAD A WHIRLWIND ROMANCE. When she moved to Providence, we still had so much to learn about each other. I told her about some of the swerves my life and career had taken over the years. Even a cursory Google search of my name could fill in many of the blanks. She knew I had been a conservative, then a liberal, and had more recently grown disillusioned with the left and moved back in the other direction. I became aware of LaJuan's political views only gradually. I noticed a copy of Noam Chomsky's *Manufacturing Consent* on her nightstand, and I also noticed that the long list of podcasts she consumed had a leftist bent to them. We had different ways of looking at things. Nothing wrong with that. We loved each other. That was the important thing.

LaJuan and I were each attracted to the passion we saw in each other. That passion extended to everything, from music to politics to food. LaJuan has an encyclopedic knowledge of music, and when we were first getting to know each other, we'd try to outdo each other.

"Have you heard this Earth, Wind and Fire B side?"

"No, but do you know about this Mingus cut?"

Each of us wanted to show the other something they hadn't seen before. When it came to music, it was fun. Although she usually outdid me, when the two of us were sitting around the living room playing our favorite songs for each other, both of us won.

But the same competitiveness and passion that brought us together could also get between us. I did not appreciate just how our political differences would manifest until we were living together. This was the

Trump era, and as it turned out, not even love could fully insulate us from the political polarization that was affecting the rest of the country. LaJuan couldn't stand Trump. I, on the other hand, often found myself watching footage of his rallies with a grin on my face.

There is the cover story and there is the real story.

The cover story is that in 2016, I thought that Trump gave voice to unaddressed grievances that many white working-class voters felt in their gut. These voters felt alienated by the mainstream of both parties. Republicans seemed concerned mostly with lowering taxes on large corporations and wealthy individuals, while Democrats spent their time on superficial displays of support for people of color and upper-middle-class women. The critiques of Trump were obvious. He was unqualified for high office. He was boorish and undisciplined. Some of the people he surrounded himself with were shady, to say the least. There was a legitimate case to be made that some of his actions were corrupt. And yet, millions of people in the country saw him as an authentic representative of their concerns. Liberal elites (and a good number of conservatives) portrayed these Americans as racists, yahoos, and deplorables, as though they were too ignorant to understand their own interests. Maybe you could write Trump off as a Barnumesque huckster, but to do the same to his supporters was condescending, which was exactly the sort of thing that drove them to Trump in the first place. It was on Trump's opponents to persuade those voters over to their side, not to bash them.

That is the cover story. And it's true, so far as it goes. The real story is that I liked Trump. I understood what people found appealing about Trump's sparring with the press and his hectoring of the elites. Not only did I understand it, I felt it. I got visceral pleasure out of watching Trump standing on stage and hurling insults at smug, self-satisfied liberals and conservatives who had lost touch with the people whose support they relied upon. Despite being something of an elite myself, I identified with Trump's supporters. None of the disqualifications of Trump that his critics listed—ceaselessly, day after day, year after year—could negate the gut-level satisfaction I got from watching him. Sure, he lied constantly, but Americans had become so inured to the dishonesty of their politicians that it was actually a relief to hear someone lie with brazenness and glee, instead of prevaricating and equivocating while pretending they had a claim on moral authority. Trump revealed the hypocrisies of the political class for what they were even as he embodied them. His behavior was an indictment of the failures of that class as much as it was an indictment of himself.

Then he took things too far. If I enjoyed seeing him torment liberal elites from the rally stage, I was dismayed by his denial of the 2020 election results. Joe Biden won the election, and Trump should have followed precedent and conceded. But as Trump continued to discredit the election results, and as he failed to do anything to halt or meaningfully censure the rioters who stormed the Capitol on January 6, 2021, I had to admit—and did admit to John McWhorter on an episode of *The Glenn Show*—that I had been wrong to grant Donald J. Trump the benefit of the doubt.

Discussions with LaJuan about politics would turn into disagreements. Disagreements would turn into arguments. Without warning, our breakfast table could turn into a caricature of a cable news show, with both of us attempting to shout over the other one to make our points heard. Didn't I understand that, as a rich country, we needed to be doing more to help out the downtrodden? Didn't she understand that we wouldn't be a rich country for long if we ignored the perverse incentives of overly generous welfare programs? Conversations about trivial matters in the news could escalate without warning. We at least agreed on one thing: the Democrats had no idea what they were doing. We just had different reasons for thinking so.

Whatever the issue, we both thought we were right. But because we disagreed, we couldn't both be right about being right. Maybe one of us was right and one of us was wrong on a given issue. It came to the same thing: us both fuming at each other, often in separate rooms. This, we knew, was unsustainable. We didn't want to be angry at each other. And really, most of the time, we were quite happy together. Our political differences weren't going to go away. I wasn't going to one day wake up and realize that Howard Zinn was right, and she wasn't going to read Gary Becker and become a neoliberal overnight. But the atmosphere of the culture was such that we both had politics on our mind constantly. An argument could flare up at any moment, throwing an ordinary afternoon into chaos. Under those conditions, we each grew wary of setting off the next dispute, and enforced silence in a marriage is just as unsustainable as rancor.

We were both determined to find a solution. Maybe the country was going to hell. We each had our reasons for thinking so. But that didn't mean our marriage had to go down along with it. So we sought counseling. Thankfully, we found a wonderful therapist to help us through our dilemma. We had something worth preserving. If staying together required only a little humility, it was worth the price. It didn't come naturally to me, and maybe it never would. But I had to believe I could learn, if not for my own sake, then for ours.

Conclusion

We've been playing a game, you and I, reader and author. Now the game is over. The gambit has worked, or it hasn't. Perhaps my strategy for circumventing the problem of self-regard, the artful deployment of discrediting information, has allowed me to get through to you. Or perhaps you've come away thinking I'm little more than a self-justifying narcissist. Time will tell.

By considering the latter reaction on the part of the skeptical reader, I only reveal my own anxieties. For, if I've been playing a game with you, I've also been playing one with myself—a game where I'm the Player and I'm the mark. I'm the agent in pursuit of his genuine self and the target who seeks to evade him. I am the author of the cover story and its primary audience. I am the one who, even at this late date, must choose between the pain of self-knowledge and comfort of self-delusion. That game never ends.

The cover story is that an aging black economist and conservative social critic constructs a theory of his own memoir in order to encourage the skeptical reader to see past his missteps and to consider his achievements and his humanity. The real story is that this humanity and those achievements were sometimes cover stories of their own, narratives that allowed this aging black economist and conservative social critic to justify doing as he pleased, whatever the costs.

I said I had to tell it all, but in truth I cannot tell it all. I cannot tell of all the affairs and all the deceptions because there were simply too many to list. I cannot tell of all the occasions I allowed my ego to compromise my judgment, because the book would never end.

The skeptical reader may well have noted that no meditation on the nature of black identity and group loyalty can explain why a man would carry on an affair with his best friend's wife. No love note a man writes to his own wife, no matter how eloquent and sincere, can make up for the adultery that follows. No critique of injustice, no matter how apt, can purify the lust for status and acceptance that motivates it.

When I was a child, my mother taught me that, if my wife ever caught me with another woman, I should deny it. And I followed Mama's advice. But at a certain point, I was no longer denying it to another. I was denying it to myself. As a witness to my own life, I am thereby compromised.

I fought the enemy within, but in truth he was no intruder, no stranger. I cannot disavow his actions any more than I would deny my own, because his actions are my actions. I am that enemy within.

THE GAME GOES ON.

Though I have fallen away from religion, I've never shaken the feeling that I am a fallen man. I retain a sense of awe when reflecting on the meaning of this life. I still gather as much of the family together as possible every summer—my five children with their partners and my six grandchildren—these days on the Outer Banks of North Carolina. We inhabit one of those mansions by the ocean for a week. All my children have long since made their way in the world: Lisa is a clinical psychologist, Tamara a civil rights lawyer, Alden a Chicago-based journalist, Glenn II a retail banker, and Nehemiah a data scientist. None of them share my conservatism, but they are still Lourys. They sometimes carry that inheritance uneasily, just as I do that of my own mother and father. There are clashes and reconciliations, words spoken in anger and in love. Things done and said in the past do not always stay there. Recriminations and accusations sometimes upset the delicate equilibrium that holds the three generations of my family in balance. I cannot know what the future will bring for them, but I remain ever hopeful, and I will always be proud. Like any souls born into this world, they have had nets flung at them, and my greatest hope is that they will learn to fly by those nets.

Adlert and Alfred and Eloise and Moonie are all gone. My mother, Gloria, is gone. Linda is gone. My sister, Leanett, and her husband, Wesley, passed away. At the time of my father's death in 2018, we were barely on speaking terms, a consequence of either some inadvertent offense I visited on him or his wish, in his undying pride, for his son not to see him in such a diminished state. Whatever the cause was, he would not let it go, and he would not allow me to plead my case. Stubborn to the end, or perhaps obeying the mysterious dictates of his private code of honor, he wrote me out of his will. I did not care about the money he might have left me. I did not need it. But it would have meant something to see myself remembered in his final testament. I have not been able to shake the thought that the infant Everett Lowry who became the man Everett Loury was simply unable to forgive me, his only son, for repeating his father's sin by abandoning his grandson at birth. As did William Lowry with Everett, Glenn Loury refused to acknowledge Alden until he had grown into adulthood. My dad and I never spoke of this.

After I delivered the W. E. B. Du Bois Lectures in 2000, I mailed a copy of the tapes to my father so he could see what his son, after all his troubles, had achieved. Six months after his death, I received a package in the mail from his widow Constance. It was those tapes. It was the only thing of his that she chose to share with me, which, I gathered, was some sort of coded message, her way of letting me know where I stood. I was devastated by that, as well as by her decision to invite Alden to write my father's obituary for our hometown newspaper, the *Chicago Tribune*. When Alden called to inform me of this, I encouraged him to do his best, and shared, as a model, the text of the obituary I penned for the funeral program after Linda's death.

There are fewer and fewer of us left who remember the black South Side at midcentury. The streets where Woody and I rode our bikes and the alleys where we played stickball, the homes in whose backyards stood the apple trees we pilfered are now, most of them, overrun by poverty and crime. I would not walk through those neighborhoods myself, much less allow a child to play in them unsupervised. There are many such neighborhoods in America's cities, black neighborhoods that must have felt, seventy-five years ago, as though they were on the upswing and that now lie fallow and half-abandoned.

In my seventies, I have nothing left to prove and nothing to hide. Whatever promise the young man showed sitting in Mr. Reffels's solid geometry class at John Marshall Harlan High School has long since come to fruition. I now find myself receiving honors that point backward to what I have accomplished in the past rather than garnering grants that anticipate what I might yet accomplish in the future. If I have made any lasting contribution to the field of applied economic theory, my first and enduring love, time will serve as the arbiter.

I can no longer take refuge in my secrets. There is now no place for me to hide, not even from myself. Nor is there any need to.

It sometimes seems acceptable to do that which I, inspired by Václav Havel, had fought so hard against: "to merge with the anonymous crowd and to flow comfortably along with it down the river of pseudo-life." After all, I have nothing left to prove. Still, I find myself reaching for an oar. Whether out of compulsion or conviction, I do not know. Sometimes the two feel the same. The fire I felt roar inside me in my younger days when I stood before the old guard and declared the Civil Rights Movement to be over still calls out for stoking, and in stoking it I still feel the same rush.

When the protests over the murder of George Floyd erupted into riots in 2020, a truth needed telling. Flowing along with the crowd would have been fatuous cowardice. Anguish was certainly appropriate. State power may have needed to be called to account, but the conflagrations that burned across the country were not recompense for injustice. They were further injustices, injustices that were out of all proportion to the crime that had been perpetrated against George Floyd.

I was not the only one saying so. My friend John McWhorter, with whom I continue to share a remarkable intellectual partnership and an extended public conversation that I now host on Substack, saw the riots for what they were. We received wide recognition for our criticisms of and skepticism about the "racial reckoning" of which those riots were purportedly a part. Our arguments were given their due, but the fact that we are both black men played a substantial role in raising our voices above the fray. In online comments and personal correspondence, viewers thanked us for helping them maintain sanity. Some even said that they seldom (perhaps too seldom) heard such things from the mouths of black observers. Perhaps, these viewers sometimes remarked, it would be helpful to our nation if more African Americans spoke up in the way we did.

Feedback like this is always flattering, but at the same time it was disquieting. It caused me to question what was really being said. It became obvious that, along with my status as an authority on race in America, my own race had something to do with how my comments were received. White conservatives who called out the rioters found themselves accused of racism. Such charges would not stick to me. I was therefore in a nearly unique position to offer a moral and political critique of the riots that would have to be dealt with on its own terms, even if it could be (and typically was) brushed aside with mere ad hominem attacks by adherents to the Black Lives Matter party line.

Truth-telling and blackness: in my case, these two elements cannot be disentangled. For all my desire to see America get past its resurgent obsession with racial identity, I cannot disavow the central role my experience, my social being, as a black man played in my critique. It is a reprise of a familiar theme. To be an economist and to be a black economist, to be a conservative and to be a black conservative, to be a man and to be a black man. I am a man of the West, and accordingly I can lay claim to the cultural heritage of the West. Tolstoy is mine, Shakespeare is mine, Einstein is mine, just as Charles Mingus and Muhammad Ali and David Blackwell are mine. And yet, as I have felt compelled to insist, the unique history of African-descended peoples on the North American continent has ineradicably shaped my consciousness and self-understanding. My blackness is at the core of my being.

Navigating the varied professional, political, and social locations I have occupied as a black man has given me a unique angle of vision, to be sure. I have tried not to let it define me. Even so, one feature of my racial condition has been my constant concern with what observers might be thinking about "people like me." I've felt shame over the social dysfunction in black communities, and I've felt guilt for how my personal failures might discredit "the race." And even when I've persuaded myself that I do not care what others think, the tortuous struggle to affect that posture of indifference has exacted its own toll. Often, I have been unsuccessful in disregarding the surmises of others about "my people," even as I have deluded myself by refusing to acknowledge this failure. Often my cover story has been to inveigh against the slings and arrows of "the black man's" outrageous fortune, even though the real story was that this specific black man, Glenn Cartman Loury, had simply choked. Such self-aggrandizing departures from reality have served me poorly. They have been an invitation to live in bad faith. That way lies dishonor. Ultimately, I am convinced, that way lies a kind of madness.

Standing on stage in front of a cheering crowd, I still feel the rush. But now I know the rush for what it is, not the emanation of a righteous cause but the stirring of some hunger deep within me that seeks satisfaction. I am not yet satisfied and may well never be—unless, that is, I can find a way to convert the problem of self-regard into a positive-sum game. I once believed that the divinity of Jesus Christ offered me precisely such a solution. But I now have my doubts.

In a zero-sum game every loss is a gain, and every gain is a loss, which means that when a single player occupies both sides of such a contest, and when no external force intervenes, then nothing can truly be lost and nothing truly gained. I cannot defeat the enemy within, not entirely. To do so would be to defeat myself; to deny my true nature. For now, we hold an uneasy truce, one that requires long negotiations to maintain. I have my strategies. But the game never ends.